The Complete Book of

PERENNIALS

	DATE DUE	

The Complete Book of

PERENNIALS

Reader's Digest

The Reader's Digest Association, Inc.

Pleasantville, New York • Montreal

First published in Great Britain as *The Gardener's Guide to Perennials*

A Reader's Digest Book
Edited and designed by Mitchell Beazley

Library of Congress Cataloging in Publication Data

Rice, Graham
  The Complete Book of Perennials / Graham Rice.
        p.   cm.
  Includes index.
  ISBN 0-89577-825-4 (hardcover)
  1. Perennials.   I. Title.
SB434.R528   1996
635.9'32—dc20   95—13645
ISBN 0-7621-0360-4 (paperback)

Printed in China
13579108692
Front jacket: Andrew Lawson;
Back jacket: Octopus Publishing Group Ltd.

CONTENTS

FOREWORD

This book portrays the vital contribution that perennials make to our gardens, describes the very best choice of plants, and reveals how easy they are to grow.

Covering every aspect in detail, *The Complete Book of Perennials* begins with a comprehensive section on growing perennials. After an assessment of the various ways of acquiring plants, it spells out the important practical steps you can take to ensure that perennials give their best in the garden. Soil preparation and planting methods, the various cultural techniques that help perennials to thrive, propagation methods, and controlling pests and diseases are all explained in a clear and logical way. Step-by-step illustrations guide you through the details of each technique.

This practical information is followed by inspirational advice on how to use perennials in the garden to the best effect. Perennials are adaptable plants that can be used in a great many ways, and this section is full of ideas for every type of garden and situation. The many different styles that are discussed range from the organized chaos of the cottage garden to more formal herbaceous borders and from modern mixed borders to easy-maintenance island beds. Wildflower plantings and growing perennials in containers are also covered. A broad range of attractive and imaginative planting designs are beautifully illustrated and reveal the many ways in which perennials can be used successfully in the garden.

Finally there is a comprehensive alphabetical listing of the best perennials available today. Each plant is concisely and clearly introduced with an outline of its general characteristics, and this is followed by a selection of the best forms, chosen for their quality, availability, and ability to stand the test of time. Their special features are described, and any individual cultivation requirements are pointed out. A glossary, an explanation of hardiness zones, and a guide to where to buy perennials complete the book.

Right: This border of fall-blooming perennials, including solidago, helenium, asters in many colors, and *Sedum* 'Autumn Joy' ('Herbstfreude'), is backed by an old brick wall to provide shelter from fall winds and support for climbers.

WHAT ARE PERENNIALS?

Perennial plants are long-lived plants that have no permanent woody growth above the ground. Although trees and shrubs are also long-lived, their woody stems and trunks exclude them from this group. There are some weeds that come within the perennial category, but these are usually not encouraged to grow in gardens.

Unlike annuals, which usually die as soon as they have produced seed, perennials go on living. The life span of perennials varies from one species to the next. Some species, such as pinks, can be short-lived, lasting for a period of 2 to 5 years; others may last for 15 to 20 years or more. The life span of plants of the same type also varies depending on many factors,

Delphinium spires contrast well with bushy perennials that also hide the bare delphinium stems.

including the state of the soil in which they are planted and the care taken to protect them from pests and diseases. In practical terms, a perennial dies if it becomes starved, overcrowded, or outgrows its planting position.

A perennial's life cycle starts in early spring, when new growth appears. In the spring and summer the plants grow quickly to display their leaves and flowers. A few varieties flower for up to six months; others are in their prime for less than six weeks. The top growth of most perennials dies down to dormant buds in fall, although there are exceptions to this rule. Many hellebores, for example, have leaves that remain green over the winter but die away in the spring as new leaves emerge.

Left: These informal perennial borders, seen in midsummer, tumble onto the grass path and lead the eye to the sundial and white gate set against the background wooded area. The display was carefully planted with variations in color and height to create a harmonious effect.

TYPES OF PERENNIAL

Over the centuries perennials have become known by a variety of other names. *Herbaceous perennials*, the oldest term, originally referred only to plants whose growth dies down completely in the cold months of winter, but now it is used more generally. The term *border perennials*, also frequently used, refers to the traditional positioning of this group of plants in the border of a garden. *Hardy perennials* designates perennials with the ability to withstand cold winters; in contrast *tender perennials* describes perennials that are unlikely to survive cold winters. Hardiness and tenderness are both relative qualities; for specific information relating to a plant's ability to survive at a certain temperature, check its zone indicator (see pages 230–231).

PERENNIALS IN THE WILD

Perennials are found all over the world in a wide variety of natural habitats, but most of those covered in this book grow naturally in cool or warm temperate areas. Some are found in open situations, where there is little shade, except perhaps from their taller neighbors. These open places may be sunny meadows in river valleys, alpine pastures, dry

The range of perennials

Perennials vary enormously in size and growth habit. The range of mature perennial plants shown here reveals their diversity.

1 *Traditional delphinium hybrids develop from a tight crown and produce bold leaves followed by tall spires of flowers.*

2 *Many euphorbias have upright, semi-woody, overwintering stems carrying cylindrical heads of yellowish flowers.*

3 *Garden pinks are woody at the base with low, bushy growth of blue-gray leaves and single or double flowers on floppy stems.*

4 *Bugle produces leafy runners that creep over the soil, rooting as they go. The short spikes of flowers stand up vertically.*

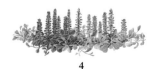

1   2   3   4

prairies, mountainsides, or seashores. Other perennials thrive in shaded situations: for example, in woods and groves, in deep gullies, or on relatively sunless hillsides. Perennials also vary in their requirements for moisture: some grow in dry, inhospitable places; others flourish beside streams or in bogs. Their growth habits in these diverse habitats vary considerably. In woodland clearings a single species may become dominant to the exclusion of most others, while in moist meadows a rich tapestry of species may develop.

PERENNIALS IN THE GARDEN

The fact that perennials grow in such a wide array of natural habitats ensures that there is a type for almost every situation in the garden. And because these garden perennials are derived from such a huge range of wild species, the diversity in size, vigor, habit of growth, flowering season, and color makes it possible to choose exactly the right plant for any seasonal planting and any color scheme. Perennials are also both tolerant and adaptable, often thriving in garden situations noticeably different from those in which they grow naturally. For these reasons and because

5 Fall anemones have vigorously spreading roots, foliage gathered toward the base, and tall, airy heads of flowers.

9 The fat, fleshy roots of agapanthus produce long, slender foliage and rounded heads of flowers on stiff, upright stems.

8 The upright stems of coreopsis carry finely cut foliage with neat daisylike flowers. The roots spread steadily.

6 Many hardy geraniums grow out from a central root-stock to form a low, bushy dome or a spreading carpet of flowers.

7 Primrose leaves emerge in early spring as a neat rosette; the flowers are carried singly or in loose clusters.

5   6   7   8   9

they are among the easiest plants to grow, perennials have gained great popularity and are often the most important constituent of many successful gardens.

Traditionally, perennial plants were used in two main ways. In large gardens they stood on their own in the border, known as the herbaceous border, in which bold groups of brightly colored plants created an impressive display. In more humble surroundings, perennials were frequently mixed with bulbs, annuals, and even fruit bushes in the more informal displays characteristic of the cottage garden. Today, we are open-minded in our approach to growing perennials and mix them with shrubs, bedding plants, hardy annuals, bulbs, climbers, and tough alpines. Each can complement the other, providing an attractive and diverse range of color and form throughout the year.

This mixed planting shows today's most popular approach to growing perennials in the border.

NAMING PERENNIALS

Perennials, like other garden plants, are named by professional horticulturalists, botanists, and gardeners. Botanists usually give plants their Latin names, based on specimens found growing in their natural habitat. Internationally agreed-upon rules govern how this must be done. Similarly, the variety or cultivar names of garden plants are given by both professional and amateur gardeners, and here too international rules apply.

Plant names are a form of shorthand, a concise way of referring to a plant without having to repeat a full description every time that the plant is mentioned. The botanists' plant names, which follow a system originated by the 18th-century botanist Linnaeus, are made up of two or three parts. Take, for example, *Campanula persicifolia* 'Telham Beauty.' The first name, *Campanula*, refers to the plant's genus, placing it in a group of broadly similar plants with fundamental features in common. The second name, *persicifolia*, indicates the plant's species, identifying it as one distinctive type of campanula. A cultivar name, 'Telham Beauty,' is used to denote a distinctive form of a species, which is cultivated for one or two particular features—usually qualities that are valued in gardens, like flower color.

RENAMING

Problems often arise when botanical research reveals fundamental differences, not originally apparent, in plants that for hundreds of years were considered closely related. Then a new name is given to a plant whose old name was in use for many years. Take, for example, *Chrysanthemum*: some species in the genus have been renamed *Dendranthema*; others have been renamed *Leucanthemella*; and the few that remain as *Chrysanthemum* are all annuals.

Another problem, dating from a period in which travel in wild terrain was unusual and communications were poor, is that the same plant may have been discovered in more than one country by different botanists, who each gave it their preferred name. When the plants are eventually studied closely and perhaps grown side by side, they are found to be identical and one name has to be selected for official use.

Difficulty also arises when a cultivar that should be propagated by division, to ensure that all the offspring are the same, is raised from seed. The seedlings may then differ, from both the parent and each other, but they may have the same name.

In all these cases, botanists look at individual problems in the light of the international rules and make decisions accordingly. The most significant of these rules is that the first name that was given to a particular plant is the name that should be used, provided it has been published in a book, journal, or catalog with an adequate description.

COMMON NAMES

There are many opportunities for botanical names to create confusion, but common names can cause even more problems. In the Pacific Northwest the name *bluebell* is sometimes used for *Mertensia longifolia*; in Scotland the bluebell is a small perennial, *Campanula rotundifolia*; and in England it is a bulb found in woodland, *Hyacinthoides non-scripta*. Three entirely different plants are known by the same name; botanical names suddenly seem far more dependable.

The bluebell in England, *Hyacinthoides non-scripta.*

The bluebell in Scotland, *Campanula rotundifolia.*

The bluebell in the Pacific Northwest, *Mertensia longifolia.*

GROWING PERENNIALS

There are perennials to suit every garden, whatever the situation and climate. Perennials are among the most accommodating of plants. As long as their basic requirements are met, these plants usually repay a little care with much pleasure.

Given the opportunity, perennials can provide pleasure for many years, but they are most likely to thrive when you start with strong, healthy plants. A weak or diseased plant is likely to languish, although careful nurturing may sometimes rescue it.

Choosing plants to suit both the soils and situations into which they are to be planted is an important consideration. There is no doubt that it is always a gamble to buy a plant that appears attractive and to plant it where there happens to be an available space in the garden. Instead, first assess the site to determine its suitability for different perennials; then make improvements to help ensure that the plants grow well once they are planted. A plant in the wrong place will never thrive.

Planting in the right manner and at the right time helps to give the perennials a healthy start. Giving careful attention in the first weeks after planting ensures that they acclimate well. But over the years they need regular attention. Weeds must not be allowed to smother them, and perennials also need to be watered, fed, deadheaded, staked, and, from time to time, revitalized. Like all plants, perennials can be vulnerable to attack from pests and diseases, and these must be prevented as far as possible or dealt with promptly when they appear. Some troubles affect a wide range of garden plants, others are more specific. But if left to multiply, the pests will weaken your plants and may kill them altogether.

Shrubs make a colorful background for perennials in this cottage garden.

Left: This informal double border with its slightly meandering path features a wide range of perennials augmented with a few shrubs and annuals to add variety.

ACQUIRING PLANTS

Taking a serious interest in perennials is closely linked to the enjoyment of acquiring plants, which may be given by friends and neighbors or bought from mail-order catalogs or local garden centers. Often as interest grows and tastes develop, gardeners find that they become more exacting in their requirements and look to specialized nurseries and seed companies for the more unusual plants that are not generally available.

PLANTS FROM NEIGHBORS

Taking cuttings from the gardens of family, friends and neighbors not only encourages the spread of good plants but preserves them too. An advantage of exchanging plants with neighbors, particularly for newcomers to gardening, is that if the plant is already thriving in the garden next door, it will probably thrive in yours. However, exchanging plants is not entirely without problems. For example, few plants respond well to being transplanted in full flower, so whether you are giving or receiving a plant, wait until its best propagation time (see Plant Directory).

PEST AND DISEASE CONTROL
A more serious problem concerns pests and diseases. There is no garden that is entirely free of pests, but that is no reason to import your neighbor's pests to add to your own. Keep a close watch on all new acquisitions, for even when no problems are apparent, insect eggs or fungus spores may be present. Be prepared to spray if a specific problem should arise.
Soil-borne problems Some problems can be more insidious. Root-feeding insect pests such as vine weevil may be hidden in the soil, and spraying the plant's foliage will not destroy them. For those plants that are especially susceptible to these pests, wash the

soil from the roots as soon as you return home. Primulas, heucheras, peonies and epimediums are particularly vulnerable to attack from vine weevil. There is also a lesser but still noteworthy danger of introducing soil-borne problems into your garden. Fungus diseases of vegetables or trees that are not present in your own garden may be in your neighbor's soil and could start an infection in your own. Pests such as eelworms, which attack fruit bushes, may be living in the soil around the roots of a columbine plant transplanted from a friend's fruit garden.

SEED CATALOGS

Perennial seeds are available from stores, garden centers, and nurseries, but often the choice of cultivars is poor. Mail-order seed catalogs offer the widest selection and extremely good value, since a large number of plants can be raised for the price of a single plant bought from the garden center or nursery.

ADVANTAGES OF SEED
Economy is the main reason for raising perennials from seed, and when planting a new garden this can be an especially important factor. But there are other advantages. Some species are available from seed companies in mixed colors, so a range can be raised from a single packet. Seed provides

an economical way of filling beds and borders in a new garden. Then, as the garden fills up, you can discard the plants in colors that you find less attractive and allow those you prefer to spread. Many of the more recent perennial plant introductions into seed catalogs are specially bred for vigorous growth and often flower prolifically in their first year after sowing. They can thus serve as bedding plants in their first year and then continue to give many more years of pleasure. Some new introductions may be available only as seed in the first few years, before nurseries sell them. It is also true that some uncommon species, which are hard to find on sale as plants, may be found in seed catalogs. And, of course, from a seed catalog you can purchase by mail, avoiding time-consuming trips to nurseries.

PERENNIALS TO GROW FROM SEED
In general, selections from seed catalogs most likely to be successful are those intended to be raised from seed. These types are often the most

Coreopsis 'Early Sunrise' flowers well in its first year after sowing; it continues to bloom every year but on taller stems.

vigorous growers, the most prolific, and the most tolerant of less-than-perfect conditions. Examples include *Achillea* 'Summer Pastels,' *Campanula carpatica* 'Clips,' *Coreopsis* 'Early Sunrise,' *Delphinium* 'Southern Noblemen,' *Echinacea* 'White Swan,' *Gaillardia* 'Kobold,' *Geum* 'Lady Stratheden' and 'Mrs. Bradshaw,' *Kniphofia* 'Border Ballet,' *Lobelia* 'Compliment Scarlet,' *Lupinus* 'Gallery,' *Salvia farinacea* 'Porcelain' and 'Victoria,' also *Salvia × sylvestris* 'Blue Queen' (Blaukönigin) and 'Rose Queen,' and finally *Sidacea* 'Party Girl.'

Unusual species not listed in nursery catalogs are also worth trying. Special consideration should also be given to plants that have received awards, and these are often mentioned in the catalog.

PROBLEMS WITH MAIL ORDER

There are however some drawbacks to buying seed by mail. The seed of some plants, like hellebores, has a short life, so by the time it is sent out in the normal winter mail-order season it may have already deteriorated. The chances of raising a good crop of seedlings from such seed will be slim. Other plants, such as peonies, are difficult for home gardeners to germinate successfully, so these too may have to be excluded. Even when these difficult plants are listed in catalogs, they are best avoided until you have some experience of raising plants from seed.

There is another problem that affects a much wider range of plants: when seed is collected from many of the very best perennials—the cultivars that are usually propagated by division—the offspring that are produced are rarely as good as the parent. The unpredictability of seed collected from these plants means

Sown in spring, *Achillea* 'Summer Pastels' flowers prolifically in summer. The best colors from the mixture can be propagated by division.

that seed companies cannot state exactly what their seed will produce, so they tend not to list it at all. So for the very finest forms of *Delphinium, Helleborus, Phlox, Aster,* and *Monarda,* it pays to buy the actual plants. In general, avoid forms that require special facilities (such as heated propagators and cold frames), which you may not have, and those usually raised by division, as these will not come true from seed.

ORDERING BY MAIL

When ordering seed from mail-order catalogs, use the following rules to help the process flow smoothly.

Send off for catalogs as soon as they are advertised, and try to place your order as soon as possible after the catalog arrives. The newest and best selections may sell out quickly. Keep a photocopy of your order in case of problems later.

Check the figure given for the number of seeds in each packet before deciding how many packets you need. The seed content may vary from one cultivar to another: you may find that you need two packets of some cultivars to raise the number of plants you require, while just a single packet of another cultivar may contain enough seed to share with friends.

If your order arrives incomplete, without any explanation, or if the seed has not arrived within the time stated in the catalog, contact the company promptly, sending them a copy of your order.

If the seed arrives before the correct time for sowing, do not leave it in a hot kitchen or a damp basement until sowing time; it is best stored cool and dry. The most effective way to store seed is in a screw-top jar placed in the bottom of the refrigerator. Add a few crystals of silica gel to the jar to absorb excess moisture and help keep the seed fresh.

GARDEN CENTERS

The first port of call for most gardeners buying plants is the local garden center, which has the great advantage of convenience and sometimes offers good prices. But, unfortunately, the range of plants available in garden centers is usually restricted to well-established and well-known types together with ones that are easy to propagate and thus relatively inexpensive. A high proportion of the perennials on sale in centers are seed-raised plants, so it may be difficult to find the best cultivars of lupines, delphiniums or hellebores, for example.

Fortunately, an increasing number of larger garden centers now have an area devoted to special plants. The better-quality cultivars can often be found here, but these plants may also be more expensive or a little more difficult to grow than other perennials. They are often accompanied by detailed explanatory labels to help you choose and grow them well.

SPECIALIZED PLANT CENTERS

In recent years things have moved a stage further with the development of plant centers. Here the balance has shifted, and the plants take precedence over everything else. There are no watering cans, patio sets, spades, or sprays available. Apart from seed and perhaps books, these stores concentrate on plants. The result is a far wider range of cultivars, and it is often the selection of perennials that benefits most.

CHOOSING GARDEN CENTER PERENNIALS

Perennials are not ideally suited to selling in garden centers. Contrary to the situation with shrubs, small perennials in the small pots in which they are so often sold may attempt to reach the same height as they would in the garden. As a result, the perennials become starved and top-heavy, and they may blow over and look bedraggled by flowering time. Fortunately, a trend toward growing them in larger pots is developing.

The best approach is to buy perennials as strong, young plants in spring or fall and to plant them at once, before they fill their pots with tightly packed roots. Such plants are often presented in neat pots, sometimes topped with gravel and with a helpful color label. Choose those plants with the most growing points, as this is a sign of a potential rapid increase in size. Sometimes these plants will be in flower, but selecting a strong and bushy plant that is likely to grow vigorously in the future is more important than taking home a plant in flower. Plants that have been in their pots too long will have lost their lower leaves, have only a few small flowers struggling to open, and look generally tattered.

Seed-raised mixtures, like these Russell hybrid lupines, can be spectacular; but an individual plant from the garden center may prove to be any of these colors unless you buy it in flower.

Plants that are in good-sized pots and have been well cared for can look impressive, especially if they are displayed in a sheltered area, where they are not battered by wind. You can then see clearly how they grow and how they will look in the garden. Sometimes these more established plants can be unexpectedly good buys, for although they are more expensive, you may be able to split the plant into two pieces for planting—giving you two plants for the price of one.

Before you buy, inspect all plants closely for pests and diseases, especially aphids, and examine the pots in case some of the stems have died off at soil level. Check that the roots, which may have grown through the drainage holes in the base of the pots, are not too well rooted into the gravel or sand on which the plant containers are standing.

SPECIAL PROMOTIONS

There are two other ways in which perennials are sold in garden centers, as special promotions and as seed. Some new introductions are given a showy presentation with display boards, colored pots and labels, and a great deal of publicity. These lavish campaigns are usually reserved for particularly good new cultivars, although the plants may not be quite as good as the publicity leads us to believe. They are usually sold in larger-than-average pots and at premium prices, costing more than other high-quality perennials that are usually as good. Garden centers also sell seed, but the range of perennials they offer is usually restricted. A few rows on the seed racks are sometimes reserved for perennials, but a far wider choice is available in the mail-order seed catalogs (see p.16).

Specialized nurseries will advise on which rock plants are tough enough for perennial borders. These blue and white *Campanula carpatica* flowers are ideal.

SPECIALIZED NURSERIES

All over the country there are nurseries, often small family businesses, that specialize in perennial plants. Unlike garden centers, which buy their stock from wholesale nurseries, these small, specialized nurseries propagate most of their plants themselves and grow them until they are ready for sale. As a result, they have a more intimate knowledge of the plants they grow and usually stock a wide range of cultivars. Being specialists, they also have a deeper understanding of perennial plants in general. The standard of advice available in garden centers may be improving, but the staff at specialized nurseries will be familiar with a wider range of perennials and how to grow them successfully.

KNOWING A GOOD SPECIALIST

The success of a specialized nursery depends on two things: the choice of plants they grow and how well they grow their plants for sale. Specialists who know all about their plants are in a good position to select the best forms. They often raise new cultivars themselves and may have a network of contacts who bring them new plants to introduce. As these specialized nurseries tend to grow all or most of their plants themselves, they can also ensure that their plants are of good quality. They may stagger propagation so that different batches of the same cultivar are at their best at different times of the season, and if they sell out of a particular cultivar, they should know when the next batch will be ready.

Another advantage of using specialized nurseries is that many of them have display gardens where mature specimens of the cultivars on sale can be viewed in a realistic garden situation. You can see firsthand the features and faults of the plants you may be tempted to purchase.

The best specialized nurseries are very good indeed. Being a regular customer and getting to know the people who run the nursery will enhance

When building up a collection of a specific plant, such as these fall asters, visiting a nursery with a good display garden will make choosing less difficult.

your enjoyment of growing and buying plants; some enthusiasts for perennial plants buy only from specialists. Of course, there are some specialists who are not good, but you can often tell the good from the bad at first glance. Weeds are a bad sign. The problem with a weedy nursery is that even if the cultivars it has are well chosen, you will almost certainly be buying weeds or weed seeds along with the plants. And you may well buy other problems as well, for not only do weeds harbor pests and diseases that attack perennials, but they are also a sign of a careless attitude, which will probably affect other aspects of the nursery. There are other factors to consider. Is the staff helpful? Does the catalog have good descriptions and advice? Is the nursery organized logically? Are the sales beds laid out clearly? Are the plants well labeled?

VISITING SPECIALIZED NURSERIES

When considering a visit to a specialized nursery, send for the catalog first. This will not only give the hours it is open, but will also provide directions and probably a map; many specialized nurseries are in rural areas and may be difficult to find. Often these nurseries allow you to order plants to collect when you visit, and as most also stock a small number of plants not listed in the catalog, these can be your focus when you arrive.

When choosing plants do not always pick those in flower; bushy habit and the potential for flower in the future are more important. Check for pests, diseases, and weeds, and avoid plants whose roots have grown through the drainage holes and developed outside the pot.

One problem that can arise when visiting specialized nurseries derives

from the sheer number of selections available; newcomers to growing perennials may find it difficult to choose among, say, 15 different types of phlox. Always ask for advice; explain what you like and describe the situation and soil in your garden, and you will usually benefit from suggestions of which forms to try. You may also pick up some tips on how to grow them. Establishing a good relationship with a specialized nursery will ensure that you take home the right plants with the right advice—and if anything should go wrong, it will increase the chances of resolving difficulties amicably.

MAIL ORDER

For many gardeners, especially those living in rural areas, buying live plants by mail order is the only way to obtain any but the most commonplace types. Postal and courier services give access to a huge range of plants from nurseries all over the country. There are two ways of using them. One way is to request catalogs from the nurseries and order plants directly from them (see p.234); the other is to respond to advertisements for plants in magazines.

NURSERIES AND CATALOGS

Mail-order nurseries advertise themselves in gardening magazines and journals, or they may be mentioned in articles. But they vary in the quality of the plants they supply and the care with which they pack the plants, so a recommendation from a friend is worth a great deal. If you are interested in specific plant types, specialized journals and society bulletins are the most likely places to find appropriate advertisements. Many are smaller operations run by one or two people, so you can save them unnecessary work and speed up the service by finding out what they charge for their catalog and sending the right amount. Requests for catalogs that are not accompanied by the payment required may be ignored.

Catalogs vary enormously. Some are fully illustrated in color, although the more colorful the catalog and the more lavish the descriptions, the fewer selections it contains. At the other extreme, some mail-order catalogs are little more than a list of plant names; to get the best from these catalogs you need a good reference book on hand when ordering.

Each mail-order nursery has its individual way of doing business, so it is vital to read the advice to customers in the catalog before sending off your order. Some nurseries send plants only at certain seasons or mail only certain plants from their collection and not others; some have a minimum order charge or suggest you pay in particular ways; some have codes to indicate plants that will not be available until late in the season. Ignoring these points can lead to confusion and frustration—for both you and the nursery. Once your order is made out, photocopy it before

Try to order pot-grown fall anemones, as they dislike disturbance.

sending it and mark on your calendar the date by which the catalog indicates your plants should arrive.

ORDERING FROM AN ADVERTISEMENT

When you order from an advertisement in a magazine, you usually fill in a coupon and send it off with your money. These advertisements are often for collections of plants and rarely let you choose from a large number of individual varieties. Read the small print, and take special note of the size of plants you will receive and relate this to their cost. Again, keep a copy of your order and mark the last delivery date on the calendar. Complain promptly if you don't receive your plants by that date.

WHEN PLANTS ARRIVE

As soon as your plants are delivered, unpack them; be sure to check what has been sent against your original order and the packing list that may have come with the parcel. If you plan to be away when the plants are due to arrive, then ask a neighbor to look after them for you. If, on unpacking your parcel, you discover that the wrong plants have been sent, if you are dissatisfied with the quality of the plants, or if they have been damaged in transit, try to photograph the plants; if possible, use a camera that can print the date in the corner of the picture. Complain promptly to the nursery concerned, sending a copy of your order and a photograph of the damage. Most nurseries will quickly respond with a fresh consignment or a refund.

Problems may arise some time after your plants arrive. You may have ordered a white iris, and when it flowers it turns out to be blue. Photograph the plant and make a

complaint. Good nurseries guarantee their plants to be true to name, but some mail-order companies are little more than brokers and don't know a dandelion from a dogwood. You may have to wait a very long time for a refund or replacement.

After unpacking, plants still in their pots can be stood in a sheltered place for a few days before planting. Bare-root plants and those knocked out of their pots need planting more quickly. Plants that have suffered in transit may need a period of recuperation and can be potted and grown in a cool but bright window until they are ready to go outside. Plants are sometimes supplied with temporary labels, so write permanent ones as soon as the plants are unpacked. Check them for pests, diseases and even weeds, and spray if necessary.

When buying plants by mail order, you have to take a certain amount on faith: you trust that the plants are correctly named and of high quality. Fortunately, most suppliers are eager to supply good plants and in this way build up a base of regular customers. So if you find a nursery that you can depend on, tell your friends; on the other hand, if you find one that cannot be trusted, warn them.

Well-established hostas are better value than expensive newcomers.

SITE AND SOIL

Conditions vary from one garden to another and from one border to another in the same garden. Although perennials are not fussy, they do grow better in some places than in others. It is thus important to assess the site where you intend to plant perennials and the soil to ensure that the right types are planted in the right place. In smaller gardens, where planting options are limited, the suitability of the site is critical, but conditions can often be improved to ensure that the plants thrive. In large gardens, a number of sites may be considered, so that each plant may be grown in a spot that best suits it.

PLANTING SITES

Once a site has been selected, any factors that pose problems must be considered. The areas of sun and shade and the position of immovable features, such as walls, cannot usually be changed, so you must adapt your plans to take them into account.

SUN OR SHADE
Although many perennials thrive in varying degrees of shade, most do best in plenty of light. In a sunny and open location, the soil needs plenty of extra organic matter to increase its capacity for retaining water; this enables plants to cope with the drying effects of the light, warmth, and wind. In an especially exposed spot, choose short, self-supporting plants that will be relatively resistant to damage from the wind.

WARM AND COOL SITES
A south-facing site is often very hot. This suits perennial plants that come from Mediterranean climates but increases the danger of the soil drying out, so less tolerant plants may suffer from drought. East-facing sites are good for tough perennials that flower in midsummer, although plants may

be scorched by cold winds unless a form of shelter is provided. If the wind is combined with frost, it can be devastating. The plants may also be damaged when frost is followed by a quick early-morning thaw; soft, new shoots and early flowers are especially vulnerable.

In north-facing sites use tough, late-emerging plants. Cold in winter and warming slowly in spring, these sites subject plants to long periods of frozen ground that not all can tolerate. Although shade-loving plants may do well in winter and spring, in summer, when the sun is high, these plants may be scorched. West-facing sites warm up slowly in the spring, but they are valuable for fall perennials, as plants remain undamaged by frost until relatively late in the year.

Planting sites
Conditions vary in different parts of even the smallest garden. Although perennials are not fussy, they grow better if they are sited according to the conditions they prefer.

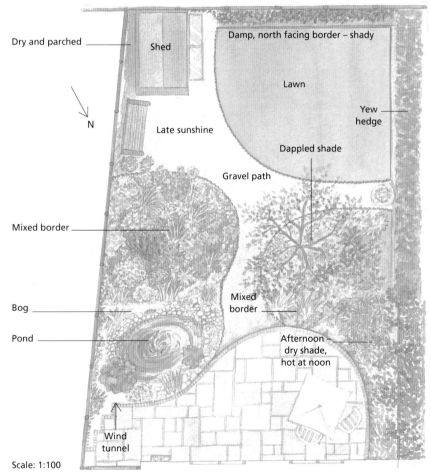

Dry and parched — Shed — Damp, north facing border – shady — Lawn — Yew hedge — N — Late sunshine — Dappled shade — Gravel path — Mixed border — Mixed border — Bog — Pond — Afternoon – dry shade, hot at noon — Wind tunnel — Scale: 1:100

Left: An open, sunny site will suit the widest range of flowering and foliage perennials.

PERENNIALS UNDER TREES

Introducing perennials under trees requires careful consideration. Trees vary in the nature of the shade that they cast: the dappled shade cast by high-branched deciduous trees for part of the year is attractive to many plants, but the dense, permanent shade created by an evergreen tree is very inhospitable. Evergreen trees present further problems in that they keep rain off the soil all year, causing drought conditions, and the needles of some conifers increase the acidity of the soil and deplete nutrients—conditions that suit few perennials. Removing low branches and thinning the crown can help a little, but it is more realistic to accept the fact that few perennials will succeed under evergreen trees. If the deciduous trees

Planting around roots

The dry, rooty soil under trees presents difficult conditions in which to grow perennials. These can be improved by using logs to raise the level, then adding organic matter to create the right conditions for a wide variety of woodland plants.

in your garden are planted very close together, increase the light by cutting down poor specimens and by sensitively removing the lower branches or thinning the crowns of the stronger trees. These jobs are best left to a skilled tree surgeon, who will take care not to destroy the overall character of the trees.

Planting around roots The roots of trees are often shallow and intrusive. Finding space among them to plant perennials may be a problem, and if you do establish a planting, competition for both water and nutrients will follow. The simplest way to reduce root competition under trees is to make raised beds and fill them with moisture-retentive soil. Most of the tree roots that are actively taking moisture and nutrients from the soil are at the edge of the root system, which is usually under the tips of the branches, so position raised beds near the trunk to minimize the sapping of nutrients by the tree. Use lengths of log to raise the level of the bed by 6–9 in (15–23 cm), and get the plants off to a strong start by mixing

fresh soil with plenty of leaf mold or compost. Before filling the bed with soil, loosen as much of the underlying earth as is practical.

DRAINAGE

Drainage is a site characteristic that is not easy to assess. If water lies on the surface in winter or especially in summer, the soil is not draining properly. This may be the result of a heavy clay soil, which naturally holds a great deal of water. Alternatively, it may be the result of poor soil structure, which prevents water from draining easily. Heavy clay soil can be made more suitable for growing a range of perennials by the addition of organic matter. Poor soil structure is often the result of compaction, in which case deep digging will greatly improve the situation by loosening the soil.

WALLS AND FENCES

If the border is positioned in front of a wall or fence, the wind may cause difficulties as it swirls past the solid barrier, creating eddies among the plants; a hedge will filter the wind

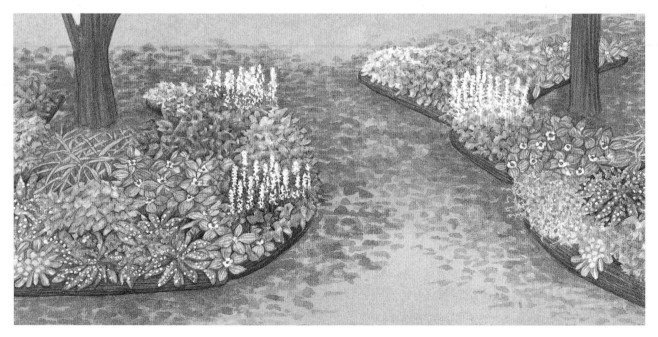

Walls versus hedges

A wall makes a solid barrier and creates turbulence, which may damage plants on both sides in stormy weather.

A hedge filters the wind and creates gentler conditions.

and prevent this problem (see illustrations above). Plants growing at the front of walls and fences may also need support to prevent them from leaning toward the light and to counteract swirling air currents. Plant perennials at least 1½ ft (45 cm) from a wall and 1 ft (30 cm) from a wood fence to avoid problems arising from poor soil, drought, or excess moisture. If climbers are trained against a wall or fence, the competition from their roots for moisture and nutrients should be considered before introducing other plants in the border.

HEDGES

Hedges provide pleasant backgrounds to borders but pose a number of problems. They develop an extensive but shallow root system, so space must be left between the hedge and the plants to reduce root competition. Also, access to the hedge is necessary for clipping; ideally leave a strip 3 ft (90 cm) wide between the hedge and the perennials. In a small border a space of 1½ ft (45 cm) will suffice.

WEEDS

Weeds are a problem, in the early stages of establishing a new planting and also when revitalizing a neglected site. There are two types of weed: annual and perennial. Annual weeds are relatively easy to deal with, but perennial weeds are more difficult.

Annual weeds Annual weeds are prolific but are generally soft in texture. Although they flower and seed quickly, they are easy to pull or dig out because they have no substantial underground roots. Remove annual weeds when preparing the soil, then leave it fallow for several weeks to allow more annual weeds to germinate. Once you have eradicated the second growth of weeds, plant the perennials. Finally, apply a sterile mulch around the plants to prevent further annual weeds from appearing.

Perennial weeds Perennial weeds have roots that grow deeply into the soil and spread, and although the top growth may be pulled off, shoots inevitably spring up again from the roots. Competition from perennial

weeds for space, light, moisture, and nutrients can be a significant problem, so it is essential to eliminate them before planting garden perennials. Care must be taken to remove the entire weed root because many of the most harmful weeds will grow from small and apparently insignificant pieces. If an area intended for perennials is severely infested, use chemical or other methods of control before working on the soil itself.

SOIL FOR PERENNIALS

Good soil is fundamental to growing good perennials. Whatever the state of the soil when you start, it can usually be improved. When assessing your soil for the first time, start by digging a hole about 1½ ft (45 cm) square. Take out 9 in (23 cm) of soil—about the depth of the blade on the digging spade—and pile it on one side, then continue down another 9 in (23 cm) and pile the soil on the other side. Examining the soil and the hole from which it has come can tell you a great deal.

In a few cases it will be impossible to dig a hole this deep. If the spade hits rock a few inches below the surface, then you must resign yourself to having a problem that can only partially be solved. The soil may not be so shallow across the entire garden. Use a crowbar to go over the whole area at 6 ft (1.8 m) intervals, driving it into the soil to locate areas with deeper soil, which can then be marked out as areas for beds; in this way the garden will design itself. If the whole garden is made up of a thin layer of soil over solid rock, however, the only solution is to build raised beds to increase the depth of soil.

If the hole proved very difficult to dig, it may be because the soil is compacted. This condition may have been created by the use of heavy equipment during construction, by regular traffic across the same part of the garden, or through regular shallow plowing or rotary tilling over a period of many years. In such cases deep digging is the only answer to the problem. Known as double digging, this involves loosening the soil to two spades' depth, or about 1½ ft (45 cm). Although hard work, it not only improves root penetration and drainage, but also facilitates the addition of organic matter.

ASSESSING THE SOIL

If the soil is deep enough to excavate the hole, note how the color and consistency of the soil change from top to bottom. If the earth remains a dark color and is crumbly from the soil surface to the base of the hole, then you have potentially fertile soil. Usually, however, the deeper you look, the less dark and crumbly the soil becomes. The greater the depth of dark topsoil the better, and the darker the better.

Inspecting the soil below about 9 in (23 cm) usually reveals the fundamental characteristic of the soil: at this depth it is often obvious. Pure sand or gravel may appear, indicating a dry, fast-draining soil but one that is usually easy to work. If you find red, yellow, or gray clay, the drainage will be slower; the soil will dry out less quickly after heavy rain and will retain moisture for longer in dry weather. To confirm this, take some damp soil and rub it between your thumb and forefinger. If it smears smoothly, it contains a great deal of clay; if it feels gritty and rough, it contains grains of sand or grit. The way in which it crumbles is also a useful clue. If the soil tends to stick in a lump or falls into fine grains, it is more likely to need improvement than if it crumbles into granules.

IMPROVING THE SOIL

Organic matter is the most valuable soil improver, as it has the capacity to improve both clay and sandy soils. It breaks up clay soil from solid lumps into crumbly granules that allow water to drain through, yet it also helps bind sandy soils together, so that both rain and plant foods drain through it less quickly. Organic matter needs constant renewal. Even if the soil is found to be rich, dark, and crumbly to a good depth and needs little to bring it up to an acceptable standard, regular additions of organic matter will be necessary to maintain a high level of fertility.

ORGANIC MATTER FOR SOIL IMPROVEMENT

Many types of organic matter are available for soil improvement. Compost is often the most accessible; you can make it yourself in the garden from weeds, trimmings, and vegetable kitchen waste. Unfortunately, unless it is made well, it may contain weed seeds.

Animal manure is an excellent form of organic matter but must be well rotted before use. Peat should be avoided, since not only is it a

Loamy soil: naturally rich and fertile and good for many plants.

Heavy clay: sticky and difficult to work, best improved with organic matter.

Alkaline soil: dry, hungry, and limy, but some plants love it.

Stony soil: well drained, needs regular enriching with fertilizer.

diminishing natural resource, but it also contains almost no plant foods. Many of the so-called peat substitutes are, however, excellent. These are made from a variety of composted materials, including wood and paper waste, bark, spent mushroom compost, coir (coconut fiber), and straw. They are weed free, last well in the soil, and also contain valuable plant foods, which are usually released slowly. Other, less familiar forms of organic matter are sometimes available locally, and any type is usually better than none at all. Some materials, however, may be unusually alkaline or have an imbalance of plant foods, so caution is advisable.

LIME

Some aspects of soil fertility are not immediately apparent. The amount of lime, or alkalinity, in the soil is less crucial for perennials than it is for many shrubs, but some perennials, such as lupines, are particular, preferring lime-free soil. One of the easiest ways to find out what soil type you have in your garden is by looking at the plants in your neighbors' gardens. For example, if the local hydrangeas are blue, the soil is likely to be acid; if they are pink, it is more likely to be alkaline. If rhododendrons and azaleas are widespread and grow well, the soil will be acid; but if they are rarely seen and then only in tubs or raised beds, the local soil will probably be alkaline.

A more accurate measure can be made by using a simple test kit that can be purchased at most garden centers. While not one hundred percent accurate, soil test kits do give a general indication of the acidity or alkalinity of the soil, and information on how to interpret the results of the test is usually supplied with the kit.

The pH scale

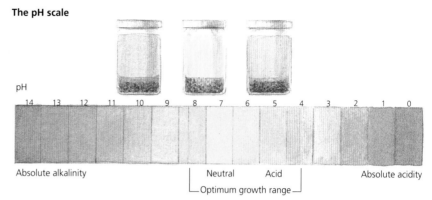

Test kits can assess the alkalinity or acidity of the soil and show the result on a colored chart. A pH of 6.5 is suitable for the widest range of perennials.

Soil acidity is measured on what is known as the pH scale. Most garden soils are between pH 5 and pH 8: pH 7 is neutral; figures below indicate an increasingly acid soil, and higher figures indicate increasing levels of lime. The best level for most perennials is about pH 6.5.

The test kit gives information on how much lime to apply to reduce soil acidity, and this varies according to the soil type. For average soil, one application of garden lime, using 6 oz (190 g) per sq yd/m, will reduce the level of acidity from pH 5.5 to the ideal of pH 6.5. Wearing gloves, apply on a still day; rake it in and do not plant or sow seeds for at least one month. Although it is generally easy to make soil more alkaline by adding lime as explained above, but it is much more difficult to make soil more acid. There are few perennials that are like rhododendrons and insist on an acid soil. Those, like lupines, that prefer lime-free conditions usually grow on neutral soil.

PLANT NUTRIENTS

It is also helpful to know how much nutrition there is in the soil. A look at the plants already growing can give a good indication of the amount of nutrients present. Roses or shrubs with a mass of dead and twiggy growth, small leaves, and a sparse show of small flowers may indicate a starved soil. Neglected borders showing patches of bare soil in midsummer may also point to a shortage of plant nutrients. Weeds that flower when tall and lush often indicate rich soil, but if they rush into flower when just a few inches high, the soil may be low in nutrients.

Kits are available that test for the main plant nutrients: nitrogen, phosphorous, and potassium. Although less accurate than the pH test kits and also more expensive, these kits may be worth using in small gardens. The levels of nutrients in the soil are usually increased by the addition of organic matter, but fertilizers are often necessary as well. Fertilizers may be organic or inorganic in origin, but both are effective, so the choice is yours. If a soil test reveals a significant shortage of any one material, the kit usually includes advice on how to deal with it. But perennials are generally easy to please, and a balanced general fertilizer, such as Growmore, applied in the spring in accordance with the manufacturer's instructions usually works well.

PLANTING

Planting is the most exciting of the many tasks associated with growing perennials, full of promise and anticipation. Often perennials will grow despite being planted thoughtlessly or at the wrong time of year. But when planted properly, perennials respond with speedy growth, a profusion of flowers or foliage in their first season, and a tendency to increase.

PREPARATION

It is easiest to prepare thoroughly for planting when you are putting in a new bed or border rather than a few plants into an already established border. The main aim of the preparation process should be to bring the soil into the best possible condition for the plants. In practice this means reducing compaction, breaking the soil up to create a friable texture, improving its drainage, increasing its organic content, and ensuring that there are adequate nutrients for the plants. These goals are best achieved by digging, which also provides a chance to eliminate perennial weeds.

PREPARING WHOLE BORDERS BY DIGGING

The soil and therefore the plants will be best served by deep or double digging, to a depth of 1½ ft (45 cm). This gives you a chance to incorporate plenty of organic matter into the soil, which is valuable to plants even when the soil is already in good shape. Perennials vary in the depth to which their roots go in search of moisture and nutrients and in the extent to which they appreciate rich conditions. In general, however, thorough preparation is invaluable.

Left: By dealing with all of the border at the same time, the preparation can be extremely thorough. All the varieties will benefit and develop well together.

Digging is best carried out in spring on sandy soil, but on clay soil it should be timed for when the soil is neither so dry that a spade will hardly penetrate nor so wet that it sticks to your boots in clumps. Digging heavy soil in fall to leave over winter is preferable, as the frost helps break up the clumps into smaller granules. Digging, combined with frost action, helps improve drainage.

Large stones should be removed, but both smaller stones and pebbles improve drainage on heavy soil, so they are best ignored. Weeds, though, should not be ignored, and the fleshy roots of perennial weeds must be removed and disposed of. The roots of many perennials run deep, and a few produce shoots that emerge at the surface after growing from 1½ ft (45 cm) or more deep in the soil, so it pays to remove every piece.

Preparing for planting in enriched soil

1 *Fork over the soil, taking care to remove the roots of perennial weeds.*

2 *Rake off stones and other debris, and leave a reasonably level finish.*

3 *Tread the soil well to remove air pockets and prevent uneven settling.*

4 *Scatter fertilizer evenly, rake it in lightly, and the border is ready to plant.*

ORGANIC MATTER

The type of organic matter used is worth considering. The traditional technique was to use coarse, bulky materials, such as farmyard manure, and after forking over the lower 9 in (23 cm) of soil during digging, to place the manure in a 3 in (7.5 cm) layer before covering it with the topsoil. This approach was well suited to the days of large-scale borders, when both manure and labor were plentiful. In today's gardens it is preferable to use a finer, crumblier material, such as manure or compost that has rotted thoroughly, or a locally available material, such as brewery waste or mushroom compost. Either way, the material's fine texture allows it to be worked evenly through the full depth of soil using a garden fork, so that its benefits are enjoyed by plant roots at all depths.

Once digging is finished, level the soil off and tread the area to remove air pockets, unless you are digging in winter. Then rake it roughly and, if possible, leave the area for a few weeks to allow weed seeds to germinate and any remaining pieces of weed root to sprout. These weeds can then be hoed or sprayed off before perennials are planted. As planting time approaches, final preparations can be made. Rake the soil surface again, correct any bumps and hollows, remove the last of the weeds, then give a dressing of a balanced general fertilizer and rake it in. The bed is now ready to plant.

PLANTING SMALL POCKETS

The same principles apply to planting two or three plants into a small part of an existing border, although the presence of nearby plants imposes restrictions. For a small planting space the process can be simplified, as there is little point in extending it over many months. The quick way is to remove existing plants or weeds; fork over the site to a depth of 9 in (23 cm), mixing in some organic matter; tread; and rake in fertilizer. Clearly this method does not allow the addition of organic matter to the lower level of the soil, but it does minimize disturbance to neighboring plants.

It still pays to excavate all the soil to a depth of about 9 in (23 cm) if possible, then pile the soil on a sheet of plastic spread out nearby. Next, remove a small amount of the soil from the base of the hole; otherwise once organic matter is added, the final level will be higher than that of the neighboring soil. Fork over the base of the hole and mix in organic matter. Next, replace the topsoil, fork in more organic matter, tread the area, dress it with fertilizer, and rake. You can then begin planting.

PLANTING SEASON

Most perennials have a great urge to grow, but whether your new plants come in pots or have been dug from the open ground at the nursery, a few basic points on timing apply. Never plant into soil that is frozen or likely to be frozen soon after planting; also avoid waterlogged soil. Planting into dry soil in summer is another mistake, as is planting when icy winds are forecast or just before you go away for a long vacation.

CONTAINER-GROWN PLANTS

Now that most perennials are grown and sold in containers, they can, in theory at least, be planted at almost any time of year. It is often tempting to buy them in spring or summer, when they are in full flower, for at that time you can see exactly what

Plant lupines from pots in spring. Those dug from open ground may not transplant well.

you are buying. They usually survive at this time of year, but planting in summer is not good practice. Most perennials make fresh roots in early spring or fall, and these are the best times to plant. In particular, by planting in early spring, you allow new root growth to take hold quickly in the garden soil, let the plant take advantage of natural seasonal moisture as it grows, and ensure that, by the time water stress threatens in summer, the roots are established in the garden soil. Another consideration is that if plants are bought in early spring, the nursery rather than the gardener will have taken responsibility for them during the winter.

The only plants that are not suitable for spring planting are those, such as hellebores, that start to make their growth in winter or even in fall and flower in late winter or early

The best time to plant *Tanacetum* 'Brenda' is in spring rather than fall, as it dislikes winter wetness when newly planted.

spring; these are best planted in the fall. Spring planting is especially necessary for fall-flowering plants, like asters, which are often still in flower at a time when other perennials are being planted and which make strong root growth in spring. In warmer climates it is also sensible to plant varieties that withstand a little frost in the spring, giving them a chance to become well established by winter, when the frosty weather arrives. Planting in fall is generally more appropriate for plants that are dug from the open ground, as they can then establish new roots without the increasing spring temperatures, which cause too much moisture to evaporate from the new leaves. Fall is less suitable for planting container-grown specimens, as the plant sits in its water-retentive potting soil during the season when it is most likely to

remain sodden, and this can cause the roots to rot. In general, it is best to plant early-flowering species in fall, and mid- to late-flowering ones in spring. Perennials best planted in spring include *Aster, Catananche, Gaillardia, Lobelia, Monarda, Penstemon, Schizostylis,* and *Tanacetum.*

PLANTS DUG FROM OPEN GROUND

Perennials dug from the ground before being sent from the nursery must be considered differently. The first thing to keep in mind is the necessity for the plants to remain out of the soil for as short a time as possible. Nurseries may send out bare-root plants at almost any time from early fall until well into spring. They will always try to lift plants when their soil is in the right condition, although if you live in another

part of the country, your soil may be frozen and you will still need to deal with the plants whenever they arrive. If bare-root plants arrive in the fall, they can often be planted right away.

Sometimes less well organized nurseries send out plants dug from the open late in spring, when they are already growing. Apart from complaining about this, you need to give the plants special care. You can plant them at once, perhaps with the protection of shade netting, and then water them. Alternatively, you can pot them and keep them in a shaded spot until established, then plant them later. One or two plants, in particular bearded irises, are dug from the ground and sent out in late spring or summer, just after flowering. This sounds strange, but these irises make strong root growth at this stage and so establish themselves quickly.

PLANTS FROM YOUR OWN GARDEN

When you do lifting and replanting in your own garden, you can choose the timing of the operation to suit the circumstances. It is true that perennials replanted within a few minutes of being lifted stand a better chance of acclimating quickly than those that are lifted and left for some time. Taking the opportunity to retain as much soil on the roots as possible always increases the chances of success. It is possible to lift and replant some perennials, such as asters, hardy chrysanthemums, hellebores, and even lupines in full flower, but successful replanting depends on watering them thoroughly first, retaining a great deal of soil on the roots, replanting and watering them in quickly, and providing protection from strong sun and winds. Except in emergencies, it is not a recommended practice.

PLANTING TECHNIQUES

Choose a day for planting when the soil is moist but not wet and, preferably, when there is little wind and no sun. This is especially important for large-scale plantings, for if conditions are wrong, young plants could be lost; for a single plant, it is less crucial. Water plants in pots with liquid tomato food the night before planting; water clumps of perennials in the garden that are to be moved to the border at the same time.

PLANTING MIX

Even if the whole border is prepared in advance, individual plants still appreciate good treatment. The best policy is to use a planting mix, either bought or made up at home. Ready-made soilless mixes from a garden center, such as those sold for potting houseplants, are ideal and can be bought in compressed bales. The most useful homemade mix is made up of used potting soils, which can be stored in plastic bags until needed. Any used soil from potted plants that have died, the previous year's hanging baskets, and the like should be saved for use in a planting mix. If this old soil is mostly peat based, the addition of a little sand is a help. Take a 2 gallon (9 liter) bucketful, and combine this with 2 oz (60 g) of a balanced general fertilizer, such as 6-9-6, to make the final planting mix.

PLANTING INDIVIDUAL PLANTS

To plant perennials from large pots or those that have come in big clumps from another part of the garden, you must use a spade. Dig a hole 9 in (23 cm) deep and clearly wider than the pot size or the root ball of the clump. Then fork some planting mix into the base of the hole. It is difficult

Planting individual plants

1 *Using a trowel, dig a hole that is big enough for the root ball of the plant.*

2 *Grip the plant between your fingers, and loosen the pot with a tap from the trowel.*

3 *Set the plant in the hole at the right depth, then refill with soil and firm gently.*

4 *Water in thoroughly, adding some liquid fertilizer to give the plant a good start.*

to be precise about how much mix to add: it depends on the soil condition. As a guide, when planting a mature hosta, which demands a hole 1½ ft (45 cm) wide, into average soil, use a bucket of planting mix. Add more planting mix to the soil removed from the hole before refilling.

Much smaller potted plants need a different treatment. If the ground has already been prepared, no extra work may be required, but it is a good idea to spread and fork in a 2 in (5 cm) layer of planting mix over the area where the plants are to go. Then put the plants in with a trowel.

Planting depths The level at which plants are set is important. Some perennials will rot at the crown if planted too deeply, but none should be planted too shallowly. If the intention is to mulch the bed after planting to conserve moisture and suppress weeds, the plant should be set so that

Planting depths

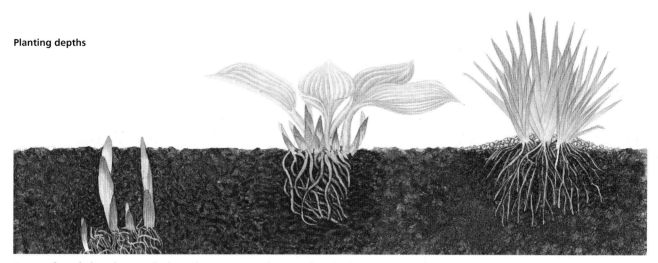

Perennials with deep dormant buds, such as polygonatums, should be planted deeply to imitate the way they naturally grow.

Many plants, such as this hosta, should be set either at about soil level or just above if they are to be mulched after planting.

Perennials that like a dry crown, such as Sisyrinchium striatum *and irises, are planted with the crown just above soil level.*

the top of the root ball is at soil level. Apply 2 in (5 cm) of mulch between the plants; do not cover the crowns. If a mulch is not to be applied, the plants can go deeper and the root ball can be covered with soil from the bed. This same rule applies to clumps dug from the garden, but small, rooted divisions are less tolerant. Plant them at the same level as they were growing previously if they are not to be mulched, and plant them more shallowly if a mulch is to be applied. Having much less in the way of food reserves in their roots, they are less tolerant of a deep mulch. Set the plant at the right depth and filter improved soil in around the roots; firm this with your fingers in stages so that it is uniformly compacted. Using your foot to firm perennials, which is sometimes recommended, may result in overcompaction of the soil, especially if it is heavy.

WATERING AND MULCHING

After planting, remove debris and then rake the soil over to remove footmarks and leave a neat finish; then water the plants. When a new bed has been planted, a sprinkler can be used, which has the advantage for the plant roots of ensuring that all the soil is at the same level of moisture. It has the disadvantage, however, of not allowing the new plants to be fed at the same time. When one or a few perennials have been planted, they can be watered in with liquid tomato food from a watering can. It is especially important to check regularly on perennials planted in summer in full growth, as it is difficult to tell how much the roots have dried out until the leaves collapse and damage is already being done.

After planting either a whole bed or a single plant, a mulch is helpful in keeping the roots moist and preventing the germination of weed seeds. Many materials are available for mulching, but garden compost should be last on the list. Unless it is unusually well made, it will contain weed seeds, which will then germinate and engulf the new plantings. Use the planting mix as a mulch for small plantings or any weed-free, bulky mulch for larger areas. It should be spread after watering.

PLANTING BEDS AND BORDERS

Planting a new bed or border all at once can be daunting as well as exciting. A systematic approach is the key to increasing the pleasure and reducing the stress on both the gardener and the plants.

ASSEMBLING THE PLANTS

Once the soil is prepared, the plants can be brought to the site. Lay out a sheet of plastic on a nearby path or lawn, and assemble all the plants that are in pots. Group plants of the same type together, with their labels still in view. It is sound practice to feed all plants in pots the day before planting with a weak liquid fertilizer—such as half-strength 10-10-10—so that their roots are moist and they have a little extra plant food to stimulate growth immediately after planting. If plants are to be lifted from other parts of the garden or from neighbors' gardens, this can be done next. To protect the roots from damage or drying out, each one can be placed in a plastic shopping bag with its label.

ORGANIZING THE PLANTS

The next stage is to group the different plants together in the pattern in which they will finally be planted. If you are working from a plan, it can be helpful to first organize the different varieties on your plastic sheet in the same pattern as they will be planted in the bed—only without spacing them out. Then, if you decide to make some adjustments to your plan, you can make them before transferring the plants to the border.

If you adopt a less structured approach, it can still be useful to organize the plants on your plastic sheet before transferring them to the bed. In this way you can avoid the tiresome task of actually moving plants from one end of the bed to the other, and perhaps back again, as you decide on the best arrangement.

SETTING OUT THE PLANTS

Once you have settled on exactly how the planting is to be organized, you can move the plants to the border itself. Many gardeners find it helpful to mark out the extent of each group on the border before moving the plants, especially if working from a plan. To do this, you can pour dry sand gently from a wine bottle to mark the area set aside for each variety. A simple alternative is to use the point of a stick to draw the boundaries of the groups in the raked soil, but these lines are easily scuffed out.

The individual plants can now be moved to the border itself. First, place the plants of each type together in the area in which they are to be planted; do not space them out right away, as it will be simpler to move them if you decide to swap them around at the last minute. When you are satisfied that all the varieties are where they should be, space out those in pots to fill their allotted areas. Depending on the selections and their size and vigor, you may have just a single plant of some varieties and perhaps seven or nine plants of others. When planting a group of one variety, try to space the plants out evenly but not in regular shapes, like squares or circles, as this can look too regimented. The spacing between individual plants depends on their vigor and height (see the Plant Directory).

When the plants in pots have been set out, remove the transplanted or bare-root plants from their bags and set them out in the same way, dividing them up as necessary (see p.65). Plant those plants that are not in pots first to ensure that their roots have the minimum possible time to dry. Put their labels in place immediately, and remove the bags from the scene. Next, deal with the plants in pots; label them and collect and stack the pots as you go. When all the plants are planted, water them (see p.46),

Organizing border planting

1 *Gather all the plants together on a plastic sheet in roughly the spots they will have in the new border. Mark out the groups if it helps you visualize the end result.*

2 *Plant the bare-root plants and those at the back of the border first, then put in the pot-grown plants. Water the plants when they are in their final positions.*

and use a hoe or rake to tidy up the soil and remove footmarks. Finally, it is a good idea to mark any changes made during the planting process on your original paper plan. If you did not start with a plan, it is wise to make one now. This sketch can be a great help later if labels become lost and names of plants are forgotten.

MIXED AND MATURE PLANTINGS

Planting a completely new border presents one sort of challenge, but planting perennials into an established border requires a different approach. Clearly, the whole border cannot be planned and prepared at once, so individual pockets must be prepared separately as described on page 32. Planting perennials into a traditional herbaceous border in which different varieties are grown in individual, self-contained clumps presents few difficulties. Other perennials are rarely so temperamental as to resent the disturbance when soil is prepared alongside, especially if their own soil is enriched in the process and the space where the new plants are to go is clearly defined. At times, though, you may want to lift and replant neighboring perennials when you plant new ones to ensure that the relationship between them is exactly as you wish.

One thing that can help in a number of situations where perennials are being planted into existing borders is to use small plants. Perennials from small pots, approximately 3½ in (8 cm), are preferable to those from larger pots, as they need much smaller planting holes and so the preparation creates less disturbance. A good alternative is to use rooted divisions taken from the edge of existing plants in your own garden, or you can split perennials in large pots into two or three pieces before planting them. In spring these will grow and quickly establish themselves. It is sometimes suggested that new plants can be established in mature borders by sowing seeds where they are required. This is rarely successful because of competition from existing plants.

PLANTING PERENNIALS AMONG SHRUBS

Planting among shrubs may present problems. With small plants, which face competition from existing shrub roots, pay special attention to watering and feeding to ensure they thrive. Take care in preparing the planting site. The roots of roses, for example, often throw up suckers when damaged. Rather than disturbing the roots, it is usually better to dig less deeply and to mulch and feed well after planting. Magnolias languish if

their roots are disturbed. Rather than digging out the soil, work carefully with a fork to determine where the main roots are, and avoid them.

Where roots are encountered, the tougher, nonsuckering shrubs, such as forsythias, will not object to one or two being carefully removed. Cut them away with pruning shears; never chop them through with a spade, as this leaves rough edges and splits, which are more likely to rot.

PLANTING PERENNIALS AMONG BULBS

When planting a new group of perennials or even a single plant into part of a border where bulbs are already growing, there is a risk of damaging the bulbs. But growing bulbs and perennials together can be very effective. Two techniques can be used to minimize any damage to the bulbs.

One way is to plant the perennials while the bulbs are in growth. At this stage it is clear exactly where the

Planting perennials among bulbs

1 *As the bulb foliage dies down, decide where the perennials are to go and transplant any bulbs that are in the way.*

2 *Choose small perennials and plant with a trowel; the remains of the foliage will indicate the presence of bulbs.*

bulbs are growing and the perennials can be planted between them. You cannot always plant at the ideal spacing, and you cannot prepare the soil as thoroughly as usual, but you should be able to spare the bulbs. Another approach is to wait until the bulbs' foliage dies down. This technique is especially useful if the bulbs are densely planted or if the soil needs improvement. Spring bulbs, such as daffodils, die down in late spring and early summer; summer bulbs, such as galtonias, die down in late summer and fall. As the leaves die down, but before they have disappeared altogether, the position of the bulbs is clear, and it is also a good time to move them. Dig up the bulbs and place them on one side, then prepare the soil. Plant the perennials, then replant the bulbs between the perennials. It is important to plant the perennials first; otherwise the bulbs may be cut by the trowel as you make the planting holes for the perennials.

PLANTING SEQUENCE FOR NEW MIXED BORDERS

When planting a completely new mixed border with shrubs, climbers, and bulbs as well as perennials, the preparation should be the same as that for a traditional herbaceous border, and the plants are best laid out on a sheet of plastic in much the same way (see p.34). First, plant wall shrubs and climbers on any wall or fence at the back of the border and tie in with wires. Then put in any posts as support for other climbers, and plant the climbers themselves, followed by the evergreen and deciduous shrubs. Single specimen perennials should be planted next, followed by groups of perennials and any tough alpines as frontal plants, with the bulbs going in last.

WILDFLOWER PLANTINGS

Gardeners are increasingly interested in making wildflower gardens, partly because they are beautiful in themselves, but also because they attract a large number of birds and insects. Plantings of native wildflowers, especially wildflower meadows, require a very different approach from that used for growing garden cultivars in beds and borders. In particular, if the soil is prepared lavishly in the way described for other perennials, grasses and weeds usually take over and smother the choice flowers. For wildflowers the opposite approach is needed, with the creation of conditions of low fertility to prevent the invasion of these coarser plants. Nevertheless, weeds can still be a problem. Whether they spread by perennial roots, like some of the coarse grasses, or by seed, like the undesirable annuals, weeds remain a real danger to wildflowers.

SITE AND SOIL

Rather than choosing a site to suit the plants you wish to grow, it is often more appropriate to choose the plants to suit the site you have available: use woodland plants for shade and meadow plants for sunny places. The ideal site will have soil that is somewhat impoverished, as in rich soil, vigorous weeds may swamp the more restrained, though more attractive, wildflowers.

Converting existing borders The soil in borders in which cultivated perennials or other plants have been grown is likely to be too rich for wildflowers. One way of remedying this is to remove the topsoil (using it to improve the soil in another part of the garden) and to replace it with

Reducing soil fertility

To prepare for wildflowers, remove the lawn or topsoil to reduce the soil's fertility.

poorer soil. An alternative approach would be to sow a succession of green manure crops, such as mustard, winter grazing rye, or alfalfa, but instead of digging these plants into the soil when mature, remove them and dig into the soil elsewhere. This results in a steady reduction of soil fertility. Then dig or fork over the site (without adding manure), and leave the area fallow for one growing season to assess the weed situation. Hoeing may be sufficient to remove annual weeds, although in some cases a total weed killer is valuable to ensure the destruction of all weeds. Gardeners who prefer not to use weed killer can cover the area with an old carpet or thick black plastic for a year to smother weeds as they come through. **Converting lawns** A lawn that has rarely or never been fed and has been regularly mowed, with the clippings removed, has the potential to be turned into a wildflower meadow. The absence of feeding and the removal of clippings create a steady reduction of the fertility and, at the

Removing weeds

1 *Cover the area with old carpet or black polythene to smother perennial weeds.*

2 *The weed roots will exhaust themselves searching for light.*

same time, finer grasses disappear and broad-leaved plants move in. Often, ceasing to mow allows a tapestry of flowers to appear from plants that have been there for some time, their flowers cut off by regular mowing. Low-fertility lawns can be converted into wildflower plantings in one of three ways. Seed can be sown directly into the grass; wildflowers can be established by planting young plants; or the top 2 in (5 cm) of lawn can be removed and the soil dug and treated as a new site.

SOWING AND PLANTING

Plants of some wildflowers are difficult to find in nurseries, and it is often more practical to raise them from seed. While it is possible and sometimes useful to raise them in pots, you may have more success if you sow them in the spot where they are to flower.

Mixtures of perennial wildflowers are available from seed companies, formulated to suit different soils and situations. They often contain annuals to provide color in the first season and to create cover to prevent the invasion of weeds.

Making new plantings Dig the soil, then tread and rake to create a fine seedbed before sowing the seed. Check the seed packet for advice on the amount of seed required for a given area. It is most convenient to sow in rows because the rows of seedlings will stand out clearly when the seed first germinates, and you can easily distinguish any weeds growing between the rows and remove them. As the plants develop, the row pattern disappears. In most areas, spring is usually the best time to sow, although in areas with mild winters, fall sowing is successful.

Sowing wildflowers

1 *Make a drill with the edge of a hand trowel in friable soil.*

2 *Sow the seeds thinly, gently tapping them out of the packet.*

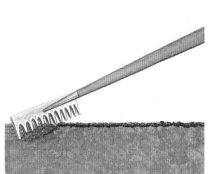

3 *Cover the seeds carefully with soil using a rake, and tap down gently.*

Daisies, violas, and poppies make a colorful and lively wildflower planting.

Planting a lawn requires care, mainly because the developing roots of the new plants face competition for moisture and nutrients from the roots of the existing lawn grasses and other plants. Relatively small plants are often most successful. Use a bulb planter to remove a cylinder of soil, fill the hole with used potting soil, then plant the seedlings. They may need occasional watering during their first summer until their roots have had time to develop.

WILDFLOWERS IN CONVENTIONAL BORDERS

Wildflowers can also be grown in more organized beds and borders in exactly the same way as cultivated plants. They can be either grown among garden cultivars or given a border of their own.

The rich soil can cause wildflowers to grow taller than they would in their natural habitats, so they may need staking in borders but not in meadows. They may also spread more vigorously and seed themselves freely.

Converting lawns Wildflower seed can be sown directly in a lawn, although because of the competition from the existing plants, this can be an unpredictable method. Cut the grass short, then rake the lawn to remove moss and the layer of fibrous matter, such as roots and grass stems, known as thatch. Make seed drills 6–9 in (15–23 cm) apart using the corner of a metal hoe, the tip of a trowel, or a similar sharp tool. This can be hard work, as the soil under lawns is often compacted. Now, thinly sow the seed in the drills and lightly cover it with sand. As the seedlings mature, the rows will at first be obvious, but the random distribution of many species in the seed mixtures ensures that, after a year or two, the pattern will disappear.

Planting young plants Wildflower plantings can be created by raising the plants in pots and planting them in prepared soil or lawn. Young plants are also available at some garden centers, by mail order, or from special wildflower nurseries. Starting with plants rather than seed helps to establish plantings more quickly. If the soil has been prepared, planting young plants in clumps rather than sowing seed gives you another season to deal with weed problems by hoeing and spot treatment, before the coverage of wildflowers is too dense.

Planting wildflowers in a lawn

1 *Use a bulb planter to neatly remove a cylinder of grass and soil.*

2 *Set the young plant in the hole, and refill with used potting soil.*

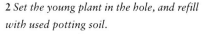

CONTAINER PLANTINGS

Growing perennials in containers successfully depends on choosing the right plants and the right containers for the individual situation, then using the appropriate potting soil and drainage materials. It is important to state at the outset that many perennials are unsuitable for growing in containers. Some, such as hellebores, have such deep root systems that they do not adapt well to restricted root space. Others, like delphiniums, look entirely out of scale and out of place. Still others have a restricted season of interest; attractive for a few weeks, they are then best moved out of sight—a tedious task. The best perennials to grow in containers have the following qualities:

• They are modest in size, making them naturally the right scale for most containers.

• They have an unusually long flowering season.

• They have attractive foliage for many months or are evergreen.

• They have good foliage *and* good flowers, maximizing their appeal.

• They have the character to make specimen plants.

• They benefit from close inspection of their flowers.

Perennials for containers include *Acanthus, Ajuga, Astilbe, Epimedium,* ferns, hardy geraniums (low or trailing), *Hemerocallis* (especially dwarf types), *Heuchera, Hosta, Lamium, Primula, Pulmonaria, Sedum,* and variegated grasses.

CONTAINERS

Containers made of natural materials are generally more attractive than those made of synthetic materials, and they usually look better in the garden. Matching the size of each container with the size of its plants is crucial; putting a small plant in a large container is not only wasteful but may even result in rotting roots, since the potting soil may stay too wet. A large plant in a small pot will need constant watering and with insufficient root room will never develop naturally. Also, it will probably blow over. It is a mistake to put even the smallest perennials, such as primroses, in pots smaller than 5 in (13 cm) in diameter. At the other extreme, some of the more vigorous hostas, like 'Krossa Regal,' will eventually need a pot 1½ ft (45 cm) wide or more to look and grow their best.

Frost-resistant, earthenware flower pots are the most suitable containers for perennials along with stone or terracotta urns and containers cast in a stone and concrete mix. Wooden tubs are also very attractive and are inexpensive if made at home; deep wooden boxes, at least 9 in (23 cm) wide and as deep, are also good for smaller plants.

POTTING SOIL

Always start with fresh potting soil; never use old soil from the garden. A mix containing some loam is preferable. Use one part sterilized potting soil, one part sharp sand, and two parts soilless potting mix. For plants that appreciate moisture, potting soil with 25 percent additional peat can be mixed in; for those preferring unusually good drainage, 25 percent extra sand or perlite can be added.

Before filling the container with potting soil, drainage material must be added. Any large drainage holes should be covered with fine plastic mesh, such as small squares of window screen, to keep out insects, and then covered with a layer of gravel, which should be at least 1 in (2.5 cm)

Container planting

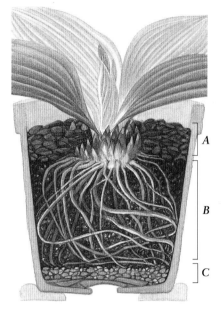

A maturing specimen hosta grown in a container with its extensive root system and expanding crown of shoots: A Mulch, B Roots in potting soil, C Drainage material.

deep but need be no more than 2 in (5 cm) deep in even the largest pots. The gravel helps excess moisture drain away quickly. To prevent the potting soil from filtering into the gravel and clogging it, the gravel should be covered with a layer of landscape fabric. The fabric allows moisture through; it also allows some roots through but prevents the potting soil from filtering downward, blocking the drainage. The fabric provides an additional barrier to worms and other soil dwellers.

PLANTING STYLES

There are two ways of planting containers. They can be planted with a single, carefully chosen plant as an attractive specimen. The same effect can be created by planting three plants of the same type in a neat triangle so that they grow together and look like one plant. This is often the most effective way of planting pots up to about 1 ft (30 cm) in diameter. Alternatively, larger pots and long boxes can be planted with a carefully chosen selection of perennials. In this case consideration must be given to the eventual location of the container. If it is to be viewed from all sides, a symmetrical arrangement may be best, with the tallest plant in the center, surrounded by lower, bushier plants and perhaps sprawling ones around the edge. If it is to be backed by a wall or fence or placed in a corner site, the tallest plant is better toward the back. Whichever style is adopted, it is important to choose plants carefully, for plants in containers always come in for close scrutiny.

PLANTING CONTAINERS

Before planting a large container, move it to its final site. At this point containers that are to stand on the ground should be set on low blocks about 1 in (2.5 cm) high to lift the base off the ground and allow unimpeded drainage. Now assemble all the drainage materials, potting soil, and plants. Cover the drainage hole, add the gravel, and start to add the soil mix. Firm the soil gently as you go. Then set the plant in place in the center of the container to check its level. If possible, leave a 1 in (2.5 cm) space between the top of the soil and the top of the container. Once the plant is sitting in place at the right level, it can be removed from its pot, set back in the container, and more soil mix added and gently firmed until the required level is reached. Finally, the surface of the container should be mulched. The space between the soil and the top of the pot can be filled entirely with washed medium or coarse gravel or very coarse bark to reduce moisture evaporation, prevent the potting soil from being splashed out during watering, and enhance the appearance of the container. When planting a mixed container, perhaps using plants from different-sized pots, fix the position of the plant in the largest pot first, then add more soil mix, then the smaller plants until the planting is complete.

WATERING AND FEEDING

After planting, the container should be watered using a plant starter fertilizer until it drips from the base. As the roots fill the container, particularly in warmer months, water regularly, sometimes as often as every day. Although potting soil contains some nutrients, after the first few weeks water every week in the growing season with a liquid tomato fertilizer to encourage robustness and steady growth.

Planting a mixed container

1 *Set the container in its final position; prop it on blocks to help drainage.*

2 *Place drainage material in the base of the container, and start to fill with soil.*

3 *Put the plants in place as the container is filled, firming the soil around them.*

4 *Finish off with a mulch of coarse bark or gravel, and water thoroughly.*

Right: Place the tallest plant in the center if the arrangement is to be viewed from all sides.

CARE AND CULTIVATION

Perennials are not demanding plants, but regular care helps them to give their best for as long as possible, to increase, and to resist the attacks of pests and diseases. Much of the care required is routine watering, weeding, and removing dead flowers, but the more occasional tasks, such as feeding, mulching, and staking, are no less vital. The periodic need for replanting is crucial: while some perennials survive for decades without division, others need to be replanted every other year.

MULCHING

Mulching is the spreading of a layer of sand, gravel, or organic matter onto the surface of the soil. This treatment, repeated periodically and depending on the material used, replicates the natural cycle in many plant habitats, where a dense covering of fallen leaves or dead stems accumulates every fall. It also suppresses weeds, provides nutrients, retains moisture in the soil, and offers a simple and attractive background for the plants. Sand and gravel mulches are used in relatively few situations, usually only on beds prepared with good drainage and in drought gardens and Mediterranean plantings. Sand helps water drain away from the crowns of plants, which may be susceptible to rotting in wet winters.

ORGANIC MULCHES

Most mulches are organic, and here the most important characteristic is that they should be weed free. The time and effort spent removing weeds from the soil, then mulching in order to keep it that way, are wasted if the mulch itself is full of weed roots or weed seeds. An organic mulch is less permanent than a gravel mulch, but as it rots the organic material releases nutrients that benefit the plants.

Garden compost Most garden compost contains weed seeds unless it has been made to a very high standard. The compost needs to heat up to at least 120°F (49°C), preferably higher, during the decomposition process to kill weed seeds. To achieve this, use a large wooden box as a container, building the pile in layers, using a commercial compost activator, and ensuring a good supply of air and moisture. Unless you can be sure your compost is of the highest quality, it is usually better to dig it into the soil than to use it as a mulch.

Manure Raw, lumpy manure is sometimes used as a mulch, but it does not cover the soil sufficiently to be effective and may also burn plant roots. Animal manure must be well rotted before being used on the garden, and it can take over a year to break down into a suitably crumbly texture. It is usually free of weed seeds, unless the straw upon which it is based contains seeds.

Peat Peat can be used; its texture is good, it is usually weed free, and it can be bought in handy plastic bales. However, as well as being a diminishing natural resource, it contains almost no plant nutrients, dries out on the surface; and may blow away on windy sites. Its cost may also be a limiting factor for large borders.

Compost bin

A compost bin constructed of treated wood will last well and keep the compost at a high temperature to help kill weeds.

Bark Coarse bark, partly composted to darken its color and help create a better nutrient balance, is an attractive and popular mulch. Unlike peat, bark is more persistent, lasting a great deal longer before rotting. Its one drawback is that unfortunately it provides almost no nutrients. Some

Manure mulch

gardeners also use shredded bark or wood chips, which are effective, although unattractively pale in color. There is concern that as fresh wood chips decompose, they may take nutrients from the soil, but this fear has been exaggerated.

Leaves Commonly used, leaves can be applied in the fall either whole or partially composted. Worms pull them into the soil, which gradually improves in texture.

Other materials In different parts of the country, other bulky organic materials, such as brewery waste or the waste from local farm crops, may be available. These materials are always worth investigating and are often good value. Some gardeners spread grass clippings on their borders, but while this may suppress weeds growing in the border soil, grass clippings usually contain so much grass seed that the border may soon be carpeted in green. Shredded garden prunings are becoming more popular, as efficient shredders have come down in price, and the shredded material can be applied directly to borders or composted first. It decomposes and disappears more quickly than bark or wood chips.

TIMING

A mulch should be applied only to damp soil that is free of weeds. Initially, a mulch should be applied immediately after planting, to a depth of at least 1 in (2.5 cm). A depth of 2 in (5 cm) is often more effective in terms of water conservation and weed prevention but will smother small plants. Established herbaceous borders should be mulched in the fall, after the border has been tidied for the winter, but if the border contains a high proportion of late-flowering plants, tidying and mulching can be left until the spring.

Timing a mulch for mixed borders that also contain fall and spring bulbs is more difficult. The trick is to put it on the border when there is little in flower or likely to be damaged, so the best time to mulch is immediately after the fall bulbs fade but before the spring bulbs start to grow.

Apply the mulch in late fall or early winter in northern areas, or during the winter months in more temperate climates. If possible, the mulch should be renewed regularly. Annual mulching is valuable on poor soil, but mulching every other year is usually adequate.

FEEDING

In nature, the dead plant stems and leaves that fall around the plants rot, and are taken back into the soil to provide nutrients for the plants in succeeding years. In gardens we cut down the top growth in the fall and remove it, so we must replace the nutrients lost in that process.

Most perennials are neither demanding nor unusually fussy about feeding. The process starts with thorough preparation of the soil before planting, ensuring that the soil contains good reserves of nutrients to which roots will have access as the plants develop. In succeeding years, regular additions of nutrients, either as bulky organic matter or as fertilizers, are essential to keep plants healthy and growing strongly.

PLANTING TIME

Adding bulky organic material to the soil at planting time not only improves the structure of the soil but also provides a reservoir of nutrients, which are steadily released over the years as the organic matter decomposes. A general fertilizer is also usually applied shortly before planting to ensure that the plants have access to nutrients in the shorter term (see p.30). Applying a liquid fertilizer immediately before or after planting gives the plants a flying start.

REGULAR FEEDING

An annual mulch of organic matter can provide most of the nutrients that perennials require. Unfortunately, materials vary in the amount of nutrients that they contain. Some, such as bark and peat, are relatively low in nutrients; manure is a richer source. Even then, the precise balance of nutrients in manure can vary from

Bark mulch

Leaves used as mulch

batch to batch. Many gardeners rely solely on regular annual mulching to provide all the nutrients their plants require. In most gardens, however, and especially when the soil is not already fertile, additional annual feeding using a dry organic or inorganic fertilizer is beneficial.

Fertilizer and mulch The frequency with which fertilizer is required depends to some extent on the regularity of mulching and the material used.

• If materials that contain little or no nutrients, such as peat or coarse bark, are used as mulch, annual applications of fertilizer are advisable.

• If good mulching materials are difficult to obtain, a mulch can be applied every other year and a dry feed at full strength can be used in alternate years.

• If mulching materials are not available at all, fertilizer is best applied every year.

• Even if beds and borders are mulched on a regular basis, an occasional application of fertilizer helps redress any imbalances created by the continual use of one type of mulch. This is especially true in the early years of a new planting, when fertility can be built up by applying fertilizer immediately after the border has been tidied and then also applying a mulch.

Timing In general, fertilizer is best applied in late winter or early spring, just as plants are starting to grow. If it is applied in fall, the winter rains may wash some of the nutrients away through the soil while the plants are dormant and unable to absorb them. It is not always possible to follow the best practice, however. In warmer regions, where such plants as hellebores and bergenias grow during the winter, spring application is less crucial. Also, where beds are carpeted with early spring bulbs, it is often more convenient to apply fertilizer in fall or winter, when the bulbs will not be trampled.

Materials Perennials do not demand a special fertilizer. A well-balanced general fertilizer which contains nitrogen, phosphorus, and potassium—the three main plant nutrients—is ideal. These fertilizers come in a variety of strengths, so it is important to follow the instructions on rates of application. The most commonly found ratios are 6-9-6 and 7-7-7. Try to choose a brand that includes minor or trace elements in its formulation, especially if you are unable to mulch regularly. Perennials rarely show signs of being deficient in such minor nutrients as manganese and zinc, but their availability does help keep the plants healthy. Organic and inorganic materials are equally effective, so if you prefer to garden without artificial fertilizers, plenty of effective organic dry feeds are available.

Technique First, check the rate of application on the fertilizer package; this is usually given in ounces per square yard (grams per square meter). Note and follow any safety warnings. Although fertilizers are among the least dangerous of garden chemicals, they can irritate or dry your skin so it is wise to wear disposable plastic gloves when handling them.

Applying fertilizer

1 *To help apply fertilizer evenly, use bamboo stakes to mark out sections.*

2 *Spread the fertilizer evenly holding the hand 1–3 ft (30–60 cm) above the soil.*

3 *Rake the fertilizer into the soil's surface to keep it from drifting away in the wind.*

Take a comfortable handful of fertilizer and weigh it. Check the weight against the application rate, and adjust the handful accordingly until you can confidently grasp a handful containing approximately the amount required for 1 sq yd/m.

To ensure that the fertilizer is distributed at the correct rate, tie four bamboo stakes 4 ft (1.2 m) long into a square with each side 1 yd/m long. Lay the square on the soil in one corner of the bed then spread the fertilizer on this area. Move the square along, and continue until the bed is completed. You may find that you can soon visualize 1 sq yd/m fairly accurately and dispense with the bamboo square.

Apply fertilizer on a still, dry day. Move your hand from side to side, releasing the fertilizer about 1–2 ft (30–60 cm) above the soil. Aim to spread almost all of each handful in one pass, retaining a little to cover any bare patches.

Some perennials will be in leaf when fertilizer is applied, and in this case try to spread it beneath the leaves. After spreading the fertilizer, take time to rake or hoe it in lightly into the surface to prevent the wind from blowing it away. If rain does not fall within a week of a spring application, watering will help to activate the fertilizer.

SPOT FEEDING
Occasionally the poor growth of a plant may tempt you to consider giving it a boost. This is best done with a liquid fertilizer, which can be directed more precisely and so encourage the growth of an individual plant rather than boosting all the plants in the area, whether they need it or not. Use a liquid fertilizer containing plenty of trace elements.

WATERING

As water becomes an increasingly scarce natural resource in many areas and as summer climates become less predictable, often including long hot spells, gardeners must think more carefully about how to keep their perennials supplied with moisture during the growing season.

MOISTURE-RETENTIVE SOIL
Organic matter retains water; one of the main reasons for adding generous amounts while preparing for planting is to increase the moisture-holding capacity of the soil. This ensures that, during dry spells, the soil contains reserves of water that help keep the plants growing. Levels of organic matter drop as it decomposes over the years, however, and so it needs replenishing. Regular mulching is important. Although the organic matter is applied to the surface, earthworms soon draw it down into the soil, and cultivation eventually

results in it being mixed into the lower levels. In addition, regular mulching has the advantage of helping to prevent the soil from losing moisture directly from its bare surface. Thorough preparation of planting sites when perennials are replaced or replanted also helps keep the soil rich in humus.

WIND AND SHELTER
Strong wind can increase evaporation of moisture both from plant leaves and from the surface of the soil, so shelter can be helpful in preventing water loss. A fence is one way of providing shelter. Even a hedge can be worthwhile, as the benefit from the shelter it provides outweighs the fact that its roots take moisture from the soil. Many traditional herbaceous borders are backed by an evergreen hedge and fronted by a low boxwood hedge. The shelter that these hedges provide to developing plants is as valuable as their role as a background against which to view the flowers.

In shady, moisture retentive situations choose plants that enjoy the conditions like these primulas, ferns, meconopsis and hostas.

WHEN TO WATER

Newly planted perennials appreciate a good soak to ensure that their roots do not dry out and to encourage new roots to grow into the garden soil. But once they are established, be cautious about watering. Watering at the first sign of a dry spell encourages the roots to remain in the surface layer of the soil rather than to grow more deeply in search of water reserves. The time may come, however, when watering is necessary. Look out for these signs of water shortage:

• Growth slows almost to a stop.
• Leaves and flower heads wilt.
• Lower leaves shrivel.
• Leaves lose their gloss.
• Newly opened flowers seem unusually small.
• The plants in the border look limp.

Ideally, watering should be carried out before these symptoms become visible. With experience, you will become increasingly sensitive to the needs of your plants.

The time of day you apply water is important if it is to be used efficiently. Water on calm days so that wind does not distort the area of coverage or hasten evaporation. If possible, water in the evening, so that moisture has time to penetrate the soil before the heat of the sun the following day increases evaporation.

HOW TO WATER

Watering individual plants with a watering can is usually futile, except for sensitive varieties, like candelabra primulas, growing among more tolerant plants. Even then many canfuls of water may be needed to help the plants. If the moisture soaks only a few inches into the soil, the roots will grow up toward it, making them more vulnerable to future drought. Only the use of a hose can ensure that sufficient quantities are applied.

There are four main ways to water: a sprinkler, a soaker hose, a porous hose, and a drip irrigation system.

Sprinklers Sprinklers come in various designs, all intended to apply an even covering of water without constant attention. The most common types are the following:

• Simple static units that water a small circular area with a constant fine spray. Although inexpensive, these are difficult to adjust and may create puddles by constantly watering the same small area.

• Adjustable rotating pulse-jet sprinklers that cover a circular area and generally apply the water more evenly than other units. They are often the most expensive, but both the area of coverage and the fineness of the spray can be adjusted.

• Adjustable oscillating units that cover a more or less rectangular area, which can be varied to suit the shape of the border. While more expensive, they do not puddle the soil and are also the most effective type to use when water pressure is low.

All of these waste a lot of water in evaporation during hot weather. In addition, the oscillating units can cause compaction due to the large droplet size. It is essential when using any of these sprinklers to apply plenty of water. It is not possible to be specific about how long a sprinkler should be left watering one area because the rate of application depends on the nature of the individual unit, how the sprinkler is set, the water pressure, and the nature of the soil. But the water must penetrate deeply, preferably deeper than the roots of most of the plants, to a depth of at least 2 ft (60 cm). Excavating a hole the day after watering will give an indication of the degree of penetration. Finally, always make sure that the sprinkler is adjusted to water exactly the right area: when watering a large area, move the sprinkler so

Many shade- or moisture-loving plants, such as these primulas and meconopsis, thrive in open, sunny locations if the soil is kept sufficiently damp.

Types of sprinkler

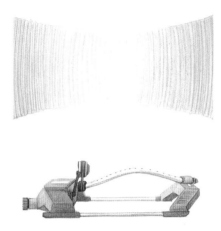

Simple rotating sprinklers are inexpensive. They water a circular area but are uneven in their distribution of water.

Pulse-jet sprinklers are expensive. They water a circular area or part of a circle, are very adjustable, and water evenly.

Oscillating sprinklers vary in price. They water a rectangular area, are partially adjustable, and water fairly evenly.

that there is no overlap with areas watered earlier, and when placing the sprinkler in the border rather than at its edge, raise it above the level of surrounding plants.

Soaker hose Available in different lengths, these hoses have a double row of small holes on one side. When connected to a water supply, they give a fine spray of water on either side. Being flexible, they can be snaked through the border, bending to pass around plants. If placed with the holes facing up, they water a wide strip, but a lot of water is lost through evaporation. When the holes face down, the water soaks down to the roots in an inverted "V" pattern.

Porous hose In recent years another useful way of applying water has become available: perforated hose is manufactured with a large number of tiny holes through which water seeps. It is laid on the soil or even buried under a mulch, connected to a standard supply line, and water oozes from the hose into the soil. The great advantage of this system is that little water is lost through evaporation, so the amount of water required is

reduced. The disadvantage is that in alkaline areas the pores of the porous hose can become clogged with lime deposits, reducing the amount of water that penetrates to the soil. Furthermore, it can be difficult to assess just how thoroughly the soil has been watered. Perforated hose is useful for watering rows of young plants or cut flowers, because if it is laid directly along the row, you can be sure water will reach the roots.

Drip irrigation system It is also possible to water plants individually rather than soak the soil. From a supply line in the center of the bed, small "spaghetti-tube" pipes can be run to each plant. An emitter on the end of each pipe keeps the water from washing holes in the soil. If winters are mild and severe freezing unlikely, these can be left in place year-round and hidden beneath the mulch. Where winters are severe, they need to be removed or emptied before frost.

CHOOSING THE RIGHT PLANTS

One way of reducing the demand for water in regions where droughts are common or there are frequent

restrictions on garden watering is to use drought-resistant plants. These usually grow naturally in areas with hot, dry summers and so are best able to thrive in such conditions in the garden. Drought-resistant plants include *Armeria, Dianthus, Diascia, Elymus magellanicus, Erodium, Festuca, Helianthemum, Iris unguicularis,* and *Phlox douglasii* cultivars.

In damp or well-watered gardens, a drought-loving plant, such as this *Euphorbia characias* subsp. *wulfenii,* can be grown in a container and so kept in the drier soil it prefers.

WEEDING

Keeping perennial borders free of weeds demands thorough preparation and constant vigilance. The seeds of some weeds, like poppies and nightshades, can remain viable in the soil for decades, so the old saying "one year's seeding brings seven years' weeding" is more than true.

PREPARATION

Planting a new border that has not been cleared of perennial weeds is asking for trouble. Part of the point of digging the soil before putting the plants in is to remove the roots of perennial weeds. Unfortunately, some weeds, such as quack grass, regenerate from a piece of root less than ¼ in (5 mm) long if a bud is present, so it is important to try to remove every piece during the digging process. Inevitably some small pieces of root will be missed, but waiting a few months between digging and planting allows these pieces to sprout and then they can be removed individually. When adding organic matter to the soil, it is important not to add more weeds at the same time. The roots of perennial weeds should never be added to the compost pile in the first place, but ensuring that compost is made properly, heating up and killing weed seeds, is a valuable preventive measure.

Another way of dealing with perennial weeds is to kill them all using a systemic weed killer before the ground is dug. This technique is especially useful when you are creating a bed in an area that has not previously been cultivated. Apply a broad-spectrum systemic weed killer to the whole area in late spring or early summer, or at any time when weeds are growing strongly. After a few weeks, you can clear away the dead material and dig the bed. When difficult weeds, such as bindweed, are present, you may need a second application in order to kill any regrowth. An alternative total weed treatment is to cover the area with an opaque material to smother the weeds. Old carpet is often recommended for this and is very successful; heavy-duty black plastic also works well. But the covering must be left in place for at least a year to ensure that the weeds are killed, and this demands some advance planning.

GROUND-COVER PLANTS

Once a bed is prepared and free of perennial weeds, planting can begin. If you wish to minimize the time spent on weeding, think about planting perennials that are particularly good at smothering weeds. Many hardy perennials have such dense growth that weeds find it difficult to penetrate. Hostas, for example, have foliage that is so broad and dense that weeds stand little chance of establishing themselves underneath, and many hardy geraniums make mounds of crowded shoots that have the same effect. It is important to remember, however, that no ground-cover plants will smother weeds if they are planted into ground that is already weedy. Weed-smothering perennials include *Alchemilla, Astrantia, Bergenia, Geranium, Heuchera, Hosta, Lamium, Nepeta, Rheum,* and *Symphytum*.

WEEDING TECHNIQUES

However careful the preparation, weeds are bound to grow. Weed seeds that have been lying dormant in the soil may germinate, the wind may blow them in, or they may even be introduced with plants bought at a nursery or garden center.

Hand weeding Many gardeners find removing weeds by hand a satisfying experience. Working through the border with a hand fork is not only an effective way of dealing with weeds, as long as there are not too many of them, but it also provides an opportunity to look at the plants at close quarters.

Annual weeds, such as groundsel and chickweed, are easy to pull out; the soil can be knocked off the roots, and they can be added to the compost pile. Be sure to remove these weeds before they go to seed. Keep a separate bag or bucket just for perennial weeds, and when you do come across them, a little more excavation may be needed to ensure that the root is completely removed. These weeds should not be added to the compost pile.

One of the advantages of hand weeding is that when seedlings of garden plants are discovered, they can be left in place or moved to a more suitable situation. Other methods of weed control do not discriminate between flowers and weeds.

Hand weeding

Use a hand fork to help remove weeds, then shake the soil off the roots.

Mulching Applying a layer of weed-free mulch is a good way of preventing weed growth. Weed-free organic matter will make an effective weed-suppressing mulch but the most useful materials are dense enough to prevent germination of weed seeds already in the soil, yet sufficiently coarse to provide a poor seedbed for weeds blown in. Bark chips and coconut shell are good examples. The soil should be cleared of weeds before the mulch is applied, as established weeds may have the strength to grow through the mulch and then spread.

Hoeing When no mulch is applied, hoeing can be a useful method of weed control, especially in the early months after planting. Hoeing is not advisable when a mulch has been applied, as it disturbs the mulch, reducing its effectiveness. Hoeing between plants when the surface of the soil is dry slices off the weeds, and they usually shrivel in the sun. Take time to remove perennial weeds individually, since they almost always regrow from their roots.

Take care when hoeing through a border not to damage the stems of your perennials. As the perennials grow, their foliage fills the space between the clumps. It becomes increasingly difficult to use a hoe without damaging the plants, and eventually it becomes impossible.

Weed killers Weed killers can be invaluable aids in the battle against weeds, but it is vital to use them carefully. There are two main groups: nonselective weed killers, which kill all plants, whether they are weeds or precious perennials; and selective weed killers, which kill some plants and not others. Nonselective weed killers themselves come in two types: systemic weed killers, which travel through the sap to all parts of the plant, and contact weed killers, which kill the leaves and stems they touch.

Systemic nonselective weed killers These kill foliage, stems, and roots of annual and, more usefully, difficult perennial weeds. They are used to kill weeds in areas where there are no garden plants, particularly if you are preparing the ground for a new planting. They can also be used on perennial weeds in mature borders if applied carefully and selectively with a hand sprayer or brush. Some weeds may need two treatments.

Contact nonselective weed killers These affect any green tissue they touch, so they kill annual weeds, which have no perennial roots, but kill only the top growth of perennial weeds and not the roots. They have limited use in perennial plantings.

Systemic selective weed killers These, too, have limited use in perennial borders and are mostly used for killing broad-leaved weeds in lawns. There is, however, one product that kills couch grass and similar perennial grasses but can be sprayed on other garden plants without harming them. This is useful when couch grass invades perennials. In general, weed killers are of most value in the early stages of preparing a border and as a spot treatment to kill individual perennial weeds in mature borders.

Guidelines for using weed killers
• Always read the instructions on the package and follow them carefully.
• Never increase the concentration at which you apply weed killer; it will not necessarily work better.
• Unless using the appropriate selective weed killer, always ensure that none falls on your perennials.
• Use a spot treatment, employing a hand sprayer or brush, when possible.
• When spraying, choose an overcast, cool, dry, windless day.

Weeds and their roots

Groundsel *has many fibrous roots that carry a lot of soil; shake them well.*

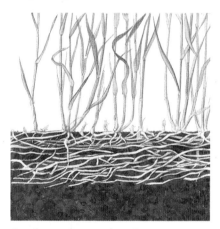

Quack grass *roots make a dense mass; almost every small piece will grow.*

Dandelions *have a stout taproot that shoots again if the top is broken off.*

STAKING

Plants growing in the wild often fall over, and although they may look untidy, it usually makes little difference to their general health. But in the garden you want your plants to look their best, and preventing perennials from flopping over by providing support is an important part of their care. Their tendency to flop is increased by the fact that in rich garden soils plants tend to grow taller than they do in the wild, and cultivars bred specifically for their large or double flowers are also naturally less self-supporting.

MATERIALS

Brushwood Traditionally, twiggy branches of deciduous trees and shrubs were used to support perennials. They had the advantage of looking natural, and local forests provided an annual supply that could be cut each winter. In some areas, brushwood is still available, often from local conservation organizations, and some gardeners with plenty of space plant hazel shrubs specifically to provide plant supports. To do this, cut twigs to a little less than the eventual height of the plant to be supported. When the plant is still less than a quarter of its final height, push the twigs into place in a ring around the edge of the plant. Large clumps also benefit from a few pieces of twig being placed within the clump. When pushed in firmly, the tops of the brushwood should be about three-quarters of the eventual height of the plant. To complete the operation, loop twine from one brushwood stem to the next to give extra strength.

Stakes and twine In gardens where brushwood is not available, bamboo stakes and twine make a practical alternative. Choose stakes a little shorter than the eventual height of the plant. Spacing them evenly around the clump, approximately 15–18 in (38–45 cm) apart, push them into the soil by about a quarter of their depth. Place a rubber cap (available from garden centers) on the top of each stake as a safety measure. Next, run the twine all the way around, looping it around each stake and then taking it across the center of the clump from stake to stake. The result will be a ring of stakes and twine around the clump, with a crossing pattern of twine over the clump itself. This arrangement ensures that both the edge and the center of the clump are supported. One lower piece of twine is put in place first, with another higher up as the plants grow. At the end of the season the stakes can be cleaned and stored in a dry place for the following year; they will usually last at least two years.

Metal supports Ever since the 19th century, metal supports have been manufactured specifically for use with

Peonies and lupines need support or they will blow over in the wind or collapse under the weight of rain. The simplest system is to use stakes and twine.

plants, and these are the easiest of all types of support to use. They come in three forms. One consists of two uprights with a loop between and is best used to prevent naturally floppy plants from falling too far forward. An alternative design consists of a wire mesh mounted on four legs and placed over the clump early in the season; the plant grows through the mesh as the season progresses. A third type involves a series of interconnecting stakes and crosspieces. All these designs are quickly and easily fitted over the plants, need no special preparation, and last for many years if they are cleaned at the end of the season and stored in a dry place. But they are less versatile than brushwood or stakes and more expensive.

Other plants The most natural supports, especially for climbers, are other plants. Perennial climbers, such as *Lathyrus latifolius*, can be planted under or next to stout shrubs, such as elders, and will be supported by their branches. Smaller climbers like herbaceous clematises and *Codonopsis clematidea*, can be trained through such dwarf shrubs as potentillas.

Staking methods

Brushwood: *Place the stake in the soil so that it is close to the plant, but not so close that it damages the bulb or roots. A wire hoop can be fixed around the stem and adjusted for height.*

Stakes and twine: *Push bamboo stakes firmly into the soil around the plant, and twist twine between them to form a cat's cradle. If the plant is a large one, use some additional stakes in the middle of the clump for extra support.*

Metal supports: *Place the stakes around the outside of the plant to make a continuous support that follows the outline of the clump. Simply link the hook of one stake into the loop of the next.*

Tying individually: *Plants with tall spires of flowers can be tied to individual stakes with soft garden twine. Make a figure eight between the stem and the stake to prevent chafing, then tie the knot behind the stake.*

TIMING

The most important rule is to stake plants before they need it. Nothing looks worse than a plant that has collapsed and is then tied up to its supports afterward. A plant that has grown through its supports will eventually look so natural that it appears unsupported; this is the ideal. Staking early is crucial, but it means that the stakes themselves will dominate the border for some time, until hidden by the plants. Because plants grow at different rates, it is impossible to be specific about exactly when to stake them, and a balance must be struck between putting supports in place early enough to be really effective, but not so early that the stakes are obtrusive for too long.

TECHNIQUE

Most plants that grow into increasing clumps do not need to have their stems supported individually—the clump as a whole can be supported. Some plants—*Crambe cordifolia*, for example—appreciate a single tall stake to support each stem. In windy situations delphiniums, too, can be staked in this way. The drawback with staking individual stems is not only the time that it takes and the cost of the stakes, but the fact that even when the plants are in full flower the stakes may not be hidden. Another disadvantage is that tall, top-heavy flower stems may snap at the point where they are tied to the stake. In general, it is preferable to provide support for a whole plant or a whole clump rather than for individual stems. At the end of the season when the plants are cut down, the stakes can be retained for use the following year. Brush off the soil, cut off the base if it shows signs of rotting and store in a dry place.

DEADHEADING

There are three reasons why removing the dead flowers from perennials is a good thing. First, many perennials will continue to produce more flowers if the old ones are removed regularly. If dying flowers are left on the plant, a great deal of its energy goes into the development of seedpods, which usually add nothing to its attractiveness. If the dead flowers are removed, however, this energy is usually diverted into producing flowers; in some plants, while deadheading may not result in more flowers, it will encourage the growth of a mass of new foliage. The second reason for deadheading is simply tidiness. Gardeners vary in their attitude toward this: some hardly notice a few deadheads; others pounce with the shears as soon as petals drop in their eagerness to keep the borders looking neat and tidy. The final reason for deadheading is that many perennials produce so much seed that their seedlings can be a nuisance. Foxgloves, alchemillas and lamiums, for example, can become weeds if their seed heads are not removed.

DEADHEADING DIFFERENT PERENNIALS

For the purposes of deadheading, perennials can be divided into two main groups. Those like phlox, salvia, and anthemis, which produce leaves on the lower part of their stems and flowers at the top, should have the dead flower heads cut off just above the leaves. Plants like hardy geraniums, pulmonarias, and hellebores, which carry flowers on relatively bare stems with the leaves growing separately from the base, should have the old flower heads cut at ground level.

Perennials vary so much, however, that it is worth considering a few groups separately:
• Delphiniums, which produce their flowers in spikes, should have the

Deadheading plants, such as this anthemis, as the petals drop not only improves the look of the plant but also encourages further flowering.

Deadheading

Flowers on individual stems are snipped off above foliage or a branch.

When flowers come in spikes, the whole spike can be cut off above the basal leaves.

Plants with a few large flowers can be deadheaded individually as each fades.

whole spike cut off low down, but above most of the foliage, when the last flowers fade. Cutting the spike off at ground level will encourage a second flowering, but this may be at the expense of good flowers the following year.

• Some plants, like hardy geraniums, doronicums, astrantias, and alchemillas, can be cut to the ground after the main flush of flower, and will then produce lush new foliage, which may be followed by more flowers. It is important, however, to ensure that the plants are kept moist immediately after they are cut back.

• Hardy chrysanthemums and other plants that produce a long succession of flowers in the same flower head should have the individual flowers snipped off as they fade, then the whole flower head cut off when all the flowers are over.

• Oriental poppies produce single flowers on bare stems and should have the stems cut out at ground level as soon as the petals drop. Their leaves die away soon after, at which time they too can be cleared away.

• Plants with large numbers of small flowers, like gypsophilas, are impossible to deadhead individually. Some gardeners simply leave them untouched; others clip them to leave them looking neat.

RETAINING SEED HEADS

Although it is generally wise to cut off dead flowers, some plants are so attractive in seed that the seed heads are best left in place. For example, the seed heads of many grasses can remain a feature until winter; the fluffy heads of pulsatillas and herbaceous clematises are very pretty; and the berries of *Iris foetidissima* are its most colorful feature.

Another time to be cautious about deadheading is when you would like a plant to spread by seed or when you wish to collect seed from plants to give away or to raise seedlings yourself. In this case leave a few seed heads in place but remove most.

REPLANTING

After growing in the same place for some years, many perennials begin to deteriorate. Growth becomes less vigorous, stems shorter, foliage less luxuriant, and flowering less prolific.

WHY REPLANT?

Perennials deteriorate partly because the roots exhaust the supplies of nutrients in the soil. Another reason is that as the plant spreads outward from its original planting site, its center becomes starved, leaving a ring of healthy growth surrounding a weak center. As this growth takes place, the overall size of the clump increases, unevenly, and it eventually becomes too large for its position. Plants with a strongly spreading habit, such as Oriental poppies and *Campanula takesimana,* may begin to invade their neighbors. The solution is to dig up the whole clump, improve the soil, and then replant healthy pieces in the required area. Although generous mulching and feeding may keep a plant healthy and vigorous when it would otherwise languish, these treatments are not a long-term solution, as they only hasten the day when the plant outgrows its space and needs replanting as a smaller group.

WHAT TO REPLANT

Plants that grow quickly and are hungry feeders need to be replanted most frequently of all. Some peren-nial plants should be divided every other year in order to keep them looking their best, but those that naturally form tight, dense clumps can be left for a period of many years to develop into substantial specimens.

Plants needing frequent replanting include *Anthemis, Aster, Bellis, Campanula,* (particularly *C. glomerata, C. takesimana,* and 'Elizabeth') *Doronicum, Iris, Lobelia, Monarda Phlox, Tanacetum,* and *Viola.*

Plants best left to form mature clumps include *Bergenia, Clematis, Eremurus, Euphorbia characias, Foeniculum, Helleborus, Hosta, Kniphofia, Paeonia,* and *Rheum.*

TIMING AND TECHNIQUE

The rules for the timing of replanting are much the same as those for planting (page 30): some plants prefer to be lifted and replanted in spring; others prefer the fall.

The technique is not difficult. First, dig up the whole clump and lay the plants on a plastic sheet nearby, covered with polyethylene or damp burlap to protect them from the sun or drying winds while you work on the soil. Then fork the soil or dig it in the same way as when preparing for planting new plants (page 29). The dug-up plants should then be examined and, using the traditional two-forks technique (see page 66), broken up into manageable pieces. Any dead, weak, or unproductive growth, especially from the center of the clump, should be discarded and the strongest, most vigorous pieces from the edge kept.

The treatment of the remaining plant material varies enormously, since different plants grow in different ways. This procedure is covered in more detail in the section "propagation by division" (pp. 65–67). To replant an existing clump in its original space rather than expanding its area, split off pieces with a number of strong shoots using the two-forks technique and pruning shears, then replant. When material is scarce or the clump must be expanded, smaller pieces may be required.

Lifting and replanting

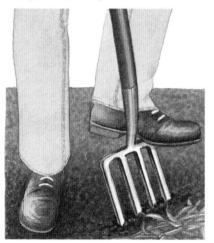

1 *Dig up long-established plants with a fork, retaining as much root as possible.*

2 *From the resulting shoots choose healthy growth from the edge of the clump.*

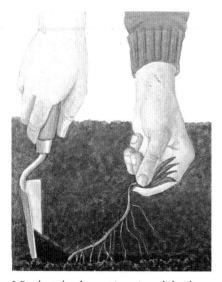

3 *Replant the chosen pieces in soil that has been improved with organic matter.*

4 *The newly replanted area showing seven evenly spaced leafy shoots.*

Right: Mature clumps, such as these, will deteriorate unless the plants are lifted, divided, and replanted regularly.

PESTS AND DISEASES

However well you look after your perennials, they may still be attacked by pests or diseases. You can, however, take steps to prevent such an attack. And if pests or diseases strike, choosing the appropriate method of control and going about it in the right way can greatly reduce any damage.

PRINCIPLES OF PEST AND DISEASE CONTROL

An appreciation of the general principles of pest and disease control is always helpful. In particular, understanding how to prevent trouble from arising in the first place will ensure that far fewer plants are attacked.

PREVENTION
The first principle to keep in mind is that a healthy plant is less likely to suffer from pest or disease attack than a sickly one and it will also prove more resilient if it should be attacked. Follow these rules as a first step in preventing perennials from being attacked by pests and diseases:
• Always grow plants in the type of soil they prefer. For example, a plant needing good drainage will be more likely to suffer from root rot if grown in damp soil.
• Always grow plants in the amount of light they prefer. For example, a sun-loving plant may be more likely to suffer from mildew or rot if grown in full shade.
• Make sure that plants are given the feeding and watering they require, and remember that plants vary in their requirements; treat each specimen as an individual.
• When they are available, choose cultivars that are resistant to problems that have been troublesome.

Another way to prevent pest and disease attack is to reduce the possibility of introducing infection:

• Keep the garden free of weeds. Weeds can be reservoirs of infection, and insects and fungal diseases may spread from weeds to reinfect plants after initial problems have been solved.
• Do not leave a pile of garden debris in an odd corner; compost it.
• Inspect all new plants carefully to be certain that new pest and disease problems are not introduced from either neighbors or nurseries.
• Be aware of problems suffered by neighbors, and be prepared to take preventive action.
• Learn to recognize how the weather may affect your plants. For example, in long, hot, dry spells powdery mildew and spider mites are more likely to be troublesome.

CONTROLLING PESTS AND DISEASES
However thoroughly you try to prevent problems from occurring, plants will still be attacked. The most important way to ensure that they suffer as little as possible is to be watchful. Dealing with the very first signs of a problem, before it has had time to cause too much damage, will ensure that plants remain as healthy as possible. As soon as you notice worrying symptoms, identify the problem, then treat it promptly.

Once plants have been attacked, there are three practical ways of controlling pests and diseases: cultural methods, which involve practical techniques like simply picking off caterpillars; biological methods, which include introducing a predatory insect to kill pests (although there are more applications for this in the greenhouse than the perennial border); and chemical control methods, which use pesticides and fungicides.

Cultural control This method includes many of the techniques described above for ensuring that plants thrive, but there are also a number of other valuable procedures:
• Examine the leaves of susceptible plants for the egg clusters of caterpillars and squash any eggs before they have had a chance to hatch.
• Pick caterpillars off plants where the leaves are being eaten.
• Fork over the soil between plants in order to expose soil-living pests to predatory birds.
• Pick off the leaves affected by leaf miners, which burrow under the skin of the leaf.
• Collect slugs and snails by flashlight on damp evenings when they are most easily visible.
• Erect fences or put up netting to prevent attack from large animals, such as rabbits or birds.
• Try scaring devices, such a silhouettes of cats or birds of prey, which are useful in some situations.

Biological control This method involves using a creature that does not harm plants to control another that does. These beneficial creatures are either parasites or predators, and even simple measures such as encouraging garden birds can often have a noticeable effect on the caterpillar and aphid population.
• Provide birdhouses, shelter, and winter food in order to encourage garden birds.
• Both ladybugs and praying mantises are available by mail. Ladybugs eat aphids, while praying mantis eat almost anything that flies.

• Encourage beneficial insects by growing their favorite food plants. Flies, for example, which help in the control of aphids, appreciate fennel and annual convolvulus.

• Choose from a number of forms of biological control that are available for controlling spider mites, whiteflies, and other pests in the greenhouse during propagation.

• If mice are a problem, keep a cat.

Chemical control There are various chemicals available to control pests and diseases. Some of these are derived from natural substances, while others are synthesized from chemicals. Even the natural, organic chemicals can be dangerous if used incorrectly or at the wrong dosage. In general, chemical controls are best used as a last resort, when the buildup of the pest has reached unacceptable levels. Be sure the chemical you intend to use will control the problem; insecticides are no use against a fungal attack, for example.

USING CHEMICALS SAFELY

• Always read the instructions and guidelines on the package carefully and follow them precisely.

• Always wear any protective clothing recommended. Wear gloves when handling concentrate.

• Never mix a stronger concentration than is stipulated; there is a risk that you may damage the plant and still not solve the problem.

• Use granular formulations, rather than concentrated liquids, whenever possible; try to choose premeasured chemicals or those supplied with a measuring device.

• Always store chemicals in a locked cupboard.

• Never mix different types of chemicals together unless the package instructions specifically suggest it.

• Keep as much of your skin covered as possible while spraying, and never inhale the vapor.

• Keep pets and children away when spraying the plants.

• Always spray in calm conditions, preferably on an overcast day.

• If it becomes necessary to spray open flowers, do so if possible in the evening to prevent the chemical from affecting bees.

• Try to cover the whole plant with spray, including both the undersides and tops of the leaves.

Selinum wallichianum attracts many insects that are useful in the garden.

THE ORGANIC APPROACH

Many gardeners now feel that using garden chemicals to control pests and diseases is unnecessary and that these problems can be dealt with effectively without using products that may harm pets and wildlife. For many gardeners, the organic approach works very well, although it is often true that gardening without chemicals is more time-consuming than simply resorting to a spray. The use of organic methods can be divided into six parts:

1. Choosing resistant cultivars
2. Effective prevention by using good growing techniques
3. Encouraging natural predators
4. Cultural control
5. Biological control
6. Using safe sprays

CHOOSING RESISTANT CULTIVARS

Unfortunately, although many cultivars of food crops, such as vegetables and fruits, have been developed to be resistant to important pests and diseases, few cultivars of hardy perennials have been specially developed with this in mind. This is partly due to the fact that it can be a long, time-consuming, and expensive enterprise to develop these plants and partly because the same disease can vary very slightly from one part of the country to another, so a cultivar resistant in one area may be attacked in another. One approach that can help is to plant cultivars that local gardeners find are able to resist infection successfully, even if they are not generally described as resistant ones. Another, of course, is to seek out those varieties which have been found to have general resistance.

For example, although most cultivars of *Phlox paniculata* are susceptible to mildew, forms of *Phlox maculata* are all resistant.

GOOD GROWING TECHNIQUES

All the ideas discussed under "Prevention" (p.56) are doubly important when avoiding the use of garden chemicals. For if the plants are growing well, they will be less likely to be attacked and more likely to survive the infection if they should happen to be attacked.

ENCOURAGING NATURAL PREDATORS

There are many creatures living in the garden that can be a great help in controlling pests. Sometimes the predators and pests will set up an uneasy balance naturally, with just enough pests around to keep the predators fed, but not so many as to cause much damage. Yet the pests often multiply too quickly for their enemies to deal with, so gardeners must intervene by setting out to attract beneficial creatures. Some useful strategies include:

- Planting annuals such as annual convolvulus, poached-egg plant (*Limnanthes;* also known as meadow foam), and buckwheat (*Fagopyrum*) among perennial plants in order to attract flies, whose larvae eat aphids in large numbers.
- Planting perennials such as purple-leaved fennel and *Selinum tenuifolium,* which also attract flies.
- Using a shallow dish of water and some flat rocks to attract toads.
- Hanging up nuts during the winter months for chickadees near perennial borders, so that they will eat over-wintering insect eggs and aphids and larvae on the plants while waiting their turn at the nuts.
- Leaving logs in out-of-the-way corners as cover for carnivorous beetles.

CULTURAL CONTROL

Cultural methods, such as picking off caterpillars and collecting slugs by hand, can be effective ways of controlling pests, but it is important to check the plants frequently to be sure of catching and dealing with infestations before the have the chance to cause too much damage.

The poached-egg plant (*Limnanthes douglasii*), also known as meadow foam, attracts hoverflies, whose larvae eat large numbers of aphids.

This can be time-consuming, and if a few days of bad weather keep you inside, or you spend a weekend away, problems may build up. (See also p.56.)

BIOLOGICAL CONTROL

Most biological controls have the enormous advantage of affecting only the target pest and not harming beneficial insects or other wildlife. Unfortunately, most work best in the greenhouse, but there are several which are useful outdoors. These include the eelworm that carries the bacterium to control vine weevils and some other soil-dwelling pests, the predator that controls spider mites, insects such as ladybugs and praying mantises which eat aphids and leafhoppers. But perhaps the most effective biological control for pests of perennial plants is the bacterium that kills caterpillars. Perennials are attacked by a wide range of caterpillars, but the damaged can be controlled by spraying plants with this bacterial preparation.

USING SAFE SPRAYS

Many organic gardeners are happy to use natural pesticides, and indeed, most associations of organic gardeners approve a certain number. It must be remembered that a substance of natural origin will not necessarily be harmless to people or wildlife. It is quite safe to use water from a hose as a spray to knock pests off a plant physically, but employing the plant extract rotenone, a natural material that is an effective treatment for a wide range of pests, can be dangerous to fish. The safest sprays are the soap extracts used as insecticides, but they have the disadvantage of being indiscriminate in their action and so they harm a wide range of insects. It is just as important to read the instructions and warnings on packages of natural pesticides as it is on packages of artificial products.

PESTS OF PERENNIALS

Pest problems are caused by insects and other small creatures eating the leaves, flowers, stems or buds of plants, sucking their sap, or creating problems indirectly for example, by undermining roots or spreading disease.

actual size: ¼ in (6 mm)

ANTS

Ants excavate the soil from among the roots of perennials. They also "farm" aphids, which provide secretions on which ants feed. They do this by carrying the aphids to new shoots, where the aphids multiply.
Damage: Plants grow poorly and collapse in hot weather due to drought caused by removal of soil from roots.
Prevention: Vigilance and prompt control reduce the spread of ants.

Ensure that containers are set on blocks to deter infestation.
Control: Pouring boiling water into nests is sometimes recommended but is rarely completely effective. Powders and baits are effective, but it is important to continue treatment until all activity has ceased. Precious plants that are severely affected can be lifted, all soil washed off the roots, and then the shoots cut down, potted, and grown until they are ready to be replanted.

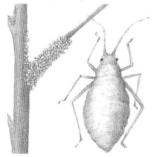

actual size: ⅛ in (3 mm)

APHIDS

Aphids cause damage by sucking sap from their hosts. Some types attack a wide variety of plants; others are more selective. Aphids also transmit viral diseases.
Damage: Plant growth is stunted, and the shoots, leaves, buds, and sometimes flowers are deformed. Large numbers of insects congregate, especially under the leaves and on the shoot tips.

Prevention: Encourage such natural garden predators as ladybugs, flies, and lacewings. Avoid using broad-spectrum pesticides, which kill these beneficial predators as well as the aphids.
Control: Spray with insecticidal soap or with an aphid-specific insecticide. It is important to ensure that the buds, the undersides of the leaves, and the shoot tips are coated with the insecticide as this is where the insects congregate.

actual size: ½ in (10 mm)

CAPSIDS

Tiny pale green grubs and the larger green adults attack a wide range of perennials, particularly early in the season. They suck sap and are often concentrated in the unfurling shoot tips.
Damage: Small, rather ragged holes, often edged in yellow, are found in the new leaves around the shoot tips, often becoming larger as the leaves expand.
Prevention: Prevention is not possible but prompt attention at the first signs of attack is the best way to limit damage.
Control: Pinch off shoot tips or spray with a systemic insecticide. Contact insecticides are less effective as they do not always reach the grubs on the inside of the tightly closed shoot tips.

actual size: ¾ in (20 mm)

CHAFER GRUBS

These soft, white, brown-headed, C-shaped grubs eventually develop into beetles. They attack plant roots, causing plants to wilt or grow poorly.
Damage: Grubs eat through roots and eat bulbs and tubers. They are especially troublesome when lawn or grassland is dug up to make flower beds.
Prevention: Regular cultivation reduces numbers by exposing them to birds.
Control: Use a soil insecticide when planting. Little can be done when established plants are attacked.

actual size: 2 in (5 cm)

CRANE FLY LARVAE

These soft, fat, gray-brown grubs are the larvae of the crane fly, or daddy longlegs. They are most troublesome when new flower beds are created in a lawn or meadow but may also cause problems in beds near rough grass.
Damage: Plants appear weak and may collapse completely or partially because of the grubs feeding on the roots below the soil.
Prevention: Repeated cultivation before planting exposes the grubs to predatory birds.
Control: Soil insecticides and some slug killers also control crane fly larvae.

actual size: 2 in (50 mm)

CUTWORMS

These fat gray or brown grubs eventually hatch into moths.
Damage: Stems are eaten through at ground level. Cutworms are most often seen on young plants and seedlings.
Prevention: Cultivate the soil in winter to expose the grubs to feeding birds.
Control: Use a soil insecticide when planting young plants or sowing seed.

actual size: ⁶⁄₁₀-¾ in (15-20 mm)

EARWIGS

These small, brown, very mobile insects have noticeable pincers at the rear.
Damage: Flowers with fleshy petals, especially double chrysanthemums and dahlias, are eaten.
Prevention: Keep the garden tidy, and promptly remove any debris.
Control: Trap the insects in pieces of orange peel laid on the soil, in rolls of corrugated cardboard, or in inverted flower pots stuffed with straw. Alternatively, spray with a systemic insecticide in the evening.

actual size: 0.004 in (1 mm)

EELWORMS

These microscopic wormlike creatures feed on stems or leaves. Different species attack different plants.
Damage: Distortion of foliage in phlox; browning of lower leaves in penstemon.
Prevention: Buy healthy stock. Propagate phlox by root cuttings, and penstemon only by shoot tips.
Control: Apart from removing and then destroying infected plants, there is no means of control.

actual size: 1 in
(25 mm)

LEAF CATERPILLARS

The caterpillars of a variety of butterflies and moths can attack perennials. They come in many sizes and colors. Some feed only on specific plants; others are less fussy.

Damage: Leaves, flowers, buds, and sometimes stems are eaten, at times from the edge and at times less discriminately.

Prevention: Squash the clusters of eggs if you find them on the undersides of leaves, and actively encourage insect-eating birds.

Control: Pick off caterpillars by hand; spray with parasitic bacteria or with an appropriate insecticide.

LEAF MINERS

Tiny white dots appear on leaves, and these are the sign that an adult fly has laid its eggs.

Damage: The eggs hatch into small grubs, which tunnel just under the leaf surface, through the tissues, leaving characteristic blisters or a maze of tunnels. In several species the larvae make large brown, hollow blisters, which are known as blotch mines.

Chrysanthemums and aquilegias are especially prone to attack.

Prevention: Control weeds in the daisy family, such as sow thistle and groundsel, which may host this pest.

Control: Pick off affected leaves. If the attack is severe, remove and dispose of the leaves. Chemical control is difficult; inspect susceptible plants regularly and spray with a systemic insecticide at the first sign of any tiny white dots.

actual size: 1¾ in
(45 mm)

MILLIPEDES

These are slim, slow-moving, usually black grubs. Do not confuse them with the very active, usually reddish centipedes, which are useful carnivores.

Damage: Seedlings and the fleshy parts of plants are eaten.

Prevention: Clear away garden debris. Look in dark hiding places and remove any millipedes that are found.

Control: Soil insecticide can be forked into the soil when planting.

actual size:
3¼ in
(90 mm)

SLUGS AND SNAILS

These familiar creatures can cause an enormous amount of damage. It is said that snails are more common on alkaline soil and slugs are more troublesome on acid soil, but many gardens suffer from too many of both.

Damage: Seedlings, tender new shoots, or any soft and succulent growth—including flowers and leaves—are eaten, as well as roots and fruits.

Prevention: Keep the garden tidy; clear away long grass and other cover that provides damp spots in which slugs and snails can hide during the day.

Control: Many controls are available, including orange skins or traps baited with beer laid on the soil. Pellets are effective, and most contain a repellent to stop pets and wildlife from eating them.

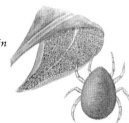

actual size:
0.002-0.004 in
(0.5-1 mm)

SPIDER MITES

This almost invisible pest can be very destructive in hot, dry seasons by sucking sap and disfiguring the plants with their webs.

Damage: Fine, pale mottling of leaves is followed by the development of gray webs. Spider mites particularly attack crocosmias, penstemons, and especially primroses, which may be killed.

Prevention: Do not plant susceptible plants in hot, dry conditions.

Control: Control is very difficult, partly because some strains of the pest have developed resistance to chemicals. Some insecticides are partially effective.

actual size:
¼ in (6 mm)

SPITTLEBUGS, OR FROGHOPPERS

Common froghoppers are small green sap sucking grubs. They surround themselves with white protective foam known as "spittle" that can be found on many plants in late spring to early summer. Eventually they become insects resembling tiny green frogs.

Damage: Attacking a very wide range of perennials, they are usually more unsightly than damaging but may cause distortion and some wilting.

Prevention: None.

Control: Wash off with a jet of water from a hose dislodging the pests, or pick off by hand; or spray with a systemic insecticide if the attack is severe.

actual size:
³⁄₁₀ in (8 mm)

VINE WEEVIL

These are becoming increasingly troublesome pests because they have developed resistance to many of the chemicals which were previously used to control them. They are most commonly found in warm climates. Most types of herbaceous plants are potential hosts.

Damage: Adult weevils eat foliage, characteristically by taking semicircular notches out of the leaf edges. Orange-headed white grubs feed on roots and tubers, especially damaging for primulas, Michaelmas daisies, phlox, peony, cyclamens, heucheras, and tiarellas.

Prevention: Wash the soil off susceptible plants and repot in new potting soil.

Control: Some insecticides will control adults. Use biological control: a parasitic eelworm seeks out and penetrates the vine weevil larvae; it carries a bacterium that infects and kills the larvae.

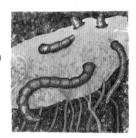

actual size:
1 in (25 mm)

WIREWORMS

These slim cream-colored grubs eventually develop into click beetles and are especially common in new flower beds made in grass and lawns.

Damage: The wireworms feed on fleshy roots, bulbs, and tubers, usually weakening the plant rather than killing it.

Prevention: Cultivate a number of times before planting to give predators an opportunity to eat them. Regular hoeing of established borders will help to reduce wireworm numbers. Control weeds, which may nourish them.

Control: Protect individual plants by forking in a soil insecticide when planting or by forking it in lightly around established plants.

DISEASES OF PERENNIALS

These are caused mainly by fungal organisms. The likelihood of occurrence is increased by poor or inappropriate conditions or extremes of weather.

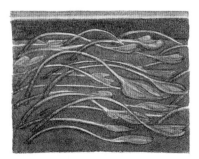

DAMPING–OFF

This problem is caused by a number of soil-living fungi, the presence of which can be detected only by the damage they do. It occurs most often when seedlings are grown in wet, compacted potting soil and when seed is sown too thickly.

Damage: Seedlings collapse as the result of fungus attack, usually at the soil surface. Perennials that have been raised in a propagator or a warm greenhouse are the most likely to suffer.

Prevention: Always use clean pots or flats together with fresh, bagged seed-starting mix; never use garden soil. Do not overfirm the potting mix; sow seeds thinly; water with tap water, not water from a water barrel. Handle seedlings gently when pricking out.

Control: Water the potting mix with a liquid copper fungicide after sowing and when seedlings have emerged.

GRAY MOLD, OR BOTRYTIS

This widespread problem is less troublesome in the perennial border than it is in the greenhouse. The fungus is especially virulent in cool, damp conditions, but some plants may suffer even at the height of summer if conditions are damp and humid.

Damage: Especially dangerous to fully double flowers with soft or succulent petals. Dahlias and chrysanthemums are particularly susceptible. Sometimes the infection is confined to spotting, but it may attack old flowers as the petals collapse, then spread through the flower stem.

Prevention: Regular deadheading of susceptible plants is crucial. Remove flowers which have been damaged by either bad weather or frost.

Control: Remove diseased parts, and spray the plant with a systemic fungicide.

LEAF SPOT

This is caused by a number of different fungi and bacteria, each of which attacks only one type of plant. It is most troublesome in warm, wet weather.

Damage: Dark blotches or spots disfigure the foliage of a wide range of perennials, including pinks, delphiniums, irises, and hellebores. In some cases there is little serious damage, but severe infections can be fatal.

Prevention: None.

Control: Picking off the infected foliage restricts the spread of the disease; spraying with a systemic fungicide is sometimes effective.

MILDEW

The dusty white coating of powdery mildew is especially troublesome in hot, humid weather and in locations with poor air circulation. Pulmonarias, aquilegias, asters, delphiniums, monardas, and phlox are among the plants affected.

Damage: Fungus attacks the foliage, buds, flowers, and stems, covering them with a disfiguring white coating. The leaves may then turn yellow, and the whole plant may even die.

Prevention: Divide susceptible plants frequently to keep the clumps small, so that the air can circulate freely.

Control: Spray with a systemic fungicide.

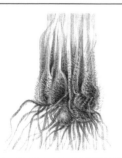

ROOT ROT

Many perennials are subject to root rot caused by a variety of fungi. This condition is often the reason for otherwise unexplained collapse.

Damage: Soil-borne fungi attack roots, causing reduced growth and leaf yellowing at first, then poor flowering, and sometimes, eventually, sudden collapse.

Prevention: Keep plants growing well in conditions they enjoy. Some forms of root-rotting fungi can lie dormant in the soil for years, so never replace an affected plant with another of the same type.

Control: No chemical treatment is yet available to control this disease.

VIRUSES

These microscopic organisms can cause severe damage to some plants and are becoming increasingly common.

Damage: Viruses can cause a wide range of symptoms, including stunted growth; distorted flowers, foliage, and stems; pale or yellow streaking; spotting; and mottling in many different forms.

Prevention: Sterilize the pruning shears or knife when taking cuttings of susceptible plants, as the virus is spread in sap. Control aphids, which are the main carriers of viral diseases.

Control: Dig up and then dispose of the infected plants.

PROPAGATION

For many gardeners, propagation is the most exciting of the practical tasks associated with perennials, but it is also a subject that creates doubts and uncertainties. Fortunately, hardy perennials are among the easiest of all plants to propagate, and most types can be increased using basic techniques without the need for too much special equipment. There are two main kinds of propagation: by division or cuttings and by seed. Propagating perennials by division or cuttings results in the new plants being exact replicas of their parent; when plants are raised from seed, they may be identical to both the parent plant and to each other, but they may also vary significantly.

DIVISION

Division is the most basic and most valuable of all methods of propagating hardy perennials. No special equipment is required, success is all but guaranteed, and division is suitable for the vast majority of perennial plants. Many perennials also benefit from being dug up, split into small pieces, and replanted every few years, even if there is no need to increase the stock (see p. 54). The increased vigor that results from fresh divisions often means that the plants are more productive.

SEASON
Perennials are best divided in either spring or fall. Although many can also be split during the winter, where climates allow, more losses are likely to occur at that time of year. The majority of cultivars will divide well in either season, but there are other factors to consider.

Where the soil is unusually heavy and in areas of high rainfall, spring is usually the best season. When divided and replanted in fall, the new divisions must spend three or four months in cold, wet soil before it is warm enough for them to grow, and this can lead to losses. In very dry soil and in areas of unusually low spring rainfall, new divisions may be slow to establish themselves without adequate moisture; in these cases dividing in fall is often preferable.

A few plants do have distinct seasonal preferences. Bearded irises, for example, are usually divided in summer, soon after flowering, as this is when a burst of root growth takes place. New roots can then grow into the soil at once, allowing the plants to acclimate quickly. Hellebores are best divided in late summer or early fall, just before their main burst of root growth, and primroses are best split in late spring or early summer, immediately after flowering. Peonies are also best divided at this time to give them time to make new roots before winter.

More plants prefer being divided in spring, and they fall into two groups. First, there are those that naturally flower very late in the year and so may well be at their best in the fall, when other plants are ready for division. Second, there are plants that are particularly unhappy spending the wet winter months without a well-established root system.

Plants to divide in spring include *Agapanthus, Alstroemeria, Anthemis, Aster, Chelone, Delphinium, Dendranthema, Gaillardia, Helenium,*

Left: For a varied and colorful display fill your border with home-grown perennials.

Some perennials, such as these asters and sedums, are best divided in spring, as they are often still in full flower in the fall.

Helianthus, Imperata, Kniphofia, Lobelia, Morina, Sedum, Tanacetum, Tricyrtis, and *Viola.*

A few plants, while not difficult to divide, make better specimens in the garden if left in place to mature. Plants best left undisturbed for some years include: *Bergenia, Clematis, Cortaderia, Helleborus, Hosta, Kniphofia,* and *Paeonia.*

TECHNIQUE

Dealing with the whole plant With a digging fork, dig up the whole clump with as much root as possible. Take another, similar fork (perhaps borrowed from a neighbor) and insert the two forks vertically, back to back, through the middle of the clump. Some effort may be required to penetrate plants with tight root systems. Now press the handles of the forks together, which results in the tines forcing the two halves of the plant apart. Working the handles backward and forward should eventually split the plant into two pieces. You can then repeat the process on each half, and either pull apart the resultant pieces by hand or cut them up with a

pair of pruning shears. Strong, vigorous pieces, usually from the edge of the clump, are the best choice for propagation. Each piece should have one or two strong buds or emerging shoots and a good portion of young root system attached.

Using the pruning shears, trim the chosen pieces to remove any dead foliage, old or dead roots, and ragged cuts. The size of the pieces selected depends, to some extent, on whether they are to be replanted in the open or potted and kept for later planting. If the aim is simply to extend a clump in the border or make a second clump elsewhere in the garden, the pieces chosen can each have three or four shoots or buds and an established root system, although the majority of roots should be relatively young. Try to use material from the edge of the clump. These pieces can be planted into the open ground at once, as described on page 31. If a large number of new plants are required, perhaps to provide stock for a plant sale, smaller divisions can be used; it may be necessary to cut the best growth into small pieces, each with a

single good shoot and a piece of root. It is advisable to wash the soil off any pieces that are to be potted to prevent the soil in the pot from being contaminated with pests or worms.

The new portions will establish themselves in 3½ in or 5 in (9 cm or 13 cm) pots of commercial potting soil, as long as they are protected from hot sun and drying winds in, for example, a greenhouse or cold frame, for the first few weeks.

Weak plants and plants you wish to increase quickly from a young original plant can be propagated in the same way. Very small pieces, which may struggle to survive when replanted directly into the garden, often establish themselves well in pots if given a little protection. In some cases it may be necessary to use old growth from the center of the clump. While this may be tough or weak, when potted and protected, it often recovers sufficiently to make a good young plant.

Dealing with only part of the plant Sometimes, if only a small number of new plants are required, it is not necessary to dig up a whole plant in

Propagation by division

1 Insert the tines of two forks close together, back to back, in the center of a clump of perennials.

2 Push the handles together, then work them back and forth to split the crown and tease the roots apart.

3 To provide further divisions, use pruning shears to cut the resulting clumps into smaller pieces, then discard the oldest.

order to propagate from it, and the majority of the clump can be left in place. In the case of kniphofias, for example, shoots with roots can be detached from the side of the clump and potted up. Propagating material can be removed from hostas by using a spade to cut out a wedge-shaped section, as if you were cutting a slice of cake. The pieces removed are washed and pulled apart, then the individual shoots are potted. The hole in the main clump is then filled with old potting soil. Shoots with roots can easily be cut from the edge of clumps of some plants, like asters. There is a danger, however, in repeatedly removing propagating material from the edge of a clump. The old original growth in the center becomes increasingly weak and eventually you may find that, although you have propagated many new plants, the original dies.

STEM CUTTINGS

Raising perennials from cuttings may not be the first method that springs to mind, but it has the great advantage of allowing a perennial to be propagated without disturbing it by digging it up. A little more equipment is required than for division, but like division, taking cuttings ensures that all the new plants will be exactly like their parent.

EQUIPMENT
Cuttings need protection from the natural environment to encourage rooting, and this is best provided by a thermostatically controlled propagator. Its clear cover admits light while at the same time creating a humid environment that prevents the cuttings from collapsing and dying in the weeks before roots are formed. Its

Equipment for cuttings

Cuttings often root most quickly in a heated propagator but they should be misted regularly with a sprayer to keep them moist.

Cuttings of many perennials can be rooted under a plastic bag on a windowsill or in the greenhouse.

heated element speeds up the rooting process so that roots are formed before the cuttings rot.

Ideally, the propagator should be situated in a greenhouse for extra protection from the wind and cold. A sunny windowsill is also an option, although if the cuttings are lit from just one direction they may become stretched and weak. In both situations, shading may be required to protect the cuttings from bright sunshine, which can cause overheating and scorch the foliage.

It is possible to root some perennials (especially the tougher varieties) in an unheated propagator, which may be useful in the house, where the environment is naturally warmer. If sited on a windowsill, the propagator can easily be turned to ensure that the cuttings are exposed to light on all sides. Perennials can also be rooted indoors or in a heated greenhouse in individual 3½ in (9 cm) pots, each covered with a clear plastic bag.

SEASON AND TECHNIQUE
Cuttings of hardy perennials are almost always taken in the spring, often early spring, although a few

can be taken later in the season. The best growth to use for cuttings is the newest spring shoots, soon after they emerge at the base of the plant. Sever each shoot from the plant as near to the base as possible; a craft knife is often more effective for cutting away shoots cleanly than a garden knife or pruning shears. The size of cuttings required varies among species: 2–3 in (5–7.5 cm) is the usual length, but a slightly shorter cutting is sometimes required for plants that are naturally dwarf.

A few plants, such as delphiniums and dahlias, tend to develop a hollow stem as their shoots lengthen. Cuttings that have hollow stems rarely root well, so only the shortest, earliest shoots that still have solid stems should be used. Plants from which cuttings are to be taken should be protected from attacks by slugs. When the shoots have grown sufficiently, sever cleanly and place immediately in a plastic bag with a label.

Now take the cuttings indoors and trim them at the base, just below a leaf joint. On cuttings of this sort, the leaf joints may be quite difficult to see, as the leaves are sometimes

Taking cuttings of hardy chrysanthemums

1 *Remove strong young shoots from the base of the plant in spring.*

2 *Trim each cutting just below a leaf joint, and trim off any lower leaves.*

3 *Dip the base of each cutting in rooting powder, then insert in a soilless mixture.*

greatly reduced in size at the base of the stems. If cuttings have normal leaves at the base, nip these off to discourage rotting. Then dip the base of each cutting in rooting powder and insert the cuttings to about half their length in pots of moist soilless mix.

A commercial rooting or seed-starting mixture should be used, never garden soil, although it is often advisable to add extra sand or perlite, at a proportion of up to 50 percent, depending on the drainage capacity of the original mixture. Relatively small, 3½ in (9 cm) pots are adequate. If there are more cuttings of one type than will fill a single pot, use two pots rather than a larger one or a seed flat. This minimizes the risk of any rot spreading between cuttings.

Insert cuttings using a dibble or pencil to make a hole in the rooting medium the same depth as the distance between the base of the cutting and the lowest remaining leaf. Then place each cutting in a hole, and when the pot is full, tap it sharply on the table or bench to settle the rooting medium. Do not firm the rooting medium with your fingers. On average, six to ten cuttings will go in a 3½ in (9 cm) pot, depending on their size. After a thorough watering the pots should be placed in a propagator; if there is a thermostat, set it at 70°F (21°C). Alternatively, you can stand the pot in a plastic bag and close the top above the tips of the cuttings with a wire tie.

During the period before rooting, it is essential to keep the rooting medium moist and the atmosphere around the cuttings humid. Cuttings rooted in an unheated propagator or plastic bag often need little watering until rooting has begun, but they may still require regular spraying with a hand mister containing warm water

to keep the air around them damp. Cuttings in a heated propagator dry out more quickly and require watering as well as misting.

AFTER ROOTING

Cuttings vary in the time they take to root: while some may root in a week, others may take much longer. Rooting is usually indicated by the shoot tips beginning to grow, root tips emerging from the drainage holes in the pot, and a slight resistance when the cutting is gently pulled. When the cuttings have developed roots ½–1 in (1–2.5 cm) long, depending on the size and vigor of the plant, they should be moved into individual pots of commercial potting mix. It is advisable not to let the cuttings stay in their original pots for too long after rooting, as this will retard their growth. They should be given protection immediately after potting—in an unheated propagator, for example—and then as they grow they should be moved into increasingly unprotected conditions, or hardened off, before planting out.

OTHER WAYS WITH CUTTINGS

Some perennials can be rooted later in the season using the same general technique. It is often more convenient to use slightly longer cuttings. While tip cuttings give the best results, it is sometimes also possible to root lower portions of the stems. This technique is valuable when you acquire a new plant and wish to make as many offspring as possible in the shortest time.

Sometimes it is even possible to root the stems of cut flowers. Penstemons, *Phlox maculata,* variegated forms of *Phlox paniculata,* chrysanthemums, dianthus, achilleas, and veronicas can all be propagated from longer stems in this way.

ROOT CUTTINGS

A few perennials are not easy to divide and cannot be raised from stem or tip cuttings but produce viable shoots from short pieces of root. This tendency is found in the most pernicious perennial weeds, but it can be turned to advantage in the propagation of some perennials and enables gardeners to propagate large numbers of plants that would otherwise be slow or difficult to increase. It is also possible to raise large quantities of certain varieties in a shorter time than is possible by the usual methods. It is not, however, suitable for variegated cultivars, as plants grown from root cuttings usually produce green leaves.

TIMING, EQUIPMENT, AND TECHNIQUE

Take root cuttings during late winter or early spring, before the plant naturally starts into growth. A thermostatically controlled propagator is useful, but a cold frame will provide protection until the vulnerable roots have established shoots. The precise techniques vary slightly according to the nature of the plant.

Plants with fat roots Plants like Oriental poppies (*Papaver orientale*) and *Echinops* have fat, fleshy roots. Dig up the plant in late winter and wash off the soil so that healthy roots can easily be identified. Roots about the thickness of a pencil are the most suitable, and they should be undamaged and disease free. Cut off a length of root with sharp pruning shears, then immediately cut it into 2 in (5 cm) lengths. Make a horizontal cut at the end of each piece nearest to the crown of the original plant, and make an angled cut at the end nearest the root tips. These cuts help to identify

Taking root cuttings of Oriental poppies

1 *Lift the plant using a spade, and dig up as much of the root system as possible. Any roots left behind may grow.*

2 *Wash off the soil, then cut off lengths of young healthy roots about the thickness of a pencil. Replant the plant.*

3 *Cut the roots into 2 in (5 cm) lengths, making a straight cut at the top of each one with a slanting cut at the base.*

4 *Insert each cutting vertically with the straight cut at the top, cover with sand, and place in a propagator or cold frame.*

the top and bottom of each cutting. When a large enough number of cuttings has been taken, the plant can be replanted, but try not to take more than a third of its roots for cuttings.

In some cases it is possible to take root cuttings without digging up the parent plant. Scrape the soil away from the roots, cut off one or two roots for propagation, and then replace the soil. Place the cuttings vertically, no less than ¾ in (2 cm) apart, in 5 in (13 cm) pots of rooting medium with the flat cut level with the surface. Then cover the cuttings

with ¼ in (5 mm) of compost and a further ¼ in (5 mm) of sand. Stand the labeled pot in a propagator, with the thermostat set at about 55°F (13°C), or put it in a cold frame.

Shoots may quickly appear, but as the roots often have sufficient reserves of nutrients to produce shoots before growing new fibrous root, do not pot them on at once. When both new roots and new shoots are growing well, however, the young plants can be potted individually into 3½ in (9 cm) pots, then grown over summer for planting outside in fall.

PLANTS WITH FIBROUS ROOTS

Plants with fibrous roots, such as phlox, can also be raised from root cuttings, but a variation in technique is required. Phlox and other plants with slender, more fibrous root systems should be dug up in late winter and the soil then washed off so that the roots are clearly visible. Snip off sections of root approximately 2–3 in (5–7.5 cm) long for use as cuttings. These may have a few fine, fragile roots attached, which can be left in place; branched roots can also be used if necessary.

The simplest way to deal with these fibrous cuttings is to fill a seed flat with potting soil and to lay them out flat on the surface of it. Then cover them with a fine sprinkling of potting soil and ¼ in (5 mm) of sand. Next, place the flat in a propagator or cold frame. Pot the young plants up into 3 ½ in (9 cm) pots later in the spring, when both roots and shoots are growing.

There is an alternative for plants with fibrous roots if space is tight: group the lengths of roots together in a small bundle of 10 to 20 roots with their tops level, tied loosely with twine, and insert them vertically in the center of a 5 in (13 cm) pot of soil mix. The top of the bundle should be level with the surface. Cover this with a little potting soil and ¼ in (5 mm) of sand. When shoots begin to grow, remove the bundle from the pot, gently tease it apart, and pot up the root cuttings individually in 3½ in (9 cm) pots of potting soil.

Plants that can be raised from root cuttings include *Acanthus*, *Anemone* (fall-flowering types), *Catananche*, *Echinops*, *Eryngium*, *Geranium* (some) , *Papaver orientale* cultivars, *Phlox paniculata*, *Pulmonaria longifolia* cultivars, and *Pulsatilla*.

SEED

There are two substantial advantages to raising perennials from seed. The first is that growing from seed enables you to acquire a large number of plants for a very modest outlay, because a seed packet usually costs less than a single plant of the same variety. This is especially important when planting a new garden on a tight budget. The second advantage is that you can order unusual cultivars from seed catalogs without having to travel to specialized nurseries to find them. But there are also disadvantages. Many of the best cultivars are not available as seed, so they must be propagated by other means. Another problem is that some popular types, such as New York asters, are available only as mixtures. The final drawback, although some would see it as an interesting bonus, is that when you raise perennials from seed, the plants may not always be the same. Of course, some may be unusually good, but others may be poor.

Achillea 'Summer Pastels' flowers well in the same year as the seed is sown.

SOWING SEED OUTDOORS

The most basic method is to sow seed outside during the summer months. This approach, however, is not suited to forms where the seed packets contain only a small number of expensive seeds. To ensure an adequate number of seedlings in this case, more care is advisable. But if large numbers of seeds are supplied, the plants can be raised outdoors successfully.

Sowing technique The best time is usually early summer, when the soil has warmed up and when there is still a good part of the growing season remaining for the plants to become established. Choose a sheltered, open site with good, fertile soil. A site protected from the heat of the midday sun is best but rarely available; avoid sites that are overhung by trees and where the soil is heavy and badly drained. If the soil is in good shape, ensure that the site is weeded and forked over, trodden lightly, and raked level.

Check the instructions on the packet before going any further, as plants differ in the spacing and depth of sowing they require. The packet may give advice on how thickly to sow, but the thinner the better is usually the best guide. For many types, aim to sow seeds ½–1 in (1–2.5 cm) apart. After cutting open the seed packet with a pair of scissors, check the contents. Then, keeping in mind whether you require only half a dozen plants or wish to raise much larger numbers, make a rough estimate of the length of row required. Using the point of a stick, draw a narrow row, or drill, in the soil to the depth specified on the packet and of a length that seems suitable for the number of plants you wish to raise. Always use a longer row to raise more plants in preference to sowing thickly, and do

Sowing lupine seeds outside

1 *Make a drill ½–1 in (1–2.5 cm) deep, sow the seeds about 1 in (2.5 cm) apart, then cover them carefully.*

2 *In good seasons most seeds will germinate, and when they do, hoe between the rows to control weeds.*

3 *As the seedlings develop, thin them to about 3 in (7.5 cm) apart to prevent overcrowding and spindly growth.*

4 *As they continue to grow and again become crowded, transplant the seedlings 6–9 in (16–23 cm) apart.*

not be tempted to sow all the seed if it is not necessary.

In dry weather it pays to water the drills before sowing. Fill the watering can, remove the rosehead, and with one finger partly covering the spout to lessen the flow, gently fill the drill with water along its length. Now sow the seed. There are a number of ways of actually sowing the seed, and everyone has a preferred method. One of the simplest is to pour some seed from the seed packet into the

palm of your left hand (if you are right handed) then take a pinch in the fingers of your right hand and gently release it as you move your hand along the drill. Watch carefully to see that the seed is evenly distributed and spaced as recommended on the packet. Large seeds, like those of lupines, can then be moved individually to a more accurate spacing. Once the seed is sown, insert a label at the end of the row and, with the back of the rake, draw a little soil from the

sides to cover the drill. Firm gently with the flat part of the rake. If a spell of hot weather follows sowing, water to encourage germination.

When seed germinates When the seed germinates, the row can be weeded by hand as the seedlings develop. This method allows you to see how many seedlings have germinated. If germination has been good, the seedlings will need to be thinned to give them more space to develop. The seed packet usually offers guidance, but in general aim to thin the seedlings to about 3 in (7.5cm) apart. The unwanted seedlings can be discarded, given away, or planted elsewhere. If germination has been poor, little or no thinning may be required.

As they develop, the seedlings of different plants perform in different ways. Some grow quickly and can be lifted and replanted at a spacing of 6–9 in (15–23 cm) by the fall. Others grow more slowly and are probably best left undisturbed until the spring; again, the seed packet gives advice. Finally, remember that plants of many perennials raised from seed will not necessarily be identical, so it is advisable to see the plants actually in flower before choosing which ones to transfer to borders.

SOWING SEED IN PROTECTION

Sowing seed in a protected environment is a more efficient way of raising perennials than sowing outside, but you need the right facilities. Some gardeners are successful in raising perennials using a propagator on a windowsill in the house, but the low light levels and the difficulty of controlling the temperature make it more difficult than is often suggested. A cold frame or a greenhouse is far more likely to ensure success.

Cold frame

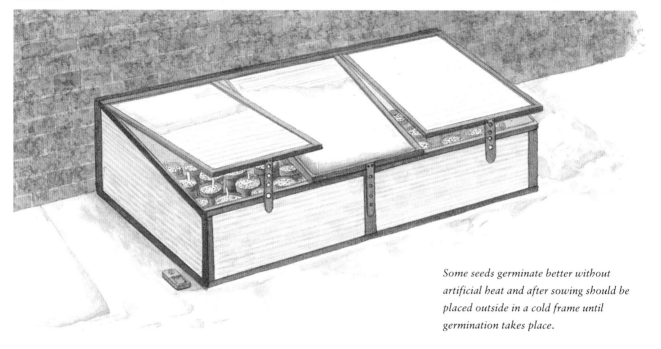

Some seeds germinate better without artificial heat and after sowing should be placed outside in a cold frame until germination takes place.

Cold frame A cold frame, which is usually rectangular in shape, serves as a box in which plants can be grown under cover or protected during winter. It has a plastic or glass lid, and some types also have transparent side walls. A cold frame is an important asset, for it provides sufficient protection to ensure good germination of seed and growth of seedlings, yet it is inexpensive, easy to manage, and requires little space. In particular, it provides an opportunity to give expensive seeds better conditions than those found in the open garden, and this is especially important when the packet contains only a small number of seeds. The added protection of a cold frame also allows plants to reach greater maturity before the end of their first growing season. The vast majority of perennials can be raised in this way. For some, such as hellebores, primroses, and pulsatillas, sowing in a cold frame in summer is really the only way to ensure good germination. A few plants, however,

like perennial lobelias, require not only the additional warmth of a greenhouse but also a long growing season following a spring sowing.

Most cold frames are suitable for raising seeds. You can construct a wood or aluminum structure from a kit, or you can make your own model using old boards. It is best sited in an open spot, where it is not overhung by trees, but if the only place available is in full sun, then shading is necessary to prevent the temperature inside from rising too high.

Seed is best sown in summer, when most other plants, like half-hardy annuals, have been taken from the cold frame for planting. Always check the packet for specific advice, but most types can be sown thinly in 3½ in (9 cm) plastic pots using a soilless mix. Try to find the grade specific to seed sowing. It is advisable to add 20 percent extra sand or perlite to the mix to improve drainage. Perennials vary enormously in the time they take to germinate, so after sowing, it is

good practice to cover the seed with coarse sand to deter the growth of moss. Water the pots of seed, and place them in the cold frame, which should be closed to keep the temperature high enough to encourage germination. However, some plants, especially primroses and other primulas, dislike hot conditions, and for them it usually pays to site the frame in a place that gets no sun whatsoever.

It is important to prevent the cold frame from overheating, or seedlings may be scorched. Thus, unless the cold frame is sited in a naturally shady place, you need to open it partially. In many areas the cold frame also requires shading with plastic netting or shade cloth during the warmest months. It is also vital to ensure that the seeds and seedlings never dry out, so check them daily and water when necessary. Because seedlings are vulnerable to slug damage from the moment they germinate, pellets or some other form of control should always be used. Some seedlings may be eaten by mice, so a mousetrap or a bait should also be placed just outside the cold frame.

After germination, the seed pots should be moved to an unshaded part of the cold frame. When the first true leaves have developed, prick the seedlings out into a commercial potting soil. They can be moved into seed flats, or the more vigorous types can go straight into individual 3½ in (9 cm) pots. Then grow them for planting later in the year or the following spring.

Finally, there are a number of perennial plants that require either cool conditions or frost to promote germination. These include gentians, hellebores, some primulas, and pulsatillas. These, too, are best sown in a cold frame, but they may not germinate until early in the winter after sowing or even until the following spring. The most practical approach is to sow the seed as soon as it is available from seed companies, then place the pots in a cold frame in a cool place and wait, ensuring that they never dry out. After germination has taken place they can be treated like other seedlings.

Greenhouse The greenhouse can be used in much the same way as the cold frame, but it can be put to better use for sowing in spring. There are quite a few perennials which flower in their first year if sown in spring and raised in much the same way as you would raise half-hardy annuals. The sowing routine is the same as for seed sown in a cold frame, but since sowing in early spring in a warm environment ensures prompt and more complete germination, expensive seed is used to the best advantage by this method. A temperature of 60°–65°F (16°–18°C) is ideal, and although this can be provided in a heated greenhouse, a thermostatically controlled propagator is much more economical.

After germination remove seedlings from the propagator and place them either on a greenhouse bench or in a propagator set at a cooler temperature. After pricking out, they can be grown on at a cool temperature (minimum 45°F/7°C), and then hardened off in an unheated cold frame to accustom them to outdoor conditions before planting out in late spring. Many perennials are sufficiently tough to allow them to be planted out before the last frost if they are hardened off well.

There is one disadvantage but two great advantages to raising perennials in this way. The main difficulty is that in spring there is often competition for space in the greenhouse and propagator, as half-hardy annuals and greenhouse vegetables require sowing at the same time. A major advantage, however, is that many perennials sown early provide a good display in their first year, although sometimes a little later than their usual flowering season. The second advantage of early sowing is that plants available from seed only in mixed colors can be planted in a spare piece of ground for the summer, and the plants with flower colors that are especially attractive can be selected for transplanting to the border the same fall.

Perennials that flower in their first year The following plants are among those that flower well in their first year provided they are sown in warm conditions in early spring: *Achillea* 'Summer Pastels,' *Centranthus ruber*, *Coreopsis* 'Early Sunrise,' *Dephinium* 'Southern Noblemen,' *Geum* 'Lady Stratheden' and 'Mrs. Bradshaw,' *Lobelia* 'Compliment Scarlet,' *Lupinus* 'Band of Nobles' and 'Gallery,' *Polemonium caeruleum*, and *Salvia × sylvestris*, 'Blue Queen' (Blaukönigin) and 'Rose Queen.'

Types of propagator

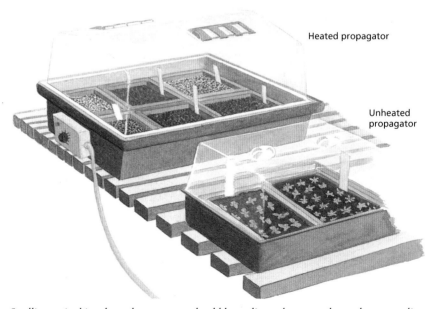

Heated propagator

Unheated propagator

Seedlings raised in a heated propagator should be acclimated to normal greenhouse conditions by giving them an intermediate stage in an unheated propagator.

USING
PERENNIALS

Perennials can be used effectively in many settings, from traditional perennial borders to containers on a patio but, whatever the scale, every situation benefits from a thoughtful approach.

The single most important factor in ensuring the success of any planting style is planning. Even if the aim is to achieve a less formal style, a natural looking or cottage garden, simply rushing ahead with no plan of any sort is usually a recipe for disappointment.

Planning does not always mean drawing a plan to scale on a piece of paper and then transferring it to the patch of land outside. It also means thinking carefully about the desired effect and making sure that this effect will look appropriate in the place available.

The upright spikes of delphiniums and lupines with Oriental poppies are fronted by bushier hardy geraniums.

Choosing the plants that are most likely to create the effect required and ensuring that they will thrive in the soil and situation that is available is also an important factor when planning the border. Once all this has been thought out, the way that the plants are arranged with each other in the border is crucial. Selecting colors that complement each other or contrast attractively; taking account of factors such as the plants' height on maturity, foliage color, habit and respective seasons of flowering, should ensure a successful planting.

Most important of all, as you enjoy the beds and borders you have created, look critically at them, and think about how you can improve them. Gardens change continuously: make sure yours changes for the better.

Left: This skillfully planned herbaceous border in midsummer is graded in height from the tall rudbeckias at the back to the shorter sedum and artemisia at the front. The colors link up along the border, with yellows and pinks repeated in different plants, and foliage colors calming any clashes.

PLANTING STYLES

Traditionally perennials were grown in formal herbaceous borders in large gardens, where tall plants and plants with a short season could be easily accommodated. In contrast, an informal cottage garden was filled with perennials growing in the company of herbs, fruit trees, and bulbs. As gardens became smaller, mixed borders in various styles became more popular. Today, perennials are grown alongside a variety of other plants.

The many different ways in which perennials can be grown caters to the full range of gardens and individual tastes. Island beds, for example, were introduced as a response to the need for shorter, self-supporting plants in the confined conditions of smaller gardens. At the same time imaginative gardeners began to develop other ways of growing perennials, adapting their planting ideas to their own situations and tastes. Today's gardeners may showcase collections of specific perennials, highlight individual specimen plants, opt for naturalistic plantings and wildflower gardens, or feature permanent plantings of perennials in containers.

Above: This spectacular midsummer border is split into two color-themed sections. In the foreground the flowers are mainly bright yellow with an occasional red highlight; in the distance they are red with some bronzed foliage.

Above: This cool and restful tapestry of purples, lavenders and lilac, with occasional white highlights, contrasts well with the darker, shadier area beyond. The planting is kept low to allow a view of the distant shade from the top of the path that looks down to the clipped holly, and is softened by billowing perennials.

Above: Seasonally themed borders, where plants with the same flowering time are concentrated together, provide a colorful display. Here the tall white daisies of *Leucanthemella serotina* tower over other fall flowering perennials.

HERBACEOUS PLANTINGS

In the past large formal gardens usually had a herbaceous bed or border, which was intended to be one of the glories of the year's displays. Certainly, this is the most spectacular way to grow perennials, but they can also be attractively organized on a much smaller scale.

TRADITIONAL HERBACEOUS BORDERS

The herbaceous border was usually a long, straight border, sometimes up to 10–12 ft (3–3.6 m) deep and occasionally hundreds of feet long, depending on the size of the garden as a whole. It was normally backed by a wall or by a hedge of yew or another evergreen, which provided shelter from potentially damaging winds while at the same time offering an attractive neutral background against which to view the plants. In many large, grand gardens, a pair of parallel borders was planted with a broad grass walk between them, terminating in a view of the surrounding countryside, the house, a garden feature, or some highlight of the distant landscape.

Generally these grand herbaceous borders were summer features. In displays of this scale the plants had to be colorful if they were to have a significant impact, so among the most popular were groups of delphiniums, Shasta daisies, phlox, lupines, and Oriental poppies—all of which are summer-flowering-plants. The fact that the main display was concentrated into two or three summer months also ensured that the color was intense—at least for the period that the border was in flower there were no spaces where earlier plants

had faded. Displays for other seasons were often accommodated in other parts of a large garden.

These traditional borders were usually arranged in a straightforward way. All individual varieties were planted in broad groups, scaled in proportion to the overall size of the border. The tallest plants were placed at the back, with others decreasing in size to the shortest at the front. Bold clumps of particular plants were sometimes repeated at intervals along the length of the border to create a more coherent feeling. Where a double border was planted, the two sides might be arranged as mirror images of each other.

Most of the plants grown were chosen for their colorful flowers. Foliage plants were used much less often, their prime function usually being to separate clashing colors. In fact, foliage plants in general were uncommon compared with the wide selection available today.

THE DECLINE OF THE HERBACEOUS BORDER

Large-scale herbaceous borders were labor-intensive. The necessary staking, weeding, and deadheading involved many hours of work for a team of gardeners. It was also a customary practice for one-quarter or even one-third of the border to be replanted each year; this involved removing the plants, digging the border, incorporating large quantities of rich organic matter, then splitting the plants and replanting them.

Times changed, and gardens became smaller and labor more expensive. Setting aside a large area of the garden for a short seasonal display became difficult to justify: for much of the year there was little to see, and in winter the soil was almost

bare. At the same time, given the cost of labor, it became impossible to provide all the regular attention such borders require.

As a result, grand herbaceous borders began to disappear. They are still found in some public and historical gardens, but most gardeners now adopt a different approach to growing perennials.

MODERN HERBACEOUS PLANTINGS

In recent years the herbaceous border has been revived in a style radically adapted to modern gardens. Many gardeners now plant small herbaceous borders but ensure they make a significant contribution to the garden by making a careful choice of plants.

One approach is to set the plants much closer together, so that more varieties can be grown in the same space. This is the opposite of the traditional approach, where plants were grown in their own individual clumps and regular lifting and replanting kept them from growing into one another. Though the choice of plants is crucial in the modern method, planting tightly—even allowing two types to mingle—ensures that, as one variety finishes flowering, another is just coming into its own.

This is almost impossible to manage on a large scale, but in a small space it is both manageable and effective. Another way of adapting the traditional herbaceous border to smaller gardens is to choose perennials with an unusually long flowering period. As a result, the border is colorful from early summer until the middle of fall, instead of providing a few short weeks of summer splash. A group made up of only a dozen varieties can give a very impressive long-season display.

The scale of such plantings can be reduced even further, so that as few as six carefully chosen cultivars are used to make a feature in a special place within the garden. Alternatively, you can choose perennials that have valuable features in addition to their flowers. At its most basic, this means growing plants, such as pinks, that have evergreen foliage.

Plants with colorful or unusually handsome foliage are particularly valuable in the border, as they provide a long season of interest before and after the main flowering period. Varieties that have either colorful fruits or attractive winter stems are another good choice. In addition, there has been a strong trend toward growing perennials alongside other plants, such as shrubs, bulbs and annuals, that provide color and interest outside the perennials' flowering season.

The herbaceous border

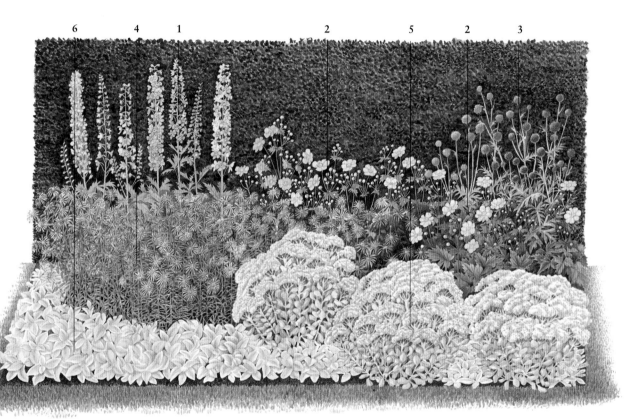

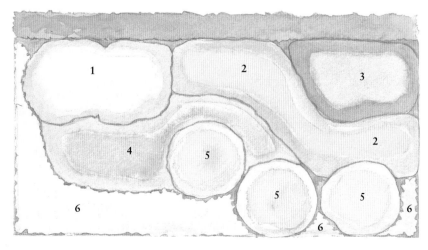

Key
1 *Delphinium 'Blue Bird'* × 1
2 *Anemone × hybrida* 'Queen Charlotte' × 2
3 *Echinops ritro* × 1
4 *Aster × frikartii* 'Mönch' × 1
5 *Sedum* 'Autumn Joy' × 3
6 *Stachys byzantina* 'Primrose Heron' × 3

COTTAGE STYLE

In contrast to formal herbaceous borders, which developed in gardens belonging to affluent families, cottage borders originated in humble circumstances and smaller spaces. Their creators had limited resources and were taken up with the day-to-day pressures of surviving in the countryside. They saw little need to separate different types of plants and so planted what they liked, or whatever cuttings and seeds were available from friends' and neighbours' gardens. The result was a joyful mix.

Lifestyles have changed, and today cottage gardens are more consciously planned. A disorganized appearance is now more the result of thoughtful foresight. We have adapted the style to an age in which resources are more plentiful but time to spend on gardening is more limited.

TRADITIONAL COTTAGE STYLE

The views of cottage gardens in Victorian paintings, while often idealized, give a flavor of the way they were: billowing color in a rural setting, unexpected combinations of plants with the cottage as a backdrop, and often work, rather than relaxation, in progress. Toward the back of the border fruit bushes or even large fruit trees were found with rows of vegetables; access paths were often

The cottage border

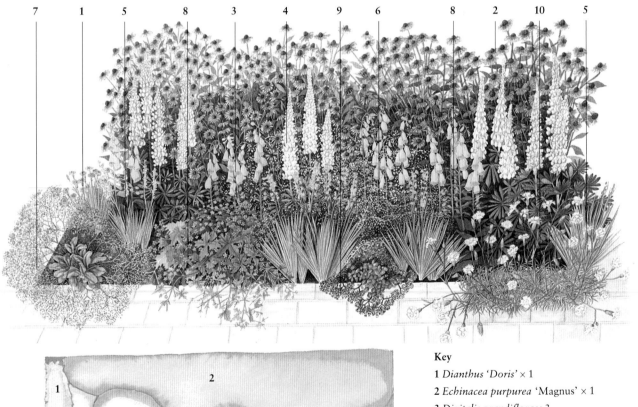

Key
1 *Dianthus* 'Doris' × 1
2 *Echinacea purpurea* 'Magnus' × 1
3 *Digitalis grandiflora* × 3
4 *Lupinus* 'Noble Maiden' × 3
5 *Sisyrinchium striatum* 'Aunt May' × 4
6 *Gypsophila paniculata* 'Bristol Fairy' × 1
7 *Limonium platyphyllum* × 1
8 *Geranium endressii* × 1
9 *Sedum* 'Ruby Glow' × 1
10 *Dianthus* 'Haytor' × 1

stone or brick. The beds might have been edged with boxwood hedges to keep the chickens from scratching among the plants, or there might have been a line of garden pinks or mossy saxifrages edging the path.

The planting consisted of an apparently chaotic jumble. Useful plants were set close to hand, where they could be looked after and picked easily, and ornamental plants were placed where they would grow well. Climbing or rambling roses, sweet peas, and honeysuckle might grow up trees, shrubs, a fence, or a cottage wall alongside runner beans. Annual plants such as love-in-a-mist and godetia, and biennials, such as sweet rocket and forget-me-nots, self-sowed where their seedlings could find space and thus flowered in unexpected places, making colorful combinations with perennial neighbors. Bulbs, such as daffodils and lilies, grew steadily into ever-expanding clumps.

Holding all this together were the perennials, spreading into clumps, only to be split and replanted in smaller groups whenever they began to occupy too much space. The varieties most commonly grown were resilient—they had to be tough enough to survive. They were also usually easy to propagate; divisions were passed from neighbor to neighbor, so often many of the gardens in a locality had the same kinds of perennials. Anything and everything could be cut, taken indoors, and placed in a jar of water to brighten the house.

The care cottage garden plants received was rudimentary at best. Manure provided the nutrients, waste water was tipped over plants that needed it, pruning was done when there was time or not at all, and the plants that grew well in the soil and climate of the area survived the best.

Lupines, delphiniums, and self-sown foxgloves make spires in the early summer cottage garden.

Traditional cottage garden perennials
The following perennials have long been cottage garden favorites and are still popular choices today.

Aquilegia Columbines self-sowed in many colors.

Aster New York asters of the past suffered from mildew. Many modern cultivars are more resistant.

Dendranthema Tough garden chrysanthemums, such as 'Clara Curtis,' are still grown today.

Dianthus Every cottage garden had its scented pinks. Many more recent cultivars have no scent.

Iris Tall flag irises flowered in early summer and were usually fragrant.

Lathyrus latifolius This perennial with its typical pea-shaped flowers scrambled over fences and tough shrubs.

Leucanthemum The striking, white Shasta daisies are now more often seen in short, characterless forms.

Lupinus The slim spikes of the older cultivars were less overpowering than today's tall, fat spikes.

Paeonia Left alone and fertilized occasionally, peonies flowered ever more prolifically.

Primula Primroses in particular were happy to provide a little early color in the shade of taller, later perennials.

MODERN COTTAGE GARDENING

While the unaffected gardens of the past can still sometimes be seen, cottage gardens have become more deliberate in recent times, as rural life has changed. Although many gardeners concentrate on traditional cottage garden plants, rather than growing the more up-to-date cultivars, the results tend to be planned: they consciously strive for a confused effect. Suburban and city gardeners re-create cottage gardens in unlikely situations, while both urban and rural gardeners try nostalgically to copy a style that derived from the circumstances of a different age. In these modern adaptations of the old-style cottage garden, fruit trees—except perhaps trained forms like cordons or dwarf trees grown on dwarfing rootstocks—are less often seen, while flowers and vegetables are more often confined to their own separate areas.

PERENNIALS IN MODERN COTTAGE GARDENS

At the turn of the century the choice, highly bred types of perennial plants were cultivated in the large scale gardens and simpler forms, including wildflowers, were grown in cottage gardens. At times plants from affluent estates found their way into cottage gardens, but as they often required more careful attention, they did not always thrive.

The perennials best suited to today's informal cottage style must be tough; we now try to pack even more varieties into our borders, so there is vigorous competition. Short, stocky plants with disproportionately large flower heads should be excluded in favor of types with a more open habit. Those that have been cultivated to produce bold blocks of color should be passed over in favor of those with a less dominant style.

Perennials with a tendency to run, allowing other plants to seed among them, were once appreciated. This open growth is still not necessarily a bad thing, but a balance must be struck between, on the one hand, letting plants spread and mingle and, on the other, preventing them from crowding out their neighbors.

Modern cottage garden perennials These perennials have become more popular in recent times yet fit well into cottage-style borders:

Alchemilla The green-flowered *A. mollis* is now frequently grown in many cottage gardens.

Allium Once alliums were merely kitchen onions run to seed, but today they are thought of more highly and many ornamental forms are grown.

Astrantia Generally rather demure, these can self-sow all too well.

Crocosmia Brilliantly colored modern forms still retain elegance.

Eryngium The open habit of these suits cottage-style plantings well.

Geranium Hardy geraniums, rarely grown a century ago, are ideal cottage garden flowers.

Helleborus Lenten roses, in particular, now come in many clear colors, with or without spots.

Linaria The wild yellow form with its running root was once a favorite. Now the slender pink 'Canon Went' is more common.

Nepeta Many new catmints are now available to complement the traditional form.

Penstemon Although often short-lived, these natives fit perfectly into cottage plantings.

The less chaotic style of modern cottage gardens, with salvias and a range of penstemons.

MIXED PLANTINGS

The mixed border, in which perennials are grown alongside other plants, has become increasingly popular since the 1950s. It can vary from a few shrubs being used to form a background and provide protection for the perennials to a more fully integrated planting incorporating a wide range of plant types.

Deciduous and evergreen shrubs or even small trees serve as the main structure, the backbone, of the mixed border. They also provide early flowers, fall leaf color and fruits, and a consistent presence throughout the season. Perennials usually provide the most color and variety in both flowers and foliage, while annuals and bedding plants are carefully chosen to blend in rather than dominate. Bulbs are an essential constituent, especially as they can grow through perennials and produce attractive color combinations. Climbers are set to scramble through shrubs and trees.

The whole border is planned so that the many different constituents knit together harmoniously. Choosing and placing plants so that they will not overpower each other, either in the vigor of their growth or the color of their flowers, ensures an attractive and balanced effect.

ADVANTAGES OVER HERBACEOUS BORDERS

Mixed borders have many advantages over borders composed entirely of hardy perennials. First, by adding shrubs and bulbs to perennials it is possible to have plants coming into flower for much of the year—indeed, the whole year in southern climates. Most herbaceous borders look empty between late fall, when most of the plants are cut down, and late spring,

Perennials are now grown with other types of plants like these alliums and bedding pansies.

when the first full flush of flowers takes place. Shrubs, climbers, bulbs, and biennials can be used to provide color in that otherwise relatively colorless period.

Second, the enormous range of different plant types that can be included in mixed borders allows you to create a wide variety of interest. Shrubs, climbers, and bulbs offer a diversity of shapes and styles of growth you cannot find among the perennials alone. Perennials are grown primarily for their flowers, with foliage as a secondary attraction, whereas shrubs provide bark,

fruits, and fall color in addition to their flowers and leaves. But the single most important advantage of the mixed border over the herbaceous border is that, by choosing from the full palette of plants, a small garden can be made more colorful and more interesting for considerably longer. One possible disadvantage, if you prefer a traditional style, is that the mixed border is a more modern arrangement. With a greater range of plant types, mixed borders are also less straightforward to look after, but this could be seen as a challenge rather than a disadvantage.

PLANNING MIXED BORDERS

Mixed borders can be as simple or as intricate as you wish. In practice they are often organized in a straightforward way at first, but soon become more complicated as plants are added and self-sown seedlings appear.

Choose the shrubs and small trees (if any) first. Use some to create a solid presence at the back of the border, and let smaller forms add substance toward the front. You can select climbers to clamber through them, either to flower with and complement the shrubs or to flower at another time of year, extending the season of that particular group.

Next, consider your perennials, looking both for those that will combine well with the shrubs and climbers at flowering time and those that will extend the flowering season.

Some should be long-flowering types; some should be good foliage forms; and some should be chosen for their short but spectacular display.

Now you can plan spaces for annuals, summer bedding plants, and biennials. The varieties of these you choose can be changed from year to year to bring additional diversity, and bulbs can be selected to grow up among the perennials, so that more

The mixed border

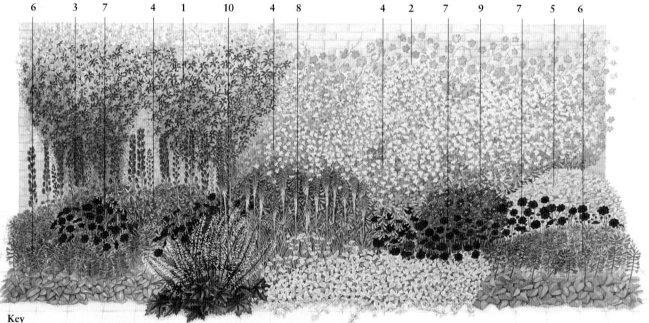

Key

1 *Clematis viticella* 'Madame Julia Correvon' × 2
2 *Tropaeolum peregrinum* × 1
3 *Aconitum carmichaelii* 'Bressingham Spire' × 5
4 *Nicotiana langsdorfii* × 5
5 *Spirea* 'Goldflame' × 1
6 *Stachys macrantha* 'Superba' × 4
7 *Cosmos atrosanguineus* × 7
8 *Kniphofia* 'Bressingham Comet' × 4
9 *Aster amellus* 'Violet Queen' × 4
10 *Heuchera macrantha* 'Palace Purple' × 1
11 *Helichrysum petiolare* 'Limelight' × 2
○ Spring flowering bulbs underplant the aster

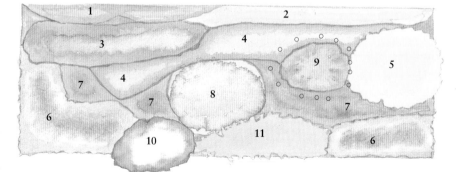

than one plant flowers in one place during the course of the year.

Perennials in mixed borders in small gardens The most important advantage of using perennials in mixed borders in small gardens is that by choosing from such a wide range of plants, you can do a great deal of interplanting, making every inch of the border as colorful as possible for as long as possible.

Perennials and shrubs Although shrubs provide the backbone of the mixed border, perennials are generally the most important plants.

Tall perennials that might otherwise require elaborate support, such as the white daisies of *Leucanthemella serotina,* can benefit from the shelter afforded by large shrubs at the back of the border. Perennial climbers, such as peas (*Lathyrus latifolius*) or herbaceous clematises, can be planted under shrubs to scramble up through them.

Perennials and bulbs Some perennials are very effective when interplanted with bulbs. Spring bulbs, for example wood anemones, can be planted in a carpet among summer-flowering perennials, such as *Salvia × sylvestris.* Evergreen perennials, such as bergenias, can provide a good background for spring crocuses, while the very attractive foliage of hostas can mask the leaves of ornamental onions, which may shrivel when their flowers are at their best.

Perennials and annuals Annual climbers, such as canary creeper (*Tropaeolum peregrinum*) and sweet pea, can be planted to climb into shrubs, but they will also trail attractively through perennials and will often provide color after early flowering perennials have been deadheaded. Summer bedding plants with good foliage, such as the silver-leaved

Helichrysum petiolare, can be used to hide the bare basal stems of some perennials, such as phlox, while at the same time providing a harmonious association of color.

Dual-season perennials Perennials that have more than one attractive feature are especially valuable in mixed borders. For example, the clump-forming *Geranium renardii* starts the season with a new flush of sage-green leaves, which look delightful covered in dewdrops on spring mornings and make a good background for late spring bulbs; then, in summer, its purple-veined white flowers appear; and, in early fall the mature mound of its leaves makes an excellent background for the pink or white chalices of the fall-flowering colchicum, a bulb which shares the geranium's preference for well-drained soil.

Self-sown annual opium poppies mingle with delphiniums, salvias and potentillas in this most manageable of mixed plantings in which hardy bulbs are used for the main spring display.

85

ISLAND BEDS

Three important trends have altered the ways in which we grow perennials in recent decades. First, gardens have become smaller and beds and borders have correspondingly decreased in scale, so many of the larger perennials, such as delphiniums and rheums, are not as easy to accommodate. Second, gardeners are not able or willing to spend as much time looking after their gardens. Third, there has been a drift away from formality to a more informal style of garden and border design. The combination of these three factors has led to the development of the island bed.

WHAT ARE ISLAND BEDS?

Island beds are freestanding beds, most often in lawns but sometimes in gravel or paving. They are usually designed in informal-looking, flowing curves around which it is easy to mow. Sometimes a number of beds may be cut out of a lawn, their size depending on the scale of the garden.

The traditional border is usually viewed from only one side, but significantly, island beds are intended to be seen from all around, introducing a greater variety of views into a small area. If a number of island beds are created together, it is possible to give each a different color or seasonal theme, adding even greater variety.

Island beds are often unsuitable for taller plants, as their more open position—away from hedges and walls—leaves them exposed on all sides to strong winds. Besides, you don't want to spend your limited time on staking. A further reason to be wary of tall plants is that they are likely to be out of proportion to the scale of the beds themselves. Many of the stately traditional perennials are therefore unsuitable for island beds; plants that are shorter, stockier, and bushier are more appropriate choices. With enthusiasm for island beds continuing to grow, many new dwarf cultivars have been developed to meet these requirements.

These island beds cut out of a well-kept lawn are densely planted to help keep down weeds.

ADVANTAGES OF ISLAND BEDS

This radical change of approach to using perennials in the garden has created many advantages:

• Small beds fit more effectively into today's smaller gardens.

• The all-around view creates more interest in a small space.

• Smaller plants with stockier growth allow a greater variety of cultivars to be grown in the available space.

• Dwarf, bushy cultivars require little or no time-consuming staking.

• The informal design suits today's tastes and allows scope for composition that can be viewed from all sides.

• Island sites create conditions for a wide range of plants.

PLANNING ISLAND BEDS

The traditional one-sided herbaceous border is usually a long rectangle set against a background. Island beds are often kidney-shaped or laid out in flowing curves in an open area. In the traditional herbaceous border the tallest plants must go at the back, scaling down to the smallest at the front; in island beds the tallest plants go in the middle.

Taller plants look too formal if planted in a line along the backbone of the bed; they are more effective if set in clumps interspersed by groups of smaller plants. The clumps are best situated where the bed is widest, with smaller plants grouped around them.

Only where big, sweeping island beds are created in large gardens is a strong backbone of substantial plants likely to be effective. Otherwise, it is more successful to use shrubs instead as the backbone, so that you create two one-sided borders back-to-back. These can be different in character, not the least because one will probably be sunny and the other shady.

The key plants The taller, more substantial plants set the main theme for the planting in terms of either color or season and influence the choice of nearby plants. Key plants should have a long season or good foliage and, when their flowers are over, should help to provide a background for

The island bed

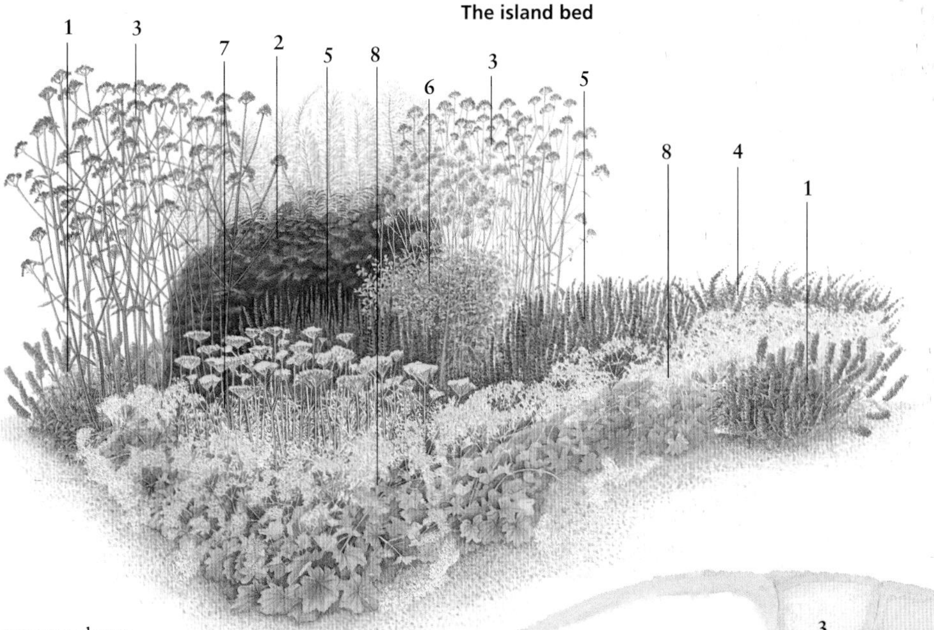

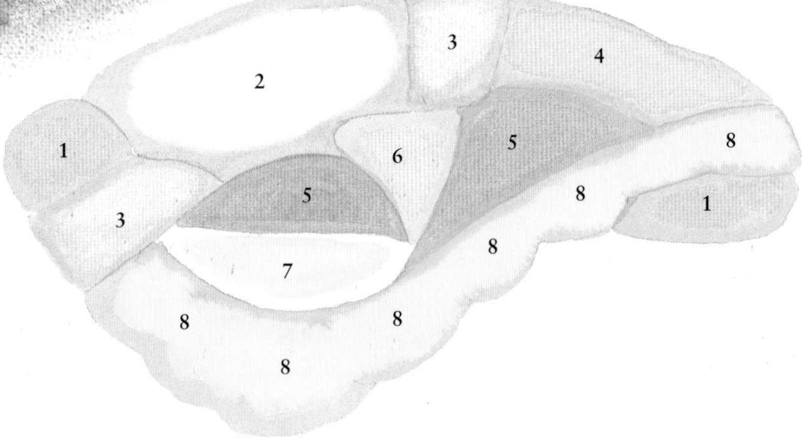

Key

1 *Nepeta nervosa* × clump
2 *Aruncus dioicus* × 2
3 *Verbena bonariensis* × 2 clumps
4 *Nepeta* 'Six Hills Giant' × 3
5 *Salvia nemerosa* 'East Friesland' × 2
6 *Thalictrum aquilegifolium*
7 *Achillea clypeolata* 'Moonshine' × 1
8 *Alchemilla mollis* × 7

other plants. Some gardeners choose flowering and variegated shrubs rather than perennials for these positions, as they offer a greater selection of plants that combine these features.

There are several alternative ways to deal with these key points in the border, although they involve more work. Instead of planting bold long-season perennials or using shrubs, you can opt for a tall early-season plant, such as a delphinium, and interplant or surround it with tall late-season plants, such as asters; the delphinium flowers can then be cut down when they are over, leaving the aster to develop and fill the space as the season progresses. Yet another approach is to construct a tepee of stakes and use it to support such perennial climbers as *Lathyrus latifolius* or annual climbers.

The filler planting Planning the planting around these key plants is more difficult than for one-sided borders, with their single viewpoint. Not only must the varieties chosen combine well with the key plants, whatever the angle of view, they must also associate well with each other, follow the planting theme and style (if there is one), and be suitable for the different conditions around the key plants. As an example of this last consideration: because substantial long-season feature plants cast shade, a filler that does well on the sunny side may languish on the shady side.

With an island bed, your planning must take into account the fact that the bed has no solid backbone, so that it is often possible to look right across the planting from one side to the other. You must pay attention to the color and character of plants that will appear in the same view, though they may actually be set some distance apart.

As with the other plants in the bed, you can extend the season of the filled-in area through interplanting.

SMALL GARDEN, SMALL SCALE
There are two other features to consider with island beds, especially those in small gardens. First, as beds are reduced in size, the size of the plants must be reduced in proportion. Second, in a small garden the plants and plantings are examined more closely and more regularly than in larger gardens. It is therefore worth keeping the following points in mind:
• Try to choose only the very best cultivars.
• Replace promptly any plants that do not appear to be thriving or prove to be poor choices.
• Choose forms with secondary features, such as attractive foliage or fruits, in addition to their main display, so that their period of interest is much longer.
• Deadhead and trim the plants frequently to keep them at their best.
• Avoid gaps in the planting—if a plant is slow to become established or if it dies, then fill the resulting space in the bed temporarily, with foliage annuals if necessary.

Small island beds like this can contain a good range of varieties and still fit the scale.

WILDFLOWER PLANTINGS

The increasing enthusiasm for wildflowers has developed along two distinct lines. First, there is the interest in growing those less highly developed perennials whose natural grace has not been destroyed by plant breeders trying to "improve" them. Second, many gardeners find that growing perennials in a naturalistic way is a more satisfying approach to gardening than formal and highly planned strategies.

WILD SPECIES

The attraction of wild species over their more highly developed descendants is that they often have a more elegant habit, are less gaudy in color, and display a simple charm that is missing from modern, highly bred cultivars. Not having been developed in and for gardens, they also enjoy that intimate connection with the natural world that appeals to today's environmentally conscious gardener.

But they also have disadvantages. Some wild perennials are exceptionally vigorous and may overwhelm less rampant neighbors. Some produce too many self-sown seedlings, which can be a nuisance. Some, while undeniably charming, suffer from features that in the wild would not be considered deficiencies but are less desirable in the garden, such as tall growth, small flowers, or a brief flowering season.

In short, while some wild species integrate well into herbaceous garden plantings in many styles, others are better used in more conscious attempts to create a wildflower habitat.
Native and wild There is a distinction between wild species and native plants. Wild species are unchanged species found growing in natural habitats around the world. Native plants are those wild species that grow in and are particularly suited to a given area—a country, state, or county. Just as gardeners have become more interested in wild species generally, so interest in native species has also increased. Beds, borders, or even whole gardens are sometimes devoted to them.

In addition to their aesthetic attractions and their associations with unspoiled nature, native plants have one particular advantage. As the natural plants of the area, they are best adapted to local conditions and are most likely to attract insects, birds, and other wildlife. Many gardeners find this the most important reason for growing them.

WILDFLOWERS IN THE GARDEN

Creating garden habitats that replicate the environments in which wildflowers grow naturally is appealing but also challenging.
Natural habitats Creating replicas of natural habitats is the opposite of the usual approach to gardening, which is inherently an artificial process. The first step is to prepare the site in a

Cornflowers, field poppies, corn marigolds and other wild cornfield annuals make a sparkling summer display and thrive in poor soil.

Wild primroses and anemones make an attractive spring group in a shady corner.

different way from the way that you would prepare for more conventional plantings (p.29). You must strike a balance between letting the habitat develop in its own natural way and preventing weeds or very aggressive species from taking over. What you are attempting to create is something of a contradiction in terms: an artificial natural environment.

• Prepare the site carefully (p.36) to ensure that the plants have the most appropriate habitat and to minimize the chances of weeds becoming established and smothering them.

• Check the balance of the different species regularly. If one has a tendency to dominate, you can deadhead it to prevent it from self-seeding, or you can restrict its spread by digging up some of its roots.

• Some species may prove short-lived; this may be natural or it may be the result of inappropriate growing conditions. In either case, regular reintroduction may be the answer.

• Invasive weeds can quickly become established in plantings that are not managed in a conventional way. Watch for them and remove them as soon as they appear.

• At the same time keep an eye out for welcome arrivals of native species you did not yourself introduce. Not all newcomers are unwanted weeds.

• Pay attention to the health of native plants by inspecting them regularly. They may be attacked by unfamiliar pests and diseases, which do not usually strike garden plants.

Wild species in beds and borders
Some wild species are sufficiently colorful, accommodating, and well behaved to be grown with other perennials in traditional borders without requiring special treatment. Such wild species can be found in the Plant Directory (pp.144–227). Undeveloped forms of wild species, which may offer uncommon colors, can be integrated in the same way.

To create a less managed, more natural look in traditional border plantings, space the original plants more widely than usual and then interfere as little as possible with their

natural spread by root and seed, allowing more mingling and integration. When you let plants spread freely in this way, covering any patch of bare earth, it is a good idea to put some stones in the bed to give you access when you want to tend the plants. Borders of this sort cannot be left to run wild; they require careful and detailed management to offer a good balance of varieties and look pleasing from different viewpoints.

Recently a new approach was developed that integrates selected forms of wild species and suitable garden cultivars into natural-looking stands of plants. Although in herbaceous beds and borders it is common to grow individual plants or clumps of plants in one place, separate from one another, this arrangement is rarely seen in nature. Individual groupings are found in the wild, but there is usually a greater mingling of species, often in broad swathes covering whole fields or mountainsides.

This style is now being replicated in gardens. Gardeners plant broad drifts that comprise a number of different wild species or garden cultivars mingled intimately together. These may flower successively to give a series of sweeps of color through the season, or they may flower together, providing an intensely rich and sometimes dramatic effect.

Such an approach to planting requires not only space but also careful management to ensure a balance of different plants. It can, however, create an extremely satisfying display, combining the best features of natural wildflower habitats with the demands of the garden.

Right: Moisture-loving perennials, both wild and cultivated, can be allowed to grow naturally and to spread and self-sow freely.

SHOW BEDS

Many gardeners have groups of plants that are special favorites and like to build up collections of these. There are two ways of accommodating collections of perennials.

The first is to plant the individual selections where they naturally grow well and look best; this is the way in which collections are usually built up initially. Integrating a collection into a garden works only if the plants are small and not too bright or overpowering; for example, if you spread a collection of delphiniums around the garden they will, when flowering, attract such attention that the garden will seem to contain little else. By contrast, hardy geraniums, smaller in size and softer in color, can be integrated with greater success. They adapt to a variety of situations, so spreading them around the garden will cause few problems. Collections of primroses or water irises, on the other hand, need special conditions.

COLLECTIONS IN SHOW BEDS

Show beds are a second way of accommodating a collection of perennials. If the selected plants are grouped in one place, the particular conditions the plants require can more easily be provided, looking after them is less demanding and time-consuming, and it is easier to compare the different plants within the collection. The collection becomes a feature in its own right. A planting of delphiniums or phlox is spectacular in early summer; a collection of hellebores is intriguing and beautiful in late spring; hostas are interesting for more than half the year.

But there are three problems associated with presenting plants in this way. First, you need a substantial area throughout which the conditions suit the plant in question. Second, if one individual is attacked by a pest or disease, this easily spreads to the others. Third and most important, when the collection is not at its peak, there may be little to see.

Clearly it would be foolish to collect plants whose requirements cannot be met in your garden. However, in some instances you may decide it is worth indulging in a degree of special soil preparation—for example, if your chosen group has unusual members that are fussier than the more common ones. If a group of plants is vulnerable to a particular pest, it can be advantageous to grow them together because at least you confine spraying to a single area of the garden.

SHOW BEDS OUT OF SEASON

The problem of out-of-season interest can, with some collections, be solved easily. You can interplant with other varieties whose main interest comes at a different season. This interplanting is best kept very simple to ensure that the bed does not have various care requirements.

Bulbs are often the most suitable plants to use in order to prolong the season. For example, collections of summer or fall perennials, such as peonies, phlox, or New York asters, can be interplanted with species crocuses; these will often self-sow throughout the bed, making a delightful spring carpet before the

Hostas, with their harmonious leaf tones, make a good collection in a bed of their own.

summer plants come into their own. Similarly, winter and spring plants, such as hellebores, can be interspersed with clumps of lilies, or an easy hardy annual, such as love-in-a-mist, can be allowed to self-sow among primroses or irises.

COMBINED COLLECTIONS

Sometimes two collections can be integrated to make a display in a single bed that provides conditions both plants enjoy. Both hostas and ferns enjoy similar cool, shady situations, and the broad hosta leaves make an attractive combination with the feathery ferns. Daylilies and Siberian irises also look good together and like similar conditions.

It can be difficult to give some plants the care they require when their companion plants are in the way, so collections that need a great deal of staking, deadheading, and spraying, not to mention regular replanting, are best grown in isolation; examples include phlox and delphiniums. Plants that have a tendency to spread rapidly, such as anemones, are best grown either on their own or in widely separate locations with other plants between.

THEMATIC DISPLAYS

There is another way of planting attractive show beds. An unusually spectacular display can be created with a substantial planting of a few carefully chosen forms.

A collection of asters also makes a fine feature as their colors harmonize well.

Instead of planting a small bed or border with a range of mixed perennials, using a single plant of each, you can restrict yourself to three or four types planted in larger numbers to create an impressive show. You can opt for plants that produce a short but brilliant flash of color, perhaps to coincide with a birthday, annual party, or anniversary, or you can select unusually long-flowering plants to bring constant color to an important part of the garden, such as the view from the kitchen window.

Many other themes are possible. A planting can be made of cultivars with the same names as family members, for example *Dianthus* 'Diane' and *Sisyrinchium* 'Aunt May.' To celebrate a silver wedding anniversary, you could display silver foliage plants. Or you might want to remember a special vacation by growing plants from that area together. Themed collections of this sort can give you a great deal of fun and ensure that your garden is unique.

FEATURE PLANTINGS

Some perennials are such naturally impressive plants that they can be used as a feature in their own right rather than as just part of a border. They may be large or colorful, such as *Gunnera manicata,* and rheums. Like specimen shrubs or small trees, these plants are often better viewed from afar and without surrounding distractions. Alternatively, they may be smaller plants that naturally grow into elegant specimens, like some of the larger hostas. Or they may be intimate specimens—plants that display an attractive feature or combination of features, such as habit, foliage, and flowers, when grown in isolation.

There is one problem. Unlike shrubs, most perennials die down in winter, so you are left with an uninteresting gap in your garden's display. Plan to counteract this either by ensuring that there are attractions in other parts of the garden or by underplanting winter or spring bulbs or a low evergreen ground cover.

DRAMATIC SPECIMENS

Some perennials are so bold and imposing that their structure, habit, and brilliant color is best appreciated when viewed from a distance. They may be best used as focal points in beds or borders of other plants; this is the case with, for example, tall species, such as *Leucanthemella serotina,* that may loose their lower leaves or whose attraction is mainly at the top of the plant.

Others, like pampas grass (*Cortaderia selloana*), can look superb in a more solitary situation. They can be used to fill a prominent angle between fences or walls, as the focal point at the end of a path or grass walk, or in splendid isolation toward the edge of broad gravel driveways. In larger gardens they can be used in a more traditional manner in beds cut out of grass, although some may benefit from a low ground-cover edging.

When perennials are deployed as dramatic specimens, it is especially important to look after them. A plant in a prominent position can look magnificent, but if it is not cared for or is planted in unsuitable conditions, it will languish, creating a worse effect than if it had been grown as one of several attractions in a border. **Plants to grow as dramatic specimens:** *Cortaderia selloana, Cynara cardunculus, Eryngium* (tall species), *Foeniculum vulgare* 'Purpureum,' *Gunnera manicata, Kniphofia* 'Prince Igor,' *Macleaya cordata, Miscanthus sinensis* cultivars, *Rheum,* and also *Stipa gigantea.*

INTIMATE SPECIMENS

Moving farther down the scale, a number of smaller plants derive particular benefit if isolated from distracting neighbors. These, too, can be grown in spaces made in paving or in gravel; some can also be grown in containers. Choose plants that look attractive in the scale and setting in which they are to be grown, and make sure the plants have an elegant habit, or at least one that is not ungainly. Most important, select plants that repay close inspection.

These varieties may have especially interesting flowers, such as double primroses, or flowers that are delicately veined or spotted. They may have nodding flowers that reveal a surprise when turned up, like some of the hellebores, or possess an especially intriguing scent, like many pinks. Foliage whose delicate coloring is especially attractive at close quarters might be the special feature, as with the Japanese painted fern (*Athyrium niponicum* var. *pictum*). Any plant with some quality that benefits from close inspection can be displayed as an intimate specimen. **Plants to grow as intimate specimens:** *Ajuga reptans* 'Variegata,' *Aquilegia viridiflora, Athyrium niponicum* var. *pictum, Bellis perennis* 'Prolifera,'

A bed devoted entirely to delphiniums makes a spectacular summer feature.

These bold clumps combine to make a striking feature, with the iris in the wettest soil, and the hosta and euphorbia in slightly drier soil.

Campanula punctata cultivars, *Dianthus* (laced and scented types), *Geranium renardii, Helleborus, Primula* (particularly double primroses), *Saxifraga fortunei* 'Wada.'

ELEGANT SPECIMENS

Perennials that are not exceptionally large but nevertheless develop into specimens with a strong, distinctive character can be effective when grown on their own. You can do this in a number of ways.

You can remove a single slab from an area of paved terrace or patio to make space for the plant; the neutrality of the surrounding paving often makes an ideal background. The space can be in a corner of the patio or toward the side, or the plant can be sited as a focal point. In these situations you must ensure that the light is even so that the plant develops in a balanced way. If the paving is strongly colored, choose your plant carefully: flowers or foliage in equally strong colors may clash.

Gravel is another good background for elegant specimens, and it has the advantage of suppressing weeds. However, it also encourages self-sown seedlings to appear, and these may need to be removed so that the original specimen stands out, uncrowded by any seedlings.

Plants to grow as elegant specimens: *Acanthus, Agapanthus, Dryopteris erythrosora, Euphorbia characias* cultivars, *Hakonechloa macra* 'Areola,' *Hosta* (larger forms), *Iris pallida* (variegated forms), *Molinia caerulea* 'Variegata,' *Polystichum setiferum* cultivars, and finally *Zantedeschia aethiopica* 'Crowborough.'

A single specimen of *Euphorbia characias* subsp. *wulfenii* develops into an imposing specimen for winter and spring.

CONTAINERS

Most perennials are best grown in the open garden, where their roots can spread and they can develop naturally. However, some perennials and some situations are better suited to the use of containers.

WHY USE CONTAINERS?
Your soil, particular features within your garden, or specific problems with the plants themselves may encourage you to explore the use of containers to grow plants.

If there is no way of transforming your garden's natural soil sufficiently to grow your favorite plants, then containers may provide the answer.
• On unusually wet soil, containers can be used to provide free-draining

conditions for plants that require drier soil. Examples include *Arabis, Asphodelus, Dianthus, Gaillardia, Iris* (many types), and *Paeonia.*
• On dry soil, containers can provide damper conditions for plants that require moisture. Examples include *Astilbe, Caltha, Dicentra,* ferns, *Hosta, Houttuynia cordata* 'Chameleon,' *Iris ensata,* and *Trollius.*

GARDEN SITUATIONS
Containers can provide planting options in areas where perennials could not otherwise be grown. For instance, they are invaluable in small paved yards, which may have little soil available for planting. Cultivars can be planted in window boxes and hanging baskets to bring perennials to unexpected sites. A specimen

perennial in a large container can make an arresting feature.
Solving problems Containers can be used to solve problems that commonly affect some perennial plants.
• Hostas are easier to keep free of slugs when planted in containers.
• Some perennials that are too rampant for the open border, such as the variegated ground elder *Aegopodium podagraria* 'Variegatum' and *Houttuynia cordata* 'Chameleon,' can be easily restricted in containers.
• In cold areas, slightly tender plants, such as agapanthus, can be grown in the open in containers and then moved into a protected place when temperatures drop in the fall.
• In very cold areas, containers should be plunged in the ground for the winter.

USING CONTAINERS EFFECTIVELY
Planting in containers requires much thoughtful planning. For a good display, it is necessary to grow suitable plants, choose compatible containers, and site them in appropriate places.

PLANTS FOR CONTAINERS
Good plants for containers fall into a number of categories.
• They should make elegant specimens in their own right and not be so tall or ungainly as to look out of place. Low, rounded, or broad plants are often very effective. Examples include *Aegopodium podagraria* 'Variegatum,' *Carex* (many), ferns, *Geranium* (some), grasses (many), and *Hosta* (most).
• Low, trailing plants are natural choices for containers. They soften the edges of tubs and boxes and, because their growth habit leaves plenty of free surface, allow additional plants to be grown in the container. Examples include *Ajuga,*

Containers are invaluable for paved areas where little soil is available for perennials.

Dianthus, Geranium (some), *Lamium, Malva sylvestris* 'Primley Blue,' and *Verbena* 'Homestead Purple.'

• Evergreen perennials are invaluable for containers, as they provide interest all year. Examples include *Ajuga, Bergenia, Carex, Dianthus, Heuchera, Lamium,* and *Luzula.*

SITING CONTAINERS

In small paved gardens, where there is little choice other than to grow plants in containers, different styles can be used in different ways to create the best effect.

• Position large wooden boxes along the bottom of walls.

• Place smaller boxes beneath windows or on low walls.

• Hang baskets along fences and from walls.

• Set collections of pots in different sizes in corners.

• Use elegant individual containers as focal points.

• Hide drains or utility box covers with low boxes or broad tubs. In larger gardens, where most perennials are grown in the open ground, only a few containers may be in use. These must be positioned carefully to blend into the setting.

• Highlight large tubs alone or in a group rather than scattering many small ones.

• Place containers as focal points at the ends of narrow paths or in alcoves.

• Use pairs of large tubs to frame doors or gateways.

• Avoid small pots in beds or borders, as they look dreadful; even large pots can look out of place.

The attractive foliage of ferns makes them ideal plants for containers.

Euphorbia characias subsp. *wulfenii* is a striking plant to grow in a container, and it remains handsome in all seasons.

Right: The dark evergreen hedge makes a good background and sets off pale cephalarias and slim delphinium spires well. The gray foliage balances the strong colors of the geraniums, and plants with tall stems are mixed with bushier varieties.

BEDS AND BORDERS

Planning new beds and borders is one of the most exciting aspects of gardening. It is the stage at which good foundations are laid for long-term success, but it is also the time when you can make mistakes that may be difficult to correct in the following years. It is highly challenging to group perennials together so that the whole is more than the sum of the parts. There are many factors to consider over and above the style in which the plants are to be arranged: What is the scale of the border, and how does it fit in with the existing house and garden? Should you adopt a formal or informal approach? What are the heights and habits of the plants themselves? What are the flower and foliage colors? Should you confine the planting to perennials or incorporate shrubs, bulbs, and other plants?

Fortunately, there are some useful guidelines that can help you plan successfully. You will find, incidentally, that many of the ideas and principles discussed in relation to perennials are also relevant for other plantings.

Above: This truly mixed border is planted in red and orange with complimentary bronze foliage. The shrubs form a background to solidagos, monardas, heleniums, phlox, and other perennials interplanted with dahlias, verbenas and other tender plants.

Above: This spectacular planting of Russell lupines makes a wonderful feature planting for early summer. It will also work well on a smaller scale but is best isolated by a fence or hedge from other borders.

STARTING FROM SCRATCH

A large empty area, whether part of an existing garden or a new garden, presents a wonderful opportunity but can also be daunting.

While there are perennials for every situation, it makes sense not to fight against nature but to let the characteristics of each individual situation indicate the best style of planting and the most suitable plants. It cannot be stressed too strongly that it is a mistake to decide where to place specific beds or borders, or even a particular plant, and then try to fit the other garden features around them. This is the way to create a muddled garden. Every herbaceous planting should be considered not in isolation but as an important part of an overall garden plan.

You do not need to plan every feature in detail from the start. However, when presented with an empty garden and the chance to design everything without the constraint of existing features, you should take the opportunity to make a coherent general plan. Even in an empty garden, there are indications of the best places for different types of herbaceous plantings.

ASSESSING SURROUNDINGS

Assess the external factors affecting the garden and how perennials will respond to them.

Local climate The local climate will significantly influence your choice of perennials. Are the winters unusually harsh, the summers unusually hot and dry, the winds unusually scorching? Choose plants accordingly.

Wind and shelter From which direction do the prevailing winds come? Is there any shelter, particularly from a fence or wall? (If there is, the fence or wall could make a backing for a traditional herbaceous border.) Are there hedges? If so, are they sound? If not, can a solid fence be erected or an evergreen hedge planted? (If this is not possible, you might be better off with island beds of shorter plants or a mixed border in which the shrubs can provide shelter.)

Shade from trees Are there mature trees overhanging the garden? Are they evergreen or deciduous? (Few perennials thrive under evergreen trees.) Do the trees shade the whole garden, or are some areas lighter? Are they planted within the garden? If so, can the branches be thinned or lower branches removed to admit more light? (The thin shade of tall deciduous trees is the ideal cover for a woodland garden of shade-loving plants. If there is no consistently light place for sun-loving varieties, make a feature of shade lovers.)

Shade from buildings Do tall buildings overshadow the garden? Is the sun completely excluded, or are the buildings on the side of the garden that is naturally shady? Shade from tall buildings is less restricting than that from trees; because buildings cast no overhead shade and have no hungry roots, a wider range of plants

Ferns thrive in this shady bed and are brightened by the flowers of *Stachys macrantha*.

can be planted. It is important to remember, though, that the soil immediately alongside a building's wall may be drier than in the rest of the border. Short plants should be chosen, as they naturally lean less toward the light. The taller the building, the less light the plants will receive, and the greater the number of shade lovers you should choose.

WITHIN THE GARDEN

There are factors within the property that will influence the siting of features and the choice of plants and planting styles.

Views Short, seasonal plantings should not be the focus of a much-used view from the house (for example, from the kitchen), unless the view is sufficiently broad to include other features or is itself seasonal (for example, spectacular summer-season plantings can be the visual focus from a sitting area used only in summer). Specimens with a long season should be made the focal point of walks or paths. Check the views from upstairs windows as well as from the ground floor.

Neighbors Remember that your neighbors may have a view of your garden. When planning an area for relaxation, especially one in which you might sit and enjoy scented and aromatic perennials, determine whether it is overlooked.

Garden features Relating one feature to another is a mark of good garden design. A herbaceous border provides an attractive view from a terrace, for it will be at its best at a season when the terrace is most in use. The planting along a path to a garage or front gate should be less intensely seasonal, as it will be used throughout the year. A path is more interesting if it runs along the edge

This richly planted herbaceous border of silver stachys, pinks, campanulas, and Oriental poppies with its neat mowing edge forms an intriguing view from the garden terrace.

of a richly planted border than if it simply cuts across a lawn.

CULTURAL FACTORS

A new, unplanted garden gives you the opportunity to investigate soil conditions carefully before you start.
Soil Test the soil for pH and nutrients as described on page 27. In an empty garden, conduct tests over the whole area; you may find a pattern of barren and fertile areas, which could influence the overall design. Patches of particularly barren or intractable soil may be good spots for a sitting area, shed, or greenhouse.

Debris Soil is often moved during construction work. Before you start planning in any detail, dig holes at regular intervals across the garden (p.25) to find out where infertile subsoil has been brought to the surface or debris has been buried; try to discover any hidden features that may influence planning.

Previous cultivation Digging trial holes may also reveal unusually fertile areas, perhaps where vegetables were once grown or animals kept. Such soil should be valued. An area like this could be the best site for a herbaceous border.

RENOVATING AN EXISTING PLANTING

Often, however, your new garden will already have been cultivated, so you don't have the opportunity to plan new borders. Instead, you must improve or entirely renovate existing beds and borders. Established borders may have been badly neglected by a previous owner, or you yourself may have allowed the plantings in your garden to deteriorate.

After a few years of neglect, vigorous plants may have outgrown their space and invaded their neighbors and small, compact forms may have been smothered by nearby plants. Many plants may have become crowded and spindly. Because no one has done any deadheading, self-sown seedlings of some varieties may have overwhelmed others. Some plants may be suffering from lack of nutrients. Perennial weeds may have moved in, or annual weeds may have formed suffocating carpets.

ASSESSING EXISTING PLANTINGS

Moving to a new garden If you have moved and taken over a border whose history is unknown, your best plan is to do almost nothing for a year while the plants in the border reveal themselves as the seasons go by. This is the only practical way of discovering exactly which plants are there—especially if, in addition to perennials, the border contains bulbs, which remain dormant or difficult to identify for much of the year.

You should not leave the border entirely alone during this period, however. For a start, it is important to keep the weeds under control. By spot-treating perennial weeds using a systemic weed killer, you can make

Wait for a year when taking over new gardens; these *Allium sphaerocephalon* would not be visible for much of the year and could be damaged if the more obvious liatris and campanula were removed.

some valuable improvements. You can also test the soil and generate some general ideas about possible planning approaches.

As each plant comes into its season, decide whether it is worth retaining; at this stage the plant's position is not important. Plants that you do not want should be dug up; often they will be self-sown seedlings of good plants (for example, astrantias, lamiums, and hardy geraniums), which are too numerous. Do not leave unwanted plants in place after they have flowered.

Occasionally you may find that a good plant is struggling to grow. In this case it is often wise to lift it at once. Pot it, then keep it in a sheltered place until it is growing strongly again. Otherwise, plants you want to keep should be labeled—preferably, if they are unfamiliar to you, with full

details of their height, flower color, and flowering time. A photograph can be taken to aid identification during the winter. Plants that have grown into one another need careful labeling to ensure that the correct form is retained.

It is important at this stage not to be seduced into the idea of making only a few changes because the border already has large clumps of mature plants. Be prepared to remold plantings thoroughly to your own taste, rather than change little and regret it later.

In your own garden If plantings in your own garden deteriorate through neglect, they are easier to deal with, since you do not need to spend a year discovering what plants the border contains. Dealing with weeds by spot-treatment, deadheading, and the removal of self-sown seedlings should be your priorities until the time comes for soil improvement and replanting.

The scale of renovation depends on the following factors: the period of neglect, the degree to which the plants have deteriorated, and the extent to which you feel you require a new plan rather than a simple restoration of the original planting.

IMPROVING EXISTING PLANTINGS

Moving to a new garden After a year you will have assessed all the plants and know the extent to which the planting needs renovating and changing. It may be that the plan and the plants are basically good, in which case you have little to do beyond the usual seasonal tasks plus adding favorite varieties. On the other hand, the border may contain both overgrown clumps and large spaces, so you will have to carry out a more substantial renovation.

By this time you should have developed some ideas for the future of the area. It is a mistake to be over-influenced at this stage by the size and position of the plants you wish to retain. Instead, be concerned with how the area can best be used within the context of your garden as a whole. Most perennials can be lifted, split, and replanted in the place that suits them, and this has the additional advantage of providing an opportunity to improve the soil. That said, with plants that look their best after developing for many years into substantial mature clumps—hostas, hellebores, and peonies, for example—it is sometimes most effective to leave them in place, as long as they fit into the overall design.

Once you decide on the general plan of the border and discard any unwanted plants, set about planning

Tired, mature plantings can be improved in a short time by adding quick growing plants like this anthemis, which will flower well in its first season.

in more detail. First, consider the shape of the border; make changes in its size, shape, or outline before you start improving the soil.

The following spring or fall remove those plants you want to retain, improve the soil, and then replant using a mixture of retained plants and new acquisitions.

In your own garden Restoring your own borders can involve either a radical overhaul or a more modest revival. Where the deterioration has been substantial—clumps have

grown into one another, others have all but faded away, and weeds have moved in—you need to take strong action. Remove most of the plants, kill or remove weeds, improve the soil, and then replant the healthiest pieces of the old plants.

If the neglect has been less drastic, a blitz on the weeds, plus lifting and replanting plants that appreciate regular division, such as phlox and achilleas, may be enough. After carrying out these measures, you must follow them up with regular care.

BORDER SCALE AND STRUCTURE

Scale is important in two respects when planning for perennials. First, the overall dimensions of beds and borders must be in proportion to the size of the garden as a whole and the existing features within it. Second, the size and spread of the individual plants must match the scale of the border in which they are located.

BORDER AND GARDEN

It is difficult to give definitive advice on the best size for beds and borders. However, guidance can be given for plantings of different types.

One-sided borders As a general principle, the ideal depth of a border that is set against a wall, fence, or hedge depends on the height of the background and the length of the border: the taller the background and the longer the border, the greater the depth required if the proportions are to look balanced.

Many backgrounds are approximately 6 ft (1.8 m) high; in such a case a formal border restricted to perennials will rarely be successful if less than 5 ft (1.5 m) deep. A mixed border needs to be deeper than this because it has to accommodate the size of its shrubs.

If for some reason the depth of a border along a wall or fence is restricted, it is better not to attempt a sophisticated planting of perennials. Instead, grow a collection of special plants that are well suited to the soil and likely to repay close inspection. Another alternative is to clothe the background with climbers and plant the strip at the base with ground-cover plants.

At the other extreme, a large garden may require borders 10 ft (3 m)

This one-sided mixed border backed by a hedge has tall groups of shrubs at the back grading down to smaller perennials at the front.

deep or more if they are going to look in proportion. Such borders need to be thought about in terms of both a distant viewpoint, from which they can be regarded in their entirety, and somewhere closer, from which individual plants can be appreciated.

For a large one-sided border, be sure to leave space for a path along the back to allow adequate access for maintenance.

The front edge of a border is often laid out parallel to the background, but in many situations it is more appropriate to draw it in sweeping curves, especially if you plan an informal arrangement of beds within a formal structure of walls or hedges. In such a case parts of the border can be made narrower than would otherwise be ideal, although this should not be done in an arbitrary fashion. If the front line sweeps back toward a wall at a point where there is a fragrant climber to smell, for example, or a seat in a sunny place, there is a rationale for the change of line.

Island beds Island beds are similarly less likely to be successful unless made at least 5 ft (1.5 m) wide; it is difficult to prevent narrower strips developing a strongly linear look. One or both ends of an island bed can, however, be made narrower, especially if the beds are a little broader than 5 ft (1.5 m) in the center or toward the other end.

When shrubs or small trees are added to the perennials to create a mixed planting, the beds should be made substantially wider. Otherwise, once the shrubs mature, there will be little room for perennials. The majority of the shrubs and trees can be used to form the spine of the bed, providing both shelter and a background, with the plantings on either side dominated by perennials. Each side will have its individual conditions, so it can be planted differently.

Right: This mixed border uses shrubs for height and bulk, conifers for emphasis and perennials and bulbs for frontal color.

PLANTS IN BORDERS

There are two aspects to choosing plants of the right size for beds and borders: the height of the plants and the breadth of the clumps in which they are to be grouped.

Plant height The standard rule is that the height of the tallest plants in a border should not exceed half its depth. In one-sided borders set against the background of a wall, fence, or hedge, the plants can be a little taller, but at the same time remember that where light is partially cut off by the background, plants at the back are apt to stretch a little toward the light. Other useful guides are that the tallest plants in a long border should be slightly taller than those in a short one, and plants in a one-sided bed backing onto a tall background can be slightly taller than those with a shorter background. Do not line up the tallest plants side by side along the back of a one-sided border or along the center of an island bed; to avoid a regimented look, separate them with groups of lower plants. Moreover, delphiniums and other plants with tall flower spikes need space to be shown off effectively. Taller plants also look especially dramatic when silhouetted against a neutral background.

Many interesting variations can be created by occasionally extending groups of tall plants toward the front of the border and allowing drifts of shorter plants to extend toward the rear. Position shorter, early-flowering plants toward the front, and arrange taller, spreading plants behind them to open out into their space later in the season.

In areas where strong or icy winds restrict your choice of plants, you can divide one-sided mixed borders into almost individual compartments by the careful positioning of bold ever-green shrubs. These provide valuable shelter as well as a variation in background.

Plants in clumps The size of the individual clumps of plants is something else that you need to consider. A whole border, however narrow, has a tendency to look untidy if planted entirely with single plants, unless the plants have been especially selected for their capacity to intertwine and knit together well. An arrangement of fewer, bolder clumps is usually more effective.

The number of plants needed to fill a given space varies enormously, depending on the character of the plant. For example, a single plant of a bold and naturally expansive species, such as *Crambe cordifolia,* may fill the same space as six or eight plants of a delphinium of similar height. In general, in a 5 ft (1.5 m) border, a mix of individual plants and groups of three or five will be a most effective combination.

On a larger scale, a one-sided border 10 ft (3 m) deep may require up to 10 plants of some varieties. It is wise, however, to create interest by ensuring that the clumps are not all of an identical size.

The most effective approach is to allocate different spaces to the different forms. You can do this by varying the number of individuals of each type planted while taking into account their growth habits.

Finally, remember that no two gardens are the same. Many of these guidelines should be adapted to the style of the individual garden and to your own inclinations.

Hostas are best left to grow into bold clumps; the geraniums can be split regularly.

HOUSE AND GARDEN

Perennial plantings should be planned to fit in with existing garden features and also with the style of your house to create a harmonious whole. This coordination of the plantings, the house, and the general garden environment depends partly on matching the permanent features themselves: any new stonework, paving or fencing should be executed in a similar style and with similar materials, and furniture should be compatible in style and color. But in gardens where plants are important, the design of planting must also be appropriate to the overall tone.

ARCHITECTURE AND GARDEN PLANNING

The style of perennial plantings should to some extent match the style of the house. If this proves impossible or conflicts with your taste, make a definite decision to make the style different. Doing so will enable you to plan a garden that has a clear relationship with the house.

Old houses Traditional stone or wood country houses prompt ideas of a rambling cottage garden. This combination is likely to be successful, although it may require more work than you want. Take, for example, a front garden with a path from the gate to the door. This setup can be

dealt with in two ways. The path can be edged with boxwood or pinks while the rest of the garden is planted with the full range of cottage garden plants, including vegetables toward the back. You also need paths weaving through for access. An alternative approach is to place a strip of low planting, with pinks and bulbs, alongside the path, then put an area of lawn behind and a broad border at the back. The size of the lawn can be varied depending on the amount of time you are prepared to spend looking after the borders. If your time is limited, the style of planting can shift from the organized "chaos" of the old-fashioned cottage garden toward

Cottage garden flowers such as these delphiniums are well suited to the garden surrounding this traditional-style thatched cottage.

Asters, lavatera, and crocosmias crowd the windows of this country cottage giving a cosy rural feel.

a more modern mixed border, with broader drifts of plants and effective ground covers—but be sure to grow some classic cottage plants, such as peonies, to keep the theme alive.

If the house is especially attractive in itself, you might choose to treat the garden around it in a more modern way. Gravel or stone chips, in a color chosen carefully to match or complement the building, can make an attractive weed-suppressing surface, across which the house can be appreciated without the clutter of plants. Then you can site borders or specimen roses with underplantings in strategic corners, and allow foxgloves, verbascums, and poppies to self-sow into the gravel (though do not let them take over). You can use rustic containers as features, making sure that their colors and styles are in keeping with the house. Choose some old-fashioned wood, wrought-iron, or steel garden furniture.

One reason why cottage-style gardens go especially well with many types of country houses is that the wealth of detail in the planting matches the degree of detail often seen in the design of the house itself. For a larger, bolder house you might instead opt for a more expansive planting on a bigger scale, featuring large clumps of the same type of plant, with plantings in other styles confined to small areas subdivided from the overall prospect by hedges.

The narrow gardens of small urban houses may seem very restrictive, but they, too, often provide a range of opportunities. For a Victorian house an option would be to adopt a Victorian pattern, perhaps even using Victorian-style materials such as terracotta edging, old brick paving, and wrought iron. You could have a straight brick path, edged with tiles, and regular borders with perennials or colorful bedding. A more interesting compromise would be to create a Victorian structure and then to make the planting more modern and varied.

An alternative approach is to divide a long, narrow garden widthwise into a series of compartments using hedges, trellises, or fencing. The area immediately beside the house can be closest in style to the house itself, with the other compartments being treated more freely.

Modern houses These demand a different approach. The stark lines, clean look, and unweathered squareness of many modern houses are so dominant that they often demand a corresponding boldness in the garden in order to maintain the balance. A foundation planting of solid evergreen shrubs, especially if used to soften the angles of the building itself, is often helpful here. The shrubs have a presence that can match that of a modern building, but they are also twiggy and leafy. Because this detail connects visually with perennial planting, the evergreens can provide a link between the house and your perennials. Climbing roses on the house's walls can have a similar effect.

A garden of sweeping curves planted in informal groups, with island beds of perennials cut out of the grass, will tone down the angularity of the building. This works very well even with smaller houses, as long as there is room in the garden for the beds.

A large house needs space as balance, and the most difficult gardens to plan are the disproportionately small plots so often attached to large modern houses. Here the focus is often best turned away from the house to the boundaries which are usually in a more appropriate scale. If the garden of a large house *is* large, it is often best to adopt a formal style (p.112). Plan a formal layout in relation to the house, then plant it formally, perhaps with a traditional herbaceous border. Different and potentially conflicting styles can be segregated by walls or hedges into self-contained compartments.

One-story houses are easier to manage than more substantial buildings. Although their low height restricts your opportunities to grow climbers on the walls, this same modest stature fits in better with the scale of garden plants and, indeed, of people. One-story houses do not dominate the garden to the extent that larger houses do, and they set the tone less rigidly, so you can explore a greater range of styles. You might even combine diverse styles in the garden around a one-story house.

EXISTING GARDEN STYLE
Relating a new border to an established garden is easier. The style is set: all you have to do is ensure that the new planting fits in with the old. Match formality with formality; add an extra island bed or more containers; develop a new bed with a related color theme. However, it may be that you want something entirely different, in a new style.

Fitting an island bed into a formal setting or introducing a formal planting into a cottage garden is a more difficult affair. The solution is often to isolate the styles. This can be done in a number of ways. In a small property the only method might be to plan the front garden in a different style from the back, so that the house itself serves as a division between them. Where more space is available, different styles can be blended simply by gradually changing from one to another—although in practice this may be difficult to do successfully. One effective solution is to give large island beds a backbone of shrubs and then plant each side in a different

The mature trees cast shade that provides an opportunity to plant shade-loving plants and maintain the woodland style of the garden.

style. In general, however, the most reliable way to accommodate different styles, even in larger gardens, is to segregate them, using screens, hedges, fences, or walls. This approach has two advantages: different styles are separated effectively and cannot clash, and visitors to the garden are treated to visual surprises as each area is discovered.

Here are a few possible layouts for the garden of a modern house: An open area of gravel might open out at the rear and continue several containers near the house and, in a

sunny area, a group of Mediterranean plants, which appreciate warm conditions and well-drained soil. A rustic summerhouse might be set in a hedged area planted in a cottage style, with an arch leading through to a color-themed garden or a vegetable garden. A hedge planted to shelter the terrace might open onto a path or driveway leading to a gate with a mixed border on either side.

Even the smallest gardens can be thoughtfully subdivided, by using trellises, for example, rather than hedges, to provide separate themes.

SEASONS

In recent years, especially as gardens have become smaller, gardeners have turned to the idea of the year-round garden to generate the maximum amount of color and interest from a limited space. There are two ways of developing this theme. One is to plan each border so that there are always plants of interest to see. The other is to plan for different seasonal highlights in different parts of the garden.

THE SEASONAL BORDER

Another approach to creating year-round interest involves planning in an entirely different way. This strategy also gives you a garden where there is always something to see, but it overcomes the problem of having no seasonal highlights. In this approach you arrange the garden so that different parts are at their best at different times of the year. Plants with the same flowering time are concentrated together, creating a small but very colorful display for one period of the year. As one seasonal planting begins to lose its attraction, another is coming into its best. Such plantings do not rely so much on shrubs and bulbs, although these can add to the spectacle.

Planning these highlights is easier than working out a year-round border, and it is a much less daunting beginning if you have never planned borders before.

Advantages and disadvantages of the seasonal border The two advantages of the seasonal border are that in its season it is more colorful than a year-round border ever is and that it is easier to plan. The biggest disadvantage is that when a border is over and interest moves elsewhere, that space in your garden becomes dull.

Bugles and primroses mingle with phlox and other easy alpines in this bright spring garden.

In summer, borders should be bursting with a wide range of colorful perennials.

Summer plants linger but autumn eupatoriums and heleniums are taking over.

THE YEAR-ROUND BORDER

Where winters are not too harsh, it is possible to plan a perennial border so that there are always plants of interest. It is, however, easier to create a year-round effect in a mixed border that includes shrubs and bulbs, which are valuable for filling in during the months that are devoid of perennials.

If at the planning stage you choose plants from a variety of flowering seasons, while keeping factors like height and color in mind, this will go some distance toward achieving a year-round effect. There are other ways in which you can avoid seasonally empty areas in the border:

• Allow long-season foliage plants to intermingle with flowering plants.

• Choose evergreen plants and mix them with deciduous ones.

• Plant late-flowering forms close to early-flowering ones so that, as the early ones die away, the later bloomers fill out into the space.

• Use climbing perennials on free-standing supports.

• In mixed plantings, add plenty of shrubs for winter and bulbs for late fall and spring.

The choice of plants is crucial. Perennials with a few weeks of glory are obviously unsuitable for the year-round border; rather, in addition to or sometimes instead of the usual flowering display, you should include plants with characteristics that extend the season. Look for plants with the following features: Unusually long flowering season, attractive foliage, fall fruits or berries, fall-coloring leaves, attractive winter stems, evergreen foliage, striking growth habit, attractive or interesting buds.

Advantages and disadvantages of the year-round border The benefit of the year-round border is, of course, that there is always something colorful or

Leave the dead stems of perennials in place all winter to catch the morning frost.

at least interesting to see. Particularly in a small garden, blank spaces can be especially noticeable, so it makes sense to try to avoid them.

However, putting together an effective year-round planting using only perennials is no easy matter. The winter effect will largely depend on evergreen foliage plants, such as bergenias, lamiums, and hellebores, but if you include enough of these to make the winter attractive, you will have relatively little space left over for summer plants. As a result, at the very time when flowering perennials are expected to be at their peak, the display is not very dramatic. This is the real problem with year-round borders: while you can plan them so that there is always something to see, at no time do they ever become spectacular. Almost inevitably, you find yourself slipping in spring bulbs or summer annuals to supply a burst of color when the long-season border, with foliage as its primary attraction, looks dull. The border then becomes more colorful, but only at the expense of changing its character, so that it is no longer truly a perennial border.

Silver and yellow foliage will provide color for months before and after these summer flowers.

REALISTIC OPTIONS

Two compromise approaches exist that can almost provide the best of both worlds.

One is to plan as before for a succession of colorful displays, season by season, in different parts of the garden, but to choose the plants carefully so that when their flowers are over, they display some other feature of interest, particularly foliage. Although the impact from a given area is reduced when the plant has finished flowering, the space remains interesting.

The second approach can be combined with the first. This is to underplant each area of perennials with bulbs for a different season. For example, a planting of perennials whose display is concentrated in the main summer season can be interplanted with clumps of daffodils or other spring bulbs, either in one or in a range of colors to provide color throughout the spring. So even though the main spring display is in another part of the garden, the summer planting area provides additional spring color from these companion plants.

Long-flowering perennials: *Alstroemeria* ('Princess' hybrids), *Aster × frikartii* 'Mönch,' *Aster × frikartii* 'Wunder von Stäfa,' *Clematis integrifolia*, *Dianthus* (modern pinks), *Geranium × riversleaianum* 'Russell Prichard,' *Geranium wallichianum* 'Buxton's Variety,' *Salvia farinacea*, and *Scabiosa* 'Butterfly Blue.'

Flowering perennials with good foliage: *Achillea* ('Clypeolata' hybrids), *Anthemis punctata* subsp. *cupaniana*, *Aquilegia* 'Vervaeneana,' *Astilbe simplicifolia* 'Sprite,' *Dianthus* (pinks), *Dicentra* (woodlanders), *Eryngium*, *Euphorbia × martinii*, *Lychnis coronaria*, and *Pulmonaria*.

FORMAL AND INFORMAL

Borders or entire gardens can be planned in a formal or informal style. The choice depends partly on the nature of your house and your requirements from a garden, partly on the degree of formality displayed by existing garden features, and partly on your own preferences.

HOUSE AND GARDEN

The age and style of your house are important. An older house with a symmetrical appearance suggests a formal garden, perhaps with boxwood hedges or a pair of herbaceous borders. The elegance of such a house may itself be an important feature of the garden, and the planting must not detract from it. Conversely, a modern house in a less symmetrical style invites a less formal approach, with more curves, a lack of symmetry, and planting done in a less ordered style. The planting may even clothe the house walls, making the house part of the garden.

In many cases you will want to tailor these general principles so that the parts of the garden close to the house match it in style, while more distant areas are developed in different styles. You can do this either by creating a steady transition to a contrasting style or by instituting distinct styles in separate, self-contained parts of the garden.

WHAT ARE FORMAL AND INFORMAL STYLES?

In theory the distinctions between formal and informal styles are very clear. In practice, however, they can become blurred.

Formal style A formal style is based on strong, straight lines, which are

In a formal setting with evergreen hedges, double perennial borders look superb.

stressed in the obvious boundaries of the garden as a whole, in the divisions within the garden, and in the shapes of the beds and borders. These lines are frequently emphasized by the planting of bold, often cleanly cut evergreen hedges, such as tall yew hedges or short boxwood edging. Symmetry is important to a formal garden. Matching borders may be created on opposite sides of a straight path, with a clear focal point in the distance; this focus may be a part of the house, a garden building, a specimen tree, a piece of statuary, or in large gardens, a feature of the landscape. Within the borders, individual specimen plants may be repeated side by side or opposite each other to create an additional feeling of regularity.

Formal gardens may also include these elements:
• Rectangular beds.
• Square areas that are subdivided into smaller squares, perhaps with the corners marked by matching specimen plants.
• Matching pairs of ornamental urns, seats, fountains, or plants.

A planting that features perennials will always appear to be less strongly formal because perennials are by their nature soft and relaxed in their growth. It is possible to trim a hedge formally, but you cannot treat perennials in the same way. What is critical in establishing a formal planting style is the manner in which the perennials are arranged. Here are some guidelines:

• Grow perennials separately from other plants.
• Use pinks and other low plants as a linear edging.
• Keep tall plants firmly positioned at the back of a border, with the plants graded evenly to shorter varieties at the front.
• Plant in substantial groups that combine well with, but are cleanly separated from, their neighbors.
• Pay timely attention to the details of cultivation, such as deadheading and cutting down, so that plants always look well tended.

Informal style An informal style is based on a more natural look. This does not mean that the gardener stands back and lets the plants look after themselves, although in some settings this may be possible. The same degree of organization and planning is required, but it is directed toward a different objective.

Informality depends on a softer and less rigid approach to both gardens and planting. Curves, rather than straight lines, predominate. An asymmetrical layout gives an appropriately relaxed feeling. Wherever possible, use sweeping curves that reflect the contours of the garden and take in existing natural features, such as mature shrubs. Whereas symmetry and line are emphasized in the formal approach, here they are played down and softened or even, in a more extravagant informal planting, lost altogether; differences, rather than similarities, should be accentuated. Use a less definite division between the planting and any contiguous paving or grass. Tough perennials

can be naturalized in rough grass, while creeping types can be allowed to escape from the border across gravel or along the cracks in paving. You can relax the rule whereby tall plants are placed at the back of the border and short ones at the front. You can let plants mingle with each other, or even plant them so that their clumps overlap. If their seed heads are interesting, you do not need to cut the plants down the moment the flowers fade.

Plants such as achilleas and campanulas can be allowed to self-sow and their seedlings encouraged to create occasional surprises among other plants. Of course, you may have to remove many of their seedlings to prevent prolific varieties from crowding out others, and sometimes you may need to cheat and move a seedling to a better spot where it will

look as if it had turned up by chance, but the principle still holds. Staking can be less rigid and plants can be allowed to fall into each other a little—although do keep a watchful eye on them to ensure that shorter types are not overwhelmed.

COMBINING STYLES

Many of the most successful gardens set informal plantings within a more formal layout characterized by bold lines, symmetry, and a strong relationship with the house. This design gives the garden a clear, strong structure but permits a more informal, relaxed planting style in keeping with contemporary trends. A rectangular border may be backed by a yew hedge and edged with a low boxwood hedge, but the perennials planted in it can be organized in a relaxed and informal way and cared for without the timely precision that is required by more formal plantings. In particular, you can break the straight lines by permitting low plants, such as hardy geraniums, to grow over and through the boxwood edging or to billow out over a path of paving stones. Occasional self-sown seedlings that appear in the path may be left in place.

For many gardeners this combination of formal structure with informal planting is the most satisfying approach. It allows a transition from the solidity of the house to the natural feeling of the garden, and it provides the security of a structure within which to work, yet still allows for personal expression in the choice and arrangement of the plants.

A formal boxwood hedge encloses a tumbling cascade of colorful flowering perennials.

Right: Allowing low-growing plants to spread onto the path and placing tall plants at random in the border creates an informal and relaxed garden scene.

COLOR PLANNING

Most gardeners grow perennials mainly for their color, but while the colors themselves are obviously important, using them effectively can be a challenge. There are three main ways of using color when planning beds and borders:

• Color contrasts can create a bold, eye-catching border.

• Cooler pastel shades can set up a more harmonious effect.

• Different strengths of the same color can offer a subtle show.

You can use one, two, or all three of these techniques at different places within a border to create a highly sophisticated display.

SINGLE-COLOR BORDERS

Borders in which the flowers and much of the foliage share in the same color range can be the most effective and satisfying of all. It might seem that creating a border based on a single color should be a simple proposition; if you plan a border composed largely of yellow flowers, for example, and ensure that all the varieties flower at approximately the same time, you will indeed create an interesting display. But with a little more planning you can produce something much more striking.

As a first step, select plants of a single basic color, but choose types whose flowers or foliage varies from the rich and dark to the pale and pastel. If you planted these on their own, you might achieve the ultimate in color harmony but produce a fairly dull display. To add variety, consider the other features of the plants. The overall habit of a plant, its foliage, the shape of the flowers, and the way they are held on the plant all become more important when the color range is narrow.

You also need to decide exactly where to define the boundary between one color and another. When planning a border of yellow flowers, should you include types whose flowers are close to orange or cream? Bending the rules may cause awkward clashes, or it may add the spark that lifts the whole border.

White agapanthus and fragrant white tobacco plants create a cool summer border.

COLOR CONTRASTS

Bold color contrasts create the most striking borders: scarlet and white, for example, or purple and yellow. However, while these are undeniably brilliant, eye-catching combinations, they are not restful.

Sometimes, unless the shapes of the plants are very carefully chosen, they can look strangely unplanned. Such borders are best sited where the spectacle can be admired from a distance. They are so bold and overpowering that you should put them in areas separated from other parts of the garden by trees, a lawn, a hedge, a fence, or perhaps a fruit garden; otherwise they will dominate and in effect nullify any cooler combinations nearby.

In practice you are unlikely to want to create a whole border of contrasting perennials. However, contrasts on a smaller scale work well, offering endearing and effective surprises in containers or small corners.

SOPHISTICATED COLOR BORDERS

Bringing together all these themes into one planting is a real challenge. It is often wiser to start with more limited objectives and then to build on early successes as you feel your confidence develop.

Planting to coordinate contrast and harmony in color, plus all the other variables of season, flower, foliage, shape, texture, and style—not to mention possibly including shrubs, climbers, bulbs, and annuals alongside the perennials—is certainly a great adventure.

When it works well it can be a triumph; the very fact that so much care has gone into the planning ensures that the result far surpasses the average, unplanned border.

Pink, mauve, and white perennials contrast beautifully in a cottage garden.

HARMONIOUS COLORS

Borders with broader color themes, such as two or three harmonious flower and foliage colors used together in a single bed or border, are much simpler to plan and more likely to be successful. Bringing together harmonious colors creates a more restful feel. The softness of pastel colors, such as blush-pink and pale sky-blue, linked by gray foliage, is best suited to a modest scale. When seen from a distance, large plantings in harmonious colors may enhance the overall atmosphere of the garden and draw the eye but are too subtle to be impressive features. Harmonious color combinations are most rewarding when closer inspection allows you to appreciate the subtlety.

A harmonious arrangement of purple lupines, salvias, and catmints with fresh green foliage.

PLANT
COMBINATIONS

The success of planting designs for beds and borders depends not only on how well the plants are cared for, but also on the way in which individual plants are grouped together. Putting the right colors of flower and foliage side by side; creating interesting juxtapositions of plant habit, form, and texture; and integrating other features, such as fruits, into the overall planting design can transform a border from a muddle to a work of art.

Above: Careful color harmonization in this mixed border sees purple echinops and hibiscus and bluish perovskia grown with silver-leaved stachys and artemisia, pale mauve phlox and white highlights from antirrhinums.

Left: In this summerlong perennial border the blue spikes of delphiniums are echoed in the purplish salvias and yellow thalictrums providing a lightening effect. Behind the salvia, crocosmias and heleniums will continue the display into fall.

Left: A simple grouping of just two plants can create a most impressive effect. Here the yellow leaves of *Catalpa bignonoides* 'Aurea' provide the perfect background for the mahogany red flowers of 'Stafford,' an old variety of hemerocallis but still one of the best.

FLOWER COLOR

Grouping flower colors effectively is fundamental to creating a satisfying perennial display; while there are planning guidelines that can help the newcomer, personal taste is paramount. The principles involved in the three basic approaches to color planning were outlined on page 116; here more detailed ideas involving popular plants as examples are discussed.

COLOR CONTRASTS

Bold contrasts are best seen from a distance—the full effect is at its most impressive when seen across a lawn. Choosing contrasting flower colors is the first priority, but you can add emphasis by paying attention to other types of contrast.

A clump of a delphinium, such as the bright 'Blue Nile' with its distinct white eye, stands out and reaches 5–6 ft (1.5–1.8 m) in height, so the deep butter-yellow heads of the shorter *Achillea* 'Coronation Gold' can be set slightly to one side. Here more than color is involved: the flat heads of the achillea contrast with the upright spikes of the delphinium. The feathery, brick-red plumes of *Astilbe* 'Red Sentinel,' a cultivar that also features unusually dark foliage, can go alongside the achillea.

At the front you could add smaller summer cultivars—perhaps placing *Leucanthemum* 'Snowcap,' with its bright, yellow-eyed white daisies, alongside the long-lasting, slender bluish-violet spikes of *Salvia* 'Ostfriesland' and the greenish-yellow foam of *Alchemilla mollis*. If there is space, you might complete the picture with the addition of short edging

Left: Contrasting white and blue campanulas with purple lythrum work well in this damp bed.

plants, such as the salmon-pink *Dianthus* 'Doris,' the vivid red and yellow daisies of *Gaillardia* 'Kobold,' or the multicolored foliage of *Houttuynia cordata* 'Chameleon.'

This grouping of strikingly dissimilar flower colors also offers contrasts in the habits and forms of the individual flowers. The result is an undeniably colorful assemblage, but because of the careful choice of plants, it avoids any garish clash of color. Such clashes can sometimes result from juxtaposing strongly colored flowers.

HARMONIOUS COLORS

The use of softer, more harmonious pastel shades creates a cooler, more restful atmosphere. Although from a distance the effect may seem hazy, it is very satisfying closer up.

Asters and anemones are two of the most important perennials of the fall garden. *Aster × frikartii* 'Wunder von Stäfa' is a long-flowering, soft lavender-blue aster with yellow eyes. Of the anemones, the pure white single-flowered *Anemone × hybrida* 'Honorine Jobert,' also with yellow eyes, is especially lovely. If you set silver foliage in front of both, this will help tie the two shades together and connect them with the rest of the planting. Artemisias are always useful in this role, but here *Anaphalis margaritacea* var. *yedoensis* is a better choice: its downy foliage is slightly whiter, and it offers the bonus of small, silvery white everlasting flowers. Moreover, its slightly spreading habit helps link it to its neighbors. In front of the aster you could put the white pompom chrysanthemum 'Purleigh White,' which develops pinkish tinges as it ages. On the other side of the anaphalis try *Phygelius × rectus* 'Pink Elf,' which has crimson-tipped pale pink tubes held in elegant open sprays. The net result is that the silver links lavender blue, pure white, pinkish white, and pale pink.

This combination might look too pale, so running along the very front, you could have the dwarf, double, darker blue *Aster* 'Professor Anton Kippenberg,' which fits in with the flat heads of the rich reddish-pink *Sedum* 'Autumn Joy.' These two plants in slightly more definite colors will also connect well to the many other, stronger fall hues. As a bonus, this group should prove attractive to butterflies, which are particularly fond of the asters and the sedum.

SINGLE-COLOR BORDERS

Choosing the majority of the plants in a border from a narrow range of flower colors may seem too restrictive. Yet, surprisingly, single-color borders offer a straightforward way of creating an interesting planting. Where it is possible to include foliage in the same range, continuity of color is maintained throughout the season.

Red borders There are two important questions you must try to answer before tackling a red border. First, what exactly is red? You must decide whether to include rich crimson shades and how far to go in the direction of orange, ginger, and gold. To some extent your answer to this first question depends on how you answer the second: Should bronze and copper foliage be included? Red flowers and bronze foliage go together well; indeed, plants like *Lobelia* 'Queen Victoria' combine the two colors in a single plant. However, if you bring red flowers and bronze leaves together, the result is a very dark border in both color and atmosphere. Here your response to the first question is relevant, for including brighter, fierier shades of ginger and orange adds a refreshing sparkle.

If you decide to use a narrow range of brilliant red flower colors, the best advice is to restrict the foliage colors mainly to green; this helps to create a bright and effective planting. However, a more satisfying

In this single-color border red and bronze perennials are mixed with dahlias and other tender plants.

planting can be created with the addition of bronze foliage. It then pays to incorporate additional cultivars with yellow and orange flowers to create a hot and fiery display.

Yellow borders Yellow is such a cheerful color that borders of perennials selected from yellow-flowered cultivars are very popular. There are other reasons. Flowers of this color look good with green foliage, and there are many yellow-leaved perennials that can be used to carry the color theme when flowering varieties are out of season.

It is sometimes said that too many yellow flowers belong to the daisy family and flower in late summer. Certainly many of them do, but in spring there are primroses, euphorbias, and irises; in summer there are more irises, hemerocallis, kniphofias, and achilleas, so there is certainly a sufficiently wide range of other possibilities for you to be able to create an effective long-season border.

Although many flowers come in clean, pure yellows, some lack richness. The addition of gold- and even orange-tinted forms can give the border extra substance and provide a greater depth of color.

White borders White flowers look cool and seem very refreshing in sunny places on sultry summer days. They are also valuable in areas that are dark, so it is hardly surprising that white borders represent the most popular choice among these single-color approaches.

White flowers have the added advantage of being set off especially well by foliage: they form an effective contrast with green leaves and give a soft impression with silver foliage.

Once you have assembled a few white-flowered cultivars, you will soon notice a distinctive feature of white flowers: some are significantly whiter than others. In part this may derive from color changes as the flowers age: some are greenish or

blushed slightly pink in bud; others may blush as they age, and the results can be attractive. Still other flowers are never pure white but always have a hint of cream—and when several whites are planted together, the differences show.

Some gardeners enjoy this slight variability and design to exploit it. For example, if you intersperse foliage plants that have a creamy variegation, such as *Symphytum* 'Goldsmith' or *Hosta* 'Shade Fanfare,' among the flowering plants, you can achieve very pleasing effects.

So you have two alternatives. You can choose forms with clean white flowers and use them with fresh green foliage, or you can add creamier shades and select foliage to match.

Blue borders Unfortunately there are comparatively few blue-flowered perennials, a disproportionate number of which are delphiniums and salvias, which tends to unbalance the selection. Also, you have to take care when choosing among the purplish-blue varieties, such as some of the darker penstemons, as their coloring may not blend well with the clearer, sharper blues of some of the bushy belladonna delphiniums.

By way of compensation for these difficulties, blues look especially good against fresh, bright green foliage, and indeed foliage in general can add a great deal to a blue border. In particular the blue-leaved hostas make excellent companions for blue flowers as long as the soil is not allowed to dry out and the foliage of other perennials provides enough shade. From small cultivars, such as 'Halcyon' and 'Blue Moon,' to the more substantial *Hosta sieboldiana* 'Elegans' and the enormous 'Krossa Regal,' they can contribute considerably to the overall effect.

Yellow flowers create a sunny effect and are at their best in late summer.

SOPHISTICATED COLOR BORDERS

Bringing all these different elements of color planning together into a single sophisticated planting is not easy to do successfully. The result, however, is an extremely satisfying display, so most gardeners will want to make the attempt.

Starting with an evergreen hedge behind, a group could be built up with a background of a huge cloud of the slightly creamy white flowers provided by *Crambe cordifolia*.

In front of these, and contrasting in habit, could go the solid, upright heads of the pink border phlox 'Eva Callum' and alongside the phlox, belladonna delphinium 'Peace,' whose strong blue contrasts boldly with the phlox in color but whose open, airy habit is similar to that of the crambe at the back.

In between the phlox and the delphinium you could tuck the creamy yellow daisies of *Anthemis* 'E. C. Buxton,' which connects in color to the crambe while contrasting with the phlox and delphinium.

Central to the next rank of shorter plants could be the silver foliage of *Artemisia* 'Silver Queen,' which will extend toward all its neighbors, serving to link them together. On one side, in front of the phlox, could go the flat yellow heads and pewtery green foliage of *Achillea* 'Moonshine'; on the other side you could put the white bells of *Campanula persicifolia* 'Hampstead White.'

For the front rank of smaller plants you might choose *Agapanthus* 'Lilliput,' with its rounded heads of blue flowers; bronze-leaved *Heuchera* 'Palace Purple,' with its creamy sprays; a pair of border pinks, such as the highly scented white *Dianthus* 'White Ladies' and the pink and deep red 'Houndspool Ruby'; and the long-flowering, pink-petaled *Geranium endressii* 'Wargrave.'

Your resultant border, a blend of mainly early-summer-flowering plants whose color continues into fall, would display a pleasing mixture of contrast and harmony, as well as interesting shapes and textures.

Brilliant flower colors are softened by looking through *Verbena bonariensis* and by pale yellow golden rods and limy tobacco plants.

FLOWERING AND GROWTH HABIT

Flower color may be the first feature you consider when planning perennial borders, but other factors are also important. The shapes of the plants and the ways in which the flowers are carried on them have a significant effect on the liveliness of any planting.

Plants come in six main growth styles: Upright, Arching, Flat-topped, Rounded, Sprawling and Spreading.
Upright plants Many tall plants, like delphiniums, lupines, and macleayas, and shorter ones, such as *Salvia × sylvestris*—plus kniphofias, which come in many sizes—have noticeably straight stems with a strongly vertical

Harmony in color and variation in plant habit create an interesting planting.

look. They create a bold, slightly military impression, although this is sometimes softened by the shapes of the flowers themselves. Planting too many upright plants together can look ridiculous, especially if they appear aligned in rows or ranks instead of growing in more natural-looking irregular groups. They are, however, excellent for setting behind such perennials as achilleas, which have flat-topped flower heads: the angles made between the vertical stems of one and the horizontal heads of the other are very pleasing.

Arching plants There are few arching perennials, and many of them are ornamental grasses. The taller sorts, such as the gray-leaved grass *Helictotrichon sempervirens*, have a special elegance best revealed when not cluttered by other plants nearby; only types that hug the ground make suitable neighbors. Smaller grasses with an arching, fountainlike habit, such as *Hakonechloa macra* 'Alboaurea,' make good container plants and look attractive hanging over low walls.

Flat-topped plants As with arching perennials, there are few flat-topped forms. In most cases it is the flower head rather than the whole plant that is flat. Achilleas and fall sedums are the most frequently seen, along with *Lychnis chalcedonica*. In addition, some plants, including several of the shorter asters, develop a flat-topped habit of growth; also, clumps of hostas often develop into a plateau of foliage as they mature.

Vertical stems positioned near flat-topped plants make a good contrast and work together well, while rounded, billowing plants, such as gypsophilas, can effectively soften the strong horizontal line.

Rounded plants A large number of perennials have a generally rounded

look, although some are tighter in growth than others. Border pinks in many colors, the shade-loving *Geranium macrorrhizum*, the spring-flowering *Lathyrus vernus,* and the yellow *Euphorbia polychroma* all create a fairly solid, rounded look—although as a single plant spreads into a large group, the effect may change so that the clump becomes flat-topped and rounded at the edges. *Alchemilla mollis* and gypsophilas develop a softer, foamier look.

Sprawling plants These have a looser, more open habit, and their stems naturally spread into neighboring plants to create attractive informal associations and perform a useful linking function, drawing plants together into a cohesive group. These are the natural blenders. In this context think of the red bells of *Campanula punctata* 'Elizabeth,' the angular shoots of *Malva sylvestris* 'Primley Blue,' the long-flowering *Geranium* 'Johnson's Blue,' and the more vigorous magenta of *Geranium* 'Ann Folkard.'

Spreading plants Perennials with almost flat growth are for the front of the border. They will knit in around the crowns of more upright plants, make flat mats at the border edge, and creep out across gravel or paving (they must be restrained from creeping out across the lawn). These are plants such as ajugas, with their variety of colored foliage and usually blue flowers; the almost-white-leaved *Artemisia stelleriana*; *Potentilla × tonguei*, with its crimson-centred apricot flowers; and *Stachys byzantina* 'Silver Carpet,' which produces an attractive silvery mat.

Right: Billowing limy green alchemilla fronts the contrasting spikes of *Sisyrinchium striatum*, yellow lupine spikes and bushy roses.

FOLIAGE COLOR

Foliage makes its contribution to the border for a longer period of the year than do most flowers, so it is especially important to choose foliage plants carefully. Most foliage does not cause color clashes: green, the natural color of leaves, always provides a reliable background, and even leaves in other shades commonly have an underlying green tint.

Foliage comes in the following main color groups: Green, Green with variegations, Yellow and gold, Blue and grayish blue, sometimes with variegations, Gray and silver, Bronze, red, and purple.

GREEN FOLIAGE

The natural color of leaves creates a uniquely restful background for flowers and combines well with most other foliage colors. But green comes in a variety of shades, from the deep green of a background yew hedge to the brighter shades of young hosta leaves. Furthermore, the leaves of an individual plant may change color as the months go by, and many yellow-leaved perennials become green as the season progresses.

If you have chosen to incorporate few other foliage colors, you can create visual variation by selecting types with different leaf shapes and textures (p.128).

YELLOW AND GOLD FOLIAGE

The words *yellow* and *gold* are often used indiscriminately to cover a wide range of yellow shades. In fact there are few genuinely gold-leaved plants, but the color category *yellow* does cover a wide spread of shades, from deep cream through primrose to deep, rich yellow.

Yellow-leaved perennials bring light and brightness to the border, but you have to be careful how you position them. In some varieties the leaves scorch in full sun: the edges turn brown and crisp, and the beauty is ruined. The degree of scorch depends to some extent also on the moisture content of the soil, with plants in moist soil being more tolerant. Conversely, when planted in the shade, many yellow-leaved perennials lose the strength of their color and become greener; numerous hostas change in this way.

Despite these difficulties, yellow foliage can be used very effectively with plants that have orange, blue, and even red flowers, although red should be used cautiously. It also looks good with green or bronze foliage in contrasting shapes.

BLUE FOLIAGE

Few plants have leaves that are truly blue; instead, more plants, especially hostas and grasses, show shades of bluish green and grayish blue or have a waxy blue sheen to the leaves. Often these plants are sun lovers and go well with flowers of many shades, especially yellow, blue, and white. A contrast of shapes seems to allow more opportunities; for example, a bold yellow leaf next to a bold blue one may look garish, but the blue-leaved *Hosta* 'Halcyon' looks effective with yellow-leaved grasses trailing across it.

This planting of hosta ligularias, and ferns shows a variety of green shades.

A few bluish-leaved plants, mainly hostas such as 'Frances Williams,' are also variegated in cream or yellow. 'Frances Williams,' for example, has foliage irregularly but broadly edged with yellow. This combination can look good, but it can be difficult to find pleasing groupings with other plants. Use such cultivars as isolated specimens, with green foliage, or with pale yellow or pale blue flowers.

GRAY AND SILVER FOLIAGE

The majority of gray- and silver-leaved plants originate in hot climates. The coating of hairs on the leaf, which gives them their coloring, helps protect the leaf from hot sun and reduces evaporation. In the garden many are highly drought-resistant and are good in sunny, well-drained borders.

Silver and gray have the great advantage of combining well with most other flower and foliage colors, and their neutralizing effect ensures that they clash with very few. So plants such as artemisias and anaphalis are invaluable for both creating harmonious links between pastel shades and preventing bold, primary colors from seeming too garish.

BRONZE, RED, AND PURPLE FOLIAGE

Foliage in these dark shades must be deployed carefully: overuse can make beds and borders seem too dark and create an unnecessarily heavy atmosphere. In general, brilliant blue flowers and hot-colored flowers make good companions, together with gray and silver foliage; but it is in fiery borders with scarlet, crimson, rusty, gingery, and orange flowers that bronze, red, or purple foliage is most effective, adding valuable depth to the fiery sparkle.

Heuchera 'Palace Purple' is a rich color.

VARIEGATED FOLIAGE

Variegated leaves—striped, edged, speckled, or blotched with white, cream, or yellow—are, after green, the most widespread type of foliage seen in gardens. Dull corners of the garden can benefit from bright variegations, but as a rule variegated foliage should be used sparingly as it can appear artificial when surrounded by simple greens.

The degree of variegation varies enormously, from the narrow, clean white leaf edge of the Solomon's seal *Polygonatum falcatum* 'Variegatum' to the bold cream streak of *Hosta undulata* 'Univittata'. In some plants, the brightness of the variegation creates a stark contrast with the basic leaf color. In other plants the effect is more subtle. From a distance many variegations merge to create a haze of pale color, and it is only on a closer view that you discover the details of the markings.

Some variegated perennials scorch in full sun in the same way as many yellow-leaved plants. Some produce occasional plain green, stronger-growing shoots, which will crowd out the variegated ones unless removed.

The leaves of *Houttuynia cordata* 'Chameleon' are brighter than many flowers.

FOLIAGE SHAPE AND TEXTURE

Color is the first thing that strikes us about foliage, but it is not everything. While most perennials die down for the winter, some are evergreen, and this adds interest to the garden in winter. In these and other perennials the shape and texture of the foliage are also important. If you use these two features imaginatively, you can add enormously to the success of your plantings, both large and small. In most cases, though, the interest of the foliage's shape and texture is more apparent from close up than from a distance, when such details may be invisible.

FOLIAGE SHAPE AND SIZE

Leaves vary in shape from the elephant-like ears of the bergenias and the bold, circular ones of *Darmera peltata*, each mounted on an individual central stalk, to feathery ferns and the long, hairlike strands of sedges, such as *Carex comans* 'Bronze Form.'

Size as well as shape is important. At one extreme are the vast rhubarb-like leaves of *Gunnera manicata*; at the other are the short, slender threads of *Coreopsis verticillata*. In between is the vast array of oval and divided shapes, from the tiny to the huge, which are so often overlooked in favor of flowers when choosing plants for the border.

The important rule is not to group together too many plants whose leaves are all much the same size and shape; as always with foliage, the starkest contrast is often the most successful. Delicate lacy ferns, broad heart-shaped hosta leaves, and the narrow arching leaves of *Carex pendula* provide three contrasting shapes to a group in a shady corner.

Grasses, bold hellebore leaves, and arching polygonatums make an attractive foliage combination.

Foliage shape can also be used effectively with flowering plants. Divided foliage, especially when carried on lax stems (as with many hardy geraniums), will fit neatly among the vertical stems of plants such as campanulas and help knit the planting together. For example, dense, bold foliage, such as that of the larger hostas, can be used to hide the stems of *Aster novi-belgii* cultivars, which often lose their lower leaves by late summer.

This mingling of foliage and flowers is especially valuable when planting mixed borders, where the foliage of perennials can be used both to mask the leafless stems of bulbs and to form a strong and effective angle with their upright growth.

FOLIAGE TEXTURE

Leaves can vary enormously in texture. For example, bearded irises are stiff but have a mat finish; the beautiful lobed leaves of *Geranium renardii* are soft and veined like those of culinary sage; and the marsh marigold (*Caltha palustris*) has leaves that are unusually glossy. Mixing these different textures in a planting usually works well—the contrast can be effective even when the foliage shape is similar. With many perennials it is the combination of shape and texture that creates the effect; for example, the soft leaves of many catmints are so small and neat that an overall impression of color and delicacy is all that is apparent when viewed from a distance.

FRUITS

Most flowering perennials produce fruits after they flower. Some develop very attractive fruits, which add a great deal of interest to borders many months after the main display of flowers is over.

Fruits can be divided into two groups: fleshy fruits, such as berries, and the various more familiar seed heads, which turn dry and brown. Neither will form if the plants are deadheaded, so the costs of retaining the fruits may be a reduced flowering display, as well as unwanted self-sown seedlings.

PERENNIALS WITH BERRIES

Many berry-bearing plants do not have colorful flowers. The clusters of white berries of *Actaea alba* and the corresponding red of *A. rubra* follow dowdy creamy white flowers, but they bring a real surprise to a shady border long after all the spring flowers are over. The orange lanterns of *Physalis franchetii,* with their orange berries inside, are a different case; here again the flowers are less important, but the wandering roots often invade other vigorous plants, such as *Aster ericoides* 'Golden Spray' and yellow-leaved shrubs, among which the inflated orange fruits look pretty.

OTHER PERENNIAL FRUITS

The dried pods are the main fruiting attraction of some perennials. These are less colorful than berries and need either a plain background to show them off or a position near a path, where they will be easily noticed.

The dark, slender stems of *Veratrum nigrum* last well, as do the spent pods of *Hosta sieboldiana*; when covered with the first fall frosts they are particularly attractive. Grasses last, too; and although the heads tend to fall to pieces as the weeks go by, the bleached stems and heads of *Miscanthus sinensis* 'Silberfeder,' for example, still look good in midwinter, especially if set against a dark evergreen background.

This illustrates another useful and attractive feature of perennials: their dead stems. Traditionally almost all perennials were cut down to the ground in the fall, but if they are left in place, they provide not only protection for dormant overwintering buds at the base but also additional interest for many weeks.

The structure of the bare dead branches can be attractive in itself; in the depths of winter, when covered in white frost and with glistening spiders' webs slung between the stems, they are a delight. They are especially valuable in parts of the garden that can be seen from the house or are passed through on winter mornings.

These red fruits of *Actaea rubra* are preceded by spikes of creamy flowers.

The orange lanterns of physalis look good with their own yellow fall foliage, though the plant's wandering roots mean that the lanterns sometimes appear among neighboring foliage.

Left: In small borders plants can be allowed to mingle intimately. Here the silvery blue stars surrounding the green cones of this eryngium repay close examination as they emerge through reddish stems and pink spikes of *Polygonium amplexicaule*.

Above: The slender, creamy, vertical spikes of *Kniphofia* 'Little Maid' contrast well in both shape and in color with the flat pink heads of *Sedum spectabile* in this colorful fall planting.

CHOOSING
PERENNIALS

So many perennials are available that it can be difficult to choose exactly which types to grow. Of course, personal taste must come first: there is no point growing plants you do not find attractive. At the same time there is little to be gained by trying to grow plants in soils or sites where they will never thrive, so choosing the right plant for the right place is vital.

Above: Rich, moist soil in partial shade provides ideal conditions for the brilliant blue *Meconopsis grandis* to stand tall above candelabra primulas and *Hosta fortunei* 'Aurea' with a dense cover of variegated hostas in the foreground.

THE ADAPTABILITY OF PERENNIALS

Perennials are highly adaptable plants and fit well into a wide variety of garden situations. In recent years the range of forms has increased rapidly in response to changes in gardening trends, so now more than ever there is a plant for every place.

This adaptability reveals itself in two ways. First, because perennials come from such a wide range of natural habitats—meadows and forests, riversides and seasides—there are species ideally suited to most soils and garden situations. Once adapted to gardens, these species have given rise to many more forms, with different colors or sizes. Second, some individual species of perennials are tolerant of a wide range of garden conditions. For example, many hardy geraniums will, within reasonable limits, grow in sun or shade, clay or gravel, dry or damp conditions.

It is therefore harder to make mistakes when planting perennials than, for example, alpines or annuals. However, this certainly does not mean that perennials will grow in any and every circumstance.

Perennials grow best and give their best display when planted in the soil and situation that suit them best. The most important thing to remember is that you can improve conditions that are comparatively inhospitable to perennials until the widest possible range can be grown.

SPECIAL SOILS

It is impossible to change the fundamental nature of garden soil, but often it can be made more favorable for a particular purpose. Improving the soil allows you to grow a wider range of the more adaptable plants as well as providing conditions that are suitable for many of the more specialized plants.

HEAVY CLAY SOIL

Clay soil is sticky, holds water, is often difficult to work, warms up slowly in the spring, and may open into wide cracks in dry weather. It can be improved by drainage and especially by adding large quantities of bulky organic matter. Every step taken toward reducing the negative effects of the clay will widen the range of plants you can grow, yet will have no adverse effect on the growth of natural clay-lovers. Clay soil that has been improved steadily over the years often turns out to be the most fertile and capable of supporting a wide range of plants.

Plants to grow Many of the best plants for heavy soil flower in summer or fall: mauve eupatoriums, heleniums in yellow and rusty shades, and hemerocallis, now available in enormous diversity. Many of the yellow summer and fall daisies are also good plants for heavy soil. These plants all have strong root systems, which is why they are naturally content in heavy soil; thorough preparation (p.26) will help them grow even more vigorously.

Strong-rooted spring flowers, such as *Helleborus orientalis* hybrids, also usually succeed, but spring-flowering woodland plants are less happy Fortunately, their root systems are

Helenium 'Moerheim Beauty' is one of many daisies which thrive in heavy soil.

relatively shallow, so in order to create the conditions they enjoy, you can raise the level of the bed and add leafy soil or improve just the top few inches of the heavy clay with compost. Such measures allow plants such as ajugas, asarums, ferns, and primroses to thrive.

Plants to avoid There are plants that find it hard to thrive in heavy clay, no matter how much you try to improve it. Surprisingly, a few Mediterranean plants, such as *Euphorbia characias,* grow remarkably well on heavy soil, but as a general rule you should avoid Mediterranean and drought-loving plants. The same goes for most plants that grow naturally on pebbly seashores, although *Crambe maritima* seems unexpectedly tolerant.

Plants with a tendency to rot at the crown, such as delphiniums, can be difficult to keep going. Gypsophilas often grow well on heavy soil but may live for only a few years.

Dianthus, some silvery achilleas such as 'Anthea' and 'Moonshine,' heucheras, species peonies, and scabious also dislike the wet conditions that heavy clay so often creates; it encourages rot. Plants on the borderline of hardiness can suffer in clay soil in winter; in case the main plant is lost, take cuttings and overwinter them in frost-free conditions.

ROCKY SOIL

In some gardens there is solid rock only a few inches beneath the surface. If the rock is porous, the soil is likely to be dry. However, if the rock does not let water drain through, conditions may vary enormously from wet in some seasons and after rain to dry at other times.

The most sensible solution in either case is to increase the depth of the soil by building raised beds, as this lets you grow a greater variety of plants; in some instances you can even dig rock out from the beds to make the walls. Over porous rock, the extra soil will provide a water reservoir; over impermeable rock, raising the level will lift plants above the sodden soil after heavy rains.

Plants to grow Plants that appreciate good drainage but do not have deep, vigorous root systems are your best choice. Alpines and heathers make a reliable choice, in addition to which many smaller perennials do well. In sunny areas white arabis, the shorter artemisias, *Aubrieta, Delosperma, Dianthus* of all kinds, *Diascia,* blue-leaved festucas, *Platycodon,* and *Pulsatilla* should thrive. A mulch of grit helps retain moisture.

In shady areas where the soil has been improved, many of the smaller woodland plants, such as *Ajuga reptans,* asarums, *Corydalis flexuosa,* dicentras, epimediums, some of the smaller hardy geraniums, and primroses are good bets. Here a mulch of bark is advisable. Where the shade is cast by trees whose roots invade the new bed, causing it to dry out, only plants suitable for dry shade (p.138) are likely to succeed.

Plants to avoid Tall plants, such as delphiniums and helianthus, should be avoided, not only because their roots are vigorous but also because, without the depth of soil the roots require to develop a strong anchorage, they are more likely to be blown over. Also, smaller plants with deep-growing roots, such as hellebores, hemerocallis, and *Symphytum* × *uplandicum* 'Variegatum,' may not thrive, as they will not have the root space they need and are unlikely to have access to the moisture they require at times when they should be growing strongly.

Purple flowered *Pulsatilla vulgaris* thrives well in rocky, well-drained soil in full sun.

WET SOIL

If parts of the garden have naturally wet soil or if the whole garden is badly drained, remember to work *with* the soil rather than *against* it. Draining the garden can improve matters, but this is a huge undertaking and not practicable along streams and in various other circumstances. Your best option is to choose moisture-loving plants. That said, you may want to reserve some small areas for plants that are not tolerant of moisture; you can create conditions suitable for a wider range of smaller plants by making a raised bed and filling it with sandy soil.

You can use troughs to grow alpines, and containers of various kinds (see pp.96–7) filled with well-drained soil make good homes for a wide range of other plants that do not enjoy damp conditions.

Plants to grow Many plants that grow naturally along the edges of streams and lakes or in boggy ground thrive in wet places in the garden. Some of these plants, such as astilbes and perennial lobelias, are adaptable and also grow in other spots as long as they do not dry out.

The moisture lovers include ligularias, whose leaves collapse in warm weather if grown in drier situations; the elegant globeflowers (*Trollius*); *Caltha palustris*; and irises. Irises are varied in their preferences: some,

such as cultivars of *I. pseudacorus, Iris ensata,* and *I. sibirica,* thrive in moist soil while others, such as *I. unguicularis,* prefer drier conditions.
Plants to avoid Obviously drought-loving plants, such as alpines and Mediterranean plants, will not enjoy damp soil, but they are not the only ones that hate the damp. Many other plants that thrive in ordinary border conditions will die in soil that is constantly wet, because excess moisture encourages their roots to rot. Be cautious when choosing your plants.

STONY SOIL

Stony soil can be a problem for both the gardener—cultivating soil containing too many rocks or stones is hard work—and the plants. The net effect of a stony or gravelly soil is to make it drain more freely. This can be an advantage if you feature alpines and drought lovers, but it may create difficulties for the many plants that need more moisture.

The addition of bulky organic matter is the most important measure to take, as this will build up the moisture-retentive capacity of the soil. Repeat this regularly in the form of a mulch, for in dry soil organic matter tends to disappear quickly.
Plants to grow Plants that hate wet soil and positively enjoy drier, well-drained conditions are ideal for open, sunny sites. These include plants that are sometimes classified as alpines, such as *Arabis, Aubrieta, Campanula isophylla,* and *Pulsatilla vulgaris,* as well as *Agapanthus, Anthemis, Dianthus,* and bearded irises, plus such Mediterranean plants as *Asphodelus, Convolvulus altheoides,* and *Euphorbia characias.*

The more organic matter you can add in shadier sites over the years, the more small woodland plants, even deep-rooted ones, will enjoy the conditions. In the early years only the tougher varieties can be depended upon; these include ajugas, dicentras, and forms of *Geranium × cantabridgense.* As the soil becomes richer in humus, less adaptable plants, such as primroses and epimediums, will have a better chance of survival.
Plants to avoid Moisture-loving plants rarely thrive in stony soils unless some restriction in drainage keeps the soil unexpectedly damp. So bog irises, bog primulas, and plants that are similarly dependent on

Not all irises thrive in wet soil but forms of *Iris siberica* like this 'Orville Fay' soon make tight, self-supporting plants.

moisture should not be chosen. On the other hand, apparently demanding plants, such as hostas, may thrive in shady places (note, though, that they will languish in the sun).

DRY SOIL

All plants need a certain amount of moisture, so dry soil presents an obvious problem. Fortunately it is possible in many cases to solve the problem at least partially and grow a reasonable range of plants.

If the soil is dry because it is unusually sandy or exceptionally well drained, you can improve the growing conditions enormously by adding organic matter, both by working it into the soil and by mulching as regularly as possible. Again, making a raised bed can help by increasing the depth of improved soil.

Where the reason for the soil's dryness is that tree roots are using the moisture, you have a more difficult problem on your hands, as it may be impossible to remove the roots without removing the tree. Another difficulty is that the shade cast by the tree may further restrict the range of suitable plants. Raising the soil level and incorporating a barrier to keep out roots can help.

Dry shade Dry shade is the most difficult situation for which to find good plants, as anything you try to grow will be deprived of the two things plants need more than anything else: moisture and light.

The first step you should take is to improve the site as much as possible, using any of the ideas touched on above. When it comes to the actual selection of plants, start off by considering the evergreen perennials, which can make use of what little light is available throughout the year. The shield ferns (*Polystichum*, particularly the species *P. setiferum*) are especially valuable, as is the surprisingly resilient male fern (*Dryopteris filixmas*). Other good evergreen perennials for dry shade include the elegant sedge *Carex pendula* and the stinking hellebore (*Helleborus foetidus*), with its greenish flowers and boldly fingered leaves. You might be tempted to plant the choicer woodlanders, such as epimediums and primroses, but these are unlikely to thrive in such dry conditions.

Dry, sunny places A good number of the plants that enjoy stony soils also thrive here, as the problems are similar. However, if you improve the soil, you can grow a wide range of plants, including slightly tender types for which wet, cold winter conditions usually mean death. So if the following plants are on the borderline of

Polystichium setiferum is one of the few ferns that will do well in dry shade.

135

hardiness in your area and you have a bed that is sunny and dry, improve the soil and then try them: agapanthus, diascias, the chocolate-colored and -scented *Cosmos atrosaguineus,* and the two tuberous salvias, *Salvia patens* and *S. farinacea.* Do not let the soil dry out completely.

Avoid plants that especially enjoy moisture, such as *Caltha, Trollius,* bog irises, and bog primulas.

ALKALINE SOIL

In general, the alkaline content of soil has less influence on the choice of perennials than it does on that of shrubs: fewer perennials have definite preferences, although some plants are especially happy where the alkaline level is unusually high.

In most gardens it is not practical to attempt to reduce the alkalinity of the soil. You can sometimes do it by regularly adding powdered sulfur, but in general it is better to work *with* the natural soil, not against it.

Plants to grow A wide variety of plants grow on alkaline soil, though it is important to remember that these conditions are not suitable for everything, particularly if the soil is especially alkaline. On lighter soil the many types of dianthus, including both modern and old-fashioned garden pinks, do extremely well, as do scabious and campanulas.

On richer soil bearded irises, in their vast variety, thrive along with hellebores and the delightful herbaceous clematises and peony hybrids.

Plants to avoid Few perennials have a particular objection to alkaline soil, although it is sometimes said that border phlox and lupines dislike it. However, it is more often the heavy clay or the thin, dry conditions associated with high alkalinity that cause the problem.

SPECIAL SITUATIONS

Most gardens have places that are inhospitable to plants, and on occasion whole gardens may pose problems. Sometimes the difficulty arises from the soil; in other cases it may be related to climate or geographical situation. Fortunately there are a number of measures that you can take to alleviate any difficulty, and there are always some plants that tolerate or even enjoy the conditions.

NEW GARDENS

A new and empty garden is a special challenge. When you are developing a new garden, it is encouraging if you can build up attractive beds and borders quickly. At the same time, try to avoid anything that requires unnecessary work or expense.

In new gardens the soil is often poor, especially if it has been moved around and compacted by building machinery. Not all plants will succeed in such conditions, and those that are sufficiently robust may prove too vigorous later, once soil conditions have been improved.

Bargain plants Starting with plants that are not too expensive is always a good idea when you take over and start work in a new garden:

• Bring divisions from your old garden to get you started.

• Accept plants from family, friends, or neighbors; at worst they can be replaced in a few years' time.

Dianthus, diascias, lychnis and poppies thrive in this well-drained alkaline soil.

• When visiting garden centers in spring, look out for perennials that seem unusually cramped in their pots; these can often be split immediately into three smaller plants.

• Raise perennials from seed; sometimes it is possible to buy enough seed for hundreds of plants for the same price as a single plant from the garden center.

Vigorous and tolerant plants Perennials that quickly spread to form a fat clump or become bold specimens are valuable in new gardens: they help make the garden seem more mature than it actually is. Unfortunately, plants that spread into clumps quickly often go on spreading and may later need curtailing or removing altogether if they are not to overwhelm choicer neighbors.

The tough and resilient plants that grow well in the difficult conditions often found in a new garden may not be your favorites. However, if they can tolerate poor drainage and poor soil until conditions are improved, they are valuable in the short term. Your best bet is to live with them until your garden is ready for something you prefer.

Plants for new gardens: *Achillea* 'Summer Pastels,' *Achillea ptarmica* 'The Pearl,' *Ajuga reptans, Alchemilla mollis, Aquilegia* 'McKana hybrids,' *Geranium* × *oxonianum* 'Claridge Druce,' *Lamium maculatum, Lupinus, Persicaria bistorta* 'Superba,' and, *Phalaris*.

SLOPES

Sloping sites cause problems in gardens for a number of reasons. In dry areas slopes are often drier than the rest of the garden, yet when rain comes it runs quickly across the surface without soaking into the soil. In wet areas the rain may soak in thoroughly, but the volume of precipitation may be so great that water also runs across the surface, carrying soil away in the process.

Alleviating the problem Terracing is often the most effective way to improve the problematic site. Build a series of low walls using stone, brick, wood, or whatever material is available and fits well into the garden surroundings, then fill in the newly created space behind the walls with soil to produce a series of horizontal beds across the slope. Moisture will then drain into the soil without washing the soil away.

Choosing plants Once you have built your terraced beds, select the plants that would generally be suitable for such a situation. Since you have effectively created level beds on the slope, you can treat them like any other bed, although they are likely to be particularly well drained.

Where a slope itself must be planted, your goal is to prevent rain from washing the soil away and encourage it to soak in. To achieve this, avoid plants that have a tight central rootstock and opt instead for those with runners, which will root into the soil, or ones that spread into broad clumps, which will collect leaves, retain soil, and slow down the flow of water. Often using groundcover plants in place of the usual border perennials is the best solution.

Ajugas root from every leaf joint as they run across the soil, while diascias send up stems from an

Clouds of *Erigeron karvinskianus* self-sow happily in this steep and stony bank.

ever-extending root system. Vigorous dicentras, such as 'Stuart Boothman' and 'Snowflakes,' are good in the shade, while the many grasses with spreading roots, such as *Glyceria maxima* 'Variegata' and *Phalaris arundinacea* 'Picta,' are effective.

SEASIDE GARDENS

There are two difficulties associated with gardens by the sea: wind and salt. The problems caused by wind are dealt with in the next column, but when it carries salt it can be especially destructive, and many plants cannot tolerate it. When moist air carrying salt comes into contact with foliage or flowers, the moisture evaporates and the salt causes scorch. Salt is also washed into the soil, and while this suits some vegetables, such as beets and cabbage, which are derived from seaside plants, it can be a problem for many perennials.

In some seaside gardens the soil may be unusually sandy. These gardens tend to drain rapidly, and as a result, may be low in nutrients. Some plants, especially those that are used to growing in hot dry conditions, such as *Euphorbia characias* and *Asphodelus fistulosus,* will thrive but for less tolerant plants generous applications of organic matter are necessary in order to improve moisture retention and fertility.

You can give your perennials protection by planting shelter, although you must choose trees and shrubs that tolerate the salt. In general you should rely on your choice of plants to solve the worst of the problems.

Choosing plants Plants that grow naturally by the sea are obvious choices, although few of these are in the top flight of perennials. An excellent native is *Crambe maritima,* with its bluish foliage and white flowers.

Otherwise it is a matter of choosing plants that are tough enough to cope with the salt.

Many of these, such as dianthus, eryngiums, *Elymus hispidus, E. magellanicus,* and *Limonium latifolium,* have a waxy protective coating on the leaves; this not only sheds the salt-laden water quickly but also provides a barrier to any salt that might be left after moisture has evaporated.

WINDY GARDENS

Wind can be very destructive: it can physically batter plants, scorch or tear the foliage, blow plants over, or loosen them at the roots, so that they die a slow death.

The problem is divided into two categories: some gardens are in windy parts of the country; others are parts of individual gardens that suffer particularly from exposure to wind.

Windy gardens Gardens in windy areas or in unusually windy sites benefit enormously from protection, but protecting a whole garden can be a large undertaking. Hedges and shelterbelts of trees and shrubs are generally more effective than walls and fences because they are sufficiently flexible to filter the wind yet not be damaged by it. When wind hits a wall or fence, it swirls over the top, sometimes causing damaging eddies on the leeward side; this can be especially destructive to a herbaceous border planted with a wall as a background. Unfortunately, trees and shrubs take up a significant amount of space in comparison with a fence or wall, and their roots can rob borders of moisture and nutrients.

Within the garden Sometimes a combination of features creates an unusually windy area within a garden. Often this occurs in a passage between two walls, such as a house wall

and a boundary wall. The result is effectively a wind tunnel, and the gusts generated can be particularly damaging to plants.

In some situations this problem can be easily resolved. You could, for example, fit a gate to a passage to lessen the tunneling effect. Alternatively, you might set up a trellis screen, removable if necessary, to filter the wind so that it does less damage to your plants. Another option is to plant tough evergreen shrubs or short hedges at strategic points within the garden where shelter is especially necessary.

Choosing plants Perennials for windy sites must have at least one of four special qualities:

• Some perennials are sufficiently strong and flexible to bend in the wind without breaking, and many of the grasses, especially the various forms of *Miscanthus sinensis,* fall into this category; clearly plants that are naturally fragile, such as dicentras, should not be risked.

• Another useful feature is slender foliage, which is not easily damaged; the smaller grasses, *Dianthus,* and some of the smaller irises and kniphofias score here.

• Flowers that allow air to blow through them are less easily damaged by wind; grasses, centaureas, and perovskias can cope with wind far more effectively than peonies, poppies, large kniphofias, and large double chrysanthemums.

• Finally, shorter plants that naturally keep a low profile or are sheltered by their neighbors are obvious contenders in windy situations; ajugas, arabis, aubrietas, and lamiums are worth trying.

Right: Hedges shelter the borders in this windy garden and also support perennial sweet peas.

GUIDE TO CHOOSING PERENNIALS

Listed below are plants that are especially useful in particular situations or have features of value in the garden. All are described in the Plant Directory.

Clay soil
Anemone, Doronicum orientale 'Magnificum,' *Eupatorium, Helenium, Hemerocallis, Hosta, Inula, Ligularia, Monarda didyma, Persicaria*

Alkaline soil
Bergenia, Campanula, Clematis integrifolia, Dianthus, Eremurus robustus, Iris (tall and dwarf bearded forms), *Knautia macedonica, Linaria, Paeonia,* (not species peonies), *Scabiosa*

Wet soil
Astilbe, Caltha palustris 'Flore Pleno,' *Darmera peltata, Filipendula palmata, Gunnera manicata, Iris* (*I. pseudacorus* and *I. sibirica*), *Ligularia dentata, Lobelia, Primula japonica, Trollius*

Dry shade
Acanthus mollis, Alchemilla mollis, Carex pendula, Dryopteris filix-mas, Epimedium × versicolor, Helleborus foetidus, Lamium, Liriope muscari, Polystichum setiferum

Damp shade
Dicentra (woodlanders), *Epimedium, Gentiana asclepiadea, Helleborus orientalis* hybrids, *Hosta, Primula vulgaris, Pulmonaria, Saxifraga fortunei, Smilacina racemosa, Tricyrtis hirta*

Windy sites
Achillea 'Coronation Gold,' *Ajuga reptans, Anemone, Campanula portenschlagiana Centaurea montana, Festuca glauca, Miscanthus sinensis,* 'Silberfeder,' *Nepeta × faassenii, Phalaris arundinacea* 'Picta,' *Stipa gigantea*

Sloping sites
Aegopodium podagraria 'Variegatum,' *Ajuga reptans* 'Silver Shadow,' *Convolvulus altheoides, Diascia* 'Ruby Field,' *Dicentra* 'Snowflakes,' *Geranium macrorrhizum, Glyceria maxima* 'Variegata,' *Phalaris arundinacea* 'Picta,' *Symphytum,* 'Goldsmith,' 'Hidcote Blue,' and 'Hidcote Pink,' *Waldsteinia ternata*

Seaside gardens
Artemisia, Elymus, Crambe maritima, Dianthus, Iris (dwarf bearded types), *Eryngium, Euphorbia characias, Kniphofia* 'Atlanta,' *Limonium latifolium, Persicaria bistorta* 'Superba'

Cold gardens
Achillea millefolium, Cimicifuga simplex, Coreopsis verticillata, Echinops ritro, Iris sibirica, Malva moschata, Osmunda regalis, Phlox maculata, Primula vulgaris, Tiarella wherryi

Hot and dry sites
Achillea ptarmica 'The Pearl,' *Alstroemeria,* 'Ligtu Hybrids,' *Anthemis punctata* subsp. *cupaniana, Cynara cardunculus, Dianthus deltoides,* 'Brilliant,' *Zauschneria californica, Eryngium, Euphorbia characias, Malva alcea* var. *fastigiata, Sedum* 'Ruby Glow'

Deer-resistant plants
Agapanthus, Aquilegia, Cordateria, Delphinium, Digitalis, Helleborus, Kniphofia, Leucanthemum, Lupinus, Rheum

Groundhog-proof plants
Acanthus, Aconitum, Agapanthus, Alchemilla, Anaphalis, Aquilegia, Aster, Astilbe, Bergenia, Brunnera, Delphinium, Digitalis, Euphorbia, Helleborus, Hemerocallis, Iris, Kniphofia, Liriope, Lupinus, Papaver

Quick-growing perennials
Achillea ptarmica 'The Pearl,' *Aegopodium podagraria* 'Variegatum,' *Alchemilla mollis, Convolvulus altheoides, Dicentra* 'Snowflakes,' *Geranium × oxonianum* 'Claridge Druce,' *Houttuynia cordata* 'Chameleon,' *Lamium galeobdolon,* 'Florentinum,' *Persicaria bistorta* 'Superba,' *Ajuga reptans* 'Silver Shadow'

Specimen perennials
Aruncus dioicus, Cortaderia selloana, Crambe cordifolia, Delphinium 'Southern Noblemen,' *Eremurus robustus, Gunnera manicata, Helianthus salicifolius, Hosta* 'Krossa Regal,' *Kniphofia* 'Prince Igor,' *Macleaya cordata*

Perennials attractive to butterflies
Aster amellus, Centranthus, Cynara, Echinops, Erigeron, Nepeta, Phlox paniculata, Scabiosa, Sedum, Solidago

Perennials attractive to bees
Anchusa, Anemone, Asclepias, Centaurea, Galega, Helleborus, Inula, Origanum, Salvia, Sedum

Perennials for containers
Aegopodium podagraria 'Variegatum,' *Agapanthus, Cosmos atrosanguineus, Dianthus, Diascia, Dryopteris wallichiana, Hakonechloa macra* 'Aureola,' *Hosta, Lamium maculatum, Penstemon*

FLOWERS BY SEASON
Spring flowering
Aquilegia, Dicentra, Doronicum, Epimedium, Euphorbia characias, Geranium, Iris (dwarf bearded types), *Primula, Pulmonaria, Viola*

Summer flowering
Astilbe, Delphinium, Dianthus, Hemerocallis, Iris (*I. sibirica* and tall bearded types), *Kniphofia, Lupinus, Paeonia, Papaver orientale, Penstemon*

Fall flowering
Anemone, Aster, Boltonia, Cimicifuga, Dendranthema, Eupatorium, Helenium, Leucanthemella serotina, Liriope muscari, Sedum

FLOWERS BY COLOR
White flowers
Anemone × hybrida 'Honorine Jobert,' Aster novae-angliae 'Herbstschnee,' Campanula persicifolia, 'Hampstead White,' Dianthus 'White Ladies,' Dicentra spectabilis alba, Iris siberica 'White Swirl,' Paeonia 'White Wings,' Papaver 'Black and White,' Penstemon 'White Bedder,' Pulmonaria officinalis 'Sissinghurst White'

Pink flowers
Anemone × hybrida 'Queen Charlotte,' Aster novi-belgii 'Little Pink Beauty,' Dendranthema 'Clara Curtis,' Dianthus 'Doris,' Geranium × oxonianum 'Claridge Druce,' Paeonia 'Bowl of Beauty,' Papaver orientale 'Cedric Morris,' Penstemon 'Hidcote Pink,' Phlox panicu-lata 'Eva Callum,' Sedum spectabile 'Brilliant'

Red or orange-red flowers
Aster novae-angliae 'September Ruby,' Astilbe 'Fanal,' Dianthus 'Houndspool Ruby,' Geum chiloense 'Mrs. J.Bradshaw,' Kniphofia 'Atlanta,' Lobelia 'Compliment Scarlet,' Paeonia 'Inspecteur Lavergne,' Papaver orientale 'Beauty of Livermere,' Penstemon 'Chester Scarlet,' Pulmonaria rubra 'Redstart'

Yellow flowers
Achillea filipendulina 'Gold Plate,' Anthemis 'E. C. Buxton,' Aster ericoides 'Golden Spray,' Caltha palustris 'Flore Pleno,' Doronicum orientale 'Magnificum,' Helianthus 'Lemon Queen,' Hemerocallis 'Stella de Oro,' Kniphofia 'Little Maid,' Lysichiton americanus, Paeonia mlokose-witschii, Rudbeckia 'Goldsturm'

Blue flowers
Aquilegia vulgaris 'Adelaide Addison,' Aster × frikartii 'Mönch,' Campanula carpatica 'Blue Clips,' Delphinium 'Blue Nile,' Geranium wallichianum 'Buxton's Variety,' Iris 'Jane Phillips,' Iris sibirica 'Cambridge,' Polemonium reptans, Viola 'Ardross Gem'

Purple, mauve, or lilac flowers
Aster amellus 'Violet Queen,' Campanula latifolia 'Brantwood,' Geranium phaeum , Lobelia 'Tania,' Penstemon 'Alice Hindley,' Polemonium 'Lambrook Mauve,' Primula 'Miss Indigo,' Salvia × sylvestris 'May Night,' Verbena bonariensis, Viola 'Maggie Mott'

Scented flowers
Asphodeline lutea, Astilbe 'Deutschland,' Clematis × jouiana 'Praecox,' Crambe cordifolia, Dianthus 'Mrs. Sinkins,' Hosta 'Honeybells,' Iris unguicularis, Paeonia 'Duchesse de Nemours,' Phlox carolina 'Miss Lingard,' Phlox paniculata, 'White Admiral'

PERENNIALS WITH GOOD FOLIAGE
Variegated leaves
Ajuga reptans 'Variegata,' Aquilegia vulgaris 'Vervaeneana,' Astrantia 'Sunningdale Variegated,' Carex morrowii 'Variegata,' Hakonechloa macra 'Aureola,' Hosta 'Shade Fanfare,' Eryngium bourgatii, Lamium maculatum, Phlox paniculata 'Norah Leigh,' Symphytum 'Goldsmith'

Gold or yellow leaves
Acorus gramineus 'Ogon,' Centaurea montana 'Gold Bullion,' Deschampsia caespitosa 'Golden Veil,' Filipendula ulmaria 'Aurea,' Hosta 'Zounds,' Milium effusum 'Aureum' Origanum vulgare 'Aureum,' Stachys byzantina 'Primrose Heron,' Tanacetum parthenium 'Aureum,' Valeriana phu 'Aurea'

Silver, gray, or bluish leaves
Anaphalis margaritacea var. yedoensis, Anthemis punctata subsp. cupaniana, Cynara cardunculus, Euphorbia myrsinites, Helictotrichon sempervirens, Hosta 'Halcyon,' Nepeta × faassenii, Stachys byzantina 'Silver Carpet'

Purple leaves
Ajuga reptans 'Braunherz' Bergenia 'Bressingham Ruby,' 'Brunette,' Foeniculum vulgare 'Purpureum,' Heuchera micrantha 'Palace Purple,' Imperata cylindrica 'Rubra,' Lobelia 'Queen Victoria,' Rheum palmatum, 'Atrosanguineum,' Veronica peduncularis 'Georgia Blue'

Bold foliage
Acanthus mollis 'Latifolius,' Bergenia 'Ballawley,' Brunnera macrophylla, Crambe cordifolia, Darmera peltatum, Helleborus orientalis hybrids, Hosta 'Krossal Regal,' Ligularia stenocephala, Lysichiton ameri-canus, Rodgersia podophylla

Lacy foliage
Achillea millefolium hybrids, Artemisia canescens, Aruncus dioicus 'Kneiffii,' Athyrium filix-femina, Corydalis flexuosa, Dryopteris filix-mas, Foeniculum vulgare, 'Purpureum,' Polystichum setiferum, Thalictrum delavayi

Narrow foliage
Carex, Dianthus, Festuca, Hemerocallis, Iris, Kniphofia 'Little Maid,' Liriope mus-cari , Miscanthus sinensis, Molinia caerulea 'Variegata,' Morina longifolia, Sisy-rinchium striatum

PERENNIALS WITH ATTRACTIVE FRUITS
Actaea alba and A. rubra (berries), Clema-tis integrifolia, Dictamnus albus, Hosta sieboldiana var. elegans, Paeonia mlokose-witschii, Physalis franchetii (berries), Phytolacca americana (berries), Smilacina racemosa (berries), Veratrum nigrum

A - Z
DIRECTORY

Sedum spectabile and *Aster amellus*, two of the best fall perennials, make an attractive and long lasting combination.

Left: The bright yellow of *Achillea* 'Moonshine' and the bold magenta of *Geranium psilostemon* are softened by clouds of blue catmint.

The hardiness zones

The climatic conditions of an area are of prime importance when deciding what to plant in the garden. The successful cultivation of a plant largely depends on its native climate and how easily it can adapt to a new one, if necessary. The hardiness zones on pages 228–31 indicate the degree of coldness a plant can tolerate.

ACANTHUS
Bear's breeches

This genus contains about 20 species, of which 6 are in general cultivation. They grow in fertile, well-drained soil and can be used in sun or light shade, although the former is preferred. The main problems are slugs and snails. Bear's breeches is propagated from seed in late fall or spring or from root cuttings when dormant.

A. dioscoridis

This plant has deeply cut, rigid leaves and hairy stems. It reaches a height of 3 ft (90 cm). In summer it bears dense spikes of purple-and-white flowers.

Acanthus mollis

A. mollis (above)

This is the most popular species of the genus. The deeply lobed leaves are a dull midgreen, and the flower spikes rise to 5 ft (1.5 m), carrying pink or white flowers with purple hoods. 'Latifolius' has large, shiny leaves.

Acanthus spinosus

A. spinosus (above)

This plant is similar to *A. mollis* except that the large, shiny dark green leaves are distinctly spiny and the flowers are more free flowering. The blooms are white with mauve-purple hoods and are carried on spikes approximately 4 ft (1.2 m) high. 'Spinosissimus' has more deeply divided leaves, and the spines have a silvery-white sheen.

ACHILLEA
Yarrow

These tough, vigorous plants have very attractive ferny foliage and flat heads of short-petaled, daisylike flowers. The blooms are mainly yellow, but more and more pastel and brighter colors are being introduced. The cut flowers are good for drying. These are good border plants in varying heights. They spread to form large clumps, although some types do so too readily and can become invasive.

Any good garden soil is suitable, but it should be well drained. Yarrows are drought resistant. A sunny site is needed. Propagation by division may be done any time, although yarrows can also be grown from seed.

A. clypeolata hybrids

These have beautiful silvery-gray foliage and bright yellow flowers on stems 2 ft (60 cm) high. They are short-lived and need regular replanting. 'Anthea' has very silvery leaves and paler flowers, while 'Moonshine' has similar leaves but brighter flowers.

A. filipendulina

Fern-leaf yarrow is the tallest yarrow and looks attractive grouped toward the back of a border. It has ferny green foliage and large heads of golden yellow flowers. The tall, erect stems are up to 4 ft (1.2 m) high and need staking. 'Cloth of Gold' has abundant golden yellow flowers. 'Coronation Gold' is deservedly one of the most popular yarrows. Its bright yellow flower heads are about 3 in (7.5 cm) wide. The foliage is grayer than that of other cultivars. 'Gold Plate' has large heads, up to 6 in (15 cm) wide, and greener foliage; it is one of the tallest of these forms.

Achillea millefolium 'Cerise Queen'

A. millefolium hybrids (above)

Common yarrow is not a pretty plant, but there are a number of excellent hybrids. They are up to 2½ ft (75 cm) in height, with ferny foliage and flat heads 2 in (5 cm) or more in diameter. 'Appleblossom' ('Apfelblüte') has pale pink flowers, 'Cerise Queen' deep pink, 'Forncett Fletton' orange-brown, 'Hope' ('Hoffnung'; also 'Great Expectations') creamy yellow, and 'Salmon Beauty' ('Lachsschönheit') salmon-pink.

A. ptarmica (below)

Sneezeweed can be invasive, so position it carefully. It is 2 ft (60 cm) tall with dark green leaves and looser flower heads than other types. The white flowers are double in most cultivars. 'Boule de Neige' and 'The Pearl,' which are very similar and usually considered to be the same plant, have pure white flowers of great beauty.

Achillea ptarmica 'The Pearl'

ACONITUM
Monkshood

Monkshoods make up a large genus of about 200 species, of which a dozen are in general cultivation. They are grown for their attractive, curiously shaped flowers. Each has a large upper petal, fashioned a bit like a helmet or hood. The color is generally dark blue, but there are also paler blue forms, as well as white and creamy yellow varieties. Monkshoods flower in summer and fall. The majority are stiff, erect plants up to 5 ft (1.5 m) tall, with the flowers held in spikes, but some are scramblers and need shrubs for support.

Monkshoods grow in any soil that has been enriched with plenty of well-rotted organic material so that it is moisture retentive. The taller forms may need staking when sited in exposed positions. Propagation is best achieved by division or by seed. All parts of the plant, particularly the root, are poisonous.

Aconitum 'Bressingham Spire'

Blue forms (above)

The blue forms include 'Bressingham Spire,' which has violet-blue flowers and is shorter than most. *A.* × *cammarum* 'Bicolor' has white flowers with a blue margin. *A. carmichaelii* 'Arendsii' has lovely deep blue flowers, while 'Spark's Variety' is an early-blooming form which has intense blue flowers. *A. c. wilsonii* is a taller and more vigorous variety than the others mentioned. All these forms flower in the fall.

Aconitum 'Ivorine'

Cream forms (above)

There are two main cream forms. 'Ivorine' is a creamy off-white and flowers early. It grows to only 2½ ft (75 cm). *A. lycotonum* subsp. *vulparia* is a creamy yellow and taller, growing up to 5 ft (1.5 m) in the right spot.

ACORUS
Sweet flag

Although flowering plants, sweet flags are grown more for their swordlike foliage than for their summer flowers. They grow well in shallow water, making them ideal for planting in drifts along the borders of pools and streams. The minute flowers are carried in strange spikes, shaped like horns jutting out at an angle from the foliage.

Sweet flags can be grown in mud at the edge of water or in latticework baskets. They need a sunny spot. Propagation is easily achieved by dividing the plants every 3 or 4 years.

Acorus calamus 'Variegatus'

A. calamus (above)

This species has irislike leaves growing to approximately 3 ft (90 cm). They are dark green and often wavy at the margins. When crushed they smell of tangerines. 'Variegatus' has creamy yellow stripes flushed with pink at the base of the leaves.

A. gramineus

This plant's foliage is much shorter and finer than that of other species; it is more like blades of grass. The flower spike is more upright. *A. gramineus* is not as hardy as *A. calamus*. 'Ogon' has deep yellow stripes; 'Pusillus' is more tufty than the other cultivars; and 'Variegatus' has cream stripes.

ACTAEA
Baneberry

This small genus of plants is grown as much for the colored fruit as the flowers. Baneberries make attractive foliage plants, with leaves made up of a number of leaflets. The flowers, carried in fluffy plumes, appear in late summer and are followed by the distinctive berries, which are poisonous.

Baneberries are woodland plants that grow in a cool, humus-rich soil in light shade. Propagate by division or from seed.

A. alba

Also known as *A. pachypoda*, this species has slender red stems carrying loose bunches of spherical white berries, each with a black "eye."

Actaea rubra

A. rubra (above)
The leaves on this species are fernier than those of *A. alba*. The flowers are white; the berries are a very attractive shiny red and elliptical in shape.

ADIANTUM
Maidenhair fern

These deciduous, semi-evergreen, and evergreen ferns are excellent choices for the garden. Each is characterized by a black, wiry central stem with parallel leaflets on either side. The plants always look fresh, as well as delicate.

These ferns require a moist, shady site. For the majority, the soil should be neutral or acid, preferably with plenty of leaf mold or well-rotted humus in it. They can be propagated from spores in late summer or by careful division in spring.

A. pedatum

The northern maidenhair fern, which reaches about 1½ ft (45 cm) in height and width, is a superb plant. It is normally deciduous but can be semi-evergreen in milder areas. It spreads slowly but is not a nuisance.

AEGOPODIUM
Goutweed

This small genus of plants is known in the garden mainly through *A. podagraria*, which can become an invasive weed, spreading by underground shoots. In the past it was grown as an herb, but it is rarely planted now, except in its less vigorous variegated form. It grows in any garden soil, in either sun or light shade, and can easily be propagated by division in the spring or fall.

Aegopodium podagraria 'Variegatum'

A. podagraria 'Variegatum' (above)
This plant is grown for its attractive foliage variegated with creamy white. Providing excellent ground cover, it reaches 10 in (25 cm) in height and soon covers a wide area. Grow it in a confined space to keep it under control, as it has a tendency to spread. Insignificant white flowers, borne in summer, are not particularly attractive and should be removed.

AGAPANTHUS
African lily

Gardeners can choose from an increasing number of cultivars in this genus. The fleshy roots produce a fountain of straplike leaves and balls of blue or white flowers, carried on long stems. Each flower is like a miniature lily. The blooms appear in late summer and are good for cutting.

African lilies grow in most fertile garden soils, preferably moisture-retentive ones. They need a sunny site. Avoid transplanting, as the roots are brittle and take 1–3 years to reestablish. In colder areas (zone 8) grow African lilies in containers that can be moved inside or otherwise protected during winter. Propagation is by careful division or by seed, although the latter is not suitable for named cultivars.

Agapanthus africanus

Blue-flowered forms (above)
Blue is the most common color for the flowers. It varies from very pale to deep blue. *A. africanus* has deep blue flowers on erect stems with broad, dark green leaves. 'Blue Giant' is one of the 'Headbourne Hybrids' (see **Mixed forms, next column**). It is 4 ft (1.2 m) tall and has blue flowers. 'Bressingham Blue' is

slightly shorter than 'Blue Giant' and has the darkest blue flowers of all the blue-flowered forms.

White-flowered forms

'Bressingham White' is as good as its blue counterpart. *A. africanus* 'Albus' is not quite so hardy and much shorter, but well worth growing in a container.

Mixed forms

'Headbourne Hybrids' are the most famous forms of *Agapanthus*. They are the hardiest and offer a wide range of blues and whites. Many are named cultivars, but there is also a seed strain.

Agapanthus 'Lilliput'

Dwarf forms (above)

While most forms of *Agapanthus* are 2½–4 ft (75 cm–1.2 m) tall, there are some very good dwarf forms suitable for the front of a border or rock garden. *A. africanus* 'Peter Pan,' *A. campanulatus* 'Isis,' and *A.* 'Lilliput' are all short cultivars worth considering. They grow to 1 ft (30 cm) in height, although 'Isis' is slightly taller.

AGASTACHE
Giant hyssop

These short-lived perennials all have fragrant foliage and dense spikes of flowers resembling those of the mints, to which they are related. The leaves are nettlelike in shape. The fact that these plants are short-lived is not a problem as they self-sow, offering plenty of seedlings to replace lost plants.

They need free-draining soil and a position in the sun. They do not have strong stems and need staking when not planted in a sheltered spot.

A. foeniculum (below)

This is the most commonly seen species. It grows to 3 ft (90 cm). The foliage smells of fennel or aniseed (hence the synonym *A. anisata,* under which it is sometimes listed). The flowers are mainly a dull violet color, although there are some white forms, including the ivory-white 'Alabaster.'

Agastache foeniculum

A. mexicana

This species is slightly shorter and produces flowers varying from pink to red in color. It is short-lived and should be propagated each year.

AJUGA
Bugleweed

These low-growing vigorous plants form a dense ground cover. They are grown both for their spikes of blue, pink, or white flowers, which appear in spring, and for their very decorative foliage, which comes in a variety of attractive colors. Some forms have year-round foliage.

Bugleweeds are essentially woodland flowers that need moist, humus-rich soil. They grow best in a lightly shaded spot but will grow in full sun, provided the soil does not dry out. Some of the colored-foliage forms need sun to maintain their color. The plants are invasive but are not difficult to control. Propagation is by division of the strawberry-like runners.

A. reptans

This is the common bugleweed. The species has green leaves and blue flowers carried on 6 in (15 cm) spikes. There are a large number of desirable cultivars.

Dark-leaved forms

'Atropurpurea' has deep purple foliage and blue flowers. 'Braunherz' is similar, except that the purple coloration is much browner, more a deep bronze. Both these forms can revert to green if planted in shade that is too dense.

Ajuga reptans 'Multicolor'

Patterned forms (above)

There are an increasing number of variegated forms. 'Burgundy Glow' has leaves that are a mixture of pink and burgundy, edged with cream. The cultivar 'Multicolor' (also known as 'Rainbow' or 'Tricolor') is similar, except that the colors are purple, red, and cream, often with patches of green. 'Variegata' is pale green and cream.

Vigorous forms

There are several forms that are vigorous growers with large flower spikes. 'Catlin's Giant' is the biggest. 'Jungle Beauty' has very large glossy leaves, while 'Silver Shadow' has pale leaves.

ALCEA
Hollyhock

The best known of the hollyhocks is the stately *A. rosea*, but this is now generally treated as a biennial because it is prone to the disease of rust. This and other species in the genus were, until recently, classified as *Althaea* and are still sometimes listed under this name. Their flowers are shallow funnels in a variety of colors. Double forms are available. The flowers appear on tall spikes from summer onward. There are now dwarf forms of some species.

Hollyhocks grow in any good garden soil and do best in a sunny spot. The taller forms need staking. All can be propagated from seed in late summer or spring.

A. rugosa

This has become a popular substitute for the disease-prone *A. rosea*, as it suffers less from the disease of rust. It is not as tall, reaching only 4 ft (1.2 m), and is bushy rather than single-stemmed. The flowers are a delightful pure yellow.

ALCHEMILLA
Lady's-mantle

These plants are loved for their foliage and their flowers. The leaves are round in outline; in some cases they are pleated, in others they are cut almost to the center in individual leaflets. The billowing clouds of greenish-yellow flowers appear mainly in late spring and early summer.

Alchemillas grow in any garden soil, but they look particularly attractive when planted close to water. They perform well in either sun or shade. Propagation is exceptionally easy from seed; in fact, they frequently self-sow.

Alchemilla erythropoda

A. erythropoda (above)

This species is a low-growing one, reaching only 6 in (15 cm) high. It is excellent at the front of a border or as ground cover in light shade. The blue-green leaves are partly cut.

A. mollis (below)

This is the most popular species. It has large, rounded leaves with scalloped edges and deep folds that hold the dew and raindrops in a most beautiful way. The foaming flowers are borne in spring and again in fall if the plants are dead-headed after the first flush.

Alchemilla mollis

ALSTROEMERIA
Peruvian lily

There are about 60 different species of Peruvian lily, but only a handful are in cultivation. They are very exotic-looking plants for the perennial border. The trumpet-shaped flowers often offer a fusion of colors and are spotted. The plants are 3–4 ft (90 cm–1.2 m) tall.

Alstroemerias need rich, well-drained soil and a site away from the hottest sun. Plant at least 6 in (15 cm) below the surface. Some form of support is often required. Although the roots are brittle, they can, with care, be divided to increase stock. Plants can also be grown from seed.

A. aurea

This is the hardiest species (zone 7). The flowers are a brilliant golden orange, spotted in red. The plant has a spreading rootstock and can become invasive; it needs to be kept in check. It grows well and attractively through bushes.

Alstroemeria 'Ligtu Hybrids'

A. 'Ligtu Hybrids' (above)

These hybrids offer the gardener a wide range of colors, including cream, yellow, orange, red, and pink. They are floriferous and hardy, but because they self-seed, they can become invasive.

A. 'Princess Hybrids'

This group of hybrids, bred for the cut-flower trade, is becoming popular in the garden. These hybrids, based on *A. aurea*, are available in a wide range of colors, both pastel and bright.

A. psittacina

The parrot flower has intriguing red-and-green flowers. It is shorter than most border forms, reaching 3 ft (90 cm).

AMSONIA

Blue star

As its common name suggests, this small genus is made up of species with starry blue flowers. These are carried in loose heads and contrast well with the green leaves. The plant can reach up to 3 ft (90 cm). Blue stars spread to form clumps and rarely outgrow their allotted space.

They need moist soil with plenty of well-rotted organic material added to it. A position in either full sun or light shade is suitable. They need staking in a windy spot. Propagation should be carried out in spring, either by division or from seed.

A. orientalis

Also known as *Rhazya orientalis*, this European plant is less hardy (zones 6–9) than other members of the genus. The flowers are pale gray-blue, appearing darker while still in bud.

Amsonia tabernaemontana

A. tabernaemontana (above)

This is the North American equivalent of *A. orientalis*. In summer it has willowy stems bearing drooping clusters of small, tubular pale blue flowers on slightly taller plants.

ANAPHALIS

Pearl everlasting

Even though these plants have attractive flowers, they are grown mainly for their gray-silver foliage. Unlike most silvery-leaved plants, these can be grown in moist, shady sites, which makes them extremely useful. The leaves are narrow and felted with hairs. The flowers are small buttons with yellow centers and white strawlike petals or bracts. They begin to appear in late summer and continue into the fall.

Although these plants grow in shade, they also do well in a sunny spot. A moisture-retentive soil is required, as the leaves begin to wilt and droop if the plants become too dry. Propagation is easily achieved by division in winter or spring or by seed in fall.

A. margaritacea

This erect plant grows up to 3 ft (90 cm) high. It spreads and can become invasive. The gray-green or silvery gray leaves have a few hairs above and are whiter on the undersides.

A. m. var. yedoensis (below)

This variety of anaphalis is very similar to the species, but the leaves have a distinct silver edge to them. The flower heads are also larger than those of the species.

Anaphalis margaritacea var. *yedoensis*

Anaphalis triplinervis 'Summer Snow'

A. triplinervis (above)

This species gets its name from the three distinct veins that run down each leaf. The leaves are white with hairs, and the flowers are white balls of stiff bracts with tiny yellow centers. They are carried in profusion in late summer. This is a clump-forming plant rather than a spreader. The cultivar 'Summer Snow' ('Sommerschnee') is shorter, only 10 in (25 cm) high, and covered in white flowers. It is not as resistant to drought as *A. magaritacea* var. *yedoensis*.

ANCHUSA

Bugloss

Although their foliage is coarse in texture, these plants are welcome in the garden because of their brilliant blue flowers, which appear in early summer. The flowers are carried in long spikes that uncurl in much the same way as their relative, the forget-me-not (*Myosotis*).

Bugloss needs well-cultivated, fertile soil, but if the soil is too wet or too heavy, it will die out after a year. It also needs a sunny site. The stems are stiff but can snap in wind, so staking is necessary. Propagation is by root cuttings for named cultivars. Seed can be used for the species.

A. azurea

Italian bugloss is the most commonly grown species. This tall plant can reach

5 ft (1.5 m). The stems and long leaves are clothed with coarse hairs, giving them a rough texture. There are a number of cultivars. 'Dropmore' is deep blue, flowering later than other forms. 'Little John' grows to about 1½ ft (45 cm) and is useful for exposed borders.

ANEMONE
Anemone

This is a very large genus with several different types of plants, including woodland species, such as *A. nemorosa,* and bulbous ones, like *A. pavonina*. While these, along with such plants as *A. narcissiflora* and *A. rivularis,* all make good plants for the border, it is the graceful Japanese anemone and its relatives that are most commonly used in borders. These particular anemones grow to about 2 ft (60 cm) and spread underground to form large clumps. They all flower from late summer through the fall. The flowers are saucer shapes colored either white or rosy pink, each with a yellow central disk of stamens. There are also double forms.

Anemones grow in either full sun or light shade but do best in the open. They thrive in rich soil but also grow in dry alkaline conditions. Propagation is by division in spring, seed sown while it is still fresh, or root cuttings taken in early winter.

A. × hybrida

Japanese anemones include several species and hybrids. *A. × hybrida* is the main group, although cultivars of *A. hupehensis* and *A. japonica* are also regularly seen.

Single white forms (next column)
White-flowered forms are particularly good at brightening dull corners. It is hard to distinguish between the various forms. *A. × hybrida* 'Alba' is a general name represented by 'Honorine Jobert' and its seedling 'Lady Adilaun,' both of which are excellent whites.

Anemone × hybrida 'Honorine Jobert'

Anemone hupehensis 'Bressingham Glow'

Single pink forms (above)
The pink forms are more variable in their color. *A. hupehensis* 'Bressingham Glow' has delicate rosy pink flowers. *A. h.* 'Hadspen Abundance' has deeper rosy pink flowers. *A. × hybrida* 'Queen Charlotte' ('Königin Charlotte') bears large flowers in medium pink.

Double forms
There are several double forms that lack the simplicity of the single varieties but have a charm of their own. *A. × hybrida* 'Margarete' is a semidouble pink.

ANTHEMIS
Anthemis

This genus offers the gardener a good range of daisies. Each flower has a typical daisy shape, with a central yellow disk surrounded by ray petals of either white or various shades of yellow and orange. The finely cut, aromatic leaves also help to make these good border plants. Their only drawback is that they are not long-lived, especially on wet soil, and so need yearly propagation to keep them going.

Anthemis needs well-drained soil and a sunny site to give its best. The taller forms need to be staked. Stock can be increased by taking cuttings in spring, and species can be grown from seed sown at the same time of year.

A. punctata subsp. cupaniana

Easy to grow, this sprawling plant roots as it spreads, but it can easily be cut back and so is not invasive. It has white flowers in spring and early summer and silver foliage.

A. sancti-johannis

For gardeners who like hot colors, this plant is an essential for the border. The flowers are a strong golden orange, and the foliage is delicately shaped. Together they make this a desirable plant.

Anthemis tinctoria 'Grallach Gold'

A. tinctoria (above)

The golden marguerite has yellow flowers. However, it is not the species but mainly its cultivars that are grown. 'E.C. Buxton' has pale lemony flowers, while

'Sauce Hollandaise' and 'Wargrave' have creamy yellow ones. As a contrast, 'Grallach Gold' has golden yellow flowers and 'Kelwayi' bright yellow ones.

AQUILEGIA
Columbine

Columbines are old-fashioned favorites. The flowers are like miniature ballet dancers with frilly skirts and arms held above their heads. They are available in a range of colors and come in double and single forms. There is also a wide range of heights, from a few inches to 3 ft (90 cm).

Columbines grow in any fertile garden soil and flourish in either full sun or light shade. The taller plants do not generally need staking. They tend to self-sow. Old flowering stems should be cut down before seed is shed. Because they cross easily, self-sown seedlings do not necessarily come true, although they frequently produce exciting new forms. Propagate from seed sown in spring or preferably in summer when fresh.

Aquilegia viridiflora

Species (above and next column)
A number of straight species are suitable for the border. *A. alpina* is a medium-height species which has nodding blue flowers, often with white inner skirts. *A. canadensis* is taller with small red-and-yellow flowers. *A. formosa* is similar. *A. chrysantha* is also a taller species,

with yellow flowers; many of the long-spurred hybrids are derived from this beautiful plant. *A. fragrans* is a medium-height plant with pale blue, slightly fragrant flowers and purple stems. *A. viridiflora* is one of the most intriguing; it is very short, rarely more than 1 ft (30 cm), and has beautiful lovat-green flowers. *A. vulgaris* has been grown in gardens for generations and has produced many good cultivars, mainly in blues and purples, including some delightful doubles (see below).

Aquilegia alpina

Old-fashioned forms
Many of the old short-spurred cultivars, derived mainly from *A. vulgaris*, are still in existence. 'Adelaide Addison' is a nodding blue columbine with double white skirts. 'Nivea,' also known as 'Munstead White,' has pure white flowers and pale green leaves. 'Nora Barlow' is a double with spiky petals in cream, red, and green. 'Hensol Harebell' is a rich violet-blue. 'Vervaeneana' has mixed flower colors, with leaves that are splashed with golden variegations.

Modern hybrids
Modern hybrids, many with long spurs, have come from a number of species. 'Crimson Star' has red flowers with white lower petals. 'Dragonfly Hybrids' are long-spurred columbines in a

mixture of red, blue, and yellow, some in one color, others bicolored. They look spectacular but tend to be short-lived and may have to be replaced after 2–3 years. 'McKana Hybrids,' also long-spurred, come in a similar color range.

ARABIS
Rock cress

This large genus has 100 species. Many should be considered weeds due to their general appearance. However, some are suitable for the garden. These are generally low-growing, carpeting plants that are best suited to the front of a border, especially where it edges a path or patio. The four-petaled flowers are small and usually either white or pink. The plants bloom in spring, but some species have sufficiently attractive leaves for them to count as foliage plants for the rest of the year.

Rock cress grows in most garden soils but does best in those that are well drained. A sunny site is required. Once the plants have finished flowering, trim them with shears to prevent them from becoming straggly. Propagate in spring by division or by taking cuttings.

Arabis caucasica 'Variegata'

A. caucasica (above)
This is the most commonly grown species of rock cress; it is also sometimes listed as *A. albida*. It forms low mats of rosettes that spread rapidly yet is not

invasive. The leaves are gray-green in color. The flowers are pure white, appearing in spring. 'Flore Pleno' has double flowers. 'Snow Cap' is particularly floriferous. 'Variegata' has cream variegations on the leaves.

A. ferdinandi-coburgii

This is a more refined version of *A. caucasica*. It forms a ground-hugging carpet with narrow green leaves and short spikes of small white or occasionally pink flowers. 'Old Gold' has golden yellow variegations on the leaves, while 'Variegata' has creamy stripes.

ARTEMISIA
Mugwort

Of the 400 species in this genus only a handful make good garden plants. They vary considerably in height and character, with the majority being grown more for their foliage than their flowers. Those with silver foliage are particularly useful, especially in creating white borders or for combining with soft pinks and purples. The foliage is often aromatic. The flowers are generally very small and dirty yellow in color. Many gardeners remove the flowers on sight, as they can destroy the otherwise beautiful foliage effect.

All artemisias need well-drained soil and a sunny spot. Many of the taller species benefit from being staked if they are in a windy site. They should be cut back in the early spring, once the new growth can be located. Propagation can be achieved by careful division or, more easily, by taking cuttings in spring.

Tall forms (next column)
A. absinthium 'Lambrook Silver' is one of the best silver-leaved plants. It grows to 2 ½ ft (75 cm) and has finely divided leaves. *A. lactiflora* is different from all the other species in that it has green foliage and attractive spikes of creamy yellow flowers. In the cultivar 'Guizhou'

the leaves are heavily flushed with purple. In *A. ludoviciana* var. *latiloba* the leaf segments are much broader than in the other tall forms and are pewter in color. In 'Silver Queen' the leaves are silvery in color.

Artemisia absinthium 'Lambrook Silver'

Bushy forms
A. canescens and its cultivars are low bushy shrubs 1½ ft (45 cm) high, with finely divided silvery foliage. They make good ground covers. *A. pontica* is slightly taller and more upright. It also makes a dense cover but can become invasive. Its foliage is gray-green.

Prostrate forms
Some forms make excellent covers for the front of a border. *A. schmidtiana* creates a compact, widely spreading mound whose flower stems reach approximately 6 in–1 ft (15–30 cm) high. 'Nana' is one of the most compact forms. *A. stelleriana* can grow a little taller than *A. schmidtiana*. 'Mori,' however, is a prostrate cultivar and has white foliage, as does 'Silver Brocade.'

ARUNCUS
Goatsbeard

The goatsbeards offer double value as plants, since they can be grown for their foliage and flowers. The foliage is deeply cut and produced in great fountains. The

tiny flowers are held in large, fluffy sprays and are either white or cream.

These plants do well in most soils and grow in either sun or shade. In a sunny spot, however, they do better in moisture-retentive soil, as the leaves wilt if the plants become too dry. They are clump forming but not invasive. They rarely need staking and can be increased by division.

A. aethusifolius

This is a less commonly seen species. It is low-growing, reaching only 8 in (20 cm) high. It has finely cut leaves and cream flowers in short spikes. It spreads to form a noninvasive carpet.

A. dioicus (below)

This is the species frequently grown in gardens. It is tall, reaching up to 7 ft (2.1 m) in fertile conditions. The leaves are composed of numerous oval leaflets. In the form 'Kneifii,' however, the leaves are very deeply cut, producing an impression of being lacerated. This cultivar is half the height of its parent.

Aruncus dioicus

ASARUM
Wild ginger

These plants are grown for their shiny green foliage, which is rounded or heart-shaped. They are low-growing plants, rarely rising above a height of 9 in (23 cm), and spread underground, making a dense ground cover. The flowers have a pitcher-like shape and are deep purple in color. Unfortunately, however, they usually appear beneath the thick covering of leaves and are not easy to see.

Wild gingers are woodland plants that thrive when allowed to creep around in moist, humus-rich soil in light to deep shade. They are very good plants for growing in a shady border. They do not tolerate dry conditions. Propagation is by division in spring. They self-sow easily.

A. canadense

Canadian ginger has large heart-shaped leaves. It is deciduous.

A. caudatum

This semi-evergreen species has very dark green, glossy leaves. The flowers have taillike lobes.

Asarum europaeum

A. europaeum (above)

This is a smaller-leaved form than the others mentioned, but the foliage is an attractive glossy green and remains on the plant throughout the year.

ASCLEPIAS
Milkweed

Native to North America, this large genus offers a few plants that make good garden choices, but others can sometimes become troublesome pests (*A. syriaca*,

for example), as they tend to spread invasively. The flowers of milkweed form a wonderful spread of color, with flat heads of bright red, pink, or orange that brighten any border. The blooms are carried on erect stems that are strong enough to stand without extra support. The seeds that follow have tufts of silky hairs. The stems ooze a milky sap when broken, hence the common name.

Milkweeds grow in any garden soil and prefer a sunny position. They can be propagated from seed or by division.

A. incarnata

This attractive plant has pink flowers that appear in summer on 3–4 ft (90 cm–1.2 m) stems. It likes a moister soil than the other garden species.

A. tuberosa (below)

In late summer this species has bright orange flowers that look exceptional in a border emphasizing hot colors. It is shorter than *A. incarnata*, growing to a height of 2 ½ ft (75 cm), and requires drier soil.

Asclepias tuberosa

A. tuberosa 'Gay Butterflies'

This is a seed strain producing mixed colors, including pink, red, gold, and orange. The "butterflies" in the name refers to the fact that butterflies are attracted to this plant.

ASPERULA
Woodruff

In this large genus of plants, the majority of the garden forms are grown in rock gardens. There are, however, a few types that are suitable for shady borders and are especially good as ground covers under shrubs or trees. Woodruffs produce masses of sprawling stems, each carrying whorls of narrow leaves and heads of tiny, starlike white or pink flowers.

Although these are mainly woodland plants, they grow in a sunny spot if the soil is moisture retentive. After flowering they may need cutting back. For propagation, they can be easily divided.

Asperula odorata

A. odorata (above)

Also known as *Gallium odoratum*, this is a woodland plant. Its white flowers can be used to brighten up a shady spot during early summer. It climbs through shrubs and reaches a height of 1½ ft (45 cm). The stems and leaves have the scent of fresh hay.

ASPHODELINE
Jacob's rod

These fascinating plants are good choices for a sunny border. From clumps of untidy, grasslike foliage emerge tall stems carrying starlike yellow flowers. These each have six or seven narrow petals and measure over 1 in (2.5 cm) wide. The flowers open successively up the spike and are followed by attractive seedpods, giving the plants a long season of interest. They will make dramatic clumps when positioned in the middle of a border and go especially well with blue-flowered plants.

Jacob's rods need well-drained soil and a sunny spot, sheltered from strong winds. They can be easily propagated by division or from seed.

A. lutea (below)

This is the main species in cultivation. It grows to 4 ft (1.2 m) high. The bright yellow flowers are fragrant and emerge from buff-colored bracts. The plants are in flower from late spring through early summer.

Asphodeline lutea

ASPHODELUS
Asphodel

This genus is frequently confused with *Asphodeline* because of the similarity of both the name and the general appearance of the plants. The leaves are slightly wider than those of Jacob's rod but are just as untidy. The spikes are much denser, but they produce the same kind of starry flowers as Jacob's rod, although they are either white or pink in color rather than yellow.

Asphodels require well-drained soil and a sunny site. Propagate by division in the spring or from seed in fall.

A. aestivus

Also known as *A. microcarpus*, this is one of the less common asphodels. It grows to a height of about 3 ft (90 cm) and in late spring carries dense spikes of white flowers that often display flushes of pink when in bud.

Asophodelus albus

A. albus (above)

This is the most common species in cultivation. It is much taller than *A. aestivus*, growing to 5 ft (1.5 m) in good conditions. The flowers are white but sometimes tinged with pink.

A. fistulosus

This is the shortest of the three species, reaching only 1½ ft (45 cm). It has narrow green leaves and, in summer, spikes of white stars flushed with pink.

ASPLENIUM
Spleenwort

This is a very large genus of ferns. The fronds, their main feature, vary in size, shape, and texture from species to species. Many have deeply divided leaflets, while in others the leaf is whole. Nearly all these ferns have a leathery appearance, and all of them are evergreen.

The majority grow best in a cool, shady location, preferably in humus-rich soil, although others do well in the barren conditions of stone walls.

A. scolopendrium (below)

Sometimes listed as *Phyllitis scolopendrium*, the hart's-tongue fern is named for its straplike, undivided fronds, which look very similar to tongues. The color is a shiny light green to midgreen. These ferns grow in cool, shady conditions and offer a good contrast to clumps of other ferns with the more usual cut-leaved fronds. The many forms of this plant include a number in cultivation since the late 19th century.

'Cristatum' has unusual forks at the tips of the blades. 'Crispum' has undulating margins; 'Undulatum' also has undulating margins, but less pronounced than those of 'Crispum.'

Asplenium scolopendrium

ASTER
Aster

A popular genus with gardeners, asters encompass a wide range of plants, from dwarf ones for the front of the border, to stately ones, which can look very attractive at the back. They flower from early summer onward, with some cultivars flowering until well into the fall, providing for a long period of color in the garden.

The majority have yellow central disks surrounded by narrow petals, mainly in blues and purples, although there are also pinks, reds, and whites. Flower size varies from 2 in (5 cm) or more to tiny ones of less than ½ in (12.5 mm), but the small size of the latter is made up for by the large quantity in which they appear. Most make good cut flowers.

Asters grow in any good garden soil but do best in soil that is not too dry. An open, sunny site suits them best. The taller forms need staking in windy, exposed spots. The main problem is mildew, which can be treated with a fungicidal spray. Propagation is easily achieved by division in fall or spring.

A. amellus cultivars (below)

The flowers of this species are among the largest in the genus. Its many cultivars make superb border plants with a very long season, from late summer onward. These asters can reach a height of up to 2½ ft (75 cm). 'King George' has large purple flowers, 'Nocturne' dark blue ones, and 'Violet Queen' ('Veilchenkönigin') rich violet ones.

Aster amellus 'King George'

A. × frikartii

These hybrids between *A. amellus* and *A. thomsonii* are excellent border plants with a long flowering season. The best include 'Mönch,' with lavender-blue petals, and 'Wünder von Stafa,' which is a slightly paler color.

A. novae-angliae cultivars

These Michaelmas daisies—the New England asters—are less prone to mildew than the *A. novi-belgii* cultivars. They are also generally taller, reaching a maximum height of approximately 5 ft (1.5 m). There is a wide choice of cultivars, all of which flower in the fall. 'Andenken an Alma Pötschke' is a superb plant with bright rosy pink flowers. 'Autumn Snow' ('Herbstschnee') has pure white flowers, 'Harrington's Pink' clear pink, 'Hella Lacy' ('Treasure') deep violet, 'Lye End Beauty' cerise-lilac, 'Purple Dome' purple, 'Rosa Seiger' mauve-pink, and 'September Ruby' ('Septemberrin') red-purple.

Aster novi-belgii 'Little Pink Beauty'

A. novi-belgii cultivars (above)

New York asters make up the largest group of Michaelmas daisies. Within this group there are several hundred cultivars to choose from. They vary considerably in height from 6 in (15 cm) to 4 ft (1.2 m). Those to be recommended include 'Audrey' (lavender flowers), 'Bonningale White' (white), 'Climax' (light violet), 'Coombe Violet' (violet), 'Crimson Brocade' (purple-red), 'Eventide' (violet), 'Goliath' (mauve), 'Jenny' (bright red), 'Lady in Blue' (blue), 'Little Pink Beauty' (pink), 'Marie Ballard' (light blue, double), 'Professor Anton Kippenberg' (midblue), 'Purple Dome' (violet-purple), 'Royal Ruby' (ruby-red), and 'Snow Cushion' ('Schneekissen'; white).

Small-flowered forms (below)

There are a number of asters that produce small flowers, which are insignificant in themselves but create a beautiful hazy effect when seen in quantity. *A. divaricatus* has interesting wiry black stems and myriad white flowers, while *A. ericoides* produces clouds of flowers: 'Golden Spray' is a tall form, reaching a height of up to 4 ft (1.2 m), with creamy white petals and a large golden central disk; 'Pink Cloud' is a haze of pale pink. On *A. lateriflorus* 'Horizontalis' the branches stick out at right angles to the main stem. It has mauve flowers. *A. pringlei* 'Monte Cassino' (previously considered to be a form of *A. ericoides*) has white flowers. In *A. spectabilis* the flowers are violet-blue.

Aster lateriflorus 'Horizontalis'

ASTILBE

Astilbe

Astilbes are colorful plants that are useful for brightening a border over a long period. The flowers are produced in fluffy pyramids and come in a range of bright reds, purples, whites, and creams—some seeming almost luminous. When not in bloom they are still attractive, as they have ferny foliage, often tinged with purple. The majority grow to 2–4 ft (60 cm–1.2 m) tall, but there are also some dwarf forms.

These versatile plants are able to grow in both sun and light shade. It is important however, to give them a moisture-retentive soil, and they grow best if placed next to a pool or stream. They do not need staking. Propagate by division.

A. × arendsii

The species are rarely grown; it is the hybrids, in particular those known as A. × *arendsii*, that are usually seen. The flowers and foliage are available in a wide range of colors.

White forms (below)

The white forms need deadheading as soon as the flowers are over. The foliage is mainly bright green. 'Bridal Veil' ('Brautschleier') is pure white, growing to 2 ft (60 cm). 'Deutschland' is similar except that it flowers earlier than 'Bridal Veil.' 'Ellie' is creamier and taller than the other white forms.

Astilbe × arendsii 'Bridal Veil'

Pink forms

These vary in the intensity of color. 'Bressingham Beauty' offers a rich pink bloom for late summer. 'Erica' is bright pink and flowers earlier. 'Ostrich Plume' ('Straussenfeder') has large plumes of coral-pink in the middle of the astilbe season. 'Peach Blossom' flowers at a similar time but is pale pink and shorter than the others. 'Rheinland' is also compact in height, reaching 2 ft (60 cm); it has deep pink flowers early on.

Astilbe × arendsii 'Fire'

Red forms (above)

These are the brightest of the hybrids and need careful placing so that they do not clash with other colors. They frequently have purple foliage. 'Fanal' has bright red flowers carried in short, dense spikes and flowers early. 'Fire' ('Feuer') has coral-red flowers and grows taller. It flowers late. 'Red Sentinel' has deep carmine-red flowers on tall stems and flowers early.

A. chinensis

This is rarely grown as a species but is commonly seen in its varieties. *A. c.* var. *pumila* is a dwarf form that grows only 1 ft (30 cm) tall. It has mauve-pink flowers. As a contrast *A. c.* var. *tacquetii* 'Superba' grows up to 4 ft (1.2 m).

A. simplicifolia

This species is known for its cultivar 'Sprite.' It is a dwarf species with pink flowers and delicately cut foliage.

ASTRANTIA
Masterwort

Masterworts have an old-world charm that makes them ideal for cottage and similar gardens. The plants are 2 ft (60 cm) in height. The tiny flowers get their character from the petallike bracts that surround the central dome of each flower, giving the impression of a pincushion. In most species

the bracts and the center are pale green, giving the plant a cool appearance. In some of the cultivars, however, these are pink or even red. They come into flower in early summer, and some forms continue until late summer or early fall.

Masterworts grow well in sunny or lightly shaded locations, although they do especially well when grown in light shade. A moisture-retentive soil, enriched with well-rotted humus, is needed. These plants are moderately tall but they do not require staking. Propagation is carried out by division or by sowing seed.

Red forms

The red forms are becoming increasingly popular, and better types are constantly being sought. They often take longer to grow into a good-sized clump than the normal green forms. *A. carniolica* 'Rubra' is an old cultivar with green-and-crimson flowers. It is being challenged for depth of color by two newer cultivars, *A. major* 'Hadspen Blood' and the red-stemmed *A. m.* 'Ruby Wedding,' which both have rich wine-red flowers.

Astrantia maxima

Pink forms (above)

The pink forms of astrantia make excellent cut flowers. *A. major* var. *rosea* is a green form flushed with pink, while *A. maxima* is a magnificent plant with rose-pink triangular bracts around a rose-pink flower. *A. major* 'Buckland' is another good form with green-and-pink flowers.

Whitish forms

There are no true white forms: they are all a very pale green, usually flushed with a slightly darker green. The species *A. major* is very pale green and makes an excellent plant for a shady spot. Even better are the extremely large heads of the pale-colored 'Shaggy' (also known as 'Margery Fish'), which is named for its long bracts.

Variegated forms (below)

There is one excellent form with creamy variegations on its leaves. This is *A. major* 'Sunningdale Variegated.' The leaves become greener as the season progresses. The flowers are greenish pink and are usually removed, as they detract from the appeal of the foliage.

Astrantia major 'Sunningdale Variegated'

ATHYRIUM
Athyrium

The graceful ferns in this genus create a striking contrast with other plants. They include some of the most popular species for growing in a shady spot. They vary in height, but most garden forms are 2 ft (60 cm) tall.

These ferns are woodland plants that need moist soil containing leaf mold or humus. However, they will grow in drier conditions if necessary. Light dappled shade, such as that provided by deciduous shrubs and trees, is a suitable situation. These ferns can be increased either by sowing spores or by division.

Athyrium filix-femina

A. filix-femina (above)

This is the famous lady fern, a highly refined deciduous plant. The finely dissected pale green fronds arch gracefully from a gently creeping rootstock.

A. nipponicum var. pictum

The Japanese painted fern is as desirable as *A. filix-femina*. Its name comes from the "painted" appearance of its red-flushed stems and its fronds washed with silvery gray. This fern spreads gently, without becoming invasive, to form a moderate-sized colony.

AUBRIETA
Aubrieta

Aubrieta is one of the colorful signs that spring is under way. The plants form low mounds that are suitable for the front of a border or hanging over the edges of walls. The gray-green foliage sets off the various flower colors, which include blue, purple, pink, red, and white. The flowers have short stems, so they lie close to the foliage, covering it completely during a good season.

Aubrietas grow in nearly all garden conditions, even dry ones. However, they are most floriferous and compact if grown in an open, sunny spot. For the best results, trim the plants with shears once flowering is finished to keep them compact. Propagation can be achieved by taking cuttings from new growth or by sowing seed.

Cultivars (below)

There is a wide range of colors from which to choose. The selection is increased by the existence of some cultivars with double flowers and others with variegated leaves. The following list is a selection of the best. 'Aureovariegata' has gold-variegated leaves and lavender-blue flowers; 'Bob Saunders' is a purple-red double; 'Bressingham Pink' is a pink double; 'Dr. Mules' has deep violet-colored flowers; 'Greencourt Purple' is a purple double; and 'Red Carpet' is the best of the reds.

Aubretia 'Dr. Mules'

BAPTISIA
False indigo

This genus of plants from North America provides a few excellent garden varieties. *Baptisia* is a member of the pea family, and the flowers strongly resemble those of the pea. The range of flower colors includes blue, yellow, and white. These tall plants reach 4 ft (1.2 m), and although they are not invasive, they can take up a lot of room and so are not suitable for small borders.

These are deep-rooted plants that like deep, rich soil. They are, however, drought resistant and succeed in poorer conditions. They grow in either sun or light shade. In a windy spot they need staking. With their deep roots, they do not like to be moved or have digging take place around them. Propagation is carried out from seed or by careful division.

B. australis (below)
This is the main species in cultivation. Its popularity stems from the wonderful blue flowers it produces in early summer. It grows up to 4 ft (1.2 m).

Baptisia australis

BEGONIA
Begonia
This genus includes nearly 1,000 species, which mainly come from the tropics or subtropics. Because of their tenderness, most begonias are thought of as annuals. Most of these tender forms are perennial but are best overwintered in a greenhouse or raised every year from cuttings or seed.

B. evansia (next column)
Often listed as *B. grandis*, this species is hardy in many areas. It is a tuberous plant with pointed heart-shaped leaves and drooping clusters of pink flowers in summer. It likes a moist, humus-rich soil and light shade in hotter areas (zones 6–8). It is not long-lived, but mulching with straw helps to bring it through a cold winter. Propagation is by division.

Begonia evansia

BELLIS
Daisy
Some daisies can prove to be troublesome, especially in lawns. Others, usually with double flowers, are desirable border plants. These plants have been grown by generations of cottage gardeners and are often used to line paths. Uniform in height and color, they are often used as bedding plants, although they are perennials.

Bellis perennis 'Dresden China'

B. perennis forms (above)
This is the weed of lawns, but there are any number of very good cultivars. The flower stems grow only 6 in (15 cm) high, and the plants form neat rosettes of leaves. If kept permanently in the border, make certain that they do not self-seed because they will produce unattractive hybrid forms. Some cultivars have large flowers, usually white with touches of red or pink, but the best are neat, buttonlike doubles, such as the soft-pink 'Dresden China.' 'Prolifera' (also known as 'Hen and Chickens') grows secondary flower heads, which appear out of the first.

BERGENIA
Bergenia
For ground-cover plants, few can surpass bergenias, yet they are also very attractive plants in their own right. They are distinguished by large, rounded leaves that are leathery in texture and often glossy. These come in various shades of green but also occur in purples, especially during winter. The flowers appear in short, bold spikes up to 1½ ft (45 cm) in height, with the predominant color being red in its various shades, although there are also white forms. These flowers appear from spring until early summer. Bergenias are good year-round plants.

Not only are they versatile in their foliage and flowering, but bergenias are also accommodating in their requirements. They grow in either sun or shade and tolerate both dry and moist soils. Every 5 years some gardeners like to dig them up, improve the soil, and then replant them, but many other gardeners leave them in the same spot almost indefinitely, another factor in their favor. They can be propagated by division or by taking sections of the rhizomes as root cuttings.

Foliage types (next column)
Although they all have good foliage, there are certainly some that are better than others. *B.* 'Bressingham Ruby' has ruby foliage throughout most of the year

and bright pink flowers. *B. cordifolia* 'Purpurea' has very large leaves that take on an attractive purple coloration in winter. It has bright magenta flowers. *B.* 'Perfect' (also known as 'Perfecta') has purple leaves and deep pink flowers on long stems.

Bergenia cordifolia 'Purpurea'

Reddish-flowered forms

There are several cultivars that are especially noted for their fine reddish colored flowers. *B.* 'Ballawley' has bright crimson flowers and good purple foliage in winter; *B. cordifolia* has deep pink or magenta flowers and large leaves. *B.* 'Evening Glow' ('Abendglut') is one of the best, with rich purple flowers and small leaves that turn purple in winter. *B.* 'Red Beauty' has red flowers.

White-flowered forms

White forms are not so numerous, and some are tinged with pink. However, *B.* 'Bressingham White' is an almost pure white form. *B. stracheyi* 'Alba' is a short form, reaching only 10 in (25 cm) high, with good white flowers.

BLECHNUM

Blechnum

There are approximately 200 species of this fern, most of them from tropical or subtropical regions. A few, however, are hardy and make good garden plants. They spread slowly to create large colonies. The fronds are deeply cut and mainly evergreen, although those that produce spores fade and become unattractive and should be removed.

Blechnums need moist, humus-rich soil, preferably in a shady spot. They do best in a slightly acidic soil. Blechnums look particularly attractive when planted next to water. They are not completely hardy and need a winter mulch to protect them in colder areas. Propagation is by division or from spores.

B. penna-marina

This fern has very slender, dark green fronds, giving it a delicate appearance. It spreads to form a dense ground cover, but it is the least hardy of the group.

B. spicant

Known as the hard fern, this is a larger version of *P. penna-marina*, growing to as much as 2½ ft (75 cm) in height. It is a hardier plant and can cope with drier conditions. Its leaves are dark green and glossy.

B. tabulare

This is a very similar species to *B. magellanicum*, with which it is often confused. It has large fronds, reaching up to 3 ft (90 cm), and leathery leaflets. It forms substantial colonies.

BOLTONIA

Boltonia

This genus is often overshadowed by its similar-looking relations, the Michaelmas daisies (*Aster*). Boltonias are attractive plants, however, and well worth growing in their own right. The flowers are typical daisies with yellow central disks and rays of white, pink, or lilac petals. The flowers measure only ¾ in (2 cm) wide but are carried in large numbers in loose clusters. The height of the plants varies from 2 ft (60 cm) to 7 ft (2.1 m).

Boltonias grow in any good garden soil but do better in well-drained soil. They grow best in full sun, although they tolerate very light shade. They need support only in exposed places. Increase by dividing the plants in spring.

B. asteroides (below)

This is the main species in cultivation. It is tall, growing up to 7 ft (2.1 m), but some of its cultivars are much smaller. The color of the flowers varies, with a choice of white, pink, or lilac. In *B. a.* var. *latisquama* the flowers are lilac and also relatively large. 'Pink Beauty' has pink flowers. 'Snowbank,' on the other hand, has white flowers and is one of the shorter cultivars available, reaching only 4 ft (1.2 m) in height.

Boltonia asteroides

BORAGO

Borage

This genus is best known for its annual culinary herb, *B. officinalis,* but there are two other species, one of which is suitable for the border.

B. pygmaea (next page)

Until recently this species was known as *B. laxiflora*. It is a loose-growing plant with rough leaves and small nodding flowers. These flowers are a beautiful soft blue. Although *B. pygmaea* is a lax plant, unable to support itself, it does well when grown through a low shrub. A taprooted plant that resents being transplanted or having its roots disturbed, it grows in any garden soil that is not too dry, and it grows equally well in sun and light shade. This species of borage is easily propagated from seed, and there are usually plenty of self-sown seedlings that can be transplanted.

Borago pygmaea

BRUNNERA
Brunnera

This is a small genus of three species, of which only *B. macrophylla* is grown in gardens. Originating in southwestern Asia, these plants have loose spirals of blue forget-me-not flowers.

Brunneras grow in any good garden soil but prefer a moisture-retentive soil. These woodland plants do best in light shade but can grow in full sun if the soil is not allowed to dry. Propagate by division between fall and spring.

B. macrophylla (next column)

This species, sometimes known as Siberian bugloss (although it does not come from Siberia), grows to 1½ ft (45 cm) high and spreads to make an effective ground cover with its large, slightly hairy leaves. Although it spreads rapidly, it is not invasive, as it can easily be controlled by pulling it up. The blue flowers make a magnificent display in

spring, when they are held in airy sprays well above the leaves. Once the flowers are over, the leaves are attractive enough to maintain the plant's interest. There are several cultivars that are widely grown. 'Betty Bowring' is a beautiful white-flowered form. 'Dawson's White' (previously known as 'Variegata') has variegated foliage with wide, pale cream, almost white margins. 'Hadspen Cream' is similar, but the variegations are creamier in color. 'Langtrees' has silver spots on the leaves. The variegated forms have a tendency to brown if exposed to strong sunlight.

Brunnera macrophylla 'Dawson's White'

BUPHTHALMUM
Oxeye

In this small genus of European plants, only one species, *B. salicifolium,* has entered general cultivation. Another, *B. speciosum,* has had its name changed to *Telekia speciosa*; it can become an invasive pest. All the species have yellow daisylike flowers, but their foliage is often coarse and unattractive, which is why only one is grown to any extent.

Buphthalmum grows in any garden soil, although it prefers a position in either sun or light shade. Oxeyes are weak plants and therefore require staking in all but the most sheltered spots. They can be propagated either by division or by sowing seed in spring.

B. salicifolium (below)

This species is named for its willowlike leaves, *Salix* being the willow genus. It grows to 2 ft (60 cm) and carries masses of rich golden yellow daisies throughout summer and into fall. It makes a very good plant for a border based on hot colors. Although it slowly spreads to form large clumps, it is not invasive.

Buphthalmum salicifolium

CALAMINTHA
Calamint

The plants in this genus are good for the front of a border. They belong to the mint family and have loose heads of typical lipped, tubular flowers, which are usually pink or white. The plants are short; they can reach 2 ft (60 cm) in height when grown in rich conditions but are often much shorter. The flowers provide an effective contrast with the dark to light green foliage, which is aromatic when it is crushed.

All calamints need well-drained soil and an open, sunny site. They dislike wetness and may die if the conditions are too damp during winter, so protect the plants if necessary. Propagate in spring from cuttings or by careful division.

C. grandiflora (next column)

This species forms a small bush with dark green, coarse-toothed, aromatic leaves. The flowers are deep pink and smother the plant in summer and fall. 'Variegata' offers leaves with a speckled creamy variegation.

Calamintha grandiflora 'Variegata'

C. nepeta

This is a smaller plant than the previous species, reaching only 1½ ft (45 cm) high. It has lighter green leaves, which have a delicate scent, and the flowers are white or blue. It is hardy but dislikes wetness in winter, so it is essential to grow it in well-drained soil.

CALTHA
Marsh marigold

These plants are the glory of spring. They produce a mass of golden buttercup-type flowers that brighten the dullest days and show up well against the dark green of the large, rounded leaves. They are spreading plants that can grow to approximately 2 ft (60 cm) in height.

As their common name implies, these plants enjoy wet, marshy conditions. Although they grow in ordinary border soil as long as it remains moist, they do best if they are planted along the edges of a pond or stream. They thrive in a sunny spot but are equally at home in light shade, especially when planted under deciduous trees or shrubs that are not yet in leaf when the marsh marigold flowers. Propagation is carried out by sowing seed while it is still fresh or by division.

C. palustris (below)

This species is widespread, being found from the Arctic to the Himalayas and from North America to Europe and on to Japan. Some authorities say that many other members of the genus are in fact this species in slightly different guises. *C. palustris* is as widespread in gardens as in the wild. The species has golden yellow flowers, but there are forms with paler petals. *C. p.* var. *alba*, for example, has almost white flowers. There is also a good double-petaled form, 'Flore Pleno.'

Caltha palustris 'Flore Pleno'

CAMPANULA
Bellflower

This genus includes 300 species, of which a surprising number are in cultivation. They vary in height from ground-hugging types to ones that reach 5 ft (1.5 m) or more. The flowers that give the genus its Latin and its common name are shaped like bells. In most species they hang down, but in some they are held up, so that you can see right into the bells. The predominant color of the petals is blue, but this varies in shade from very pale to very dark and includes some purple tones. As with nearly all blue-flowered plants, there are also white forms of bellflowers available.

Most bellflowers thrive in well-drained soil enriched with rotted organic material. These plants need either full sun or light shade, the white forms of some species looking especially good under trees. The majority do best, however, if they are planted in an open location. The species can all be propagated by seed or from cuttings, but the cultivars must be propagated vegetatively (for example, by leaf cuttings or division) if they are to come true to color and form.

Campanula portenschlagiana

Short forms (above)

There are a number of low-growing bellflowers that make admirable plants for the front of a border, especially along a path or on the edge of a patio. *C. carpatica* is a bushy plant growing to about 1 ft (30 cm) high. It has open, saucer-shaped bells that mainly face upward and come in various shades of blue, as in 'Blue Clips' ('Blaue Clips'), which has midblue flowers. White forms include 'Alba.' *C. isophylla* has smaller, shallow, upward-facing blue or white flowers. It is not so hardy (zone 8). *C. lactiflora* 'White Pouffe' has white flowers on a short form that reaches only 1 ft (30 cm). *C. portenschlagiana* is a rampant ground-cover plant with blue flowers; its cultivar 'Resholt' has larger, lighter blue flowers. An even more rampant spreader is *C. poscharskyana*. It is only approximately 6 in (15 cm) tall but can scramble up through shrubs. It carries masses of starry blue flowers.

Campanula glomerata 'Superba'

Medium-height forms (above)
There are many good garden species
that fall within this group. *C. alliariifolia*
has distinctive heart-shaped leaves and
attractive blue bell-shaped flowers. In
the form 'Ivory Bells' they are creamy
white. The species *C. glomerata,* known
as the clustered bellflower, has its flowers grouped together in clusters. The best
form is 'Superba,' which can reach
up to approximately 3 ft (90 cm) tall,
while others are only half this height.
C. punctata can spread invasively by
underground runners, but the form
'Elizabeth,' with its reddish bells, is
better behaved. *C. rotundifolia* varies in
stature and can be used as a rock or
border plant. It has delicate hanging
bells carried on slender stems. 'Alba' has
white bells. *C. takesimana* is another
runner, but its large pink bells, which are
flushed with reddish purple, make it
worth growing and controlling. It will
need to be supported.

Tall forms (next column)
Most tall forms need staking to prevent
them from falling over under the weight
of flowers. *C. lactiflora* is one of the
most spectacular of these forms, with
large heads of upward-facing bells on
5 ft (1.5 m) stems. 'Loddon Anna' has
pink flowers instead of the more usual
blue ones.

C. latifolia grows to approximately 3 ft
(90 cm) in height and has spikes of blue
flowers. 'Brantwood' is one of the best
cultivars, with deep blue flowers over a
long period. 'Gloaming' has smoky blue
flowers. The similarly named *C. latiloba*
also has flowers arranged in spikes, but
they are denser than those of *C. latifolia*;
the flowers are also more open and
saucer-shaped. They are generally blue in
color, but in 'Hidcote Amethyst' they are
lilac-pink. 'Highcliffe' is a strong plant
with lavender-colored flowers.
C. persicifolia is very similar in general
appearance to *C. latiloba*, but the flowers are carried on short stalks attached
to the main stem and the plants are less
robust. It has a large number of cultivars: 'Alba' has white flowers; 'Chettle
Charm' has pretty white flowers that are
edged with blue; the equally charming
'Hampstead White' has semidouble
white flowers; 'Telham Beauty' has large
single flowers that are lavender-blue.

Campanula latifolia 'Brantwood'

CAREX
Sedge
Sedges are very similar to grasses in both
appearance and garden use. Grasses have
hollow stems and sedges solid ones, but
the most obvious difference is the sedges'
triangular stems. Another noticeable
difference is that the leaves of the sedges
form a cylinder around the stem, whereas
in grasses the leaves wrap around the stem
with overlapping edges. In general appearance sedges look like clumps of grass
with fountains of narrow leaves. The various species of *Carex* are grown primarily
for the attractive color of their leaves,
which range from green to bronze and
can be variegated.

Sedges grow in any good garden soil
but do best in a moisture-retentive soil.
Many look especially good when grown
next to water. They can be increased by
division in spring.

Carex buchananii

C. buchananii (above)
Buchanan's sedge grows to about 1½ ft
(45 cm) high and erupts in a fountain of
narrow leaves that are bronze beneath
and creamy green or pinkish on top. It
does well when it is grown toward the
front edge of a border.

C. comans 'Bronze Form'
Originally from New Zealand, this sedge
forms a lax clump that grows up to
2 ft (60 cm) tall. The bronze-colored
leaves are fine and hairlike.

C. hajijoensis 'Evergold'
Also known as *C. morrowii* 'Evergold,'
this brightly colored sedge has gold variegations running along the center of its
green leaves. The leaves are up to 1½ ft
(45 cm) long.

C. *morrowii* 'Variegata'

This plant is similar to C. *hajijoensis* 'Evergold,' but with white variegation that runs down the edges of the leaves.

C. *pendula*

This is a large sedge with drooping flowers hanging from long, thin stems. In wet conditions the plant can grow up to 4 ft (1.2 m) tall. The leaves are broad and dark green in color. This is a graceful plant but can self-sow too readily.

C. *riparia* 'Variegata'

The greater pond sedge is usually grown in its variegated form, which produces 2 ft (60 cm) high clumps of white-striped leaves. In some cases the variegation is so strong that the whole leaf appears white. The plant is attractive but can become invasive through spreading roots.

CENTAUREA

Knapweed

Only a fraction of the 600 species in this superb genus of plants are in cultivation. Those that are make excellent border plants, with flowers that can be cut either for arrangements or for drying. The thistle-like flowers each have a central disk and an outer ring of petals, which are often dissected and feathery. They range in color from purples to yellows and whites. Most knapweeds flower in early summer. A distinctive feature of the plant is that the flowers are held in a hard, rounded calyx. The foliage is not especially attractive, although in some cases it can create a good foil for the flowers.

Knapweeds like well-drained soil and do particularly well on alkaline soil. Staking is often necessary. Propagation is either by division or from seed, although many will develop from root cuttings.

C. *bella*

This is one of the smaller species, growing to only 1 ft (30 cm). The foliage

forms a mat of finely cut silvery leaves, which are attractive in their own right. The flowers are soft purple, contrasting superbly with the foliage.

Centaurea dealbata 'Steenbergii'

C. *dealbata* 'Steenbergii' (above)

This form of the Persian cornflower has light green leaves that are gray on the undersides. The large flowers are rosy purple in color. The plant is floppy, however, and needs to be supported. It grows to about 2 ft (60 cm) in height. Its tendency to underground invasion can be a problem.

C. *macrocephala*

Commonly called the yellow hardhead, this plant has magnificent golden yellow flowers opening from large papery buds. The yellow looks good against the large midgreen leaves. The plant grows to 3 ft (90 cm) or more.

C. *montana*

The mountain knapweed is one of the first species to flower. It is a lax plant that needs support. The flowers are like large cornflowers with blue outer petals and red centers. They suffer badly from mildew and should be cut down after flowering to stimulate the growth of new foliage. 'Alba' is a good white form. 'Gold Bullion' is distinguished by the yellow on its leaves.

CENTRANTHUS

Red valerian

Although there are a dozen species in this genus, only one of them is usually grown. It is C. *ruber* (**below**), which is sometimes listed as *Kentranthus ruber*. This fleshy plant has gray-green stems and foliage and bears pyramidal heads of red flowers. It has long been a favorite in cottage gardens and often looks best when it is left to seed naturally, although it can be kept in a neat clump in the border. There is a white form, C. *r.* var. *alba,* which is sometimes listed as C. *r.* 'Snow Cloud.'

Although it grows best in garden soil, red valerian also thrives in poor conditions, where the plants are usually more compact. It does well in seaside gardens and can often be seen growing wild on beaches and adjacent wasteland. It will also grow on walls. Red valerian self-sows prolifically; cut it back after flowering to prevent this and to promote a second flush of flowers. Propagation can be from seed or by taking cuttings.

Centranthus ruber

CEPHALARIA

Cephalaria

The plants in this genus have scabious-like flowers. Indeed, many were formally considered part of the genus *Scabiosa*. They vary considerably in size, from tiny plants suitable for rock gardens, to the 7 ft (2.1 m) giant described on the next page.

The flowers are usually soft colors, mainly yellow and lilac-purple, and are very useful for pastel color schemes.

Cephalarias grow in any good garden soil and like an open, sunny site. Propagation can be achieved either from seed or by division, although this is more difficult with the larger plants.

C. gigantea (below)

This is the giant member of the genus, rising to a height of 7 ft (2.1 m) or more when grown in rich soil. The flowers appear in early summer and are a soft lemon-yellow, set off by the dark green leaves. The flowers are carried on tall, wiry stems, but in spite of its height, the plant does not require staking except in exposed areas. It has a tendency to self-sow prodigiously and should be cut back before this happens. It can have several taproots and resents being disturbed once planted.

Cephalaria gigantea

CERATOSTIGMA
Plumbago

Strictly speaking, most members of this genus are shrubs rather than perennials, but they are usually considered along with perennials as, like herbaceous plants, they die back to the ground in late fall. They are untidy shrubs, but their brilliant blue flowers are extremely appealing. Another point in their favor is that they flower in fall,

when good blues are in short supply. Their untidy habit can be countered effectively by growing them among other plants through which they can clamber.

Plumbagos need fertile, well-drained soil and a sunny site. They should be cut back almost to the ground after flowering in warmer areas, where the frost does not do the job for you. Propagation can be from cuttings or from seed, both of which should be carried out in spring.

Ceratostigma plumbaginoides

C. plumbaginoides (above)

This is a low plant only about 1 ft (30 cm) high, but it spreads and will scramble up through other plants, given the opportunity. The blue flowers stand out against the reddening fall leaves.

C. willmottianum

This plant is much taller than C. *plumbaginoides*, reaching 3 ft (90 cm). It also has blue flowers, but comes into bloom earlier, in late summer.

CHELONE
Turtlehead

The intriguing common name of this plant originates from the resemblance between the shape of the flowers and that of the head of a turtle. The flowers are fat tubes with thick lips and generally pink, purple, or white. The plants form clumps of stiffly erect stems, reaching up to 4 ft (1.2 m),

which makes them suitable for the center of a border. They generally flower late in the season, filling gaps toward the end of summer and into fall.

Turtleheads grow in any good garden soil, but they grow best in a moisture-retentive soil. They like sun but will tolerate light shade. They can be easily propagated by division in fall or spring. They can also be grown from seed.

C. lyonii

This is a pink-flowering species. The flowers are carried in dense spikes. In hot areas it grows best in shade.

C. obliqua (below)

This is similar to C. *lyonii* but is usually considered more decorative. The flowers are pink or white and appear over a long period. The plant has a strong constitution and will stand up to fall weather, flowering well into autumn.

Chelone obliqua

CIMICIFUGA
Bugbane

This plant provides tall, attractive spires of flowers late in the year and offers plenty of ferny foliage during the rest of the season. The unusual flowers have no petals but are, in fact, bunches of stamens, which when seen together make a spire of fluffy flowers, in either cream or white. The leaves are generally green, but some species have desirable purple foliage. These plants reach 6 ft (1.8 m) or more.

Bugbanes grow in any fertile garden soil but prefer a soil rich in rotted humus. A cool site that is lightly shaded is preferred, but the plants grow in full sun as long it is not too hot or too dry. They need staking only if grown in an exposed spot. Propagate by division or from seed. Plant at any time between fall and spring.

C. racemosa

This tall species grows to 6 ft (1.8 m). It has white flowers in midsummer and deeply divided fresh green leaves.

Cimicifuga simplex 'White Pearl'

C. simplex (above)

Although this is shorter than *C. racemosa*, growing to a maximum of only 4 ft (1.2 m), it is still an impressive plant, both for its flowers and for its foliage. It is the last species to flower, producing spires of white flowers in late fall. 'Atropurpurea' has dark purple foliage; 'Brunette' has bronze leaves; and 'White Pearl' has many white flowers.

CIRSIUM
Thistle

Most gardeners treat thistles as weeds, yet while some are pests, others are well behaved and attractive. They usually have pink or purple flowers and foliage that is tipped with spines.

Thistles are able to grow in any garden soil, even a poor one, but they do best in reasonably rich conditions. Sun suits them best. They can be readily increased by division or from seed, the latter in spring or when ripe.

Cirsium rivulare 'Atropurpureum'

C. rivulare 'Atropurpureum' (above)

This form of *C. rivulare* is the best thistle in cultivation. It has soft pincushion heads of the most sumptuous-looking crimson, which appear in early summer. The leaves look more prickly than they are. The plant grows to approximately 4 ft (1.2 m) high and spreads, although not invasively.

CLEMATIS
Clematis

Most gardeners think of clematis in terms of a woody, climbing plant, but there are a surprising number that are herbaceous, dying back to the ground each year, and they can be used in perennial borders. These may not be as spectacular as some of the climbing types, but they can still be very attractive. The flowers vary considerably in size and color, but those suitable for growing in borders are mainly blue or white. The leaves in some species can also be attractive.

Border clematises can be grown in any fertile garden soil, but it should be enriched with organic material. They like

to have their roots cool and their tops in sunlight, so shade the stem bases with other plants. Most border clematises are scramblers and need something to climb through; they can be supported either with twiggy sticks or by shrubs that have finished flowering. Some make attractive ground covers if left to sprawl across the ground. Propagation is from cuttings.

C. crispa

This climbing species from the Southeast dies back to the ground each winter. The single flowers on long stems are bell-shaped with reflexed petals. They are delightfully colored: blue with a white stripe down the center of each petal. The flowers appear from the summer onward.

Clematis × durandii

C. × durandii (above)

This plant is a hybrid between *C. integrifolia* and *C. jackmanii*. It is one of the larger-flowered herbaceous forms. The flowers are up to 5 in (13 cm) wide and are rich blue in color, appearing from late summer onward. The plants climb through shrubs, or they can be supported on sticks. They do best when cut all the way back to the ground each winter. If pruned to approximately 4 ft (1.2 m), however, they will act as climbers, growing to a height of 10 ft (3 m) or more.

C. × eriostemon (below)

This is a cross between *C. integrifolia* and *C. viticella*. It grows to about 8 ft (2.4 m) tall and requires a shrub for support. The flowers are nodding, open bells, colored an attractive purple-blue. They bloom from late summer onward.

Clematis × eriostemon

C. heracleifolia

This is one of the most commonly seen herbaceous clematises. It is generally left to grow over the ground from its woody base. The flowers are very similar in shape and color to those of a hyacinth. Blue and scented, they appear in fall. The foliage is large and coarse in texture, making a good ground cover.

C. integrifolia

The beautiful flowers of this clematis are like loose hanging bells, with four thin, twisted petals. They are purple-blue, with a prominent central boss of creamy white stamens, and appear in the late summer. The narrow leaves are lance-shaped. In a very sheltered site, this clematis is self-supporting, but it usually requires some form of support unless it is allowed to flop on the ground.

C. × jouiniana

This vigorous plant will clamber over shrubs and fences. The flowers are small, but what they lack in size they certainly make up for in numbers—at times the plant seems to be a haze of blooms. The soft blue flowers appear from late summer onward. There are several forms: 'Mrs. Robert Brydon' has milky white flowers; 'Praecox' has soft blue flowers that come into bloom much earlier than those of any other form.

CODONOPSIS
Bonnet bellflower

The bonnet bellflowers are not spectacular plants in terms of what they contribute to the overall appearance of the border, but looked at individually they are very attractive. They are members of the bellflower family, as can be seen from the shape of the flowers. The outside is usually blue, but when the flower is tipped up and the inside examined, an array of bright colors is exposed. They are mainly climbing plants that need a low shrub for support.

Plant in any good garden soil but preferably in moist conditions. Either sun or light shade suits bonnet bellflowers. They can be propagated by seed.

C. clematidea (below)

This is the species most commonly grown. The outside of the 1 in (2.5 cm) bells is pale blue, while inside are orange nectaries and crimson veining. The plant flowers in late summer and, in its preferred conditions, climbs to 4 ft (1.2 m).

Codonopsis clematidea

CONVALLARIA
Lily of the valley

The main species in this genus is the popular *C. majalis* (**below**). The fresh appearance and sweet scent of this plant have endeared it to generations of gardeners. It is an attractive, reliable plant. If it has any defects, it is that it can spread at an invasive rate, but it is not too difficult to control. In early spring large, erect oval leaves appear. These are soon followed by spikes of nodding bells that are held in the leaves like posies. The flowers are pure white and exude a sweet fragrance.

Lily of the valley is a woodland plant and enjoys moist, leafy soil and a cool root run in light shade. It spreads by underground shoots, which can be easily divided for propagation.

Convallaria majalis

Interesting forms

Several cultivars of *C. majalis* are worth planting. 'Fortin's Giant' is larger than the species, with broader leaves and large, stocky bells. It flowers later than its parent or other forms, making it possible to extend the lily of the valley's flowering season in the garden. 'Rosea' has soft lilac-pink flowers.

CONVOLVULUS
Convolvulus

Many of the species in this genus and its close relatives are considered weeds by a number of gardeners. The plants tend to spread underground at an alarming rate, but all have attractive flowers, even the worst pests. The funnel-shaped blooms are usually white but also come in pink and blue. *C. cneorum* (a shrub with white flowers and silver foliage) and the rock plant *C. sabatius* (blue flowers) are both safe plants to grow.

Convolvulus grows in any garden soil, even a poor one. It grows best in sun but may scramble into the light if planted in shade. Propagation is easily achieved either by division or from seed.

Convolvulus althaeoides

C. althaeoides (above)

If this were not such a beautiful plant, most gardeners would avoid it, but its soft pink flowers and finely cut gray foliage are too much of a draw. It runs vigorously underground but is often cut back by frosts. In warmer climates it must be contained to stop it from spreading.

COREOPSIS

Tickseed

Although there are over 120 species, very few of these plants are grown in cultivation. Those that are make a very valuable contribution to both summer and fall borders. They have yellow daisylike flowers that appear over a long period. All species make excellent cut flowers. The foliage is

bright green and sometimes finely cut. It contrasts well with the flowers.

Tickseeds grow in any fertile garden soil, but they do best in a sunny spot. The wiry stems are strong and need staking only if grown in an exposed location. Slugs attack the young growth, stunting the plants. Propagation is either by division or from seed, both in spring.

C. grandiflora (below)

This is one of the shorter species, normally reaching only about 2 ft (60 cm) high. It is not as hardy (zone 5) as other species and can die out in hot summers, so it is often treated as an annual. The flowers are golden yellow and 2 in (5 cm) or more in diameter. 'Baby Sun' ('Sonnenkind') is a popular cultivar that grows to only approximately 16 in (40 cm) and is suitable for a rock garden or as bedding. 'Brown Eyes' has a brown central disk. 'Early Sunrise' has frilly double flowers. 'Sunray' has very full double flowers.

Coreopsis grandiflora 'Early Sunrise'

C. rosea

Although most tickseeds need well-drained soil, this species prefers moister conditions. It is also unusual in that it has pink flowers. It grows to about 2 ft (60 cm). 'American Dream' is a popular form that is slightly shorter and has light pink flowers.

C. verticillata (below)

Of all tickseeds, this is the best species to grow. It is taller than the others, growing up to 3 ft (90 cm) in its preferred conditions, and has filigree leaves. The 2 in (5 cm) flowers are golden yellow and appear over a long season from summer onward. 'Grandiflora' has large flowers. In 'Moonbeam' the flowers are much paler than those of the parent plant. 'Zagreb' is shorter, reaching only 1 ft (30 cm) or so.

Coreopsis verticillata 'Moonbeam'

CORTADERIA

Pampas grass

This is a genus of large, stately grasses. They form huge fountains of narrow leaves, from which rise tall stems that carry large white plumes of flowers in the fall. These assertive plants are best used in isolation as focal points, although with care they can be incorporated into herbaceous or mixed borders.

Pampas grasses need moist soil that never becomes too dry. They also require a sunny location. The edges of the leaves are sharp, so do not plant them in gardens where children play. The leaves can cut the hands while weeding and can badly damage nearby plants when blown by the wind. Cut them to the ground in spring. Propagation is by division, although this is hard work because of their size and the compact nature of the clump.

C. selloana (below)

This is one of the best forms of pampas grasses, with thick, fluffy plumes in late summer and early fall. It is available in a wide variety of forms, ranging in height from 5 ft (1.5 m) to 10 ft (3 m). As well as forms with green foliage, there are ones that have gold-striped variegations. The flowers of *C. selloana* can be either white or pink.

Cortaderia selloana

CORTUSA
Cortusa

This genus is a small one, containing only eight species. Cortusas are closely related to primulas and are indeed often mistaken for them, as the flowers and foliage are similar. The flowers are either pink, purple, or yellow and are carried in drooping heads. The plants are approximately 1 ft (30 cm) high.

These are woodland plants and are not suited to hot, dry conditions. Plant them in cool, moist soil with plenty of leaf mold or other humus in it and a shady site. They can be increased either by division or from seed; the seeds should be as fresh as possible when sown.

C. matthioli

This is the species that is most commonly grown. It has reddish or purple-pink flowers and extremely hairy, dull green leaves. The small, pendent, bell-shaped flowers are held in one-sided flowering stalks. *C. m.* subsp. *pekinensis* has larger flowers and deeply cut, dull green leaves.

CORYDALIS
Corydalis

An increasing number of gardeners are discovering the delights of this genus of plants, and a large number of its species are now in cultivation.

Most types are too small or too difficult to cultivate for an open border, but there are a few that can be grown there. The flowers are tubular, each with a long spur and broad upper and lower lips. They come in a wide range of colors, with choices of blue, purple, pink, red, yellow, and white for the open border. The majority of corydalises are short, bushy plants, although some scramble up through other plants.

Most corydalis species prefer moist, leafy soil and grow best in light shade. They can be increased from seed sown as fresh as possible or by division.

Corydalis flexuosa

C. flexuosa (above)

Like many corydalis species, this one comes from China. It grows to 1 ft (30 cm) tall and has bronze-green foliage topped in spring with sprays of electric-blue flowers. Some forms have paler blue flowers than others.

COSMOS
Cosmos

Although this genus contains some 25 species, only one is cultivated in gardens as a perennial; the rest are either annuals or grown as such.

Cosmos are members of the daisy family and come from Mexico. They resemble the closely related dahlias, which also come from Mexico.

Cosmos atrosanguineus

C. atrosanguineus (above)

Known as the chocolate plant, both because of the rich brown color of its flowers and its chocolate fragrance, this is a valuable plant for the border, as there are few plants of its color.

The flowers closely resemble those of the dahlia and appear from late summer well into the fall. The foliage is also attractive. This cosmos reaches a height of up to 2½ ft (75 cm).

The plant needs deep, moisture-retentive soil and a sunny location. As with the dahlia, many gardeners prefer to lift the tubers and then store them under cover, in sand, over winter. The tubers can be left in the ground in milder areas, but remember that this plant is often late appearing above the soil, sometimes not before early summer. Propagation is by taking cuttings of the young growth as soon as possible in the year.

CRAMBE
Sea kale
These plants are very decorative in large borders, erupting in early summer in a cloud of small white flowers held in sprays that are often over 7 ft (2.1 m) high and just as wide. After it has flowered, sea kale can be considered as a foliage plant, since it forms a low mound of good foliage if it is not attacked by slugs or insects.

Sea kale likes well-drained soil; it will even tolerate poor conditions. In windy areas it may need some form of support. Taking root cuttings is the best method of propagation.

Crambe cordifolia

C. cordifolia (above)
This is the largest member of the genus, with enormous sprays of sweetly scented flowers. The leaves are large and dark green in color.

C. maritima
This sea kale is a much shorter plant than C. *cordifolia*, growing to only 3 ft (90 cm). It is grown as much for its glaucous blue-green foliage as its flowers. The foliage is particularly attractive when it first appears.

CYNARA
Cynara
In this genus of thistles, a few species are in cultivation, partly for their beautiful flowers but also because of their decorative foliage. The flowers are typically thistlelike, with purple heads held in a large, scaly calyx. The foliage in the ornamental species is often silver.

Cynaras grow in any good garden soil but prefer well-drained soil. They are increased by division or from seed.

C. cardunculus
Commonly called cardoon, this is one of the best foliage plants. It forms a magnificent fountain of silver leaves, from which rise tall stems bearing large flowers in summer. Both leaves and flowers are excellent when cut. The plant grows to 7 ft (2.1 m) or more.

C. scolymus (below)
The globe artichoke is mainly grown as a vegetable, but it too has silvery gray leaves that make it a valuable foliage plant. It is not as silver or as graceful as C. *cardunculus*, and it is shorter.

Cynara scolymus

CYNOGLOSSUM
Hound's tongue
In this large genus of 80–90 species of annuals and perennials, only a few types are suitable for growing in the garden. The flowers are carried in spiraled spikes, like those of forget-me-nots, and are mainly blue. The leaves are rough, covered in stiff hairs.

These are plants for a moisture-retentive soil, although it should not be too rich. They grow in either sun or shade. Support is needed, as they are naturally floppy. Propagate from seed or by taking root cuttings.

Cynoglossum nervosum

C. nervosum (above)
This is the only perennial hound's tongue in general cultivation. It is valuable in the garden for its bright blue flowers, which appear in early summer. The plants grow to approximately 2½ ft (75 cm) high.

DARMERA
Umbrella plant
This single-species genus has D. *peltata* as its sole representative. Until recently it was generally known as *Peltiphyllum peltatum*. The common name is derived from the large umbrella-like leaves. Each rounded leaf is dish-shaped in the center and 1–2 ft (30–60 cm) wide. The leaves are carried on stems reaching 4 ft (1.2 m) tall. The clusters of pale pink flowers appear before the leaves and are carried on tall, sinuous stalks.

Umbrella plants must have a wet, marshy location, such as a spot next to a pond or stream or in a bog garden, but do well in either sun or shade. They spread by rhizomes, which can be easily divided for propagation purposes.

DELOSPERMA
Delosperma

This genus of succulents is related to mesembryanthemums. Delospermas are carpeting plants that are suitable for either a rock garden or the front of a border. The leaves are thick and fleshy, while the flowers are daisylike and usually very brightly colored.

Delospermas need a free-draining soil and a sunny site. They are easily propagated from cuttings. They are not hardy; in colder areas (zone 8), overwinter plants or cuttings indoors.

Delosperma cooperi

D. cooperi (above)

This is one of the hardier species. The daisylike flowers have white centers and bright magenta petals. The fleshy leaves are cylindrical. The plant grows only 4 in (10 cm) high.

DELPHINIUM
Delphinium

With their tall, stately spires of blue flowers, delphiniums create one of the most romantic sights in the herbaceous border. However, delphiniums have a lot more to offer than this. There are a number of different species and hybrids that produce different-looking plants—ones that are short, with clouds of flowers rather than spikes. Garden delphiniums are no longer restricted to blue; there are forms with

pink, white, yellow, and red flowers. The blues also come in a wide range, from very pale to very dark. Added to this are doubles as well as singles and flowers with black or violet "bees," or eyes, in the center. Yet they are all easily recognizable.

Delphiniums need fertile soil enriched with well-rotted organic material. Many of the smaller species will also grow in less rich, more free-draining soil. The taller forms often require staking, especially in exposed sites. In the border, plants can be supported as a whole, but flower spikes for cutting or exhibition are best supported with individual stakes.

Delphiniums can be grown from seed, preferably sown fresh, or by taking cuttings in spring. Some can also be divided.

D. x belladonna (below)

These are hybrids between *D. elatum* and *D. grandiflorum.* They are not as heavy as the border hybrids, with some branching stems reaching 5 ft (1.5 m), but others extending only 3 ft (90 cm). They produce a succession of flower spikes over a long period. Many different forms are available, and it is possible to buy mixed seed that provides a range of colors, including purple and white. Among the named forms, the best include 'Bellamosum' (dark blue), 'Pink Sensation' (white and pink), and 'Royal Copenhagen' (violet-blue).

Delphinium × belladonna

D. elatum hybrids

These are the tall, stately border varieties, some of which grow to 6 ft (1.8 m). They are available in a wide range of forms and colors.

D. grandiflorum

This was one of the original parents of the tall border cultivars, but its contribution to the hybrids is the size of its flower and not its height, as it grows to only approximately 2 ft (60 cm). It forms a loose, airy plant with dark blue flowers. There are several cultivars, including 'Blue Butterfly' (bright blue) and 'Blue Mirror' (gentian-blue).

Delphinium, mixed

Mixed—seed (above)

There is a range of seed strains that provides a mixture of seedlings. The 'Blackmore & Langdon' strain includes mixed colors and large spikes. 'Magic Fountains' are short forms, which grow to only 3 ft (90 cm) tall, and include a wide range of colors. 'New Century Hybrids' are a mixture of blues and whites of medium stature. 'Southern Nobleman' is a tall strain, with high-quality spikes in a wide range of shades, including purples.

Separates—seed

Many named forms of delphinium can be raised from seed. 'Astolat' is various shades of pink. 'Black Knight' is dark blue with a black bee, 'Blue Bird' clear midblue with a white bee, 'Cameliard' lavender with a white bee, 'Galahad' pure white, 'Guinevere' rosy lavender, and 'King Arthur' deep purple.

Separates—cuttings

Some forms can be propagated only vegetatively, by taking cuttings. 'Alice Artingdale' is the most exquisite of all delphiniums. It has fully double flowers that are bright powder-blue in color. 'Blue Nile' is midblue with a white bee, 'Faust' ultramarine, 'Fenella' gentian-blue with a black bee, 'Rosemary Brock' dusky pink with a brown bee, and 'Sungleam' deep cream.

DENDRANTHEMA

Chrysanthemum

When the genus *Chrysanthemum*, consisting of some 200 annuals, perennials, and shrubs, was reclassified, the florists' chrysanthemums were all moved to the new genus *Dendranthema*. This large genus contains many garden plants. The large variety of flowers, shapes, and colors and the evocative fragrance of the foliage have given generations of gardeners much pleasure. Although there are no blues, there is a wide range of colors, both pure and mixed. The flower heads can be delicate singles or large, blowsy doubles with innumerable petals.

Chrysanthemums like rich, moisture-retentive soil to which a good quantity of well-rotted organic material has been added. The tall forms with heavy flower heads, which are often used for cutting and exhibition purposes, generally need staking, but the stockier border forms are usually self-supporting.

Many of the border forms, such as the rubellums, are hardy enough to be left outside during the winter, but other types, especially the exhibition forms, need to be lifted and then stored in frost-free conditions. They can be replanted in spring, or new plants can be propagated from basal cuttings.

Garden sprays (below)

These chrysanthemums are the ones most commonly grown by gardeners. They can be grown either in the border or in beds reserved for cutting. The flower heads come in a wide variety of forms, both single and double. There is also a wide range of colors, including all colors except blue. Each stem carries a "spray" of five or six blooms, and each plant is restricted to approximately five stems. The plant's height is 4 ft (1.2 m). 'Madeleine' has pink reflexed blooms. 'Pink Procession' is a prolific pink single. The Pennine series is a large collection of hardy spray chrysanthemums, each incorporating "Pennine" in the name—for example, 'Pennine Oriel.' The flowers vary greatly in form and color.

Dendranthema 'Pennine Oriel'

Korean forms (next column)

This type of spray chrysanthemum displays far more flower heads than the usual sprays. The plants have a very long flowering period. They are generally hardier than other spray types and may be left outside, provided the ground is not too wet. Lift and store them under cover if there is any doubt about conditions. 'Brown Eyes' is a two-tone brown double with small flowers. 'Tapestry Rose' is a single with deep pink petals and a green center. 'Wedding Day' also has a green center, but the petals are white, while 'Yellow Starlet' is a soft yellow single.

Dendranthema 'Brown Eyes'

Pompons

These medium-height cultivars, reaching 3 ft (90 cm), have masses of delightful, small, rounded heads of double flowers. 'Bronze Elegance,' as its name suggests, has bronze flowers. 'Mei Kyo' is pink, and 'Purleigh White' is white.

Rubellums

These hardy types (zone 4) can be left outside in most areas, as long as the soil is not too wet. They form bushy clumps up to 2½ ft (75 cm) high. The flowers are usually single and daisylike in a variety of colors: 'Clara Curtis' is pure pink, 'Duchess of Edinburgh' coppery red, 'Emperor of China' silvery pink, and 'Mary Stoker' apricot.

DENNSTAEDTIA

Hay-scented fern

In this large genus of 70 species of hardy deciduous or semi-evergreen ferns, only one species is in general cultivation. This is the hay-scented fern, *D. punctiloba*, which comes from eastern North America. It is an attractive light green fern with finely divided deciduous fronds reaching approx-imately 2 ft (60 cm) high.

Hay-scented fern needs well-drained, dry soil, as well as a shady spot. Its thin rhizomes can spread invasively, so care should be taken in choosing its site. Dennstaedtia can be propagated by divi-sion or from spores.

DESCHAMPSIA
Hair grass

This genus of 40–50 species of grasses includes both annuals and perennials. They are tufted grasses with flat leaves and showy, open plumes of flowers. They grow up to 2 ft (60 cm) tall.

Unlike many grasses, these grow in both sun and light shade and on a wide range of soils, including dry ones. They can be increased by seed or by division.

Deschampsia caespitosa 'Golden Veil'

D. caespitosa (above)

This is the species that is most com-monly grown. An evergreen grass that forms tufts, it has narrow, rough-edged, deep green leaves and minute, dainty pink or green flowers held in elegant spikes that appear in the summer. There are a number of cultivars to choose from, of which the best include 'Bronze Veil' ('Bronzeschleier'), with light bronze flower heads, and 'Golden Veil' ('Goldschleier'), which has attractive golden yellow flowers.

DIANTHUS
Pink

Although carnations also belong to this genus, it is the smaller pinks that are mainly grown as border plants. These are mostly based on the species *D. plumarius*. Pinks have been popular garden plants for a long time, and there are over 300,000 recorded types, with several thousand still in cultivation. The flowers are often fringed and vary from singles to full doubles. Besides white, the most common colors are variations of pink or red. In most cultivars the foliage is grasslike and bluish gray in color, although some have green leaves. The flower stems rarely reach a height of more than 2 ft (60 cm), while the foliage makes mats no more than 6 in (15 cm) high.

Pinks perform best in slightly alkaline or neutral soil, although they will grow in mildly acidic conditions as long as the soil is not too wet. They need a sunny site. Propagation is either from cuttings taken in summer or from seed in spring. Pinks are usually hardy as long as the winter soil does not remain too wet.

Dianthus 'Doris'

Modern pinks (above)

These cultivars have been bred since the beginning of the 20th century. They are usually repeat flowering, with larger flowers and less scent than the old-fashioned cultivars. The colors are

often brighter and the leaves coarser in texture. 'Becky Robinson' is a double that is rose-pink laced with crimson. 'Doris' is a heavily scented double col-ored pink with a darker salmon-pink zone in the center. 'Gran's Favorite' is a double that is basically white, with nar-row purple-pink lacing. 'Haytor' is a very good, pure white double with pro-nounced toothing to the petals. 'Houndspool Ruby' is a double colored bright pink with a ruby-red center. 'Old Mother Hubbard' is a semidouble that is pink with stripes and flecks of a darker pink.

Dianthus 'Mrs. Sinkins'

Old-fashioned pinks (above)

These are usually smaller and more subtly colored than the modern pinks. The foliage is also finer. The majority were introduced before the beginning of this century, but a number have been raised since in the same style. 'Brympton Red' has large single flowers colored a rich purple-pink with chestnut-red lacing. 'Dad's Favorite' is a double with white petals laced with velvety maroon. 'Inchmery' is a shell-pink double that is strongly scented. 'Mrs. Sinkins' is an all-time favorite that has fringed double white flowers with pale green centers. It is very sweetly scented. 'Sops-in-Wine' reputedly dates from as long ago as medieval times. It has blowsy white double flowers, each of which has a crimson center. 'White Ladies' is a fringed white double form that has scented flowers.

D. deltoides (below)

This species has fine foliage, often flushed purple in color, and a myriad of small flowers. These come in a variety of colors, including white, pink, and cerise, but 'Brilliant' is the brightest, with double crimson flowers.

Dianthus deltoides 'Brilliant'

DIASCIA

Twinspur

These are some of the most useful plants in the garden. Their gaily colored flowers appear from spring through to the first frosts. Growing 1 ft (30 cm) or more tall, they are excellent plants for the front of a border, especially if they are allowed to scramble up through their neighbors. The flowers from the different species and cultivars are similar to one another, with only subtle differences in the shades of pink and sizes of the blooms.

Twinspurs need a moisture-retentive soil, but if it is too rich they will tend to become loose growing and produce few flowers. They do best in a sunny spot but will tolerate light shade. Propagation is very readily achieved by taking cuttings at any time during the growing season. Most diascias tend to be short-lived.

D. barberae

This is one of the least hardy (zone 8) of the diascias, but it has beautiful rose-pink flowers and is worth the effort of taking cuttings each fall and keeping them frost free over the winter.

Diascia 'Ruby Field'

D. 'Ruby Field' (above)

This superb hybrid is hardier than *D. barberae*, one of its parents. It has purple-pink flowers and heart-shaped midgreen leaves.

D. 'Salmon Supreme'

The salmon-pink flowers of this hybrid are larger than those of many other forms, and their season is just as long. The plant has the hardiness of *D.* 'Ruby Field,' one of its parents.

DICENTRA

Bleeding heart

Bleeding hearts have long been popular garden plants. Generations of gardeners have been charmed by the curious shape of the flowers as well as the finely cut foliage. The flowers, in varying shades of pink and white, are shaped like hearts. The leaves are either fresh green or silver-gray in color, making dicentras attractive foliage plants when they are not in flower.

Bleeding hearts are extremely easy plants to grow, sometimes too easy, as they have a tendency to spread rapidly,

although rarely to the point of becoming invasive. They grow in any fertile garden soil but prefer one that is reasonably moisture retentive, such as woodland soil. Most can be grown in either sun or light shade, but in hot areas they grow better in shade. All can be divided at planting time for propagation.

Border plants (below)

In an open border the larger, up to 3 ft (90 cm), *D. spectabilis* makes an excellent plant. It has long, arching stems from which dangle large pink lockets, white in the variety *alba*, appearing from early spring onward. This species forms clumps and spreads more slowly than the smaller types. While still attractive, the foliage is not as fine and dainty as that of the woodland forms.

Dicentra spectabilis var. *alba*

Woodland plants

Although most species and cultivars will grow in the open border, many prefer a little light shade, especially in areas where the sun can be fierce. These cultivars are low-growing, up to 1 ft (30 cm) high, and quickly spread to form large clumps. They flower from spring into summer. *D.* 'Bountiful' has deep pink flowers; *D.* 'Snowflakes' has white flowers that contrast well with the crisp midgreen foliage.

DICTAMNUS
Burning bush

This intriguing plant gets its name from the fact that the plant exudes a volatile oil that on hot days can be lighted with a match to produce a spurt of flame. There is only one species in the genus, *D. albus* (**below**). In early summer, as its name suggests, it has white flowers. These are held in loose spikes that rise to 3 ft (90 cm) high. The leaves are deeply cut and smell of lemons when crushed or bruised. The cultivar 'Purpureus' has pink-mauve flowers with darker purple veins. Both make excellent plants for the center of the border.

Burning bushes can be slow to establish themselves, but once they do, they are easy plants to grow and will last for many years in the same spot. They resent disturbance and transplanting, however. Burning bushes grow in any fertile garden soil but do best in soil enriched with well-rotted organic material. A sunny site is preferable. In spite of their height, they are strong enough not to require staking. Propagation is best achieved by sowing seed in spring.

Dictamnus albus

DIGITALIS
Foxglove

Foxgloves are a much-loved genus of plants, especially for the cottage, woodland, or informal garden. The most common species is *D. purpurea,* generally treated as a biennial, although it will act as a short-lived perennial. All foxgloves are characterized by tall spires of tubular flowers, usually in soft colors that make them suitable for pastel border schemes. The flowers appear from early summer.

Foxgloves grow in most garden soils, even dry ones, although they do best in soil that is not allowed to dry out completely. They grow in either sun or shade; the latter is preferable in hot areas (zones 9–10). There is generally no need to support them, but some of the taller species may need to be staked in windy locations. Few foxgloves are long-lived, but each plant produces masses of seed, which can be allowed to self-sow or can be sown in pots in spring.

Digitalis ferruginea

D. ferruginea (above)

This is an attractive, short-lived foxglove with pouchlike flowers borne in midsummer that are a rusty yellow color inside with noticeable brown-red veins. The narrow, graceful spires grow to a height of approximately 3 ft (90 cm).

D. grandiflora

The large flowers of this species are soft yellow with traces inside of brown veining. The flowers are slightly hairy. The leaves are oval to oblong in shape. This evergreen, clump-forming plant grows to 2½ ft (75 cm) tall.

D. × mertonensis (below)

This cross between *D. grandiflora* and *D. purpurea* more closely resembles the second species. It produces large pink flowers suffused with a yellow-buff color. The oval leaves are large and held in a rosette. They are covered in coarse hairs. The plant grows to about 3 ft (90 cm) high.

Digitalis × mertonensis

DORONICUM
Leopard's-bane

The spring garden would not be complete without the bright yellow flowers of the leopard's-bane. Each flower is a perfect daisy shape held on a swaying stem above the fresh green foliage. There are 35 species, and several are in cultivation. All produce excellent flowers both for the border and as cut blooms.

Leopard's-banes grow in any fertile, well-drained garden soil, although they will not thrive if conditions are too dry. They grow in either sun or light shade but do best in the shade if grown in hot areas. The plants often die back below ground as summer progresses, but they can be easily propagated by division in fall.

D. orientale 'Magnificum'

This is one of the best leopard's-banes in cultivation. It grows to about 2½ ft (75 cm) and carries masses of very large heads of bright yellow.

DRACOCEPHALUM
Dragonhead

Dracocephalums are often confused with nepetas, which they closely resemble, and some species may be listed under either genus. The flowers are generally blue in color. Tubular with flared lips, they are carried in short spikes. The foliage is mid- to dark green and resembles the mint leaf in shape. The different species vary in height and make good plants for the front or middle of a border.

Dragonheads grow in any well-drained garden soil, preferably in full sun. They can be propagated from seed, by taking basal cuttings in spring, or by division.

Dracocephalum ruyschianum

D. ruyschianum (above)
This commonly grown species generally has violet-blue flowers, but it can also be found with pink or white blooms. It grows to 2 ft (60 cm) tall.

DRYOPTERIS
Shield fern

This genus of ferns has been divided botanically, and there are now only 150 species left within it, the remaining 1,000 or so having been put into other genera. Of those that remain there are about 60 species and cultivars in cultivation. They are tall, graceful ferns with elongated triangular fronds that are deeply cut. Shield ferns can be used as foliage plants in their own right or combined with other plants, providing a cool-colored background for flowers or attractive contrasting foliage.

These shade-loving ferns like to be grown in woodland conditions of dappled shade and in moist, humus-rich soil. In cooler areas they can be grown in full sun if the soil is not allowed to dry out. Propagation is easily achieved by sowing fresh spores on sterile potting soil in summer or by division in fall.

D. erythrosora
This species is known as the Japanese shield fern or the copper shield fern. The latter name is derived from the color of the young fronds, which become a glossy dark green as they mature. These very graceful, fountainlike plants grow to approximately 2½ ft (75 cm) in height.

Dryopteris filix-mas

D. filix-mas (above)
The male fern is a very common plant throughout much of the world, but its frequency does not detract from its beauty. The deeply cut fronds are grouped into a fountain or vase shape and can reach 5 ft (1.5 m) in this fern's preferred conditions.

D. marginalis
The marginal shield fern is a slow-growing plant and is more popular with collectors than with gardeners who like to use ferns as part of a decorative border. This species can reach a height of approximately 2 ft (60 cm).

D. wallichiana (below)
This evergreen fern has dark green, glossy fronds. It is attractive and can grow up to approximately 6 ft (1.8 m), given favorable conditions.

Dryopteris wallichiana

ECHINACEA
Coneflower

Related to *Rudbeckia,* the plants of this genus all carry daisylike flowers with large cone-shaped centers. They are coarse plants, with rough, hairy leaves and stems, but the flowers are attractive and make colorful border plants for the latter half of the season, as well as providing excellent cut flowers. They are much loved by butterflies and bees.

Coneflowers are easy to grow in that they are not particular about soil, as long as it is fertile. They prefer a sunny spot. Except in exposed sites, the stems are strong enough to support the flowers without staking. Propagation is easy, either by division in spring or by seed sown at the same time.

E. purpurea (next page)
Although there are several species in this genus, this is the only one in general

cultivation. It has large flower heads, up to 6 in (15 cm) wide, which are carried on stems up to 4 ft (1.2 m) tall. The flowers mainly have purple outer petals and bronze central cones. Several cultivars of *Echinacea* are available, including 'Bressingham Hybrids,' a seed strain in which there is a slight variation in the shade of the purple outer petals. 'Magnus' has very large flowers with deep purple outer ray petals; 'Robert Bloom' is similar, while 'White Swan' has white outer ray petals.

Echinacea purpurea 'Robert Bloom'

ECHINOPS
Globe thistle

This is a large genus with over 100 species, of which only a handful are in general cultivation. The common name originates from the shape of the flower, which is spherical. Although the leaves are coarse and prickly, they make an attractive foliage feature, especially when they first emerge. The plants will do well in the middle or rear of a border.

Globe thistles like deep, well-prepared soil but also grow well on poor, even dry, soil. They must have a place in full sun to look their best and need staking in windy locations. Later in the season they may suffer from mildew, which disfigures the foliage. Propagation is mainly from seed, but special forms can be raised from root cuttings or by division.

Echinops ritro

E. ritro (above)

This is a magnificent plant, growing to about 4 ft (1.2 m) tall, with steely blue balls of flowers and dark green leaves that are gray on the reverse (this contrast often shows, particularly in a breeze). The flowers are much loved by bees and butterflies.

ELYMUS
Elymus

Although this is a large genus of grasses, only a few species are in cultivation. These plants are occasionally invasive, so they may have to be dealt with firmly to keep them from taking over the border. As they can be beautiful, it is worth the effort to keep them under control. They are grown for their blue-gray foliage, which makes them attractive in their own right as well as in combination with a wide range of other colors.

The main problem with these plants is that some of them run underground, making them a nuisance in the border, although they are valuable for stabilizing sand dunes. Plant them in a bottomless bucket and sink this into the border in order to contain their questing shoots and prevent them from getting out of hand. Alternatively, they can be planted in a wilder part of the garden, where they can spread unchecked without becoming a nuisance to other plants.

Elymus grows in any garden soil, including a dry one, but like most grasses, it grows and looks best in a sunny spot. Propagate it by division in spring.

E. hispidus

This species has beautiful blue-gray upright foliage, reaching 3 ft (90 cm) in fertile soil. The leaves are prominently veined. Mainly clump forming, this grass rarely wanders.

Elymus magellanicus

E. magellanicus (above)

If anything, this plant is an even more magnificent color than *E. hispidus*. The leaves are smooth. This plant grows to a similar height and may occasionally be invasive in its spread. In such cases it may be necessary to contain it.

EPIMEDIUM
Barrenwort

These are increasingly popular plants both for their foliage and for their flowers. The heart-shaped leaves vary in color from light green to bronze and, in some forms, are flushed with red. They are attractive throughout the year but are at their best when the new foliage is just beginning to unfurl in early spring. The flowers are small but carried in decorative airy sprays well above the leaves, usually in spring, and vary in color from pink to white and yellow. In addition to being attractive, the foliage creates a dense ground cover through which weeds find it very difficult to grow.

These woodland plants like moist, humus-rich soil and light shade, although they can be grown in an open location as long as the soil is not allowed to dry out. All species should be cut back during midwinter, including the evergreen forms, so that the new growth can be easily seen and appreciated. Propagation is by division in spring or fall.

Epimedium alpinum

E. alpinum (above)
This European species has yellow petals and red sepals, which appear in spring. The finely toothed, glossy foliage is deciduous. The plant grows up to about 15 in (38 cm) tall.

E. grandiflorum
Up to 1½ ft (45 cm) tall, this barrenwort has deep pink flowers with white spurs. There are also white and red forms. It has toothed evergreen foliage.

E. × perralchium
This evergreen barrenwort has sprays of large yellow flowers and glossy deep green leaves. It was originated as a cross between *E. perralderianum* and *E. pinnatum* subsp. *colchicum*. The form 'Frohnleiten' has golden yellow flowers and grows up to 1 ft (30 cm) high.

Epimedium perralderianum

E. perralderianum (above)
This is another yellow-flowered species, this time with shiny leaves that make it an excellent ground-cover plant. It grows to 1 ft (30 cm) tall.

E. × rubrum
This cross between *E. grandiflorum* and *E. alpinum* is worthy of attention for both its attractive red flowers and its foliage, which is distinctively marked with red when young.

E. × versicolor
This is another cross, this time between *E. grandiflorum* and *E. pinnatum* subsp. *colchicum*. The result is an attractive foliage plant that carries yellow flowers and reaches a height of 1 ft (30 cm). The form 'Sulphureum' is one of the best, with pale yellow flowers.

E. × youngianum
This cross between *E. grandiflorum* and *E. diphyllum* has produced hybrids with white or pink flowers and pale green leaves. It grows up to 15 in (38 cm) tall.

EREMURUS
Foxtail lily
Foxtail lilies are among the most spectacular of all herbaceous border plants. The flowers are borne in towering spires that may reach a height of 8 ft (2.4 m) or more.

Each spire is formed from a solid column of small starry flowers, which may be white, pink, yellow, or bright yellow-orange. The foliage is a fountain of straplike leaves. Foxtail lilies are useful plants for the rear of a border, where they can appear above or between other plants and then die back into obscurity.

It is important to give these plants a rich but free-draining soil and a sunny location. The taller varieties are likely to require staking. Propagation is by careful division of the crowns, although the species may also be grown from seed.

Eremurus robustus

E. robustus (above)
The giant desert candle, as it is sometimes called, is one of the best of the 50 or so species of *Eremurus*. It grows to 8 ft (2.4 m) tall and carries dense spikes of pink flowers for a long period.

E. 'Ruiter Hybrids'
Although compared with *E. robustus*, these plants are shorter, reaching a height of only 5 ft (1.5 m), they are still spectacular, with pastel-colored spikes of pink, yellow, or golden blooms.

ERIGERON
Fleabane
Fleabanes are a genus of attractive daisies suitable for a variety of positions in the border. The flowers are daisylike, with

an outer ring of two or more rows of narrow ray petals and an inner disk of usually yellow florets. The ray petals are either white, blue, purple, pink, or red. The plants vary in height from a few inches to 2½ ft (75 cm).

Fleabanes grow in any garden soil that drains freely. Some grow in poor soils, but they need a sunny location. The taller ones are not strong and need support. They can be propagated by division in early spring or fall or else from seed in fall. Alternatively, many can be grown from basal cuttings taken in spring.

Erigeron 'Quakeress'

Border cultivars (above)
The border forms vary in height and so can be used in either the front or the back of a bed, although the taller ones definitely need staking. They remain in flower for 6–8 weeks. 'Black Sea' ('Schwarzes Meer') has very dark violet flowers, as does 'Darkest of All,' the former being slightly taller. In contrast, 'Pink Jewel' has pale pink flowers. 'Quakeress' has pale lilac-pink flowers.

E. karvinskianus
The Mexican daisy, still known by many as *E. mucronatus*, flowers continuously from spring until the first frosts. It is covered with small white and pink daisies and has narrow lance-shaped leaves. It is best for the front of a border.

ERYNGIUM
Sea holly
The members of this genus are attractive as both flowering and foliage plants. Although they belong to the cow parsley family, they often bear a closer resemblance to thistles, as they have prickly leaves and spiky domes of flowers. The flowers are usually blue but can also be white or pale green. The foliage is attractive long before the flowers appear, with leaves that are often heavily veined or marbled in white. Some forms have sharp spines on their edges, making them dangerous plants among which to weed.

Sea hollies have taproots and do best in deep, well-drained soil, preferably in full sun. They are strong plants and rarely need staking. Most can be propagated from seed; root cuttings are a good alternative.

Eryngium agavifolium

Tall forms (above)
There are a number of tall species, some reaching about 6 ft (1.8 m) tall, although the majority are shorter than this. One of the taller forms is *E. agavifolium*, with swordlike leaves that are sharply toothed and flowers shaped like small, pale green globes. *E. proteiflorum* is shorter but has similar leaves and gray-blue flowers.

Medium-height forms (next column)
There are a large number of medium-height species that are suitable for the front half of the border. *E. alpinum* has large heads of intense blue flowers surrounded by frilly ruffs of similar-colored bracts. While *E. bourgatii* is attractive in flower, it is grown mainly for its white-veined leaves. The pale green flowers are surrounded by silvery bracts. *E. planum* grows to about 2 ft (60 cm) tall and bears heads of light blue flowers, which are accentuated by pointed silver bracts. *E. variifolium* has beautiful rounded foliage with pronounced white veins. The small thistle-like flowers are gray-blue and produced in late summer. They are surrounded by pointed silver-white bracts.

Eryngium variifolium

EUPATORIUM
Boneset
These are mainly tall, clump-forming plants suitable only for larger borders. They are grown not only for their flowers but also for their colored stems and leaves, which are often an attractive purple. The flowers are carried in fluffy heads and are very enticing to butterflies, bees, and flies.

Bonesets like moisture-retentive soil and do best if situated near a pond or in a bog garden, but they grow well in any good garden soil as long as it is not too dry. They prefer a sunny position but will also grow in light shade. Propagation can be easily achieved by dividing the plants in spring or fall.

E. cannabinum

A native of British ditches, hemp agrimony is suitable only for the wild parts of a garden. The form 'Flore Pleno,' however, has soft pink double flowers that look beautiful in the border. It reaches a height of 4 ft (1.2 m).

Eupatorium purpureum

E. purpureum (above)

Joe Pye weed is a good flowering plant for the end of the year. Its tall purple stems grow to 7 ft (2.1 m) and carry fluffy sprays of rose-pink flowers.

EUPHORBIA

Spurge

Spurges make up one of the largest genera, with up to 2,000 species and many subspecies and cultivars. Many of these, however, are tropical and include trees as well as spurges that are best treated as houseplants. In spite of this, there are still a large number that make excellent border plants. These are grown both for their attractive foliage and the colorful bracts that surround the petalless flowers. The leaves are usually a cool green, although there are some that are flushed with red or purple. The bracts are yellow-green, sometimes gold, and impart a fresh-looking quality. The plants range in height from just a few inches to as much as 5 ft (1.5 m).

Spurges grow in any garden soil, and most are suitable for either shade or sun.

A few need staking, but the majority are self-supporting. They can be grown from seed in early spring, or they may be increased by division or from cuttings of basal shoots in late spring.

Deciduous forms (below)

Some forms are deciduous and die back during winter. They need to have all the old vegetation removed before the new growth starts to appear in the spring. *E. dulcis* 'Chameleon' is an extremely attractive plant with bronze-purple foliage surrounded by greenish-yellow bracts. It is short-lived but grows readily from seed. *E. griffithii* 'Dixter' and 'Fireglow' are two taller forms that have red-tinged foliage and bracts. Unlike *E. dulcis*, they run freely and soon form large colonies. *E. polychroma* is one of the earliest to flower, creating a rounded mound of bright yellow in early spring. In contrast, both *E. schillingii* and *E. sikkimensis* flower in late summer; they are both tall, slender plants with large, bright yellow-green flowers. *E. sikkimensis* can form colonies.

Euphorbia griffithii 'Fireglow'

Evergreen forms (next column)

While they do not die back each year, many of the evergreen forms benefit from having the old stems cut back to the ground in early spring. The attractive red foliage of *E. amygdaloides* 'Rubra,'

for example, often becomes mildewy by early summer and is best cut back to promote fresh growth. *E. characias* and its subspecies *E. c. wulfenii* need to have their flowering stems removed once they go brown. Both plants produce tall club-like spires of green-yellow flowers in spring, with the subspecies being the more yellow of the two. *E. × martinii* is a cross between *E. amygdaloides* and *E. characias*. It is halfway in height between the two parents and has noticeable red "eyes" on its spring flowers. *E. myrsinites* is a low-growing spurge with gray leaves arranged in spirals around its prostrate stems. It flowers in spring.

Euphorbia × martinii

FESTUCA

Fescue

Fescues are a large genus of grasses. Some of them are used in lawns and grass paths, while others, which are more ornamental, are employed in the front areas of borders. These clump-forming, tufted plants are grown for their blue or green blades.

Fescues grow on any well-drained soil, including poor soil, but avoid rich, moist sites. They like a sunny location. To keep them vigorous, divide every few years. Propagate by seed or division in spring.

F. glauca

This species is popular because of its outstanding blue foliage. One of the best forms is 'Blue Glow' ('Blauglut'), which is a wonderful silver-blue. It grows to about 1 ft (30 cm) tall.

Festuca valesiaca 'Silver Sea'

F. valesiaca (above)

This is another blue-leaved species, mainly grown in the form 'Silver Sea' ('Silbersee'). This compact plant grows to no more than 8 in (20 cm), with intensely silver-blue foliage.

FILIPENDULA
Meadowsweet

Meadowsweets are a group of plants whose common name is partly derived from the sweet fragrance given off by the summer flowers. These are small but are carried in flat, fluffy heads and are usually white or pink. The plants vary in height from about 2 ft (60 cm) to 8 ft (2.4 m), which makes them suitable for the middle of a border.

The majority of meadowsweets prefer a moist site and do particularly well if grown next to water or in a bog garden. They grow in either full sun or light shade. They can be easily divided to increase stock. This should be carried out in spring.

F. palmata

This is one of the medium-height species of meadowsweet at about 4 ft (1.2 m). It has pale pink flowers that fade to white as they age.

F. rubra

Known as queen of the prairie, this species is one of the tallest, reaching 8 ft (2.4 m) or even higher if grown in favorable conditions. It has pink flowers. Avoid planting it in a small or crowded border, as it spreads vigorously. The form 'Venusta' has darker pink flowers.

F. ulmaria (below)

This is the European meadowsweet, which is not as attractive as some of the other species. In the form 'Aurea,' however, the leaves are golden yellow. Plant this cultivar in light shade so that the foliage does not burn. Remove the pink flowers because they spoil the foliage effect and may, if left, produce self-sown seedlings with green leaves.

Filipendula ulmaria 'Aurea'

F. vulgaris

Dropwort is one of the meadowsweets that prefers dry soil and can be grown in chalky conditions. It has small heads of white flowers. The form that is most widely grown is the one with double flowers, 'Multiplex,' also called 'Flore Pleno.' It grows to only about 1 ft (30 cm) tall.

FOENICULUM
Fennel

Fennel is worth growing both for its foliage and for its flowers. It is a stately plant, often reaching 6 ft (1.8 m) or more, with arching branches of fine filigree leaves. In late summer, flat heads of small yellow flowers appear and are extremely attractive to bees and wasps. These plants can either be used by themselves as a feature in the garden or planted toward the rear of a border.

Fennels grow in any garden soil, even a poor one, but do best in soil enriched with humus and in an open, sunny spot. Cut back as soon as flowering is over or they will self-sow everywhere. Although tall, they do not need staking. Propagation is achieved by division or by sowing seed in spring or when ripe.

Foeniculum vulgare 'Purpureum'

F. vulgare 'Purpureum' (above)

This is the most popular form of *Foeniculum*; it has attractive delicate foliage that turns purple when young and then becomes bronze as the season progresses and the plant ages.

FRAGARIA
Strawberry

Strawberries are not normally associated with herbaceous borders, but there are some that are decorative, in either their leaves or flowers. One of the most popular is 'Pink Panda' (**next column**), which has bright pink flowers instead of the usual white ones. These bloom on and off throughout summer and into fall. As a bonus, edible fruit is produced. The plants are good for growing at the front of a border, in full sun or light shade, and as ground cover.

Decorative strawberries grow in any soil that does not become too dry. They can be increased, as with all strawberries, by dividing the rooted runners.

Fragaria 'Pink Panda'

GAILLARDIA
Blanket flower

If a splash of bright color is required in a border, then blanket flowers are the right plants to use. Their blooms consist of large daisies, sometimes either red or yellow, sometimes a mixture of both. The center of each flower is a red-brown domed disk. The plants are hairy and somewhat sticky, and they normally grow to about 3 ft (90 cm) in height. 'Burgundy' is bright red with yellow tips to the petals. 'Goblin' ('Kobold'; **next column**) is a short form, reaching only about 9 in (23 cm) high, with red flowers and a yellow edge. 'Monarch' is a good seed strain, with flowers of various colors.

Blanket flowers grow in any soil but do best in soil that is not too rich. They are able to sustain drought well, and a position in the sun is essential. They have a straggly growth habit and need to be staked if you want them to look neat. Propagation is by division or from seed, provided you do not mind getting color variations.

Gaillardia 'Goblin'

GALEGA
Goat's rue

Goat's rue is a large, bushy plant, attractive in its own right and also useful for creating hazy patches of color in the border, perhaps as a background for other plants. The pea-shaped flowers are produced on a myriad of spikes and are usually blue in color. The fresh-looking leaves grow in pairs on either side of the stem.

These deep-rooted plants grow in any garden soil, including a dry one. They do best in a sunny spot but also grow in light shade, especially in hot areas. They are not very sturdy plants, often scrambling through other vegetation in the wild, so they need to be staked except in the most sheltered of positions. Goat's rue can be increased by division or from seed.

G. officinalis

The species normally grown in gardens is *G. officinalis*. This has pale lavender-blue flowers. Equally popular is 'Alba,' a form with white flowers. Both bloom profusely around midsummer and reach a height of approximately 5 ft (1.5 m). They can be cut to the ground after flowering has finished.

GAURA
Gaura

Although there are a number of species in this genus, *G. lindheimeri* (**next column**) is the only one that is in general cultivation. When in flower it resembles a host of white butterflies. The upright stems carry loose spikes of dainty flowers, each with somewhat reflexed petals and prominent stamens. These contrast well with the fresh green, narrow foliage. The flowers appear over a long period during the summer and fall. The plants reach a height of approximately 4 ft (1.2 m) and are excellent for the middle of a border, especially if planted against a dark background.

Gauras grow in any fertile garden soil, although they do not grow well in one that is too wet or heavy. They grow best in full sun but also thrive in light shade. They do not need staking. Increase by taking cuttings in spring or from seed sown early.

Gaura lindheimeri

GENTIANA
Gentian

The intense blue of many gentians has entranced gardeners for centuries. This large genus contains about 400 species, the majority of which are more suited to the alpine bed than the open garden. There are a few, however, that are larger than the rest and can survive in competition with border plants. Surprisingly, not all of these are blue; there are some species that are yellow or white, but they all have trumpet-shaped flowers.

Gentians grow best in a soil that does not dry out, so plenty of humus should be added to it. They grow in full sun or shade. Propagation is by division or from seed.

G. asclepiadea (below)

The willow gentian, so called because of its willow-shaped leaves, is the main species grown in the herbaceous border. It reaches about 3 ft (90 cm) and has long, arching stems from which the blue trumpets emerge in late summer and fall. It is a useful shade plant. There is also a white form, 'Alba.'

Gentiana asclepiadea

G. lutea

Felwort is an upright-growing gentian for an open location. Its flowers are pale yellow. Do not cut back after flowering, as the seed heads are also attractive. It grows to 4 ft (1.2 m) tall.

G. septemfida

The crested gentian is a lower-growing plant, with clusters of dark blue flowers at the ends of its sprawling branches. It grows to only about 1 ft (30 cm), and the flowers appear in late summer. An ideal position is at the front of a border in a slightly shady spot.

GERANIUM

Geranium

Geraniums, or hardy cranesbills, form the backbone of any flower garden. There are several hundred various species, cultivars,

and hybrids in cultivation, presenting the gardener with plants for all kinds of situations and color schemes. They vary in height from a few inches to 4 ft (1.2 m), and the flowers come in a wide range of colors—blues, pinks, and purples as well as white. Many geraniums have a long flowering period, and those that have a shorter one often make good foliage plants when they are not in bloom. A few of the better forms are noted here.

Geraniums grow in most garden soils but do best in moisture-retentive soil. You can add extra humus to the soil to help achieve this. Most geraniums grow in either sun or light shade, although the shorter types prefer sun. The taller forms need support. Geraniums can be increased by division or by sowing seed if you do not mind variation in the resulting plants.

Geranium pratense 'Mrs. Kendall Clark'

Blue forms (above)

'Johnson's Blue' is a good violet-blue-flowered geranium for early summer. It grows to about 1 ft (30 cm) in height and soon forms a large clump. G. himalayense is one of its parents and itself makes a good border plant, especially in its purple-blue double form 'Plenum' (also called 'Birch Double'). One of the most attractive forms is G. pratense 'Mrs. Kendall Clark,' with soft blue flowers veined with silver. It grows to 2½ ft (75 cm) high and needs

support. For later in the season, G. wallichianum 'Buxton's Variety' is ideal. This rambling plant creeps over other vegetation without being invasive.

Geranium 'Ann Folkard'

Purplish forms (above)

'Ann Folkard' has purple flowers with darker centers. It spreads out non-invasively, clambering over other plants. G. phaeum is a more upright plant, forming a 2½ ft (75 cm) dome of foliage surmounted by sprays of reflexed dark purple flowers. G. procurrens, on the other hand, is unable to support itself and spreads out over an area of 4–6 ft (1.2–1.8 m), clambering through bushes and other plants. It can become invasive but is nonetheless attractive, with its pink-purple flowers suffused with dark purple. These blooms are produced late in the season. One of the brightest flowering geraniums is G. psilostemon. It forms a rounded plant, 4 ft (1.2 m) tall, which is covered in summer with bright magenta flowers, each with a dark purple center.

Pink forms

G. × cantabridgense 'Cambridge' forms a good ground cover of shiny leaves and pink flowers from spring onward. G. dalmaticum, one of its parents, is a low-growing plant suitable for the front of a border. G. endressii 'Wargrave' is a much taller plant, growing to 2 ft (60 cm). Upright at first, it soon flops over and needs support. A similar plant with brighter flowers is *G. × oxonianum* 'Claridge Druce.' *G. macrorrhizum* is an excellent ground-cover plant with fragrant evergreen foliage. Its cultivar 'Ingwersen's Variety' has soft pink flowers. *G. × riversleaianum* 'Russell Prichard' has silver foliage and purple-pink flowers. *G. sanguineum* 'Striatum' is a low-growing plant with large, pale pink flowers veined with red.

Geranium clarkei 'Kashmir White'

White forms (above)
G. × cantabridgense 'Biokovo' has shiny leaves and white flowers and grows to about 1 ft (30 cm) tall. *G. clarkei* 'Kashmir White' is slightly taller with white flowers veined in pink. *G. phaeum* 'Album' has white flowers and paler leaves than the species, known as the mourning widow, which is purple. *G. renardii* has attractive white flowers veined with purple and produced in spring, but it is grown mainly for its rounded silver foliage.

GEUM
Avens
These clump-forming plants add a lively touch to the front of a border. The flowers of many of the species and cultivars are brightly colored in strong reds, oranges,

and yellows, but there are also some forms that have subtly colored blooms, more suitable for pastel borders. The plants grow to 2 ft (60 cm).

Avens grow in any fertile garden soil. They tolerate light shade but do best in an open, sunny spot. Propagation can be carried out by division at planting time, or stock can be increased from seed sown in spring or when ripe.

Geum 'Lady Stratheden'

Cultivars (above)
A selection of the best bright forms would include 'Borisii,' 1 ft (30 cm) high, with brilliant orange single flowers that span up to 1 in (2.5 cm) wide. Two choices that are twice as tall and have semidouble flowers, 1½ in (4 cm) wide, are 'Lady Stratheden' (yellow) and 'Mrs. J. Bradshaw' (bright red). On the softer and smaller side is 'Leonard's Variety,' which is a coppery version of the pink-flowered *G. rivale*.

GILLENIA
Indian physic
This is a small genus of two American plants, but only *G. trifoliata* (**next column**) is widely grown in gardens. In appearance it looks shrubby, with reddish-brown woody stems and an open, bushy shape. The plant is, however, herbaceous and dies back to the ground each winter. In summer it has delicate white flowers that

seem to flutter over the plant's surface like tiny butterflies. The white color of the flowers is emphasized by the red calyxes. The plant grows to 4 ft (1.2 m) in ideal conditions and is an excellent choice for the middle section of a border.

Indian physic grows in any fertile soil, although it has a slight preference for acidic soil. In most areas it grows best in sun, but in hotter places (zone 8) it should be grown in light shade. It is best propagated from seed, but it can also be divided.

Gillenia trifoliata

GLYCERIA
Glyceria
There are 16 species of this grass, but only *G. maxima* in its variety *variegata* is grown to any extent in cultivation. *G. maxima* itself is a green-leaved grass growing to about 6 ft (1.8 m) in height. It is an invasive plant, spreading by creeping rhizomes. The variety has cream and green stripes on the leaves and creates a delightful fountain effect, especially when topped by the stems of greenish flowers. It does not grow as tall as *G. maxima,* reaching a height of 5 ft (1.5 m), and is not as invasive, but it can still become a nuisance.

Glyceria can be grown in ordinary soil, but it does best when planted in wet ground next to water. It can be planted directly in water, as long as it is not deeper than about 8 in (20 cm). Propagation is carried out by division.

GUNNERA
Gunnera

There are 35 species of gunnera, varying from prostrate plants no more than 1 in (2.5 cm) high to giants 8 ft (2.4 m) tall, with leaves 6 ft (1.8 m) wide. One of the giants—*G. manicata* (**below**)—is the species normally grown in gardens. This plant has large pleated leaves held like huge umbrellas on prickly stems. The flowers are carried on thick clublike stems reaching 2 ft (60 cm) high. Although it can be grown in a border, the plant is best as a focal point beside water or in a damp spot.

Gunneras must be grown in wet or moisture-retentive soil, which should be enriched with well-rotted humus or compost. They can be grown in either full sun or light shade. As they are not completely hardy (zone 7), cut the dying leaves and place them over the crowns to protect them during winter. Propagation is by division or from seed.

Gunnera manicata

GYPSOPHILA
Baby's breath

This intriguing common name is a reference to the tiny flowers that are carried in light, airy sprays above the leaves, creating a misty cloud. Although there are 125 species in this genus, few are grown in the garden, and those that are generally are better suited to the rock garden than the herbaceous border.

Baby's breath needs light, well-drained soil and a sunny spot. It is taprooted and resents disturbance, so transplanting should be avoided. Support is required for the taller plants. Propagation is from seed; named forms are grown from cuttings.

G. paniculata (below)

The main species grown in the open border is *G. paniculata*. This is a tall, bushy plant reaching 4 ft (1.2 m) high. The flowers are generally white, but there are cultivars in shades of pink. 'Bristol Fairy' has double flowers and is particularly attractive. 'Perfecta' is similar but is taller and has larger flowers. 'Flamingo' also has double flowers, but they are a lilac-pink. 'Rosy Veil' ('Rosenschleier') is much shorter, growing to only 1 ft (30 cm) high, and carries beautiful semi-double flowers in pale pink.

Gypsophila paniculata 'Bristol Fairy'

HAKONECHLOA
Hakonechloa

This single-species genus from Japan is represented solely by *H. macra*. Although the species is occasionally grown in gardens, the best-known form is 'Aureola' (**next column**), a superb grass with fountains of narrow blades colored a rich gold, highlighted with narrow green stripes. It grows to about 1 ft (30 cm) and spreads slightly to form a large clump. This decorative plant deserves a prominent place in a

border, especially where it can impart its radiance to a dark corner.

This grass grows in any good garden soil but prefers one that is moisture retentive. It also needs a little light shade, making it ideal for a woodland border. It can be increased by division in spring.

Hakonechloa macra 'Aureola'

HELENIUM
Sneezeweed

Heleniums are a mainstay of the summer and fall border. They form large drifts of daisylike flowers that remain in bloom for several weeks. Both the outer petals and the central disk are colored yellow or brown, or a mixture of the two, with the browns often appearing quite reddish. Heleniums are generally tall, reaching as much as 5 ft (1.5 m) in height, although some are much shorter. They are not invasive plants; instead, they slowly form large clumps and are particularly suitable for creating drifts of color.

Heleniums grow in any type of garden soil, but they tend to do best in soil that does not dry out. They prefer a sunny site. In spring, when the plants start to grow, slugs can cause a lot of damage to the young shoots and may have to be controlled. Heleniums are strong enough to do without support, but in an exposed spot staking will probably be required. Propagation can be easily accomplished by division in either fall or spring.

Different forms (below)
There are many cultivars and hybrids from which to choose, with more forms being created all the time. 'Bressingham Gold' has bright yellow flowers, while those of 'Brilliant' are brown. The flowers of 'Coppelia' are a coppery orange. 'Moerheim Beauty' is an old cultivar and still one of the best, with reddish-brown flowers that fade to dark orange as they grow older.

Helenium 'Coppelia'

HELIANTHUS
Sunflower
The perennial sunflowers are brash plants, but they nonetheless have a place in the border, even if they are only there to create a splash of color (yellow or orange-yellow) toward the back. There are by some estimates 150 species of sunflowers, and about 20 of these plants, with their daisylike flowers, are in cultivation. They are usually lanky in habit, growing up to 5 ft (1.5 m), and they spread vigorously by rhizomes. Some may be invasive. The leaves and stems have a rough, hairy surface. Most sunflowers bloom in late summer or fall.

The plants grow in any reasonably fertile soil and are suitable for poor conditions, but a sunny spot is needed. Stake the taller forms in exposed sites, as they are prone to blowing over. Propagate by division in fall or spring.

Different forms (below)
A list of the best sunflowers available should include the pale yellow, single-flowered 'Lemon Queen' and 'Loddon Gold,' an old cultivar with golden double flowers. *H. salicifolius* is very tall, growing to 8 ft (2.4 m), with narrow leaves and yellow flowers.

Helianthus 'Loddon Gold'

HELICTOTRICHON
Helictotrichon
In this large genus of grasses, only one species, *H. sempervirens*, is widely cultivated. This grass does not spread invasively but forms a dense clump about 4 ft (1.2 m) tall when in flower. Its beauty lies in its blue foliage, whose individual blades are erect and slightly hairy. The foliage reaches only up to 2 ft (60 cm) high, but above it are graceful stems with gray-blue flowers.

This grass will grow in any garden soil, including a dry one. Like most grasses, it needs a sunny spot. Remove dead leaves to maintain the overall effect of this plant's color. Propagation is by division in spring.

HELIOPSIS
False sunflower
This genus is closely related to the true sunflowers, *Helianthus,* and the species look very similar, although they are usually considered more refined in habit. The similarity is reflected in the name of the parent species, *H. helianthoides,* of the plants most commonly seen in cultivation. False sunflowers make good border plants, generally growing to 4–5 ft (1.2–1.5 m), with flowers that look like large yellow daisies. They have a long flowering period, which starts in the summer and lasts well into the fall season.

False sunflowers grow in any garden soil, including a poor one, and are drought tolerant, but a sunny site is required. Their stems are strong, and they do not usually require staking. Propagation is by division.

Heliopsis helianthoides 'Golden Plume'

H. helianthoides (above)
The species itself is rarely seen in cultivation. It is usually represented by one of its varieties or cultivars. The variety *scabra* has rough leaves and yellow flowers. 'Golden Plume' ('Goldfieder') has large, deep yellow double flowers, while 'Summer Sun' ('Sommersonne') has even bigger flowers, which are more orange in color than those of other forms.

HELLEBORUS
Hellebore
Hellebores are among the few perennial plants that flower in winter and, as such, are important in providing color and interest at that time of year. Their saucer-shaped flowers are mainly white, green, or plum-colored, although there is an increasing range of variants. They can be

grown at the back of a border, where they show up in winter but are covered by other plants during summer months, when they are not so interesting.

Hellebores need moist, humus-rich soil and a lightly shaded spot, so they make excellent candidates for a woodland border. They can be propagated from seed or by division if you wish to perpetuate a particular color strain.

Helleborus argutifolius

H. *argutifolius* (above)

Until recently this species was known as *H. corsicus*. It is a bushy plant that grows to 2 ft (60 cm) tall. The leaves are coarse and toothed, and the clusters of flowers are pale green or yellow.

H. *foetidus*

This is one of the tallest species, reaching up to approximately 2 ft (60 cm). It is clump forming and has finely divided leaves and bunches of pale green flowers, often tipped in red. 'Wester Flisk' is similar except that the stems are tinted red.

H. *niger*

The Christmas rose is a popular species that has white flowers, each with an attractive boss of yellow stamens in the center. It usually starts to bloom in midwinter. It tends to prefer slightly alkaline soil.

Helleborus orientalis

H. *orientalis* hybrids (above)

A great number of forms based mainly on *H. orientalis* have been produced. These come in a wide variety of hues, although many are plum-colored. Some are very dark purple, while others are white, green, pink, or yellow. They are often speckled with purple spots.

Helleborus × sternii

H. x *sternii* (above)

This hellebore is a cross, in fact, between *H. argutifolius* and the slightly tender *H. lividus*. It is a clump-forming plant with smoky pink flowers and blue-gray leaves. Some types are better than others.

HEMEROCALLIS
Daylily

The daylily has been popular since the late 19th century, and there is still an insatiable demand for new forms. Its common name comes in part from the fact that each flower lasts only for one day, although there are sufficient buds to ensure a succession of blooms for many weeks. The other part of the common name refers to the flowers, which are similar in shape to trumpet lilies. Their color varies from yellow through orange and pink to very dark red-brown. The plants are clump forming, with fountains of straplike leaves, from which the leafless stems bearing the flower buds rise. Although the majority bloom in summer, some species flower earlier and some later. With careful selection, you can have daylilies in bloom for much of the season.

Daylilies grow in most garden soils, although they prefer soil with plenty of added organic material and free drainage. They do well in either full sun or light shade. The clumps can become congested after a few years. To be revitalized they should be lifted, divided, and replanted. Propagate by division.

Hemerocallis 'Cartwheels'

Yellowish forms (above)

This color range presents the largest choice of plants. Among those to be recommended is the pale orange 'Bonanza,' which has a dark red center. 'Canary Glow' has bright yellow flowers, while 'Cartwheels' has similarly colored but very large, open flowers.

'Corky' bears small flowers that are rich brown on the outside and yellow inside. As its name suggests, 'Cream Drop' has cream flowers. 'Golden Chimes' is pure, deep yellow and 'Marion Vaughn' bright lemon-yellow. 'Stella de Oro' is dwarf in habit and has full petals that are golden yellow. 'Whichford' is primrose-yellow and scented. The more unusual species *H. dumortieri*, from Japan and China, has narrow golden yellow flowers that emerge, unlike those of other forms, from green bracts.

Pink forms
'Catherine Woodbury' has very subtle coloring that includes various shades of lilac-pink. 'Luxury Lace' has lavender-pink flowers with an orange-buff background. 'Pink Damask' is pink suffused with red and 'Varsity' is buff-peach with a red eye.

Hemerocallis 'Buzz Bomb'

Red forms (above)
'Buzz Bomb' is red-brown with a yellow throat. 'Cherry Cheeks' is rose-pink with red and has a yellow throat. 'Stafford' is a mahogany-red with a creamy white strip in the middle of each petal.

Purple forms
'Chicago Royal Robe' is rich purple with a yellow-green throat. 'Little Wine Cup' has dark purple-colored petals.

HEUCHERA
Alumroot
Heucheras are among the best border plants. They have attractive flowering stems, while also making excellent foliage plants. The tall, airy flower spikes contrast well with the rounded leaves. The individual flowers are mostly insignificant, mere dots of color, but when floating above the foliage they are more noticeable. The foliage varies both in its background color—sometimes green and sometimes various shades of purple—and in its markings, which can be brown or silver. Heucheras make excellent plants for the front parts of borders and are especially useful in areas that are lightly shaded.

These plants like rich soil as long as it is well drained. They grow best in either full sun or light shade, the latter being preferable in hot areas (zones 9–10). After 4 years or so it is a good idea to divide the plant and then replant the outer parts, discarding the woody central portion. Propagation is by division.

Flowering types (below)
'Bressingham Hybrids' produce flowers of mixed colors, mainly reds and pinks. 'Firefly,' as its name might suggest, has crimson-scarlet flowers, as does the species *H. sanguinea*, although it is also available in white forms. 'Schneewittchen' has pure white flowers.

Heuchera sanguinea

Heuchera 'Snowstorm'

Foliage types (above)
Some forms are noted more for their foliage than for their flowers. These include 'Pewter Moon,' with purple foliage splashed with silver and white flowers; 'Rachel,' with purple foliage and pink flowers; and 'Snowstorm,' with green leaves spectacularly speckled with creamy white and red flowers. *H. micrantha* has produced two notable seedlings: 'Bressingham Bronze,' which has brownish leaves and white flowers, and 'Palace Purple,' with its rich purple foliage and white flowers.

× HEUCHERELLA
Heucherella
This genus was created by crossing *Heuchera* and *Tiarella*, resulting in some very beautiful delicate-flowered plants, displaying characteristics from both of the parents. The airy sprays of flowers are particularly attractive, and the marbled foliage is also worthy of attention. Heucherellas make excellent plants for the front of the border, as they grow to a height of approximately 1½ ft (45 cm) when in flower.

Rich, well-drained soil is needed to produce the best from these plants. They grow in either sun or light shade, although the latter is preferable. Divide them every few years to increase the stock and keep the plants vigorous.

Main forms (below)
'Bridget Bloom,' one of the oldest cultivars, has delicate pale pink flowers.
'Rosalie' is a newer hybrid from Canada
with soft pink flowers and leaves with
red-brown veins.

× *Heucherella* 'Bridget Bloom'

HOSTA
Hosta

Most gardens have at least one hosta, as it
is one of the most popular foliage plants.
You can choose from a wide range of colors, varying from silvery blues through
many greens to yellows, and there are also
diverse textures and shapes. In many cases
the leaves are variegated, splashed or
striped with white or yellow. The texture
changes depending on whether the light is
being reflected back from a shiny surface
or absorbed by a glaucous bloom. Some
leaves are also more heavily textured with
veins than others. The shapes of the leaves
can be anything from a narrow, willowlike
blade to a huge, almost circular plate. The
flowers are often considered an after-
thought, but they can be extremely attractive, especially when seen en masse. They
are funnel-shaped and carried on tall
spikes held well above the foliage. The
color of these flowers is in most cases pale
blue, but other shades of blue and purple,
as well as whites, are available.

Hostas need rich, moisture-retentive
soil to perform best. They generally prefer
light to medium shade. Hostas will grow in
full sun, but special attention is needed to
ensure that the soil is kept moist. Slugs can
be a problem, and it may be necessary to
control them. Propagation is by division.

Blue leaves (below)
'Big Daddy' has very large, deep blue
leaves with distinctly puckered surfaces.
'Blue Moon' has very glaucous blue
leaves, which are small and rounded.
'Hadspen Blue' is one of the bluest-
leaved hostas, while the popular
'Halcyon' is not far behind. 'Krossa
Regal' has very large blue-green leaves,
which spout in a fountain. 'Wide Brim'
has rounded leaves that are blue-green in
color with a wide creamy edge, from
which it gets its name. *H. fortunei* var.
hyacinthina has leathery gray-green
leaves, but it also has several variegated
forms. *H. sieboldiana* var. *elegans* has
enormous glaucous leaves with a seer-
sucker texture.

Hosta 'Halcyon'

Green leaves
'Colossal' is so named because of its
large leaves. 'Honeybells' spreads very
quickly, as does the similar-looking
'Royal Standard.' 'Sum and Substance'
has enormous yellow-green leaves.
H. lancifolia has narrow, shiny leaves.
H. plantaginea has plantain-shaped,
glossy, pale green leaves and is fragrant.

Gold leaves (below)
'August Moon' has large leaves that
have a slightly wrinkled texture. They
are pale green when they first open but
then mature to an attractive golden
color. 'Gold Edger' is a small-leaved
gold form. 'Gold Standard' opens green
but turns to a bright gold if given
enough sun. 'Golden Sunburst' is a
golden form of the variegated 'Frances
Williams.' 'Piedmont Gold' has shiny
gold leaves that are slightly twisted.
'Zounds' has some of the largest leaves
of all the golden forms. They are puckered. This form can be grown in sunnier
positions than those preferred by many
similar hostas.

Hosta 'Gold Standard'

Variegated leaves (next column)
'Francee' has rounded leaves that are
deep green with a regular white border.
'Frances Williams' is one of the most
popular of all hostas. It has glaucous
blue-green leaves irregularly edged
with cream. 'Ginkgo Craig' is another
popular choice, with lance-shaped
leaves and narrow white margins.
'Shade Fanfare' has leaves with a light
green ground and yellow margins. In
'Thomas Hogg' the leaves, ranging
from oval to lancelike in their shape,
have broad cream edges, which continue
as a narrow cream stripe down the leaf-
stalk. *H. undulata* var. *albo-marginata*

has wavy leaves with irregular white margins; *H. u.* var. *univittata* is less wavy than the previous species and has central variegations.

Hosta 'Frances Williams'

HOUTTUYNIA
Houttuynia

This single-species genus is represented by *H. cordata*. It is a plant that grows to about 1½ ft (45 cm) and rapidly spreads to form a large colony. Since it has large heart-shaped leaves, this tendency makes it useful as ground cover. Each flower is shaped like a small cross, with four white petals and a central yellow-green boss. The leaves are normally green, but there is one very popular cultivar that has yellow and red variegations laid over the green. This is known as 'Chameleon' (**next column**), although it is sometimes listed as either 'Variegata' or 'Tricolor.' The other variegated form, 'Variegata,' is less dramatic in its coloring. 'Chameleon' is too vigorous for most formal borders but it can be used wherever ground cover is required. It also makes a fine container plant but must be watered well and not be allowed to dry out.

Houttuynia will grow in any garden soil but prefers soil that is moist, even to the extent of being boggy. It grows in either sun or shade. Planting is carried out from fall to spring, and propagation can be achieved by dividing the plants in spring.

Houttuynia cordata 'Chameleon'

IMPERATA
Imperata

This genus has eight or so species, but usually only one is grown in cultivation. This is *I. cylindrica,* grown in the form known as 'Rubra,' which does not differ greatly from the species itself. Of all the grasses, imperata is one of the most beautiful. The leaves grow upright to a height of approximately 1½ ft (45 cm). They are light green, flushed with brilliant red toward the tips—an effect that is most spectacular when sunlight shines through the blades. The foliage is complemented by silvery spikes of flowers. Imperata is a rhizomatous plant, but it spreads slowly and does not become a nuisance except in hot areas (zones 9–10).

Imperata grows in any garden soil and performs well in either a sunny or lightly shaded site. Propagation is carried out by division in spring.

INCARVILLEA
Incarvillea

The characteristically flared, trumpet-shaped flowers of the incarvillea add a touch of the exotic to the border. The genus originated in the Himalayas and China, but an increasing number of species and cultivars are now grown in the West. The trumpet-shaped flowers are pink or rose-pink, with the flared bell usually darker than the tube. The attractive leaves are arranged in pairs on either side of the stem.

Incarvilleas grow in any well-drained soil. In most areas they need a sunny location, but they should be given light shade in hot regions (zones 9–10). Protect them from slugs. Planting is best undertaken in fall or spring. Increase by division or from seed in a greenhouse.

Incarvillea delavayi

I. delavayi (above)
This is one of the more commonly grown species. It reaches 2 ft (60 cm) in height and flowers in summer, with large trumpets that are dark rose-pink. Some protection may be needed in winter (north of zone 8).

INULA
Inula

Although not everybody likes yellow daisies, this genus contains some of the better specimens. Each flower has a deep gold central disk and a ring of narrow outer petals colored bright yellow. The height of the plant varies from no more than a few inches to 6 ft (1.8 m) or more. The leaves range from narrow, willowlike types to huge, broad, rough ones. Where you place inulas will depend on their size, but all of them make good border plants, even though some are a little invasive.

Inulas will grow in any type of garden soil, but they prefer a soil that is well drained. The majority like a sunny site. The easiest way to increase stock is by dividing the plants in spring.

Inula ensifolia

I. ensifolia (above)

This is one of the medium-height species, growing to 2 ft (60 cm). It has narrow leaves and flowers up to 2 in (5 cm) wide. It grows in light shade. *I. orientalis* is similar but has deeper-colored, larger flowers and hairy leaves.

I. magnifica

As its name suggests, this is the largest species in cultivation, often growing to 6 ft (1.8 m) or more. The flowers are also large, up to 6 in (15 cm) wide. The plant needs staking in an exposed spot.

IRIS

Iris

Every perennial garden should have at least a few irises. In spite of the basic similarity between the species and the various hybrids and cultivars, there is surprising variation, particularly in flower color. The characteristic flowers are each made up of three standards (the upright petals) and three falls (the lower petals). They usually appear in early summer and, in many cases, are fragrant. The swordlike leaves are useful for creating foliage contrasts in the border. Because irises tend to finish blooming by midsummer, some gardeners prefer to create special iris beds, which can be ignored once the flowers are over.

Irises grow in most garden soils, but some species need to have moist soil and even grow in shallow water. They are mainly sun lovers, and the rhizomatous types in particular should be planted where their rhizomes can bake in the sun. The most practical way to increase stock is by division, but irises can also be grown from seed if the resulting colors are not considered important.

Iris 'Rose Queen'

I. ensata (above)

This species, previously classified as *I. kaempferi*, has produced a wealth of cultivars. Called Japanese irises, these forms grow in shallow water or very moist soil. In ordinary borders, add plenty of moisture-retentive humus. They reach 3 ft (90 cm) in height, and the swordlike leaves each have a pronounced midrib. 'Eleanor Parry' has blue flowers displaying purple markings. 'Great White Heron' bears pure white semidouble flowers. 'Moonlight Waves' has white flowers with green throats. 'Nara' has violet double flowers. The flowers of 'Nikko' are pale blue with purple markings. 'Pink Frost' has large, soft pink flowers. 'Rose Queen' offers rose-pink petals. 'Variegata' has purple flowers but is mainly grown for its attractive white-striped foliage.

Iris sibirica 'White Swirl'

I. sibirica (above)

The Siberian irises form large clumps of narrow leaves. They grow well in any border soil but perform best in moist or boggy soil. 'Caesar's Brother' bears deep purple flowers with a velvety texture. 'Cambridge' has light blue petals. 'Ego' offers rich blue flowers. 'Flight of Butterflies' has small, pale blue petals with much darker blue veining. 'Little White,' as its name suggests, has small white flowers. 'Orville Fay' displays large blue flowers with purple veining. 'Showdown' has deep violet petals with white and yellow markings. 'White Swirl' has ruffled white petals and a gold throat.

Dwarf bearded forms

These bearded irises, based mainly on *I. × germanica*, grow up to about 28 in (70 cm) high. They are best suited to areas from the front to the middle of the border because of their size. 'Cherry Garden' has cherry or wine-red flowers with contrasting dark purple beards. 'Green Spot' is white with green spots on the falls. 'Lemon Flare' has creamy white flowers. 'Lilliwhite,' as its name suggests, bears white flowers. 'Orange Capers' has orange-yellow flowers. 'Pogo' has rich yellow petals with rusty markings. 'Tinkerbell' has bright blue flowers with darker markings.

Tall bearded forms (below)
These are similar to the dwarf bearded irises except that they are taller, above 28 in (70 cm). Among the thousands available the following deserve special attention. 'Berkeley' has deep yellow petals. 'Frost and Flame' is white with a hint of purple and has a yellow beard. 'Jane Phillips' is soft blue with a white beard, and 'Pearly Dawn' is pearly pink. 'Stepping Out' is distinctive, with large white patches contrasting with dark purple edges. 'Victoria Falls' is a light blue form.

Iris 'Jane Phillips'

Pacific Coast forms
These forms were created by crossing *I. douglasiana* with *I. innominata*. They grow in full sun but prefer shade in hot areas (zones 9–10). They are of medium height, growing up to 2 ft (60 cm). There are many forms from which to choose. 'Broadleigh Rose' and 'Broadleigh Sybil' are both members of the large Broadleigh series of Pacific Coast hybrids. The former is a deep rose-pink, while the latter is brown-yellow with purple markings.

Species (next column)
As well as thousands of cultivars to choose from, there are also several hundred species for the enthusiast to explore. *I. cristata*, or the crested iris, is a low-growing form, reaching only 10 in (25 cm) high. The flowers appear in spring and vary in color from pale blue to purple. It is one of the few species that grows in shade. *I. pallida* reaches 4 ft (1.2 m) tall, has pale blue flowers, and is known mainly in its 'Aurea Variegata' and 'Variegata' forms. The leaves have golden and cream variegations respectively. *I. pseudacorus*, or yellow flag, grows in wet conditions, including shallow water. It has bright yellow flowers on a 5 ft (1.5 m) plant. *I. tectorum*, or roof iris, is a short plant, reaching 1 ft (30 cm) high, and has flat, open flowers in shades of blue, purple, or white. *I. unguicularis* flowers during winter and needs well-drained soil and a sunny spot. The fragrant purple flowers are shorter than the leaves, which can reach 1½ ft (45 cm) high.

Iris unguicularis

JASIONE
Jasione
Nearly all the jasiones make desirable garden plants, although the majority are too small for border use, except at the front. They have loose, untidy heads of blue flowers in summer, the blue varying in shade from pale blue to purple. The flowers are carried on wiry stems well above the mat of green foliage, and their hues make them particularly suitable for pastel-colored borders.

Jasiones like well-drained soil and full sun. Snip off the flowering stems once blooming is over. They can be increased by sowing seed in fall or by division in spring.

Jasione laevis

J. laevis (above)
Previously known as *J. perennis*, this jasione is the species best suited to the perennial border. It forms a low mat of foliage above which the flower stems rise up to 15 in (38 cm) high.

KALIMERIS
Kalimeris
Kalimeris is one of those odd genera that botanists regularly rename. Many still consider it part of *Aster*, and plants are still frequently listed under this name. Kalimeris are not easy to distinguish from many of the Michaelmas daisies. The flowers are approximately 1 in (2.5 cm) wide, and each has a central yellow disk and white or pale lavender ray florets. No kalimeris species is frequently grown, but *K. incisa*, which is one of the most common, grows to about 2 ft (60 cm) high. *K. mongolica*, which is less common, grows to 3 ft (90 cm) or more. *K. yomena* 'Shogun' is the form most frequently seen. It has variegated foliage.

Not only do kalimeris species and cultivars look like asters, they also need the same kind of conditions. They will grow in any soil that does not become too dry.

A sunny spot is best, although they will also grow in light shade if necessary. In exposed sites, taller plants need staking. Propagation can be carried out by division in the spring.

KIRENGESHOMA
Kirengeshoma

This single-species genus is represented by *K. palmata* (**below**). The plant is distinct, making it impossible to mistake for any other. It grows to about 4 ft (1.2 m), with black stems bearing soft yellow bells and large maplelike leaves. Kirengeshoma is an especially useful plant, as it not only flowers very late in the year, during late summer and fall, but also tolerates shade.

A woodland plant, kirengeshoma needs moist, humus-rich soil with plenty of leaf mold and a spot out of direct sun; it will grow in the open when the soil is not allowed to dry out. Young growth may be attacked by slugs. Propagate by division or by sowing seeds in spring.

Kirengeshoma palmata

KNAUTIA
Knautia

Although this is a large genus, very few species are grown in cultivation. In fact, only one species is commonly seen—this is *K. macedonica* (**next column**), a splendid plant that forms a mound of loose stems, which shoot off in all directions. The stems bear pincushionlike crimson-colored flowers. They appear in early summer and continue into the fall, although the later flowers are much smaller than those appearing earlier in the season. Knautia is 3 ft (90 cm) tall and wide.

Knautia grows in any good garden soil but prefers one that is freedraining. A sunny location is ideal. This floppy plant needs support. Propagation is carried out by division or from seed.

Knautia macedonica

KNIPHOFIA
Torch lily

Torch lilies, or red-hot pokers, are distinctive border plants. Their bright flowers are held in clublike heads on tall stems that rise out of fountains of narrow, grasslike leaves. They flower from early summer through to fall. Their height varies from about 1 ft (30 cm) to over 5 ft (1.5 m). The color of the flowers also varies. The more traditional types are bright red, often touched with yellow, but more subtle colors, including apricot, have been introduced. There are also forms that have bright yellow or yellow-and-green flowers. The vertical nature of the flowering stems can be used to provide a contrast to more rounded plants in the border. The upright flowering spikes with their bright colors draw attention, making these valuable plants for creating a focal point.

Torch lilies grow in any fertile garden soil but prefer one that is well drained.

They should be given a position in the sun. Since they are not completely hardy, torch lilies may need some protection in colder areas (zones 6–7). Propagation is carried out by division.

Tall forms (below)

The taller forms grow from 3 ft (90 cm) to 6 ft (1.8 m) high. 'Atlanta' grows up to 5 ft (1.5 m) and has heads that are bright orange-red at the top, fading to yellow at the base. It is one of the earliest to flower. 'Green Jade' has cool green flowers, fading to pale yellow, and broad leaves. 'Prince Igor' is one of the tallest cultivars, with large heads of bright red, fading to yellow at the base.

Kniphofia 'Atlanta'

Medium-height forms

These forms grow 2–6 ft (60 cm–1.8 m) tall. 'Bressingham Comet' is short, reaching 2 ft (60 cm), and is orange-red and yellow. It flowers late in the season. 'Royal Standard' grows 3–4 ft (90 cm –1.2 m) high and has golden yellow flowers that emerge from red buds, giving the flower head a two-tone effect.

Short forms

These grow up to 2 ft (60 cm). 'Little Maid' is one of the finest of all short torch lilies. It has narrow, upright leaves and creamy white flowers. 'Sunningdale Yellow' has light yellow flowers.

Mixed forms

'Border Ballet' is a seed strain, producing plants up to 3 ft (90 cm) tall, which carry flowers of red and yellow.

LAMIUM
Dead nettle

Dead nettles are good plants for creating blocks of color or ground cover. They are very easy to grow, and most will tolerate shade. They are grown for both their attractive leaves and their flowers, which are hooded and carried in whorls around the stems. The flowers vary in color from white to yellow, pink, and purple. The leaves are often delightfully variegated with splashes of silver.

Dead nettles will grow in any garden soil but tend to do best in soil that is moisture retentive. They grow particularly well in shade and also grow in the open, as long as the soil is not allowed to become too dry. Propagation can be easily achieved by division.

Lamium galeobdolon

L. galeobdolon (above)

This species shuttles back and forth between *Lamium, Lamiastrum,* and *Galeobdolon* and may be listed under any of these names. It has yellow flowers and can be invasive and should therefore be sited with care. 'Herman's Pride' has beautiful silver leaves that are veined in a contrasting dark green. 'Florentinum'

('Variegatum') is invasive but makes a good ground cover in suitable situations. Its leaves are larger than those of 'Herman's Pride,' and they are splashed with silvery white.

L. maculatum (below)

This is a low, ground-covering species, reaching a height of approximately 15 in (38 cm). It is available in several forms with attractive leaves. 'Beacon Silver' ('Silbergroschen') has silvery white markings and bears pink flowers. 'Pink Pewter' has gray leaves and pale pink flowers. 'White Nancy' is one of the best, with fresh green leaves that are liberally splashed with silver markings. They dramatically set off the pure white flowers.

Lamium maculatum 'Beacon Silver'

LATHYRUS
Pea

This large genus includes a number of species that are grown in perennial borders. Many are climbing plants that need support, but there are also several clump-forming species. All have typical pea-shaped flowers. The colors are mainly pink and purple, but there are also golden and white forms.

Peas grow in any garden soil. They mainly prefer a sunny site. They can be increased either by division or by sowing seed in spring.

Lathyrus vernus

L. vernus (above)

This low-growing species, reaching a height of just 1 ft (30 cm), has purple-blue flowers that appear in spring. It is usually grown in full sun, but in the wild it grows in deciduous woodland, and it can therefore be grown in a similar situation in the garden. The cultivar 'Albo-roseus' displays beautiful white and pink flowers.

LEUCANTHEMELLA
Leucanthemella

The name of *L. serotina* (**next page**) has been changed several times; it can still be found listed in nursery catalogs as either *Chrysanthemum serotinum* or *C. uliginosum*. It is typical of the chrysanthemums, with a daisylike flower that has a yellow central disk and white outer petals. This tall plant grows to 6 ft (1.8 m) or more. The flowers are carried at the top of the tall stems and have the curious habit of turning on their sides and following the sun throughout the day. They appear in late fall, when little else in the border is in flower, but since the plants are tall and boring when out of flower, it is best to place them at the back of a border.

Leucanthemellas grow in any fertile garden soil but it does prefer a sunny position. They slowly form a large clump, which can be easily divided for propagation. The eventual flowering height of the plant can be reduced by cutting back the developing shoots by about one-third in early summer. Unfortunately, this may delay the flowering time until later in the fall.

Leucanthemella serotina

LEUCANTHEMUM
Shasta daisy

As a result of the breakup of the genus *Chrysanthemum,* the Shasta daisies were renamed *Leucanthemum* x *superbum,* but they may still be listed under the older name *Chrysanthemum x superbum.* These are splendid plants, both as cut flowers and when grown in the border for display from summer onward. They are typical daisies, with the yellow central disk ringed by white outer petals, but there are also forms with pale yellow outer petals. The plants mainly grow to approximately 3 ft (90 cm) and have thick stems and dark green leaves.

Shasta daisies grow in any good garden soil, but they prefer soil that is moisture retentive. A sunny spot is best, but they will grow in light shade. Taller forms need support. Shasta daisies form large clumps and can be divided to increase stock. Some strains can also be propagated from seed.

Different forms (next column)
There are a number of variations in this plant, in height and in doubleness

of the flower form. 'Polaris' is a good cut-flower strain grown from seed. It has very large flowers. 'Silver Princess' ('Silberprinzesschen,' also called 'Little Princess'), which can be grown from seed, is a dwarf strain reaching only 1 ft (30 cm) high. 'Snow Lady' is an even smaller dwarf seed strain. 'Snowcap' is somewhat taller, reaching 1½ ft (45 cm) or so. 'Wirral Supreme' is one of the many taller, double forms, growing to a height of about 3 ft (90 cm).

Leucanthemum 'Snowcap'

LIATRIS
Blazing star

The flower spikes of blazing stars make a positive contribution to the late summer border, both with their upright stance and with their bright flower heads. These heads form columns of purple flowers. Those at the top of the spike usually open first, instead of those at the bottom, as with most other plants. There is not a great difference between the various species in cultivation.

Blazing stars grow in any good garden soil and need a sunny site. Propagation can be carried out by division of the cormlike rhizomes in the spring.

L. pycnostachya
This is very similar to other forms in cultivation, differing mainly in its densely clustered leaves and softly hairy stems. It

grows to 5 ft (1.5 m). There are both purple and white forms. It flowers over a long period.

L. scariosa
This species reaches the same height as *L. pycnostachya* but has wider leaves and more open flower spikes. It has a white-flowered form, 'White Chance.'

Liatris spicata

L. spicata (above)
This is the main species in cultivation. It grows to 2½ ft (75 cm) and has smooth, hairless stems. 'Floristan Violet' is a purple seed strain that is grown for cut flowers. 'Floristan White' ('Floristan Weiss') is the white equivalent. 'Kobold,' one of the main perennial cultivars, is only 1½ ft (45 cm) high and has dense spikes of bright purple flowers.

LIGULARIA
Ligularia

Yellow daisies add a touch of brightness to a border, especially one that is shrouded in gloomy shade. Ligularias are particularly useful in these circumstances. They flower from late summer onward, and unlike most other plants with similar flowers, many display interesting foliage.

Ligularias like moisture-retentive soil. If the soil dries out, the leaves soon begin to flag, indicating that they require water. Ligularias grow in either sun or light shade, but it is very important that the soil be moist if they are to be planted in sun. Propagation can be achieved either by division at the time of planting or by sowing seeds in spring.

L. dentata
This plant is 4 ft (1.2 m) tall with loose, untidy heads of large golden yellow flowers. The species and cultivars are often grown for their foliage, which in 'Desdemona' is a rich purple. The foliage is prone to attack by slugs.

L. 'Greynog Gold'
This hybrid has loose spikes of large orange-yellow flowers, which stand out well above the green foliage. It is 6 ft (1.8 m) tall.

Ligularia 'The Rocket'

L. 'The Rocket' (above)
This is one of the best of the ligularias. It is a hybrid, although it is sometimes attributed to the species *L. stenocephala* and sometimes to *L. przewalskii*. It has tall, slender spires of bright yellow flowers carried on black-purple stems, which are 5 ft (1.5 m) high.

LIMONIUM
Statice
Statice, or sea lavender, is a large genus of plants that contains a number of garden-worthy species, several of them annuals.

They are characterized by dense heads of colorful flowers, which not only make decorative features in the garden but also are good dried flowers.

These plants need well-drained soil and a sunny position. They are used to salt-laden winds, so they are particularly good plants for maritime gardens. Propagation is from seed or by division.

Limonium platyphyllum

L. platyphyllum (above)
This species is one of the most popular. Until recently it was classified as *L. latifolium,* and it is still sometimes found under this name. It produces an airy cloud of tiny mauve flowers in late summer. Reaching only 1½ ft (45 cm) high, it is suitable for growing at the front of a border.

LINARIA
Toadflax
Toadflaxes produce tall, slender spikes of antirrhinumlike flowers, mainly in soft colors. The flowers are often small, so they must be produced in great quantity to have a colorful effect. These plants are useful for filling in between other, more solid-looking plants.

Toadflaxes grow in any garden soil but do particularly well on light, well-drained soil, where they spread or self-sow, sometimes invasively. They like a sunny location. Propagate by division or from seed.

Linaria dalmatica

L. dalmatica (above)
This species is much larger in all its parts than *L. purpurea* and is a far bolder plant, where the details of the individual bright yellow flowers are easy to see. It flowers from mid- to late summer. The stems and leaves are a glaucous gray-green. The plant grows to 3 ft (90 cm). It can spread invasively, so site it with care.

L. purpurea
This plant produces slender spikes of tiny flowers from mid- to late summer. In the species they are purple, but in the form 'Canon Went' they are a delicate pink color. A good white-flowered cultivar, 'Springside White,' is also widely available. All these forms grow to a height of about 3 ft (90 cm).

LINUM
Flax
Flaxes produce beautiful blue, shallowly funnel-shaped flowers that are held on gracefully arching stems in summer. Each lasts only a day, but there is a constant succession of new blooms. Although flaxes are worth growing in the garden, one drawback is that they are short-lived and need to be renewed every 2–3 years. They should be planted toward the front of the border, where their fountain of stems is not constricted by other plants. Flaxes grow to a height of 2 ft (60 cm).

Flaxes do best when planted in light, well-drained soil in a sunny location, preferably in a sheltered position. They can be readily increased by sowing seed in fall or by taking cuttings in summer, and they often self-sow.

Linum narbonense

L. narbonense (above)

This is the larger and more vigorous of the two main perennial species and also the longer-lived. The flowers vary slightly in color from pale to rich blue.

L. perenne

This is very similar to *L. narbonense*, with which it is often confused, but it is slightly smaller in all its parts and it is not so long-lived, needing to be replaced about every 2 years. There is a white form, 'Diamant' ('Diamant White').

LIRIOPE
Lilyturf

Lilyturfs come into their own during the fall, when many of the other perennials have died back. The fact that the flowers are violet-blue is a bonus for this time of year. They appear in spikes that erupt from the clump of narrow, straplike leaves. The plants usually grow to only about 1½ ft (45 cm) high, which makes them candidates for the front of a border.

Lilyturfs grow in any fertile garden soil, including a dry one, in either sun or shade.

Propagation is best achieved by division at the time of planting, in spring.

L. muscari (below)

The flowers, small balls of violet-blue clustered around the stem, look a bit like those of *Muscari* (grape hyacinth), hence the botanical name. The form 'Majestic' has large spikes of flowers.

Liriope muscari

L. spicata

This species is very similar in appearance to *L. muscari*, but the big difference is that it spreads rapidly and can become invasive. It does, however, have a very good white-flowered form, 'Alba.'

LOBELIA
Lobelia

Although the flower shapes have much in common, the border lobelias differ from the trailing bedding lobelias that are frequently grown. The perennial lobelias are stiff, upright plants with spikes of red, blue, or purple flowers. These appear in late summer and grow up to a height of 3 ft (90 cm).

Lobelias need moisture-retentive soil to perform well. Either plant them near water or add plenty of humus to the soil. They grow in both sun and shade, but some are tender and may need winter protection in colder areas (north of zone 8). Propagate by cuttings or division.

Lobelia 'Compliment Scarlet'

Red forms (above)

'Bees' Flame' has deep purple foliage and scarlet flowers. *L. cardinalis* has green leaves and scarlet flowers; it is one of the hardier species. 'Compliment Scarlet' is a seed-raised scarlet-flowered form, while 'Queen Victoria' is an old cultivar with red foliage and bright red flowers.

Blue and purple forms

L. × *gerardii* 'Vedrariensis,' a cross between the red *L. cardinalis* and the blue *L. siphilitica*, has deep purple flowers. 'Tania' is a similar cross but has redder flowers. 'Russian Princess' has both purple leaves and purple flowers. *L. siphilitica* has blue flowers, but it also has a white form, 'Alba.'

LUPINUS
Lupine

Lupines are much loved by gardeners. The large spikes of colorful flowers, with their peppery smell, are perfect for the cottage or traditional garden. The individual flowers are pealike and come in a wide range of colors; some are a single color, while others are bicolored. The leaves are made up of many narrow leaflets arranged in a circle and are carried on plants that, when in flower, are up to 4 ft (1.2 m) high. They bloom in early summer and will go on to produce a second flush later in the year if they are cut back.

Lupines grow in any good garden soil but do best in rich soil that drains freely. They prefer full sun but tolerate light shade. They can suffer from gray lupine aphid. Most garden hybrids are short-lived and are best replaced every few years with new plants raised either from seed or from basal cuttings taken in spring.

Lupinus 'Band of Nobles'

Mixed colors (above)

Seed is the easiest method of obtaining lupines; there are a number of strains that provide a mixed selection of colors. 'Band of Nobles' is a mixture of Russell hybrids offering the complete range of lupine colors. 'Gallery' has a similar range of colors but on smaller plants.

Separate colors

Individual colors are available as named forms or as seed strains, but in the latter case the shades may vary. Plants derived from seed include 'Chandelier,' which comes in various yellows, and 'The Pages,' which are carmine. There are also bicolors available, including 'Noble Maiden' (white and cream) and 'The Governor' (blue and white).

LUZULA

Luzula

This genus of grasslike rushes contains some 40 species, but only about half are in cultivation. These plants do not look spectacular, but they are useful because they will grow in the shade. The leaves are flat and straplike, often with white hairs. The plants form either tufted clumps or spreading carpets.

Luzulas grow in any garden soil, including a dry one. Either a sunny spot or shade is suitable. Propagation is carried out by division in spring.

L. sylvatica

This woodland plant slowly spreads to form a large colony giving good ground cover. A flowering stem carrying brown flowers appears in spring and early summer. The form 'Marginata' also grows slowly. It produces attractive thick tufts of broad midgreen leaves that have hairy white edges.

LYCHNIS

Campion

Campions are easy and decorative plants to grow. They tend to have brightly colored flowers from spring to fall and can be used to enliven a border with their reds, pinks, or oranges. The flowers in some cases are up to 1½ in (4 cm) wide; in other cases they are much smaller but make up for it with quantity.

Campions grow in any garden soil but prefer well-drained soil. A sunny spot is required, and taller forms need staking. Propagation is from seed, but division is also possible. Most self-sow vigorously and need to be deadheaded to stop them from becoming invasive.

L. x arkwrightii

This short-lived plant has bronze-tinted foliage and large, bright orange flowers. It is one of the shorter campions, growing to only about 1 ft (30 cm). Regular replacement is needed, often yearly.

L. chalcedonica (next column)

The Maltese or Jerusalem cross gets its name from the cruciform shape of the flowers. They are small but are carried in a dense, domed head and make a splash in the border with their bright scarlet flowers. The plants are clump forming and grow to about 4 ft (1.2 m) in height.

Lychnis chalcedonica

L. coronaria

Rose campion is one of the most popular campions. It has startling carmine flowers that are set off by furry silver leaves and stems. The form 'Alba' has pure white flowers. 'Atrosanguinea' has dark magenta flowers, while those of 'Oculata' have pink eyes that form as they age. The plants grow up to 2½ ft (75 cm) tall.

L. flos-jovis

This is a shorter plant than *L. coronaria*, reaching up to 1½ ft (45 cm) tall. Its silver stems and foliage are beautifully complemented by the sugar-pink flowers. 'Hort's Variety' is a clear pink.

LYSICHITON

Skunk cabbage

Sometimes misspelled *Lysichitum*, this small genus has just two species, one from each side of the North Pacific. The strange flowers, which appear before the leaves have developed in spring, are clublike and surrounded by either a white or a yellow spathe. Large leaves, resembling those of romaine lettuce, soon develop and can be up to 4 ft (1.2 m) high. In suitable conditions they can spread to produce colonies of considerable extent.

Grow skunk cabbages in damp, moist soil, preferably in a bog garden or near water. Either sun or light shade is suitable. Propagate by seed.

L. americanus

This is bog arum, which has large yellow spathes and green spadices. The flowers smell unpleasant. Its leaves reach 4 ft (1.2 m) and are the bigger than those of *L. camtschatcensis*.

L. camtschatcensis (below)

This plant is slightly smaller than *L. americanus* and has pure white spathes and pale green spadices. The flowers have a faint sweet smell.

Lysichiton camtschatcensis

LYSIMACHIA
Loosestrife

Reliable rather than exceptional, loose-strifes are good plants for the border. They have tall spires of flowers in white or yellow. Site them with care, as they spread by rhizomes that can become invasive. They grow to a height of approximately 4 ft (1.2 m) and can therefore be used in a block toward the rear of a border, providing a background or serving as companions for other plants.

Loosestrifes like moisture-retentive soil and do best in damp soil near water. They flower best in sun but also grow in shade. Propagation is easily accomplished by dividing the clumps.

L. clethroides

This species grows to a height of about 3 ft (90 cm), producing a neat clump, at the top of which the short white flower spikes seem to whiz like fireworks, each bending over part of the way up the flower head.

Lysimachia ephemerum

L. ephemerum (above)

This species has flower spikes that stand rigidly upright. The flowers are white and more spaced out than they are in *L. clethroides*, but they are nonetheless well displayed against the glaucous blue-green stems and foliage.

L. punctata

Yellow loosestrife, a denizen of ditches and wet places, can spread invasively. Its foliage is coarser and not as interesting as that of the other species, but as if to compensate for this, it produces columns of larger flowers that are bright yellow. This species is much better suited for planting in a wild patch than in a formal border, unless it is kept under rigorous control. It grows to a height of about 3 ft (90 cm).

LYTHRUM
Purple loosestrife

Although this genus shares its common name as well as its liking for wet places with *Lysimachia*, the two are not related. Only 2 out of 35 species are in cultivation, but they have produced a large number of cultivars. All the forms are similar in general appearance, however, producing tall spikes of bright purple flowers. They grow about 4 ft (1.2 m) high. The plants form clumps and can eventually create large colonies. Indeed, they are rapidly taking over wetlands and moist meadows in much of eastern North America, so cultivation is banned in several states and provinces. Where legal, purple loosestrifes are good plants for the middle to rear of the border.

They perform best in boggy soils or next to water, but they can be grown in ordinary garden soil, provided it contains plenty of moisture-retaining humus. They grow in either sun or light shade, although they prefer sun. Propagate by division.

Lythrum salicaria 'Robert'

L. salicaria (above)

This species has narrow leaves and large, solid spikes of purple flowers, which appear from midsummer onward. 'Firecandle' ('Feuerkerze') grows to about 3 ft (90 cm) and has rosy red flowers. 'Robert' is a shorter form with pinker flowers.

MACLEAYA
Plume poppy

The two plume poppy species are superb plants for the large border. They grow up to approximately 8 ft (2.4 m) in height and rapidly spread to form large colonies. The tall stems and large, attractively lobed leaves are a glaucous, pearly gray. The pink or white flowers are small and petalless but are carried in quantity in loose, airy spikes. Although plume poppies are tall plants and thus best suited to the back of the border, they should be planted so that both the foliage and the flower heads can be appreciated.

These plants will grow in any garden soil but seem to prefer light, well-drained conditions. They can be grown in full sun or partial shade, preferably the latter in hot areas (zone 10). In spite of their height they do not need staking. Propagate by taking root cuttings or by division.

M. cordata

This species has pale, almost white, flowers and is generally considered to be less invasive than *M. microcarpa*, although it still spreads rapidly. The variety 'Flamingo' has pinker flowers.

Macleaya microcarpa

M. microcarpa (above)

This plant is very similar to the clump-forming *M. cordata* except that the flowers are a deeper pink. The form most commonly grown is 'Coral Plume,' which, as its name suggests, has coral-colored flowers.

MALVA
Mallow

Related to the hollyhocks, these plants have similar cone-shaped flowers. They are much smaller, however, and their colors are not as bright, yet this does not detract from their beauty. They are mainly upright plants with lobed leaves. The species vary in height, making them suitable for all parts of the border.

Mallows grow in a wide range of garden soils, including dry and impoverished ones. They prefer full sun, but in hot areas (zone 9 and warmer) light shade is appreciated. These plants are short-lived, but some tend to self-sow, so they are easily perpetuated. Propagation is mainly from seed, although stock can also be increased by taking cuttings in spring.

Malva alcea 'Fastigiata'

M. alcea (above)

This tall mallow reaches 4 ft (1.2 m) and has large pink flowers. The old cultivar 'Fastigiata' has richer pink flowers than the species and a neater shape due to its upright growth.

M. moschata

The musk mallow is much loved in old-fashioned gardens. It has a bushy habit, reaching a height of about 2 ft (60 cm), and is covered with beautiful pink flowers for a long period from summer onward. There is also an attractive white form, 'Alba.' The leaves are deeply cut and very decorative.

M. sylvestris (below)

This is a completely different plant, with its sprawling habit and purple flowers that are noticeably veined. It is grown mainly in the form known as 'Primley Blue,' in which the flowers are bluer and the plant shorter than in the species. It has round, lobed leaves.

Malva sylvestris 'Primley Blue'

MATTEUCCIA
Ostrich fern

This small genus of ferns has only three species. They are all vigorous ferns and form large colonies. Each plant produces a fountain of deeply cut fronds. The species most commonly seen in gardens is *M. struthiopteris*, which has pale green fronds and is a vigorous spreader. It grows up to 3 ft (90 cm) high. *M. pensylvanica* is very similar, except that the fronds are a darker green and, when satisfied with its conditions, it can grow much larger. Both need space to spread.

These North American woodland ferns thrive in moist, humus-rich soil and dappled shade. Next to a shady stream is ideal. Propagation is from spores or by division.

MECONOPSIS
Blue poppy

Meconopsis is a large genus consisting of about 40 species, most of which are in cultivation. The majority are blue, but there are also yellow, orange, and red species, as well as white varieties of the blue forms. The flowers have the same tissue-paper quality as poppies, and each generally has a large central boss of golden stamens. They can be used as specimen plants but look best when planted in drifts.

Blue poppies must have moist, lime-free soil, which can most easily be created by adding humus. They can be grown in the open in sun as long as the conditions are moist, but it is more common to grow them in light shade. Generally they are easiest to grow in a moist, sheltered atmosphere. Propagation is mainly from seed, but they can also be divided.

M. betonicifolia

This is the original blue poppy that first sparked interest in the genus. It grows up to 5 ft (1.5 m) tall. There is also a white form known as 'Alba.'

M. grandis (below)

This grows to the same height as *M. betonicifolia* and is very similar— the two are often confused. It generally has wider-spreading leaves and bigger flowers in a richer hue.

Meconopsis grandis

M. × sheldonii

This series of hybrids between *M. betonicifolia* and *M. grandis* manages to improve on both of them. Again, the flowers are blue. One of the best forms available is 'Ormswell.'

MELISSA
Lemon balm

The three species that make up this genus are untidy plants whose place is in the herb garden rather than the border. The main species in cultivation is *M. officinalis*. In spring and early summer it has attractive fresh green leaves with a strong smell of lemon, but once the small white flowers have appeared, it begins to become leggy and unattractive. There is a form, 'Aurea' (**below**), in which the green leaves are speckled with gold.

Lemon balm grows in any garden soil and in either sun or shade, with the golden form changing to light green if planted in shade. It should be deadheaded immediately after flowering, both to tidy up the plant and to prevent it from self-sowing invasively. Propagation is carried out from seed or by division.

Melissa officinalis 'Aurea'

MENTHA
Mint

Mentha species are better grown in the herb garden than in the border. Nevertheless, there are some very attractive forms, and as long as measures are taken to prevent them from spreading into other plants, they can make good additions to the front of the border. Mints are mainly grown for the scent and flavor that their foliage provides. The leaves give them most of their appeal, as the flowers generally go unnoticed except in borders where subtle, pale colors are required. The plants grow to about 1½ ft (45 cm).

Mints grow in any garden soil, doing best in moist sites, and they thrive in either sun or light shade. To prevent them from spreading invasively, plant them in a bottomless pail and remove the flowering stems before they have a chance to seed. Propagate by division.

Mentha × gracilis 'Variegata'

Variegated forms (above)

For the border, the variegated types are the most attractive choice. *M. × gracilis* 'Variegata' (also known as *M. × gentilis* 'Variegata') has dark green leaves which are veined with golden yellow. In contrast, *M. suaveolens* 'Variegata' has soft green leaves splashed with cream variegations. It seldom yields flowers.

MERTENSIA
Mertensia

This large genus of plants has an increasing number of species that are coming into cultivation as the beauty of their often glaucous foliage becomes more widely

appreciated. *M. virginica* (**below**), Virginia bluebells or cowslip, has been in cultivation for a long time, however. It grows to 2 ft (60 cm) and has beautiful blue-green foliage and nodding heads of bright blue flowers, which are pink in bud. It dies back after midsummer, and then there is a long wait until spring again brings forth the elegant foliage and flowers.

Virginia bluebells need moist, humus-rich, woodland-type soil to excel, as well as a cool, shady position. Propagation is either from seed or by division in spring.

Mertensia virginica

MILIUM
Millet grass
In this small genus of grasses, only *M. effusum* in its form 'Aureum' is in general cultivation. Popularly known by the name of Bowles' golden grass, this form grows into a beautiful, elegant plant. It is a clump-forming grass rather than a rapidly spreading one, and its narrow leaves form a low fountain of golden yellow, from which delicate, airy heads of pale green flowers arise. Millet grass is usually seen at its best in spring. Later in the season it can become greener, but it holds its color well.

This grass grows in any garden soil, but it produces the best results when it is in light shade. Propagation can be from division, but it also gently self-sows, providing ample seedlings for most uses.

MIMULUS
Monkey flower
This genus is a large one with a considerable number of species in cultivation. Many of the plants are treated as annuals and propagated each year. One species that is usually considered a perennial is *M. cardinalis* (**below**), the scarlet monkey flower. This has erect growth about 3 ft (90 cm) high with downy foliage and the characteristic flowers of the mimulus. As its name suggests, the flowers are mainly scarlet in color, often with a darker throat, but there are also less common varieties in yellow, pink, or sometimes a mixture.

Since they like moist soil, monkey flowers do best in a bog garden or next to a water feature. They also look best in this situation, particularly tumbling down a low bank to the water's edge. They grow in the sun or light shade. Cut them back after the first flush of flowers to encourage more blooms. Propagation can be carried out by taking cuttings, by division, or from sowing seed.

Mimulus cardinalis

MISCANTHUS
Miscanthus
This genus has 17 species of grass, of which a number are in cultivation. These are generally the tall, statuesque grasses that look dramatic when seen across a lawn or at the edge of a pool, but they can be used equally well as part of a perennial border, giving it both height and movement. These grasses are clump formers and spread slowly. The leaves are flat and straplike with a stiff, erect appearance. The decorative flower heads are usually supported on stiff stems that rise well above the leaves.

Miscanthus grows in most garden soils, including dry ones. Like most grasses, it prefers to be sited in a sunny location. Cut back the previous year's stems in late winter before the new growth begins. Propagate by division in the spring.

Miscanthus sinensis 'Kleine Fontäne'

M. sinensis (above)
Chinese silver grass provides most of the types that are in cultivation, the majority growing to 6 ft (1.8 m) high. 'Gold Feather' ('Goldfeder') has a golden sheen to its pink plumes, while 'Silver Feather' ('Silberfeder') has a silvery pink effect. 'Kleine Fontäne' has pink heads and grows to only 4 ft (1.2 m) in height; 'Malepartus' has broad leaves with a silver central line; and 'Morning Light' has variegated leaves. The leaves of *M. s.* var. *purpurascens* change to a purple-brown with a distinctive central vein as the seasons progress. This variety grows to only approximately 5 ft (1.5 m) high. 'Variegatus' has wide leaves variegated in white, while 'Zebrinus' has very distinctive yellow variegations going across the leaves.

MOLINIA
Moor grass

In this small genus of three grasses, *M. caerulea* is the main species in cultivation. Known as purple moor grass, it is 2 ft (60 cm) tall with feathery plumes of purple flowers. It has several cultivars, but 'Variegata' (**below**) is one of the best known. Its arching leaves have cream variegations along their length, and in fall they take on light brown tints. It is a good plant for lighting up a dark corner.

Moor grass grows in a wide variety of soils, including boggy ones, but it needs a sunny spot. Cut back the dead leaves and stems in late winter before new growth begins. Propagation is carried out by division in spring.

Molinia caerulea 'Variegata'

MONARDA
Bergamot

Bergamots are intriguing plants, with fascinating whorls of dead-nettlelike flowers in bright reds, pinks, and purples. They look better planted in drifts than isolated as specimen plants. Many also have fragrant leaves that have been used in tisanes and herbal teas for centuries. It is a good idea to plant monardas where you can reach or brush against a few leaves every time you pass, just for the pleasure of smelling them.

Most monardas need a sunny spot and rich, moisture-retentive soil, but they soon impoverish the soil. They must be dug up and divided, and before they are replanted the bed must be revitalized. Many monardas can suffer from powdery mildew, especially in dry weather. Propagation is carried out by division.

Monarda didyma

Species (above)

Although the hybrids are most frequently grown, there are a few species that deserve a place in the border.
M. didyma, bee balm or Oswego tea, grows to about 3 ft (90 cm), with strongly scented foliage and bright red flowers. This species, crossed with the more drought-resistant *M. fistulosa*, has been used to produce most of the hybrids. *M. punctata* has pale yellow flowers that are spotted with purple-brown and held in pink bracts.

Red forms

M. didyma provides some very attractive red forms. 'Adam' is bright cherry red, while the old-fashioned 'Cambridge Scarlet' is slightly darker. Darker still is 'Mahogany,' which has a touch of brown in it.

Purple forms

'Blue Stocking' ('Blaustrumpf') is dark mauve, despite its name. 'Loddon Crown' is a rich red-purple, while 'Prairie Night' is vibrant purple.

Pink forms

Many of the pink forms have been in cultivation a long time. An old favorite is 'Croftway Pink' with its soft rose-pink flowers. 'Beauty of Cobham' is very pale pink, while 'Pink Tourmalin' is darker.

White forms

White-flowered forms do not grow as strongly as other colors. Good forms are 'Ou Charm' and 'Snow White' ('Schneewittchen'), with the former being shorter and having a hint of pink.

MORINA
Morina

Although this is a fascinating genus of plants, only *M. longifolia* (**below**) is widely grown. It is an intriguing plant that looks like a thistle, although it is not related to the thistle family. It forms a rosette of long, spiny leaves that are dark green in color and fragrant when crushed. From this rises a tall stem, up to 3 ft (90 cm) high, bearing a spike of tubular flowers that are pale pink initially and flush darker as they are fertilized. These eye-catching plants always command attention in a border.

Morinas can be short-lived if not planted properly. They need a soil that does not dry out but is also well drained. They grow in either sun or shade and are normally propagated from seed, but can be divided. Plant them in fall or spring.

Morina longifolia

NEPETA

Catmint

Nepetas are valuable for providing hazy blue flowers for the summer border and are excellent in a soft and romantic color scheme. They are floppy plants that carry whorls of blue or purple flowers, which appear mainly during the summer months. The leaves are nettlelike, either green or a soft gray-green, and many are aromatic. Some of the larger forms are suitable for positioning farther back in the border, but the majority are best used as edging plants.

All nepetas like light, well-drained soil, and the majority require an open, sunny site. Cut them back after first flowering to promote a second flush of flowering or to encourage a crop of fresh leaves. Propagation is by division or by seed for nonnamed forms.

N. cataria

This untidy plant has off-white flowers. It is aromatic and much loved by cats, who nibble at the shoots, as well as roll on them, making it a very difficult plant to maintain.

N. × faassenii

This is the most frequently seen form of catmint and is used as an attractive edging. With its gray leaves and pale lavender flowers, the whole plant has a soft, hazy effect. It can reach up to about 2 ft (60 cm) if the lax stems are adequately supported. 'Snowflake' is a white-flowered form.

N. govaniana (next column)

In cultivation this is the only yellow-flowered catmint in existence, although in the wild it also frequently occurs in blue. It is tall with stems that can reach up to 3 ft (90 cm) or more. It is the only species that will grow in shade and prefers a moister soil to that favored by the other nepetas.

Nepeta govaniana

N. nervosa

This lower-growing species has dense spikes of bright blue flowers and leaves that are noticeably veined. Although it will grow up to 2 ft (60 cm), it is frequently shorter, making it a good plant for the front of a border.

N. sibirica

This is one of the forms of *Nepeta* in which the flowers play a positive role. The plant grows up to 3 ft (90 cm) and carries relatively large blue flowers above fresh-looking green foliage. The cultivar 'Souvenir d'André Chaudron' is shorter than the species, and its flowers continue to appear into fall.

N. 'Six Hills Giant'

This is an old cultivar that produces 3 ft (90 cm) high stems of aromatic gray foliage and clouds of lavender flowers. It is larger than other similar forms. Its lax habit can be controlled, if required, by staking.

OENOTHERA

Evening primrose

The plants in this large genus produce flowers that last only a day or a night in many cases, but they are well endowed with buds and so bloom over a very long period of summer and well into the fall. Their large dish-shaped flowers in yellow, white, or pink appear luminous in the evening light. This glow, together with their scent, attracts night-flying moths, which carry out pollination. The plants vary considerably in size: some are prostrate and are obviously best positioned at the front of a border, while others grow to 4 ft (1.2 m) tall or more so should be placed at the back of the border.

Evening primroses grow best in free-draining soil that is not too rich, and they must have a sunny spot. The stronger species are able to stand by themselves, but the others scramble through neighboring plants or have some other form of support. They are mainly propagated from seed or division in the fall or spring or by cutting in late spring.

Oenothera fruticosa 'Fireworks'

O. fruticosa (above)

This is mainly grown in its better-known forms. 'Fireworks' ('Fyrverkeri') has bright yellow flowers that are red in bud and purple-flushed foliage. *O. f.* var. *glauca* (also known as *O. tetragona*) has yellow flowers over purple foliage that is glaucous on its underside. Both grow to about 1½ ft (45 cm) tall.

O. missouriensis

Also known as *O. macrocarpa*, this sprawling plant grows to 1 ft (30 cm), with large yellow flowers that open in the evening.

O. pallida

This species flowers in the evening. It grows to about 20 in (50 cm) and has fragrant white flowers that age to pink.

Oenothera perennis

O. perennis (above)

This is also known as *O. pumila*. Its yellow flowers appear during the day, and it grows to about 1½ ft (45 cm).

O. speciosa

This plant spreads by underground rhizomes and can become invasive. It grows to about 1½ ft (45 cm) and has narrow grayish leaves and, during the day, beautiful white flowers. There is also a pink form known as 'Rosea.'

OMPHALODES
Navelwort

Navelworts are worth growing, as they bring a cheerful note to spring. Their bright blue forget-me-not flowers are charming and always a welcome reminder that summer is not far away. Given time, these low-growing plants will create a carpet of green foliage. In borders they are useful for growing between other plants, especially at the front of the bed. They are also good farther back, where they will be hidden later in the season when they are no longer flowering.

Navelworts grow in any garden soil, including dry ones. They prefer partial shade, but this can be provided by other perennials as well as by trees and shrubs. Propagation is by division or from seed.

O. cappadocica

This is the taller of the two species commonly in cultivation. It grows to 10 in (25 cm) and carries its blue flowers above the leaves in loose spikes.

O. verna (below)

Smaller in all its parts than *O. cappadocica*, this species produces fewer flowers, but it still makes an attractive ground cover. It prefers a moister soil. Its common name is blue-eyed Mary.

Omphalodes verna

ORIGANUM
Marjoram

There are numerous marjorams in cultivation; the majority are grown in either herb gardens or rock gardens. Several marjorams, however, are suitable for the open border. While these are decorative plants, they still retain the aromatic qualities of the kitchen herb. The pink, purple, or white flowers are held in loose clusters above the leaves and are much loved by butterflies during late summer and fall.

Marjorams like well-drained soil and a sunny site. They can self-seed prolifically, so it is best to deadhead them soon after flowering. Propagation can be by division or from seed.

O. laevigatum

This superb border plant has upright stems that can reach a height of 1½ ft (45 cm) or more. The stems carry airy displays of purple flowers. There are a number of good forms, such as 'Herrenhausen' with its dark purple flowers.

Origanum vulgare 'Aureum'

O. vulgare 'Aureum' (above)

This is the golden-leaved form of the common marjoram. It creates a rounded mound of pure gold foliage in spring, then begins to change to green later in the season, although some clones remain golden. The flowers are white but are often removed, as this form is grown principally for its leaves.

OSMUNDA
Royal fern

The genus *Osmunda* contains a number of species, but it is mainly known by gardeners for the royal fern, *O. regalis* (**next column**). This very distinctive clump-forming fern has large fronds with wide, light green, leathery segments. The fronds in the center of the plant are of a different type, rusty brown in color and shriveled in appearance. These are the spore-bearing fronds. The whole plant reaches 6 ft (1.8 m) or more when in ideal conditions.

The royal fern must have moist soil, such as that found in a bog garden or near water. If conditions are moist enough, it can be grown in the open; otherwise grow it in light shade. Increase stock from spores or by division.

Osmunda regalis

PAEONIA

Peony

Peonies are one of the mainstays of borders in spring and early summer. Their bushy plants add substance, and their flowers provide a burst of color. The flowers of the species and of many cultivars are single and bowl-shaped, each with a distinct central boss of stamens. There are also many cultivars that are doubles. These are the same shape as the singles, but the bowls are filled with layer upon layer of frilly petals, sometimes the same color as the outer petals, sometimes contrasting. The foliage is attractive, especially when it first emerges in spring and again later when it takes on fall tints.

Peonies are not especially tall plants, 3 ft (90 cm) at most, and are best sited in the front half of the border, accompanied by plants that flower later in the season.

Peonies need deep soil enriched with humus. Do not plant them too deeply; the crowns should be between 1–3 in (2.5–7.5 cm) below the surface of the soil. Many peonies grow best in a sunny site, but others prefer a little shade, especially in hot areas (zone 10). Propagation is by division at planting time, although the species can be grown from seed.

Single forms (below)

'Coral Charm' has coral-pink flowers, darker in bud. 'Emblem' has maroon-red flowers. 'Patriot' is characterized by deep maroon-crimson flowers. 'White Wings' has large, pure white flowers. The nearly unpronounceable species *P. mlokosewitschii* is one of the earliest to flower, opening to a clear yellow. For a dark red, *P. tenuifolia* is hard to beat, especially as it has attractive finely divided foliage.

Paeonia 'White Wings'

Double forms

P. officinalis 'Alba Plena' and 'Duchesse de Nemours' are both white doubles; the latter is strongly scented. 'Félix Crousse' is carmine. 'Festiva Maxima' is white flecked with crimson, while 'Inspecteur Lavergne' is completely crimson. 'Monsieur Jules Elie' is a soft, silvery rose-pink. 'Philippe Rivoire' has ruby-red flowers. 'Queen of Hamburg' is bright pink, and 'Red Charm' is crimson. 'Sarah Bernhardt,' one of the most popular of all peonies, is pink.

Imperial or Japanese forms

These forms all have anemone-like flowers. 'Bowl of Beauty' has large flowers that are deep pink on the outer petals and creamy white on the inner ones. 'Evening World' is similar except that the outer petals are a pale pink.

PAPAVER

Poppy

Poppies have long been extremely popular in gardens. The flowers may be transient, but people take great delight in their brief blooming. The majority are bright colors, and even the more subtle pinks and whites draw attention to themselves. The majority of the border choices are derived from *P. orientale*, the Oriental poppy. These have large tissue-paper flowers, often with black or purple blotches in the center. The flowers also each have a large central boss of black stamens.

Poppies can be grown in most garden soils but do best in rich, well-drained ones and should be planted in full sun. Many need support. Cut them down after flowering to encourage a fresh flush of the coarse, hairy, deeply cut leaves. Propagate by taking root cuttings in early winter.

Papaver orientalis 'Perry's White'

White forms (above)

'Black and White' has white petals, each with a black blotch at its base. 'Perry's White' has white petals and a purple-maroon blotch.

Pink forms

'Cedric Morris' is pale pink with a very large central black area. 'Mrs. Perry' has pale salmon-pink petals with black blotches. 'Turkish Delight' is pale salmon-pink with no blotches.

Red forms
'Beauty of Livermere' has huge, bright scarlet flowers with black blotches. 'Patty's Plum' ('Mrs. Marrow's Plum') is dark purple.

Papaver orientale 'Curlilocks'

Orange forms (above)
'Allegro' is bright scarlet-orange with coarse, hairy foliage. 'Curlilocks' has fringed petals and is bright orange-red with black spots. 'Doubloon' is an early-flowering orange double.

PATRINIA
Patrinia

In this genus of about 15 species, three are occasionally seen in cultivation. They are closely related to valerians, with loose, flat heads of small flowers. Instead of being white or pink, however, patrinia flowers are usually yellow. An attractive addition to a rock garden, these plants spread by creeping, forming either a large clump or a small colony.

Patrinias are normally grown in moist woodland soils in light shade. They can be increased by either division in spring or from seed in fall.

P. scabiosifolia

This is one of the taller forms, growing up to 3 ft (90 cm) high and carrying yellow flowers during summer. It prefers a more open and sunnier spot than

P. gibbosa and *P. triloba*, the other two similar species, which are more frequently seen in cultivation.

PENNISETUM
Fountain grass

The members of this large genus of perennial and annual grasses come mainly from tropical areas, but a few are suitable for cultivation in more temperate climates. They are grown not so much for their leaves as for their soft flower heads, which are cylindrical and look like bottlebrushes. These grasses vary considerably in height, from about 1½ ft (45 cm) to 5 ft (1.5 m), making some suitable for the front of a border, where they can be stroked as you pass, and some best farther back.

Pennisetums need light, free-draining soil and, like most grasses, an open, sunny site. They should be cut back in winter or early spring before new growth begins. Propagation is either by division in spring or from seed.

P. alopecuriodes

This is one of the taller species, growing to 3 ft (90 cm). The foliage is not very remarkable, but the flower heads are delightful: bluish with a white tuft at the top. Unfortunately, the plants flower only after a warm summer. The whole plant turns a buff color for the winter. 'Hameln' is a particularly good early-flowering form.

P. setaceum

This species is less hardy than the last. Its bottlebrush flower heads vary from pink to purple, and in 'Rubrum' they are rose-pink with foliage of the same color. The flowers of both types fade to light brown for the winter.

PENSTEMON
Penstemon

Penstemon is a very big genus with a large number of species in cultivation. Many of

these are small and do well when grown in the rock garden. However, an equally large number are tall enough to be grown in the open border. The taller penstemons are particularly valuable for the summer border, with bright, cheerful-looking flowers that continue blooming for a long period. The tubular flowers vary in color from blues through purples to reds and also include whites. Most are bicolored with contrasting, usually white, throats. The leaves are pointed and range from light to dark green, but they always have a fresh appearance that offsets the flowers beautifully. Penstemons vary in height from about 2 ft (60 cm) to 3 ft (90 cm). They look good in drifts or in small groups and are easy to propagate.

Penstemons grow in most garden soils but prefer free-draining soil. It is possible to grow them in light shade, but most prefer a warm, sunny location. Propagation is easily achieved by taking cuttings, although some plants can also be divided. Not all penstemons are completely hardy, and it is good insurance to overwinter a few cuttings.

Penstemon 'White Bedder'

White cultivars (above)
'White Bedder' is one of the few penstemons that appears as a single color. As the name suggests, it is white and has dark anthers that give it a slightly spotted appearance.

Pink cultivars (below)

'Beech Park' (also known as 'Barbara Barker') has large flowers that are creamy white flushed with pink at the mouth. 'Hidcote Pink' has soft pink flowers, paling toward the throat, which is veined with red streaks. 'Mother of Pearl' has smaller flowers that are pale pearly pink and white.

Penstemon 'Hidcote Pink'

Red cultivars

'Andenken an Friedrich Hahn' (also known as 'Garnet') has purple-scarlet flowers. 'Chester Scarlet' has scarlet flowers. 'Ruby' ('Schoenholzeri') has small flowers of bright scarlet.

Purple and lilac cultivars

'Alice Hindley' has large flowers in soft lilac, fading inside the tube. 'Sour Grapes' has small flowers with deep violet flowers, paling in the throat. 'Stapleford Gem' is similar to 'Sour Grapes' but paler.

Species

Many of the species are also suitable for cultivation. *P. barbatus* has small red flowers with yellow beards and is grown in a number of cultivars, including the less common 'Elfin Pink,' which has small pink flowers. *P. digitalis* is named for its resemblance to the foxglove. In the form 'Husker's Red' the foliage is tinged dark purple-red and the flowers are very pale pink. *P. heterophyllus* is a shrubby plant with flowers that vary from purple to bright blue. *P. pinifolius* is a low-growing form that is suitable only for the front of the border or a rock garden. It has narrow needlelike leaves and small narrow flowers that are orange in color. There is also a yellow form, 'Mersea Yellow,' a very unusual color for penstemons.

PEROVSKIA
Russian sage

The salvia-like plants of this small genus are, strictly speaking, shrubs or subshrubs. The only one of the seven species that is in general cultivation is *P. atriplicifolia*. This woody subshrub is usually treated as a herbaceous plant and cut back each winter. It has feathery foliage, which, along with the stems, is covered in soft, white hairs, giving the plant a ghostly gray appearance. The pale blue flowers are carried in whorls on the spreading branches, adding to the misty effect. They appear from late summer onward. The plant grows up to 5 ft (1.5 m). 'Blue Spire' (**below**) has particularly finely cut foliage.

This plant grows best in well-drained soil and a warm, sunny location. In spite of its height, no staking is required. Propagate by taking basal cuttings in spring.

Perovskia atriplicifolia 'Blue Spire'

PERSICARIA
Knotweed

To many gardeners this genus, which consists of at least 150 widely varying species, may be more familiar as *Polygonum,* and plants may still be found listed as such in most nurseries. It contains many excellent plants for the perennial garden, although some can spread rapidly and are more suited to growing in the wild part of your garden.

Knotweeds vary in height from low carpets 1 ft (30 cm) high to tall colonies of 6 ft (1.8 m) or more. The flowers are mainly held in tight cylinder-like spikes or balls and come in a variety of shades of pink. In most cases the leaves make a dense ground cover.

Knotweeds grow in most garden soils but do best in those that are slightly moist. They do well in either sun or shade. Plant at any time between fall and spring. Since most knotweeds spread, the easiest method of propagation is by division.

Persicaria amplexicaulis

P. amplexicaulis (above)

This is one of the best border forms. It forms a dense clump of docklike foliage, from which wiry stems rise carrying narrow heads of pink or red flowers. The plant grows up to 4 ft (1.2 m). It does spread but not at the alarming rate of some of its relations. 'Firetail' has large crimson flower spikes.

P. bistorta

This species can be grown in the ordinary border, but it comes into its own in a bog garden or beside a water feature. The flowers are bright pink and are set off well by the fresh green of the large leaves. The plant soon forms large colonies 3 ft (90 cm) or more wide. 'Superba' has larger flowers and grows to 2½ ft (75 cm) tall.

P. campanulata

This plant grows to 4 ft (1.2 m) but can be very invasive. It carries a constant display of tiny bells. The foliage is decorative with distinct veins. Plant it in a damp spot.

P. virginiana

This species is often incorrectly listed as *Tovara*, usually under the form 'Painter's Palette.' It is grown mainly for its decorative foliage, which is a mixture of cream and brown-maroon as well as green, and it rarely produces flowers. It reaches a height of approximately 2 ft (60 cm).

PHALARIS
Ribbon grass

Although there are 15 species in this genus, only one, *P. arundinacea*, usually in the form 'Picta' (**next column**), is grown. Known as ribbon grass or gardener's garters, it is a very attractive grass with fresh-looking leaves. These are green, striped with white, but the shoots are pink when young. The blades are wide and give rise to the common name of this grass. It grows up to 3 ft (90 cm). Unfortunately, it is an extremely invasive plant, particularly in rich, damp soil, and should be planted where it can spread at will or in a position where it can be contained.

This grass grows in any garden soil, but it needs a sunny spot. Planting should be carried out in spring. Propagate by division in the spring.

Phalaris arundinacea 'Picta'

PHLOX
Phlox

This genus provides gardens with popular plants, some of which flower in spring and others later in the year. Some are ground hugging, while some reach 5 ft (1.5 m); still others are in-between. Some prefer an open spot and others, shade. This wide range of habits and requirements, coupled with the wide range of colors, means that there are at least some plants for every garden. The tubular flowers each flare out into a flat disk of five petals. The colors are predominantly white, blues, purples, pinks, and reds.

Phlox like humus-rich soil that never becomes too dry. They vary in their need for shade, although the border phlox require sunshine. Propagation, between fall and spring, is best done by root cuttings, but phlox can be grown from basal cuttings and by division.

P. carolina

This species resembles *P. maculata*. It reaches 4 ft (1.2 m), flowers in early summer, and will grow in light shade. The most popular cultivar is 'Miss Lingard,' which has pure white flowers.

P. divaricata

This is a useful species for a shady border. It grows to only 1 ft (30 cm) and forms a tight carpet of foliage, from which the flowering stems rise in spring. The flowers are usually pale blue. 'Dirigo Ice' has light blue flowers, while in 'Fuller's White' they are so pale that they are almost white.

P. maculata (below)

This is a slender plant with flowers held in a spike. The plants are short, growing to 2–4 ft (60 cm–1.2 m) tall, and they flower early. 'Alpha' has mauve-lilac flowers with darker centers; 'Omega' is white with pink eyes and plain stems; and 'Rosalinde' has deep pink flowers.

Phlox maculata

P. paniculata (next column)

This species provides most of the border phlox, which can reach up to 4–5 ft (1.2–1.5 m) and have pyramidal flower heads. They require a sunny spot, and the taller types need staking in exposed areas. White forms include 'Blue Ice' (pale blue aging to white), 'Fujiyama' (large heads of pure white), and 'White Admiral' (similar to 'Fujiyama' but flowering later). Pink forms include 'Bright Eyes' (pale pink with a dark eye), 'Dodo Hanbury Forbes' (large heads of medium pink), and 'Eva Cullum' (pink with a dark center). Lilac forms include 'Amethyst' (violet-blue), 'Blue Boy' (lilac-blue), and 'Franz Schubert' (lilac, darkening toward the center). Orange-tinted forms include 'Brigadier' (reddish salmon), 'Orange Perfection' (nearly pure orange), and 'Prince of Orange' (deep salmon). Red forms include 'Aida' (violet-red) and 'Starfire' (cherry-red). Variegated forms include 'Harlequin' (red-purple flowers and cream marginal variegations) and 'Norah Leigh' (pink flowers, darker in the center, and dominating cream variegations on the leaves).

Phlox paniculata 'Eva Cullum'

PHYGELIUS
Cape figwort

There are two species from South Africa in this genus, both of which are technically subshrubs. From summer onward they produce tubular flowers in either red or yellow. In optimal conditions and grown against a wall, they can reach 20 ft (6 m) or more in height, but in the border they are normally confined to 4 ft (1.2 m) or less. They are attractive plants that flower over a long period.

Cape figworts grow in any garden soil, but they do best in moisture-retentive soil, as long as excess water can drain away. They can be increased from cuttings or by careful division.

P. aequalis

This plant produces tubular flowers that are straight with flared mouths. The species is dusky pink, but 'Yellow Trumpet,' which has creamy yellow flowers, is the form that is most commonly grown in gardens.

P. capensis

In this species the flowers curve back toward the stems and the tips of the tubes are reflexed. The flowers are colored an orangish red.

Phygelius × *rectus* 'African Queen'

P. × *rectus* (above)

This is the name given to the hybrids between the two species. There are a number of these, and they are very popular. 'African Queen' is pale red with orange-red tips. 'Moon-raker' is a similar color to *P. aequalis* 'Yellow Trumpet,' but the flowers are carried all around the stem. 'Pink Elf' has pale pink tubes with crimson tips and a yellow throat.

PHYSALIS
Chinese lantern

Physalis is a large genus, but only one species, *P. alkekengi,* is in general cultivation. This is grown mainly for its seed heads, which look like orange balloons. The white flowers that precede them are insignificant, but the foliage is a fresh green, which contrasts well with the orange coloring. This sprawling plant is 1½ ft (45 cm) tall and spreads to form a large colony. It is not a plant to be placed in a highly visible spot.

Chinese lanterns grow in any garden soil in either sun or shade. Planting can take place at any time between fall and spring, and propagation is achieved either by division or from seed.

PHYSOSTEGIA
Obedient plant

The odd name of this plant is derived from the fact that if the individual flowers are pushed to one side, they will remain there and not spring back. The tubular pink flowers are borne in spikes toward the end of summer on plants that are up to 5 ft (1.5 m) tall and stand erect. The plants spread to form large clumps.

Obedient plants grow in any good garden soil but do best in soil enriched with humus. Although they prefer a sunny spot, they can be grown in light shade, especially in hot areas (zone 9 and warmer). They are best planted in fall or spring. They can be increased by division in spring, or they can be grown from seed.

Physostegia virginiana 'Rose Bouquet'

P. virginiana (above)

This is the main species to be grown in gardens. The flowers range from pale to rose-pink. There is a particularly beautiful white form called 'Alba.' 'Rose Bouquet' ('Bouquet Rose') is a larger form with rose-pink flowers, and 'Variegata' has pink flowers and cream-variegated foliage.

PHYTOLACCA
Pokeweed

This genus consists of bold, somewhat invasive plants, which are better relegated to the wild part of your garden than to the formal border, where they are likely to become a nuisance. They are tall plants, up to 8 ft (2.4 m) when grown in suitable conditions, and have candlelike spikes of white or pink flowers that emerge from the large green foliage. They are attractive plants, but they must be used with care because all parts are poisonous. The species that is most commonly grown is *P. americana* (**below**), with white flowers. *P. polyandra* (*P. clavigera*) has pink flowers.

Pokeweeds grow in any garden soil in either sun or light shade. Propagation is by division or from seed. Self-sown seedlings are usually available.

Phytolacca americana

PLATYCODON
Balloon flower

This fascinating plant will cause much comment. The buds are the feature that generates all the attention. They are inflated in shape, like balloons, getting larger until they finally burst open to form cup-shaped flowers in a deep silky blue. They are carried at the top of stems, which grow up to 2½ ft (75 cm). As seen from the open flowers, these plants are closely related to campanulas. There is only one species in the genus, *P. grandiflorus*

(**below**), which is beautiful in itself, but there are also a number of varieties: *P. g.* var. *albus,* has white flowers, while *P. g.* var. *mariesii* has larger blue flowers.

Balloon flowers grow in rich, well-drained soil. They tolerate a little shade but do best in full sun. The new growth is late to emerge in spring, so do not dig it up accidentally. Slugs like the new growth. Propagation is from seed, basal cuttings, or careful division.

Platycodon grandiflorus

PLEIOBLASTUS
Bush bamboo

This genus was recently separated from *Arundinaria,* and its species are still sometimes listed in nurseries under that genus name. *Pleioblastus* is a genus of about 20 species, and a large number of these are in cultivation. Only two, however, are grown to any extent. One is *P. variegatus* and the other, the more popular *P. auricomus* (*P. viridistriatus*). Both are variegated, the former with white stripes and the latter with deep gold ones, and both are considered to be the best variegated bamboos of their color. Both form large clumps but are not generally invasive.

Plant bush bamboos in any garden soil, ideally in moisture-retentive conditions. They do best in full sun but grow in shade, although the golden form loses its rich color there. Propagation is carried out by division in spring.

POLEMONIUM
Jacob's ladder

These old-fashioned plants have been grown in gardens for many generations. The curious name comes from the shape of the leaves, which are each made up of a series of parallel leaflets, like the rungs of a ladder. The flowers are shallow funnels mainly in various shades of blue, but white forms are also available. Jacob's ladders vary in height from those that form loose plants only 1 ft (30 cm) or so tall to those that stand erect, reaching 3 ft (90 cm) or more. They flower mainly in spring and early summer, and it is a good idea to grow later-flowering plants next to them to cover their drab appearance during the rest of the season.

Jacob's ladders grow in any good garden soil but do best in moisture-retentive conditions. They perform best in a sunny spot, although they will grow in light shade. In hot areas (zone 9 and warmer), however, shade is the better choice. Propagation is from seed or by division.

Blue forms

Blue is the main color of many of the species. *P. caeruleum,* the tallest at 3 ft (90 cm) or more, has pale blue flowers. *P. foliosissimum* is similar but has darker flowers. *P. reptans* is smaller, growing up to 2 ft (60 cm), and is a sprawling plant with lavender flowers.

White forms

Both the taller species, *P. caeruleum* and *P. foliosissimum,* have white forms, known respectively as *P. c.* var. *album* and *P. f.* var. *alpinum* ('Album').

Lilac forms (next column)

As well as blue forms, there are several species and cultivars that produce delicate lilac-pink shades. *P. c.* 'Hopleys' is an upright form, while *P.* 'Lambrook Mauve,' a hybrid from *P. reptans,* is a low-growing sprawler.

Polemonium 'Lambrook Mauve'

POLYGONATUM
Solomon's seal

Solomon's seals have a fresh, cool quality that creates a tranquil mood. They are ideal for a shady location, doing especially well in a dappled woodland setting. The plants have arching stems, from which opposite pairs of leaves stand out horizontally. Below the stems hang the delicate white flowers. These are narrow bells that are pulled in slightly at the waist and tipped in green.

The plants run underground and, once they are settled, can quickly form large colonies. They are not invasive, however, as they can be easily controlled. There are about 30 popular species from which to choose, although the genus is more numerous than this.

Solomon's seals are woodland plants and like moist, humus-rich soil and a cool root run. Sawfly caterpillars can reduce the foliage to shreds by late summer and need to be controlled. Plant from late summer to late fall. Solomon's seals are easily propagated by division of the running rootstock in early fall.

P. biflorum
This is a smaller version of the common Solomon's seal, *P. × hybridum.* It grows to 3 ft (90 cm) but is often much shorter. As its botanical name implies, the flowers are carried in pairs.

P. × hybridum (below)
Also known as *P. multiflorum,* this is the most common type of Solomon's seal. It is taller than *P. biflorum,* and the flowers are carried in clusters of between two and five. There is a creamy white variegated form, 'Striatum.' Another variegated form, *P. odoratum* 'Variegatum,' has fragrant flowers and more delicate variegations than 'Striatum.'

Polygonatum × *hybridum* 'Striatum'

POLYSTICHUM
Shield fern

This very large genus of ferns provides some excellent garden plants. The fronds are typically fernlike, often evergreen and with a glossy leathery appearance.

These woodland natives should be grown in moist, acid to neutral soil—one with plenty of humus or leaf mold is ideal. They thrive in light to deep shade. Propagation is by division in spring or from spores in fall.

P. aculeatum
Known as the hard shield fern, this plant is delicately divided and light green when it first unfurls, darkening to a deep, glossy green. It is evergreen and grows to about 3 ft (90 cm).

P. polyblepharum
The evergreen Japanese holly fern is a shorter plant than *P. aculeatum* but no less decorative, with delicately divided fronds of shiny dark green.

Polystichum setiferum

P. setiferum (above)
The evergreen soft shield fern is one of the tallest species, growing up to 4 ft (1.2 m) in optimal conditions. It is also one of the most elegant ferns, with finely divided fronds of a soft green. It tolerates dry soil. There are several cultivars, of which 'Divisilobum' is one of the most beautiful.

POTENTILLA
Potentilla

This genus sometimes causes confusion, as it provides both shrubs and hardy perennials. The flower's shape is the same in both cases: five petals arranged in a flat dish. However, the underlying structure is woody in the shrubs, while the perennials are soft and die back each year. The wide range of flower colors, based on red and yellow, makes these plants a cheerful addition to any border. Some are semidouble or double. All potentillas tend to be scrambling plants, which perform best when growing up through another plant, such as a low bush.

Potentillas grow in any garden soil, although they prefer soils that are well drained. The majority like a sunny location. Propagation is by division or from seed in the case of the species.

Cultivars (below)

'Flamenco' has bright scarlet flowers, while 'Gibson's Scarlet' is such a bright scarlet that it is difficult to look at. 'Monsieur Rouillard' is double with deep red flowers touched with yellow, while 'William Rollison' is semidouble with orange flowers splashed with yellow. 'Miss Willmott,' a cultivar of *P. nepalensis*, has cherry-pink flowers with darker centers. 'Roxana,' another form of the same species, has deep pink flowers with dark centers.

Potentilla 'Gibson's Scarlet'

Species and other forms

P. atrosanguinea, one of the parents of many of the hybrids, has red flowers. *P. a.* var. *argyrophylla* has yellow flowers and leaves with silvery white hairs. *P. recta* has yellow flowers, while its form 'Warrenii' has flowers of the same color but brighter. *P.* × *tonguei*, with red-centered apricot-colored flowers, will grow in light shade.

PRIMULA

Primula

This large genus consists mainly of low-growing plants, the majority of which belong in the alpine garden, although a few are strong enough to be grown among perennials. Many, such as the primroses, have been grown in gardens for centuries, and few spring gardens

should be without them. Their flowers cover the whole range of garden colors, so you can easily fit them into any color scheme. They make good plants for the front of a formal border, where the early-flowering ones can be placed among plants that will cover them later in the year. A more permanent position can be found in shady borders.

Primulas like soil that does not dry out and has extra humus to help keep it moist and enrich it. Most prefer a shady spot but will tolerate full sun in cooler areas (zone 3) as long as the ground is moist. Propagate from seed, sown as soon after ripening as possible, or by division.

P. denticulata (below)

These are the drumstick primulas, so called because their spherical heads, made up of many flowers, are held on the tops of tall stems. They are typically mauve, but there are many other variations, including 'Alba' (white) and 'Rubinball' (shades of red).

Primula denticulata

P. japonica

The Japanese primula is one of the candelabra varieties. These are tall, growing to 3 ft (90 cm), with whorls of flowers, mainly in white or red, at intervals up the long stems. Some of the better forms are named. As its name indicates, 'Miller's Crimson' is red.

P. rosea (below)

This primrose-type species has rose-pink flowers held on short stems rising above veined leaves. 'Delight' ('Micia Visser de Geer') has carmine flowers.

Primula rosea

P. vialii

This is an extraordinary primula in that, in flower, it is often mistaken for an orchid. It has a tight, rocket-shaped head of mauve flowers, tipped with red buds. Unlike most primulas, it blooms in summer. It grows to approximately 2 ft (60 cm) in good conditions.

P. vulgaris

The beautiful English primrose, a yellow-flowered species, is considered the harbinger of spring. Many other colored forms have been derived from it, including a whole series of attractive double-flowered cultivars. 'Alba Plena' is pure white; 'Easter Bonnet' has lilac flowers; and 'Miss Indigo' has indigo petals delicately rimmed with silver. Many single forms are just as attractive, including 'Guinevere' ('Garryard Guinevere'), a unique old-fashioned primula with pale pink petals and a bright yellow center set against purple foliage. Cowichan Series is a seed strain that produces some richly colored plants, many of which flower later than other types of primula.

PRUNELLA
Self-heal
This is an attractive ground-cover plant for the front of a border. It forms a dense mat of evergreen leaves, from which stubby spikes of purple flowers rise. The flowers are hooded and lipped, resembling those of dead nettles. Self-heals are mainly blue or purple in color, although white forms are occasionally seen.

They grow in any garden soil, including dry soil, and prefer a sunny location but will also grow in shade. They self-sow prodigiously, so deadhead them after flowering. Propagation is by division.

P. grandiflora (below)
This is the main species in cultivation. It has large heads of violet flowers. There is a series of cultivars suffixed with the name "Loveliness." 'Loveliness' itself has lilac flowers, while 'Pink Loveliness,' 'Purple Loveliness,' and 'White Loveliness' are all named for their various colors.

Prunella grandiflora

PULMONARIA
Lungwort
The common name of this plant is derived from the resemblance of the spotted leaves to diseased lungs. However, it is these spots that make this such a valuable foliage plant. Most species have rough, spear-shaped green leaves, some with silver spots, which in some cases merge to make the whole leaf silver. Once the plants have finished flowering in spring, if all the foliage is sheared off, new foliage will appear, making the plant look fresh for the rest of the year. The plant grows to 1 ft (30 cm) high. The tubular flowers are not big but provide a carpet of color in late winter or spring. They are usually shades of blue and pink, with a few white forms.

Pulmonarias do best in moist soil with plenty of humus. They need a shady location. Propagate by division after flowering.

Pulmonaria rubra 'David Ward'

Foliage forms (above)
Although the following are mainly grown for their foliage effects, the flowers also have considerable attraction. The spotted-leaved *P. saccharata* has several good foliage forms, including 'Argentea,' with spots that merge into a silver leaf and pink and blue flowers. *P. rubra* 'David Ward' has pale green leaves, edged with cream.

Red-flowered forms
True red forms have yet to be developed, but there are some that are deep pink-red. One of the closest to red is *P. rubra* 'Redstart,' which has plain green leaves.

Blue-flowered forms
Blues vary from bright forms to pale ones. Some of the brightest blues come from *P. angustifolia*, and of these *P. a.* subsp. *azurea* is one of the best. 'Blue Ensign' is also a good form. 'Lewis Palmer' ('Highdown') displays its bright blue flowers on long stems.

White-flowered forms
Most blue forms occasionally produce white seedlings, but there is an excellent named form, *P. officinalis* 'Sissinghurst White.' This pulmonaria has long, elliptical leaves that are spotted with a paler color.

PULSATILLA
Pasqueflower
Pasqueflowers make excellent plants for the front of a border. Their attraction lies not only in their beautiful cup-shaped flowers but also in their finely cut foliage and superb display of silky seed heads. They flower in spring, with the seed heads lasting well into summer. The most commonly seen species is *P. vulgaris* (**below**). Typically this has mauve flowers, but a wide range of purple, red, and white flowers are also available, possibly introduced from other species. The plants are clump forming and grow up to 1 ft (30 cm) tall.

Pasqueflowers grow in most free-draining soils, but they should be planted in a sunny site. Increase stock by sowing the seed as soon as it has ripened. Often the plant self-sows.

Pulsatilla vulgaris

RANUNCULUS
Buttercup

This large genus has a few species that are grown in the perennial border, and several more are used in the rock garden. While many have yellow flowers, some species carry white flowers. Many of the yellow forms that are derived from native plants are invasive and should be treated with care. Some of the safer ones, however, can be used to brighten up the border, while the more invasive ones can be put to use in the wild part of a garden. The plant grows to 2 ft (60 cm) high.

Buttercups grow in most garden soils. They prefer a sunny site, but many will also grow in light shade. Increase stock by division or from seed.

Ranunculus aconitifolius 'Flore Pleno'

R. aconitifolius (above)

This is a bushy plant that in early summer produces white flowers that are carried on airy branches. It is best known in its button-flowered double form, 'Flore Pleno,' commonly called the fair maids of Kent.

RHAZYA
Rhazya

This small genus is sometimes included in *Amsonia* and listed in nurseries as such. It is represented in cultivation by *R. orientalis* (**next column**). In summer this produces heads of starry, soft blue flowers on stiff,

wiry stems. Unbranched, these reach 1½ ft (45 cm) high and are clothed in narrow gray-green leaves. Rhazyas slowly spread to form a small colony.

Rhazyas grow in any good garden soil in either full sun or light shade. Propagation is best achieved by division, although plants can also be grown from seed if it can be obtained.

Rhazya orientalis

RHEUM
Rhubarb

Rhubarb is often thought of only in culinary terms, but there are a large number of ornamental species for the perennial garden. They are distinguished more by their impressive foliage than by their flowers, although these are also noteworthy. The leaves are usually large and umbrellalike. The flowers emerge on gigantic spikes, which look as attractive in seed as they do in flower.

Rhubarbs need deep, rich soil with plenty of well-rotted organic material added to it. They grow in either full sun or light shade. Propagation is either by division or from seed.

R. 'Ace of Hearts'

Unlike many of its large relations, this big-leaved form grows best in a small garden, as it reaches only 3 ft (90 cm) or so. The leaves are roughly heart-shaped, and the flowers are pink.

R. alexandrae

This strange plant always becomes a conversation piece. The flowers are covered with large, pale yellow bracts, like handkerchiefs, which protect the flowers from the constant rains of the plant's native habitat in western China, Tibet, and the Himalayas. In cultivation the plant needs a similarly moist atmosphere in order to survive. This species grows to a height of 4 ft (1.2 m).

R. palmatum (below)

This is the most commonly seen ornamental rhubarb, particularly in its form 'Atrosanguineum.' The large leaves are attractively lobed and toothed and, when young, are deep red. The tall flower spikes are red. The plant grows to a height of as much as 8 ft (2.4 m) when the conditions are ideal.

Rheum palmatum 'Atrosanguineum'

RODGERSIA
Rodgersia

This small genus has six species, all in cultivation. They are renowned both for their handsome foliage and for their attractive flowers. Large clumps of plants form when conditions are right, becoming eye-catching features in borders or woodland gardens. The fluffy flowers are held in loose heads in much the same way as astilbe flowers. Appearing in summer, the blooms are held above the foliage. The leaves are large and noticeably veined. They vary from bronze to dark green in color and are often slightly shiny. The foliage is effective for the whole growing season, although some of the bronze forms slowly change to green.

Rodgersias must have moist soil, preferably enriched with plenty of humus. They can be planted in a position of either sun or shade. Propagation is carried out by division.

R. aesculifolia

This species has huge, very distinctive horse-chestnutlike leaves that are flushed with bronze. The flowers are cream. The plant grows to a height of approximately 5 ft (1.5 m).

R. pinnata

In this species the leaves are pinnate, made up of pairs of leaflets on opposite sides of the stem. The leaves are usually green, but in 'Superbum' they are tinged with bronze and the flowers are pink. The plant grows to approximately 4 ft (1.2 m) in height.

Rodgersia podophylla

R. podophylla (above)

This species also has horse-chestnutlike leaves, but the edges of the leaflets are distinctly jagged. The flowers are cream, and the plant grows to approximately 4 ft (1.2 m) in height.

RUDBECKIA
Coneflower

The attractive daisies in this genus flower in late summer and fall. The flowers are named for their prominent central cones of black, brown, or green, surrounded by yellow ray petals that droop. The plants spread, generally noninvasively, to form large colorful groups. Some forms are short, no more than 2 ft (60 cm), while others grow as high as 8 ft (2.4 m).

Coneflowers grow in any garden soil as long as it is not too dry, but they need a sunny location. Propagation is by division, although some seed strains are available.

Rudbeckia fulgida 'Goldsturm'

R. fulgida (above)

This is one of the main species of the coneflower, and it has produced some excellent cultivars. It has golden yellow flowers, each with a dark central cone, giving rise to its common name of black-eyed Susan. *R. f.* var. *deamii* is a floriferous variety that is more drought resistant than most. 'Goldsturm,' one of the most popular cultivars, has large flowers of a rich gold color. All these forms grow to 2 ft (60 cm).

R. 'Goldquelle'

This is a good plant for the rear of the border, as it grows to about 6 ft (1.8 m) in height. It has large double flowers of bright yellow from late summer.

R. hirta

This annual or short-lived perennial species has produced a number of seed strains. 'Mixed Single Hybrids' offer large flowers in a variety of yellows and browns on plants of different heights.

SALVIA
Sage

Salvia is an extremely varied genus of plants for the flower garden, totaling some 700 species worldwide. They offer a range of different types of plants, varying from ones treated as annuals to perennials and shrubs. Their flowers are mainly in shades of blue, but some of the more tender species produce a range of reds and reddish purples. Most have a long flowering season and are much loved by bees and butterflies. The foliage is often aromatic when crushed.

Sages need well-drained soil. A sunny site is also essential. Slugs can severely damage the emerging shoots in spring. Planting should be carried out in either fall or spring. Propagate either from cuttings or by sowing seed in the case of the species.

Salvia × *superba* 'May Night'

Summer-flowering forms (above)

There is a group of salvias—*S.* × *superba*, *S.* × *sylvestris*, and *S. nemorosa* — that are so similar that they are constantly being confused and their cultivars are frequently attributed to the wrong species. They produce rounded plants up to 3 ft (90 cm) tall, with dense spikes of blue or purple-blue flowers. 'Blue Queen' ('Blauköningen'), 'East Friesland' ('Ostfriesland'), 'Lubeca,' 'May Night' ('Mainacht'), and 'Rose Queen' are all worth growing.

S. pratensis 'Haematodes' is a short-lived perennial with airy branches of pale blue flowers. *S. verticillata* 'Purple Rain' has arching stems carrying purple flowers in pronounced whorls.

Salvia guaranitica

Fall-flowering forms (above)
S. guaranitica is 5 ft (1.5 m) tall and carries deep blue flowers. An even taller plant, which frequently needs support, is *S. uliginosa*, which has pale blue flowers.

Less-hardy forms
Many sages are hardy, but some cannot survive a severe winter and should be grown as perennials only in warm areas. In cold areas keep them in a greenhouse in winter as cuttings or young plants. *S. patens* is one of the main examples. It has large blue flowers and offers a range of cultivars. 'Cambridge' is a pale blue and 'Chilcombe' a lilac-blue. *S. farinacea* is a shrubbier plant with a long flowering season. Its form 'Porcelain' has white blooms, but 'Victoria' is the most popular, with blue flowers.

SANGUISORBA
Burnet

The sanguisorbas, which include the species that used to belong to *Poterium,* are a very distinct group of plants. They are characterized by tall, swaying stems carrying soft, bottlebrush-like flowers in pink, red, or white during summer. The fresh green leaves are pinnate, growing in opposite pairs on the stem; in some species they have a distinct smell of cucumber when crushed. Even when not in flower these plants are attractive.

Burnets grow in any good garden soil but do best in moist ones. Most grow in either full sun or light shade. Some species need deadheading after flowering to prevent excessive self-sowing. Propagate by division or from seed.

S. 'Magnifica Alba'

There are a number of white sanguisorbas, and this one is a popular choice. Its origins are in doubt, but this does not prevent it from being a good plant to grow in the garden. It grows to approximately 2½ ft (75 cm).

Sanguisorba obtusa

S. obtusa (above)
This species has gray-green foliage and pink flowers. It grows to a height of approximately 6 ft (1.8 m). It is frequently confused with a similar green-leaved species, *S. hakusanensis.*

SAPONARIA
Soapwort

This genus is grown mainly in the rock garden. There is, however, one species, *S. officinalis,* that makes a colorful if somewhat invasive plant for open borders and wild areas of a garden. This is known as soapwort because the leaves were once used as a soap substitute; it is also called bouncing Bet. The 3 ft (90 cm) plant has glaucous stems and leaves and bears 1 in (2.5 cm) flower heads of clear pink. There are a number of cultivars. 'Alba Plena' has double white flowers. 'Dazzler' has variegated leaves and pink flowers. 'Rosea Plena' is a pale double, while 'Rubra Plena' (**below**) is a darker double.

Soapworts grow in any garden soil, although often they are too vigorous and need to be contained. Either sun or light shade is suitable. Propagation is from cuttings or by division, and the species can be grown from seed.

Saponaria officinalis 'Rubra Plena'

SASA
Sasa

Bamboos not only add a touch of exotic foliage to a garden, they also add sound, as they rustle in the slightest breeze. They are not as popular as they once were but are now more widely available. *Sasa* is a large genus with several species in cultivation. One of the most attractive forms is *S. veitchii* (**next column**), which has oval leaves that are dark green with creamy white margins. It grows to approximately 5 ft (1.5 m). Its great drawback is that it is extremely invasive. For this reason, it is better either to plant it in a wild area of a garden or to contain it.

Plant sasa in any garden soil. It is a shade-loving plant. Propagate by division.

Sasa veitchii

SAXIFRAGA
Saxifrage

Only a few saxifrages are large enough for the open garden. The larger forms have graceful, arching flower stems that carry myriad tiny pink or white blooms in an airy spray. Their foliage usually forms large, close mats of ground cover, so they are suitable for clothing the ground under shrubs or trees.

The larger saxifrages like soil that does not dry out but that also does not retain excessive moisture. The soil should not be too rich. Partial shade is best. Most increase naturally by producing runners in the manner of strawberries, which makes them easy to propagate.

S. fortunei

This is a very late flowerer, whose dancing white blooms do not appear until fall. It has shiny, rounded leaves, which make an attractive ground cover. In the form 'Wada' the leaves and stems are a glowing red.

S. × *geum*

Another ground cover, this plant has rosettes of spoon-shaped leaves. In midsummer it produces sprays of tiny white flowers that have red and yellow spots decorating the petals.

S. × *urbium* (below)

This is the popular London pride. When grown in ideal conditions it spreads widely, forming extensive carpets of rosettes with spoon-shaped leaves. It is a magnificent sight when in bloom with its long-stemmed, tiny white flowers that are rose-pink in the center. The flowers appear in early summer.

Saxifraga × *urbium*

SCABIOSA
Scabious

Scabious have long, wiry stems, each carrying a pastel-colored, pincushion-shaped flower. There are species and cultivars in a range of pastel shades: pale blue, pale yellow, pale pink, and white. In some cultivars the blooms can be quite large, up to 3 in (7.5 cm) or more. The flowers are carried above delicately divided gray-green foliage. Choose these plants for romantic-looking flower borders with soft, pretty color schemes.

Scabious need well-drained soil that is slightly alkaline and a sunny place in the border. Propagation is carried out either by division or from seed.

Blue forms (below)

The most popular color is light blue, and there are several forms available. 'Butterfly Blue' has lavender-blue flowers, while *S. caucasica* has produced several good forms, including 'Blauseigel,' 'Clive Greaves,' and 'Fama'—all of which are similar in color.

Scabiosa caucasica 'Clive Greaves'

White forms

In keeping with the romantic image, there are no pure whites, but there are several subtle creamy whites. Again, *S. caucasica* has produced some fine forms, including 'Alba' and 'Miss Willmott.'

SCROPHULARIA
Figwort

Figworts are plants that are suitable only for the wild part of a garden. With one exception, they have little to offer the formal garden. That one exception is the variegated form *S. auriculata* 'Variegata' (**next page**), which provides an attractive cream variegation. The flowers look like miniature reddish-brown frogs and are not very distinguished; in fact many gardeners cut off the flower stems because the plants self-seed everywhere, producing ordinary green-leaved forms. The plants grow to a height of about 3 ft (90 cm).

These figworts appreciate moist soil and grow in either full sun or light shade. Scrophularia must be propagated from cuttings. Plants raised from seed and self-sown seedlings always produce plants with plain green leaves.

Scrophularia auriculata 'Variegata'

SEDUM
Stonecrop

Stonecrops are among the few succulent plants grown as perennials. The genus is very large, with over 600 species, but the majority of garden forms are too small for border use. There are, however, a few that are suitable for ground cover and color at the front of a border and other, taller forms that can be grown farther back. The stonecrops all have clustered heads of starry flowers. The color of the taller plants ranges mainly between shades of pink, but yellow and white flowers also occur. The fleshy leaves can also be attractive, and there are some useful purple-leaved stonecrops.

Stonecrops grow in any garden soil, including dry, poor soil. Although they can be grown in light shade, they always look best in sun. Propagation can be by division or from cuttings. Seed can also be used if it can be obtained.

White-flowered forms

White is not a common color among the taller forms, but there are two that make good plants. 'Iceberg' and 'Star Dust' are both cultivars of *S. spectabile*, the latter having a touch of pink in it.

Sedum 'Autumn Joy'

Pink-flowered forms (above)

There are many different pinks, varying from very pale pink to dark rose-pink. *S.* 'Autumn Joy' ('Herbstfreude') is one of the best known. It has large flat heads of medium pink flowers that turn to copper as they age. *S. spectabile* 'Brilliant' has deeper pink flowers.

Yellow-flowered forms

Yellow is not a common color in border sedums, but *S. aizoon* is able to provide it. The flat heads are bright yellow, but in the form 'Aurantiacum' they are a much richer, orange-yellow color with red stems.

Red- and purple-leaved forms

S. 'Ruby Glow' has red stems and leaves. It sprawls and is one of the smaller forms. *S.* 'Vera Jameson,' which has purple foliage and is larger in size, also has a tendency to spread. Larger and more upright is *S. telephium* subsp. *maximum* 'Atropurpureum.'

SENECIO
Senecio

Of this very large genus only a handful of the 3,000 species are grown in gardens. The main one that is of interest to perennial gardeners is *S. cineraria*, which is used as a foliage plant. Often known as dusty miller, it has foliage and stems covered in

soft, white hairs, giving the whole plant a silvery white appearance. A good form is 'White Diamond' (**below**). The flowers are yellow but are usually removed as soon as they appear. The whole plant grows only 2 ft (60 cm) high. It is neither long-lived nor hardy.

Dusty miller must have free-draining soil, as it will die if planted in a wet location, especially in winter. Sun is essential. Propagation is carried out either from cuttings or from seed.

Senecio cineraria 'White Diamond'

SIDALCEA
Prairie mallow

Prairie mallows are attractive plants with spikes of softly colored flowers like miniature hollyhocks. The main color is pink, but there are darker, almost purple forms, and white ones. Grown from seed, many have inferior-sized flowers, so for larger flowers, choose one of the named forms propagated by division or cuttings. The blooms appear from summer onward, with a second flush if the spent stems are cut back. The foliage makes good ground cover early in the season. The plants grow to a height of 4 ft (1.2 m).

Prairie mallows grow in any reasonable moisture-retentive garden soil. Although they prefer a sunny location, they will flower successfully in light shade. The best method of propagation is by division, but plants can also be grown from seed.

Forms (below)

S. candida is the only white-flowered form. *S.* 'Brilliant' has dark rose-pink, *S.* 'Party Girl' has pink, and *S.* 'Rose Queen' has rose-pink flowers.

Sidalcea 'Rose Queen'

SILENE
Campion

Campions make a useful, if not outstanding, contribution to the border. Many in cultivation are low-growing plants that are useful for carpeting frontal areas of the border, while the taller forms are useful farther back and for the wild or woodland section of the garden. Some forms flower in spring, some in summer, and some in fall; others continue to bloom from spring through fall. The flowers are usually flat disks of five petals. The red campion, *S. dioica*, has 1 in (2.5 cm) wide rosy red or pink flowers and grows to approximately 2 ft (60 cm) high. The double forms 'Flore Pleno' and 'Rosea Plena' are more frequently grown, the latter having the darker flowers.

These campions grow in any garden soil, in either sun or shade. Plant between fall and spring. Propagate by division. The species can be grown from seed.

SISYRINCHIUM
Sisyrinchium

Sisyrinchiums can brighten up a border. Their round blue or yellow flowers are not large, but when grown in quantity, they shine among other plants. Not all gardeners love them, however, as they self-seed. The foliage is narrow and grassy or irislike, and from these tufts the spikes of flowers arise in spring or summer.

Sisyrinchiums like well-drained soil and a sunny site. Cut off the old flower heads before they seed. Propagate by division or from seed. Propagation by division is best done in late summer; spring is the best time for seed. Planting should be carried out in either fall or spring.

S. angustifolium

One of the toughest species, this tolerates most conditions, including cold. It has dark green foliage and violet-blue, yellow-throated flowers, which appear in summer. The plants grow to 8 in (20 cm) high. This species is also referred to as *S. bermudianum*.

S. idahoense (below)

This is similar to *S. angustifolium* in that it has blue flowers with yellow centers, but it is twice the height and flowers earlier. It is also known as *S. bellum*.

Sisyrinchium idahoense

S. striatum

This is the most popular border form. It produces tall spikes, up to 2½ ft (75 cm) high, of soft yellow flowers, darkening toward the center. These bloom for a long period during summer. The cultivar 'Aunt May' has cream variegations on the leaves.

SMILACINA
False Solomon's seal

This is closely related to Solomon's seal and has inherited much of its fresh-looking appearance. The species mainly seen in cultivation is *S. racemosa* (**below**). It has the same kind of graceful, arching stems with opposite leaves as Solomon's seal, but instead of the flowers appearing along the stems, they are gathered in a fluffy cluster at the tips. They are creamy white and appear in spring. The plants grow up to 3 ft (90 cm) high. They spread to form a large clump but are not invasive. They make an attractive group for a shady spot.

Smilacinas like moist woodland-type soil, preferably on the acidic side, and a cool, shady site. Propagation is by division or from seed.

Smilacina racemosa

SOLIDAGO
Goldenrod

Goldenrods create striking drifts of yellow from early summer onward. The tiny flowers are carried in profusion in loose, fluffy heads. The narrow leaves are not particularly attractive and suffer from mildew in some cultivars. The plants vary in height between 1 ft (30 cm) and 5 ft (1.5 m) and spread to form large clumps, creating solid blocks of color when they are in flower. Golden-rods grow in any reasonable garden soil and tolerate either sun or light shade. Propagation is by division.

Cultivars

There are a large number of cultivars of goldenrod. 'Golden Baby' ('Goldkind') is a short golden yellow form. 'Goldenmosa' is taller and bright golden yellow, flowering early. 'Queenie' has yellow flowers on a plant that grows to about 8 in (20 cm) in height.

× *Solidaster luteus* 'Lemore'

Hybrids (above)

Solidago was crossed with *Aster* to produce a new genus, × *Solidaster*, with flowers larger than those of *Solidago*. One of the most popular of these crosses is a form known as × *Solidaster luteus* 'Lemore.' This has soft yellow flowers and is sometimes listed under *Solidago*.

STACHYS
Betony

This genus provides the gardener with a number of useful plants, many of which are so different it is hard to believe they are of the same genus. The difference is demonstrated by the fact that some are grown for their foliage while others are grown for their flowers. The flowers, tubular with the upper lip hooded, are similar to those of dead nettles or mints.

Most betonies like well-drained soil. Although they prefer a sunny spot, light shade is tolerated, especially in hot areas (zone 10). Propagation is mainly by division; seed can also be used.

S. byzantina

Still also known as *S. lanata*, this species is grown as a foliage plant. It has densely felted leaves and stems, giving the whole plant a silvery appearance. The flowers, carried on tall stems, are small and pink. Many gardeners remove them from the base so as not to destroy the foliage effect, while others think the pink adds to the plant's effect. 'Cotton Boll' replaces the flowers with what appear to be balls of cotton on the stems. 'Primrose Heron' has flushes of yellow on the silver leaves, and 'Silver Carpet' has no flower stems.

S. macrantha (below)

Also known as *S. grandiflora*, this species contrasts with *S. byzantina*, as it produces large heads of purple-pink flowers above pleated green leaves. The best form, called 'Superba,' has extra-large purple flowers.

Stachys macrantha 'Superba'

STIPA
Stipa

This large genus consists of grasses that are grown mainly for their wonderful feathery flower heads. Some are quite short, but it is generally the taller species that are used to make dramatic statements in the garden. While the grasses are frequently used in the border, they are also suitable as specimen plants. A particularly good situation is one that will catch the late evening sun.

Stipas grow in any good garden soil, preferably one that is not too wet, but a sunny site is required. Planting should be carried out in spring. Propagation is generally by division in spring, but the grasses can also be grown from seed.

S. gigantea

This species is the one most commonly grown. It can be up to 6 ft (1.8 m) tall and carries open, airy heads of large purple flowers that turn golden as seed is formed.

Stipa tenuissima

S. tenuissima (above)

This is a much shorter plant, growing only to 2 ft (60 cm). It has soft, feathery plumes in early summer.

STOKESIA
Stokes' aster

This single-species genus is represented by *S. laevis* (**next column**). The plant is a member of the thistle family but is not at all prickly, nor does it have any tendency to become invasive. It is a good low-growing, sprawling plant, approximately 1½ ft (45 cm) tall, with large, flat flowers, each made up of a central disk of small florets and an outer ring of larger strap-shaped purple-blue petals. Stokes' aster blooms from late summer onward. There are a number of cultivars. 'Alba' has white flowers. 'Blue Danube' has deeper blue flowers, and 'Blue Star' is distinguished by its larger flowers.

Stokes' asters prefer free-draining soil that has been enriched with organic material. They need a sunny site. Increase stock by division.

Stokesia laevis

SYMPHYANDRA
Symphyandra
This is a small genus of plants closely related to the campanulas. Unfortunately, they are not seen as frequently as they should be. This is because they are short-lived, but most produce copious amounts of seed and so are easy to propagate. *S. wanneri* is one of the most popular forms. It displays nodding, bell-shaped lavender-blue flowers in loose spikes in early summer. The oval-shaped leaves are hairy. This clump-forming species grows to only 10 in (25 cm) and is thus best suited to the front of a border.

Symphyandras grow in any reasonable garden soil, but prefer a free-draining soil. Either sun or light shade is suitable. Stock is easily increased from seed in the fall.

SYMPHYTUM
Comfrey
The flared, tubular flowers of comfrey are carried in spirals that uncurl as the flower buds open. The flowers come in a wide range of colors, including blue, pink, red, white, and creamy yellow. They are carried on thick, hairy stems above large, coarse leaves. The leaves themselves can be decorative, and there are some variegated forms. The plants grow to a height of approximately 1–3 ft (30–90 cm). Comfrey can spread underground, and it is difficult to extract once it has a hold. A small piece of root left in the ground will quickly grow again. It is best to plant comfrey where it can be contained or in a wild part of the garden rather than in a formal border full of choice plants.

Comfrey likes deep, rich soil that does not get too dry. It flowers in either sun or light shade. Cut back the plants after flowering to promote fresh foliage and also to prevent seeding. Propagation is from seed or by division.

Symphytum 'Goldsmith'

Foliage forms (above)
Some forms of comfrey are grown almost exclusively for their foliage. *S.* 'Goldsmith' has cream and yellow variegations on dark green, while *S. × uplandicum* 'Variegatum' has cream variegations set against a gray-green background.

Flower forms
Almost all species and cultivars are worth growing for their flowers. Two of the best are 'Hidcote Blue,' which has white bells touched with blue and opening from small red buds, and 'Hidcote Pink,' in which the blue tinge is replaced by a pink one.

TANACETUM
Tansy
The tansies are a group of daisylike plants that are often dissimilar in their general appearance. The plant commonly known as tansy is considered an herb and is too vigorous for the open border, but there are several other members of the genus that are worth considering. The flowers vary in size from ⅓ in (7.5 mm) to 3 in (7.5 cm), and the color of their flowers can also vary considerably.

Tansies grow in any good garden soil but generally prefer a sunny spot. Many grow from seed, but named forms are best increased by cuttings taken in the spring or division.

Foliage forms
Tansies generally have attractive foliage and command attention even when not in flower. Feverfew (*T. parthenium*) in its golden-leaved form 'Aureum' is particularly attractive. It holds its color for most of the season and can always be cut back to provide new growth. The plant is covered with small white and yellow daisies throughout most of the summer season.

Flower forms (next page)
One species, *T. coccineum*, was developed for its brightly colored flowers that appear in early summer. More commonly known as pyrethrum, it makes an excellent border plant. They are not very tall plants, reaching only up to 2 ft (60 cm). 'Snow Cloud' is a good white form of tansy. 'Eileen May Robinson'

and 'Robinson's Pink' are both excellent pinks, while 'Brenda' and 'James Kelway' are strong red forms.

Tanacetum 'Eileen May Robinson'

TELLIMA
Fringecups

There is only one species of *Tellima*, namely *T. grandiflora*. This plant is extremely useful as a decorative ground cover for areas of light and medium shade. The foliage is dark green and similar to that of *Heuchera*, to which it is related. The flowers appear on tall, thin stalks in late spring and are small but pronounced greenish-white bells that age to pink. With the flower stems, the plants can reach up to 2 ft (60 cm) tall. The form 'Rubra' has a purple tinge to the leaves.

Fringecups need woodland-type soil that is moist and rich in well-rotted humus, plus a cool, shady site. Propagation is carried out by division.

THALICTRUM
Meadow rue

In most meadow rues both the foliage and the flowers are very delicate and create a delightful hazy effect. The flowers do not have petals but are made up of a bunch of fuzzy stamens, with the color provided by the sepals. They vary considerably in height, from those that are only a few inches high to tall, stately plants that are 6 ft (1.8 m) or more high. Meadow rues do not need rich soil, although they like plenty of humus to keep the conditions moist. They grow in either sun or shade, preferring shade in hot areas (zone 10). Some of the taller species need support. Propagate from seed or cuttings or by division.

T. aquilegifolium (below)

This species derives its name from the similarity of its foliage to that of *Aquilegia*, and when not in flower, the two plants can be easily confused. The flowers are lilac and carried in fluffy profusion. The seeds hang like massed earrings and are decorative. There is a creamy white form, 'Album,' and a more purple form, 'Thundercloud.' They all grow to approximately 3 ft (90 cm) in height.

Thalictrum aquilegifolium

T. delavayi

Also known as *T. dipterocarpum*, this is one of the most delicate plants, with dainty foliage and airy heads of purple sepals filled with creamy stamens. It grows to a height of about 5 ft (1.5 m). 'Hewitt's Double' is possibly the gem of the genus, as in this cultivar the stamens are transformed into purple "petals," creating double flowers.

T. flavum

This tall plant reaches 6 ft (1.8 m) or more and is heavier in all its parts than the other species. It is a dramatic plant, especially when grown in large clumps, because of its strongly contrasting dark green leaves and yellow flowers. There is a better-known form, *T. f.* subsp. *glaucum*, which has glaucous blue-green stems and foliage.

T. rochebrunianum

This species is similar to *T. delavayi*, with purple flowers over glaucous blue-green foliage. It flowers a little later and grows to 6 ft (1.8 m).

THERMOPSIS
False lupine

False lupines have dark green foliage and bright yellow lupinelike flowers. The flowers appear in spring, and for the rest of the year the plants can be used for their foliage. However, they run underground and can be invasive, so they need to be planted where they can spread at will or where they can be contained.

The various species do not show a great deal of difference, and they are difficult to tell apart. *T. montana* (below) is a good species to experiment with. It has feathery leaves and reaches a height of approximately 3 ft (90 cm).

False lupines grow in most soils, including dry ones. Most tolerate both sun and shade. Propagate by division in spring or from seed in fall.

Thermopsis montana

TIARELLA
Foamflower

The plants in this small genus are ideal for creating ground cover in a shady place, but unlike most other ground covers, these plants have a wonderful charm. Their tiny flowers, held in loose heads above the foliage, give the plant its common name, foamflower. The leaves are hand-shaped and evergreen. The plants grow to about 1½ ft (45 cm).

Foamflowers like cool, moist soil with plenty of well-rotted humus in it. They need a lightly shaded spot. Propagation is usually by division, but they will also grow from seed.

T. cordata

This is the main species in cultivation. It has clusters of white flowers, and the plant spreads by stolons, soon forming a large colony.

Tiarella wherryi

T. wherryi (above)

This more compact plant has pink-tipped flowers in a more definitive, pyramid-shaped spike than the other species. It is not as aggressively invasive, since it does not spread underground.

TRACHYSTEMON
Trachystemon

This is a two-species genus, but only *T. orientalis* is seen in cultivation. It is an odd plant in that its flower stems always seem to be on the point of dying. This is mainly due to the way the blue flowers hang down while their petals curl back, almost as if they were wilting. In spite of this it is still a plant well worth growing for the general effect the flowers give. The loose clusters of flowers appear in spring, before the leaves open, on rough stems that reach up to 1½ ft (45 cm). The leaves are also rough and when fully open form a good ground cover. This plant can become invasive and is therefore not recommended for formal borders, but it is useful for growing in a large area under trees or bushes.

Trachystemon enjoys woodland conditions that do not dry out. It is extremely easy to grow and needs no attention once planted. Propagation is carried out by division after flowering.

TRADESCANTIA
Spiderwort

Spiderworts are mainly known by the species grown as houseplants, but *Tradescantia* is a large genus of some 60 species and a few of these make a valuable contribution to the garden. The garden choices closely resemble houseplants, with the straplike foliage clasping the round stems and the characteristic three-petaled flowers held in clusters in the uppermost leaves. In addition to white, there is a range of very bright, almost luminous flower colors, mainly blues and pinks. The plants flower over a long season, from late spring onward. When grown in the right conditions, they can spread and make large, untidy-looking clumps, reaching 2 ft (60 cm) high.

Spiderworts should not be planted in rich soil, or the foliage growth will be lush at the expense of the flowers. The soil should not, however, be allowed to become too dry. A sunny site is usually required. The best method of propagation is to divide the plants.

T. × andersoniana (below)

This is the main group of hybrids cultivated in gardens. *T. virginiana* is one of the parents of this group. The hybrids come in a wide range of colors. The best pure white forms are 'Innocence' and 'Snowcap.' 'Iris Prichard' is white tinged with blue. 'Isis' is a deep blue, while 'Zwanenburg Blue' is a royal blue. 'Carmine Glow' ('Karminglut') is bright carmine and 'Pauline' lilac-pink.

Tradescantia × andersoniana 'Carmine Glow'

TRICYRTIS
Toad lily

Toad lilies are among the most intriguing of all border perennials. The flowers need to be examined closely to appreciate their full beauty. Each consists of six straplike petals opening out into a shallow funnel, from which erupts a fountain of stamens and styles. The flowers are mainly white or yellow but heavily spotted in purple, red, or brown. They usually face upward, rising from the rigidly erect stems of the plant, and they flower in fall. The narrow foliage clasps the stem and is a shiny green. Toad lilies have roots that run and soon form a large, trouble-free colony, up to 3 ft (90 cm) in height. Once they form a large group, they look their best in the border, since individual plants are hardly noticed.

Toad lilies need moist, humus-rich soil and a cool root run. They can be grown in a shady border but look best in a dappled woodland setting. They resent being disturbed. Slugs like the young growth. Propagate by division or from seed.

T. formosana (below)

This species has flowers whose white petals are flushed and spotted with mauve. The dark green leaves are also often spotted. There are a number of cultivars, each varying slightly in color. Stolonifera Group is a collective name given to these variations.

Tricyrtis formosana

T. hirta

The foliage and stems of this plant are covered in short hairs, while the white flowers, which appear in fall, are heavily spotted with purple.

TROLLIUS
Globeflower

Globeflowers are one of the glories of spring and early summer gardens. They produce great orbs of orange or golden yellow held high above the buttercup-like foliage. In some species the flowers are cuplike, similar to those of their close relative the buttercup, while in others the petals curve into a complete sphere. These are plants of boggy areas, and they do best when grown in bog gardens or near water. However, provided there is sufficient humus in the soil to ensure that

it is moisture retentive, they make perfectly good, attractive border plants.

Globeflowers grow in the open in most areas, but in hot regions (zone 10) they do better in light shade. Deadhead regularly. Propagation is by division or from seed, which should be sown fresh.

T. chinensis

Also known as *T. ledebourii*, this species has outside petals that open to a shallow dish filled with upright, narrow petals colored a rich golden yellow. It grows to a height of about 3 ft (90 cm).

T. × cultorum

This series of popular hybrids offers variously colored flowers. 'Alabaster' is a pale green-yellow; 'Fire Globe' ('Feuertroll') is orange; 'Golden Monarch' is golden; and 'Lemon Queen' is lemon-yellow. They all grow up to 3 ft (90 cm) in height.

Trollius europaeus

T. europaeus (above)

This European native produces spherical globes of pale yellow flowers that are carried on stems reaching up to 2½ ft (75 cm) high.

UNCINIA
Uncinia

Not many sedges are good garden choices, but this genus produces one,

U. unciniata, that is worthy of attention. It belongs to a large group of sedges that come mainly from New Zealand. This one has beautiful brown leaves when young, but the plants are variable in color and it is best to see them in growth before acquiring one. Uncinia offers fountains of evergreen foliage up to 1½ ft (45 cm) high.

U. unciniata needs moisture-retentive soil. It grows in either a sunny location or in light shade. Propagation is by division in spring or from seed, although seed does not always produce good color forms.

UVULARIA
Bellwort

This small genus of curious but attractive plants is related to the Solomon's seal, although this is not apparent at first sight. The plants form colonies of arching stems, from which dangle yellow flowers that look like limp rags. The flowers appear in spring. The foliage is light green, and the plants reach up to 2 ft (60 cm) in height. While most of the species are in cultivation, *U. grandiflora* (**below**) is the only one that is regularly seen. It has 1 in (2.5 cm) long flowers of a rich primrose-yellow, but there is also a much paler form, 'Pallida.'

Bellworts need cool, moist soil with plenty of rotted humus in it. They grow in sun, but a shady spot is preferable, especially in hot areas (zone 9 and warmer). They are perfect for the woodland garden.

Uvularia grandiflora

VALERIANA
Valerian
Valerians are pleasant but not distin-guished plants, better suited to a wild area of the garden than to a formal border. They are tall plants with clustered heads of small white or pale pink flowers. There is one form, however, that is popular for its foliage rather than its flowers. This is *V. phu* 'Aurea' (**below**), which forms a mound of brilliant gold leaves in spring. Unfortunately, by summer they begin to turn green. The flowers are off-white and are usually removed before they open. Although the foliage makes a mound only 1 ft (30 cm) or so in height, grow this plant in the middle of the border so that it shows up when it is at its best but is covered by other plants later in the season.

Valerians grow in most garden soils. While most species will grow in the open, they do best in a slightly shady location. *V. phu* 'Aurea,' however, needs a sunny spot. Propagate by division or from seed.

Valeriana phu 'Aurea'

VERATRUM
False hellebore
False hellebores are good value in that they not only are superlative when in flower but also make excellent foliage plants. The only two disadvantages are that it can take up to 7 years to get a flowering plant from seed and that slugs can reduce the leaves to shreds. The leaves are very heavily pleated, and when forming a [...] resemble a pale green turban [...] 6 ft (1.8 m) tall flowering sten [...] the rosette, with small flower[s] [...] and clustered along horizonta[l] [...] some species they are white o[r] [...] but in the most popular specie[s] [...] (**below**), they are dark red. T[hey] [...] to glow when the sun is behi[nd] [...] stems are equally attractive w[hen it] is in seed.

Veratrums like moist, humus-rich soil. While some grow in the open, the major-ity, including *V. nigrum,* prefer a slightly shaded site out of the hot sun. Propa-gation is from seed or offsets.

Veratrum nigrum

VERBASCUM
Mullein
Mulleins are some of the most stately plants in the garden. They rise from large, hairy leaves to 8 ft (2.4 m) or more to form tall spikes that are usually covered in saucer-shaped yellow flowers. Most of these forms are biennial and must be sown each year, but fortunately some species are more permanent. Although short-lived, these can be grown in the perennial gar-den. They are not as tall as the biennial forms, but they are impressive.

Mulleins will grow in any garden soil, including dry soil, but they nearly all require a sunny site. Stake the taller species if they are in an exposed position.

V. phoenicum hybrids (below)
The species is not frequently grown in its own right but is one of the parents of a number of popular hybrids. The best known of these are the 'Cotswold Hybrids,' with a wide range of colors beyond the normal yellow of most mulleins, such as 'Cotswold Queen' (a deep burnt yellow). 'Gainsborough' is pale yellow; 'Helen Johnson' pink; 'Mont Blanc' white; and 'Pink Domino' rose-pink.

Verbascum 'Pink Domino'

VERBENA
Vervain
The majority of verbenas are too tender for the perennial garden and are treated as annuals. A few, however, are tough enough, and these usually produce small domed or flat heads of purple or pink flowers late in the season, loved by bees and butterflies. There is a plant suitable in height for every part of the border, from the front to the back.

Verbenas grow in any reasonable garden soil, although they do best and last longest in well-drained ones. A sunny site is also required. Propagation is by seed, division, or basal cuttings taken in spring.

V. bonariensis (below)
This is one of the more popular species. It is a tall, spindly plant, reaching 6 ft (1.8 m) or more, with wiry branches topped with clusters of reddish-purple flowers. Although it is tall, its wiry nature gives it a see-through quality, so it can be grown effectively in the middle or even at the front of a border. It is hardy but short-lived.

Verbena bonariensis

VERONICA
Speedwell
Veronica is a very large genus, with many species and cultivars in cultivation. Speedwells are one of the mainstays of the midsummer border. They provide a range of blue-flowered plants that vary in height from a few inches up to 4 ft (1.2 m). There are white speedwells as well as blue and a large number of pink forms. The majority carry their flowers in elegant spikes, which are held high above the foliage, but in a few of the lower-growing forms the flowers are in loose sprays.

Speedwells can be grown in any garden soil, but they soon look distressed if the soil becomes too dry. Taller forms need

some support. Deadhead to prevent self-sowing. Plant at any time between fall and spring. Propagation is by division or in some cases from seed.

White forms
There are white forms of the usually blue *V. spicata*, which is a low species for the front of the border. It grows up to 1½ ft (45 cm).

Veronica spicata 'Red Fox'

Pink forms (above)
A low-growing, pale pink form that grows no more than 10 in (25 cm) high is *V. prostrata* 'Mrs. Holt.' The cultivars *V. spicata* subsp. *incana* 'Minuet' and *V. s.* 'Heidekind' both have rose-pink flowers. *V. s.* 'Red Fox' ('Rotfuchs') has rose-red flowers.

Pale blue forms
Some of the best pale blues are those of *V. gentianoides*, with its shiny leaves and thin spires of large flowers. 'Variegata' has creamy variegations to the leaves and pale blue flowers. *V. spicata* 'Blue Fox' ('Blaufuchs') has lavender flowers.

Dark blue forms
V. austriaca subsp. *teucrium* 'Crater Lake Blue' is one of the best dark blues. In *V. peduncularis* 'Georgia Blue,' the dark blue flowers are carried in much looser spikes than those of 'Crater Lake

Blue' over low-growing purple-tinged foliage. The brilliant-flowered *V. a. t.* 'Shirley Blue,' at 1 ft (30 cm), is halfway in height between them.

VERONICASTRUM
Veronicastrum
Veronicastrum virginicum (**below**) is so close to *Veronica*, especially *V. longifolia*, that it is difficult to distinguish between the two species. They both grow to 3 ft (90 cm) in height, with stiffly erect stems and whorls of leaves. The pale blue flowers are carried in attractive spikes. If anything, veronicastrum is the more elegant plant, with longer flower spikes, and it has more leaves in each whorl. 'Album' is a beautiful white form in which the flowers are set off well by the dark green leaves.

Veronicastrums grow in any garden soil. They are best in full sun but take a little light shade. In exposed positions they may need staking; elsewhere the stems are rigid enough without support. Propagation is by division.

Veronicastrum virginicum

VIOLA
Viola
No garden should be without violas of one kind or another. These cheerful flowers can either be planted as a clump or used to fill in between other plants. They are easy to grow, and there is a wide range of colors. The majority are low-growing plants

that form loose or tight mounds. A few scramble up through shrubs and other plants. Violas come in a number of forms. Pansies have the largest flowers and are usually treated as annuals, although if they are trimmed with shears after flowering, they grow a second and even a third year. Violets, usually grown as one of the various species, have the smallest flowers. Violas and violettas are intermediate between the two. Violas are distinguished from violettas by the presence of whiskers radiating from the center of the flowers.

Violas grow in most soils, as long as they are moist. They do best in a lightly shaded spot out of the hottest sun. With the exception of violets, most benefit from being trimmed after flowering and will often produce a second flush of blooms. Propagate by taking basal cuttings or in some cases from seed.

Viola 'Jackanapes'

Viola forms (above)
In the perennial border it is the viola that reigns supreme in this genus. There is a large selection of colors available. 'Ardross Gem' is dark yellow and blue. 'Bowles Black' has small black flowers, while 'Molly Sanderson' has large black flowers. 'Chantreyland' is a seed strain with apricot-orange petals, darkening toward the center. 'Irish Molly' is a mixture of greenish yellow and bluish brown. 'Jackanapes' has maroon top

petals and bright yellow lower ones. 'Jersey Gem' is deep purple. 'Maggie Mott' is a subtle mixture of blues and creamy yellow.

Viola cornuta

V. cornuta (above)
The horned violet is one of the best of the species. It behaves more like a viola, with moderately large flowers, and benefits from being trimmed after blooming. The species has pale lilac flowers, but there are a large number of variations. 'Alba' is pure white and is useful for enlivening a dark corner. 'Belmont Blue' is a soft blue, and 'Rosea' has rosy purple flowers.

V. labradorica 'Purpurea'
This plant is a violet with purple-violet flowers and leaves that are a purple color, especially in spring. It makes an excellent foliage plant. It has recently been renamed *V. riviniana* 'Purpurea.'

V. sororia
This violet is popular in its form 'Freckles,' which is white and strongly spotted with purple-blue.

WALDSTEINIA
Barren strawberry
In this small genus of five species, only two or three are in cultivation. All are low-growing plants used as ground covers,

usually in rock gardens. They are, however, also used at the front of a shady border. The main species in cultivation is *W. ternata* (**below**). This has evergreen leaves and small, strawberrylike yellow flowers that appear in late spring. The whole plant grows no more than 4 in (10 cm) in height but spreads vigorously to form a dense carpet of green foliage.

This plant grows in most soils but performs best in shade. Propagation is carried out by dividing the creeping plants.

Waldsteinia ternata

ZAUSCHNERIA
California fuchsia
Once relegated to *Epilobium,* this group is once again a genus in its own right. It is a small genus of plants that are valuable for their late flowering. The most frequently grown and the hardiest is *Z. californica.* Its fuchsialike flowers are bright scarlet. 'Glasnevin' has bright flowers and dark green leaves, while 'Solidarity Pink' has pink flowers but flowers less readily. The plants grow to a height of approximately 1½ ft (45cm). Zauschnerias can be grown at the front of a border, but they look especially good when grown over the top of a wall or bank.

Zauschnerias must have free-draining soil and a warm, sunny site. They can be increased from cuttings or by division. Some run underground, and their spread must be checked.

HARDINESS ZONES

The climatic conditions of an area are of prime importance when deciding what to plant. Even within a particular garden, isolated microclimates need to be considered, as a sheltering wall or a hedge may affect the range of possible plantings. These microclimates can be altered or created by grouping plants and by using mulches. Also, careful siting can modify sun, shade, wind, and humidity.

However, how well a plant grows in an area largely depends on its native climate and how easily it can adapt to its new environment. A plant classified as tender will not endure temperatures below 32°F (0°C). A half-hardy plant can stand a few degrees of frost, but not a cold winter; in contrast, a hardy plant can tolerate considerable cold. Naturally, the degree of hardiness varies from plant to plant.

The maps appearing here have been specially devised to enable you to measure the degree of cold a plant can tolerate. They have been divided into 11 broad climatic areas or zones ranging from −50°F (−46°C) and below in zone 1 to above 40°F (above 4°C) in zone 11. Every plant listed in the Plant Directory cites a hardiness zone, see pages 230–1, indicating that it will survive and flower at the average minimum winter temperature of that zone. Obviously weather is variable, therefore hardiness zones, at best, can be considered only relative.

The United States Department of Agriculture issues a Plant hardiness Zone Map. Copies of the USDA map are available from the Government Printing Office in Washington, D. C.

NORTH AMERICA

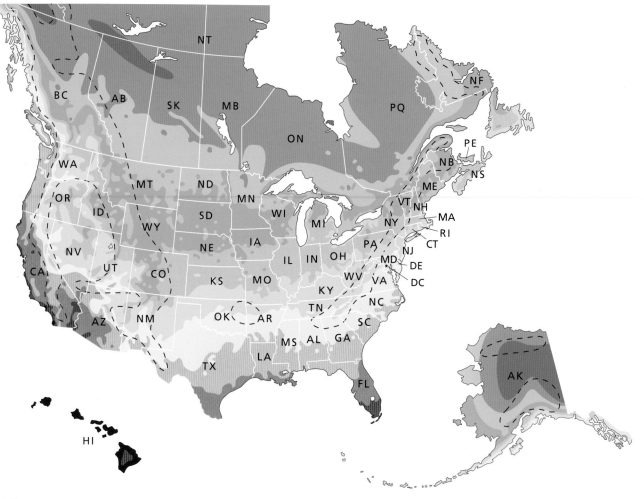

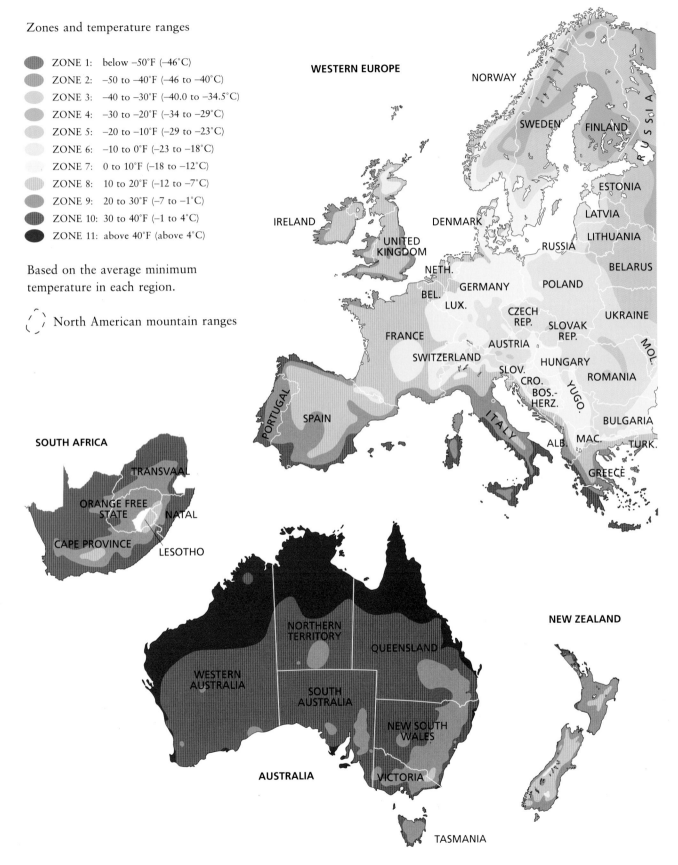

Zones and temperature ranges

ZONE 1: below −50°F (−46°C)
ZONE 2: −50 to −40°F (−46 to −40°C)
ZONE 3: −40 to −30°F (−40.0 to −34.5°C)
ZONE 4: −30 to −20°F (−34 to −29°C)
ZONE 5: −20 to −10°F (−29 to −23°C)
ZONE 6: −10 to 0°F (−23 to −18°C)
ZONE 7: 0 to 10°F (−18 to −12°C)
ZONE 8: 10 to 20°F (−12 to −7°C)
ZONE 9: 20 to 30°F (−7 to −1°C)
ZONE 10: 30 to 40°F (−1 to 4°C)
ZONE 11: above 40°F (above 4°C)

Based on the average minimum
temperature in each region.

North American mountain ranges

WESTERN EUROPE

NORWAY

SWEDEN   FINLAND

RUSSIA

ESTONIA

LATVIA

LITHUANIA

IRELAND

DENMARK

BELARUS

UNITED
KINGDOM

NETH.

RUSSIA

POLAND

GERMANY

BEL.

LUX.

CZECH
REP.

UKRAINE

FRANCE

SLOVAK
REP.

MOL.

AUSTRIA

SWITZERLAND

HUNGARY

SLOV.

ROMANIA

CRO.

BOS.-
HERZ.

YUGO.

PORTUGAL

SPAIN

ITALY

BULGARIA

ALB.

MAC.

TURK.

GREECE

SOUTH AFRICA

TRANSVAAL

ORANGE FREE
STATE

NATAL

CAPE PROVINCE

LESOTHO

NORTHERN
TERRITORY

QUEENSLAND

NEW ZEALAND

WESTERN
AUSTRALIA

SOUTH
AUSTRALIA

NEW SOUTH
WALES

AUSTRALIA

VICTORIA

TASMANIA

A

Acanthus *Bear's breeches* 6–10
Achillea *Yarrow* 3–10
Aconitum *Monkshood* 2–9
Acorus *Sweet flag* 5–9
Actea *Baneberry* 2–9
Adiantum *Maidenhair fern* 3–8
Aegopodium *Goutweed* 4
Agapanthus *African lily* 8–10
Agastache *Giant hyssop* 5–9
Ajuga *Bugleweed* 2–10
Alcea *Hollyhock* 2–10
Alchemilla *Lady's-mantle* 3–9
Alstroemeria *Peruvian lily* 7–10
Amsonia *Blue star* 3–9
Anaphalis *Pearl everlasting* 3–9
Anchusa *Bugloss* 3–10
Anemone *Anemone* 6–10
Anthemis *Anthemis* 3–10
Aquilegia *Columbine* 3–10
Arabis *Rock cress* 4–10
Artemisia *Mugwort* 4–10
Aruncus *Goatsbeard* 3–9
Asarum *Wild ginger* 2–9
Asclepias *Milkweed* 3–10
Asperula *Woodruff* 5–9
Asphodeline *Jacob's rod* 6–8
Asphodelus *Asphodel* 5–9
Asplenium *Spleenwort* 5–6
Aster *Aster* 3–10
Astilbe *Astilbe* 4–8
Astrantia *Masterwort* 4–9
Athyrium *Athyrium* 4–8
Aubrieta *Aubrieta* 4–9

B

Baptisia *False indigo* 3–10
Begonia *Begonia* 6–8
Bellis *Daisy* 3–11
Bergenia *Bergenia* 3–10
Blechnum *Blechnum* 5–8
Boltonia *Boltonia* 3–10
Borago *Borage* 7–10
Brunnera *Brunnera* 3–8
Buphthalmum *Oxeye* 4–8

C

Calamintha *Calamint* 5–10
Caltha *Marsh marigold* 3–10
Campanula *Bellflower* 3–10
Carex *Sedge* 4–8
Centaurea *Knapweed* 3–9
Centranthus *Red valerian* 3–10
Cephalaria *Cephalaria* 3–10
Ceratostigma *Plumbago* 5–10
Chelone *Turtlehead* 3–9
Cimicifuga *Bugbane* 3–10
Cirsium *Thistle* 4–10
Clematis *Clematis* 3–9
Codonopsis *Bonnet bellflower* 5–9
Convallaria *Lily of the valley* 3–9
Convolvulus *Convolvulus* 7–10
Coreopsis *Tickseed* 4–10
Cortaderia *Pampas grass* 4–9
Cortusa *Cortusa* 4–8
Corydalis *Corydalis* 7–11
Cosmos *Cosmos* 7–10
Crambe *Sea kale* 6–9
Cynara *Cynara* 6–10
Cynoglossum *Hound's tongue* 4–9

D

Darmera *Umbrella plant* 6–9
Delosperma *Delosperma* 8–10
Delphinium *Delphinium* 3–10
Dendranthema *Chrysanthemum* 4–10
Dennstaedtia *Hay-scented fern* 4–8
Deschampsia *Hair grass* 5–9
Dianthus *Pinks* 4–10
Diascia *Twinspur* 6–8
Dicentra *Bleeding heart* 3–10
Dictamnus *Burning bush* 2–9
Digitalis *Foxglove* 3–10
Doronicum *Leopard's-bane* 4–9
Dracocephalum *Dragonhead* 2–8
Dryopteris *Shield fern* 2–8

E

Echinacea *Coneflower* 3–8
Echinops *Globe thistle* 3–11
Elymus *Elymus* 2–9
Epimedium *Barrenwort* 5–8
Eremurus *Foxtail lily* 5–9
Erigeron *Fleabane* 4–9
Eryngium *Sea holly* 3–10
Eupatorium *Boneset* 3–10
Euphorbia *Spurge* 3–10

F

Festuca *Fescue* 3–9
Filipendula *Meadowsweet* 3–9
Foeniculum *Fennel* 4–10
Fragaria *Strawberry* 5–8

G

Gaillardia *Blanket flower* 3–10
Galega *Goat's rue* 3–9
Gaura *Gaura* 6–10
Gentiana *Gentian* 3–9
Geranium *Geranium* 3–10
Geum *Avens* 5–10
Gillenia *Indian physic* 4–8
Glyceria *Glyceria* 5–9
Gunnera *Gunnera* 7–10
Gypsophila *Baby's breath* 3–10

H

Hakonechloa *Hakonechloa* 4–8
Helenium *Sneezeweed* 3–10
Helianthus *Sunflower* 3–10
Helictotrichon *Helictotrichon* 4–10
Heliopsis *False sunflower* 4–9
Helleborus *Hellebore* 3–10
Hemerocallis *Daylily* 3–10
Heuchera *Alumroot* 3–10
x Heucherella *Heucherella* 3–10
Hosta *Hosta* 3–9
Houttuynia *Houttuynia* 6–10

I

Imperata *Imperata* 5–10
Incarvillea *Incarvillea* 4–10

Inula *Inula* 3–9
Iris *Iris* 3–10

J

Jasione *Jasione* 6–9

K

Kalimeris *Kalimeris* 3–8
Kirengeshoma *Kirengeshoma* 5–9
Knautia *Knautia* 5–10
Kniphofia *Torch lily* 6–10

L

Lamium *Dead nettle* 3–10
Lathyrus *Pea* 3–9
Leucanthemella *Leucanthemella*
   4–9
Leucanthemum *Shasta daisy* 5–10
Liatris *Blazing star* 3–10
Ligularia *Ligularia* 4–10
Limonium *Statice* 3–10
Linaria *Toadflax* 3–10
Linum *Flax* 5–10
Liriope *Lilyturf* 5–10
Lobelia *Lobelia* 2–9
Lupinus *Lupine* 4–9
Luzula *Luzula* 3–9
Lychnis *Campion* 3–10
Lysichiton *Skunk cabbage* 4–9
Lysimachia *Loosestrife* 3–10
Lythrum *Purple loosestrife* 3–10

M

Macleaya *Plume poppy* 4–10
Malva *Mallow* 4–9
Matteuccia *Ostrich fern* 3–8
Meconopsis *Blue poppy* 6–9
Melissa *Lemon balm* 5–9
Mentha *Mint* 5–10
Mertensia *Mertensia* 3–10
Milium *Millet grass* 3–9
Mimulus *Monkey flower* 7–10
Miscanthus *Miscanthus* 5–9
Molinia *Moor grass* 5–9
Monarda *Bergamot* 4–10
Morina *Morina* 6–9

N

Nepeta *Catmint* 3–10

O

Oenothera *Evening primrose* 4–10
Omphalodes *Navelwort* 5–9
Origanum *Marjoram* 3–10
Osmunda *Royal fern* 3–8

P

Paeonia *Peony* 3–10
Papaver *Poppy* 3–9
Patrinia *Patrinia* 5–9
Pennisetum *Fountain grass* 6–10
Penstemon *Penstemon* 3–10
Perovskia *Russian sage* 5–10
Persicaria *Knotweed* 3–9
Phalaris *Ribbon grass* 4–9
Phlox *Phlox* 3–9
Phygelius *Cape figwort* 6–10
Physalis *Chinese lantern* 3–10
Physostegia *Obedient plant* 5–9
Phytolacca *Pokeweed* 3–9
Platycodon *Balloon flower* 3–10
Pleioblastus *Bush bamboo* 3–9
Polemonium *Jacob's ladder* 3–9
Polygonatum *Solomon's seal* 4–9
Polystichum *Shield fern* 4–8
Potentilla *Potentilla* 3–10
Primula *Primula* 3–9
Prunella *Self-heal* 4–9
Pulmonaria *Lungwort* 3–10
Pulsatilla *Pasqueflower* 5–9

R

Ranunculus *Buttercup* 4–9
Rhazya *Rhazya* 6–9
Rheum *Rhubarb* 5–9
Rodgersia *Rodgersia* 4–9
Rudbeckia *Coneflower* 3–10

S

Salvia *Sage* 4–10
Sanguisorba *Burnet* 3–9
Saponaria *Soapwort* 2–10
Sasa *Sasa* 2–9

Saxifraga *Saxifrage* 5–9
Scabiosa *Scabious* 3–11
Scrophularia *Figwort* 6–9
Sedum *Stonecrop* 4–10
Senecio *Senecio* 8–10
Sidalcea *Prairie mallow* 5–11
Silene *Campion* 4–10
Sisyrinchium *Sisyrinchium* 3–10
Smilacina *False Solomon's seal* 3–9
Solidago *Goldenrod* 3–10
Stachys *Betony* 4–10
Stipa *Stipa* 3–11
Stokesia *Stoke's aster* 5–10
Symphyandra *Symphyandra* 6–9
Symphytum *Comfrey* 3–9

T

Tanacetum *Tansy* 3–9
Tellima *Fringecups* 4–9
Thalictrum *Meadow rue* 3–10
Thermopsis *False lupine* 3–10
Tiarella *Foamflower* 3–9
Trachystemon *Trachystemon* 3–8
Tradescantia *Spiderwort* 5–10
Tricyrtis *Toad lily* 5–9
Trollius *Globeflower* 3–10

U

Uncinia *Uncinia* 5–10
Uvularia *Bellwort* 3–9

V

Valeriana *Valerian* 5–10
Veratrum *False hellebore* 3–9
Verbascum *Mullein* 5–10
Verbena *Vervain* 3–10
Veronica *Speedwell* 3–10
Veronicastrum *Veronicastrum* 3–10
Viola *Viola* 3–10

W

Waldsteinia *Barren strawberry* 3–10

Z

Zauschneria *California fuchsia*
   8–10

GLOSSARY

Acid (of soil) Lime free; having a pH level of less than 7; the opposite of alkaline.

Alkaline (of soil) Limy; having a pH level of more than 7; the opposite of acid.

Alpine 1 A plant growing naturally in mountainous regions, usually above the tree line. **2** Any small plant that is grown on a rock garden. Also some times used rather too loosely to describe any small perennial plant.

Alternate leaves Leaves staggered singly on opposite sides of the stem.

Annual A plant that completes its lifecycle from germination to shedding seed in a single growing season.

Anthers The male organ of a flower, the part producing pollen.

Apex The tip of a petal or leaf or the growing point of a shoot.

Basal leaves Leaves arising directly from the crown rather than the stem.

Biennial A plant that completes its life cycle in two seasons. It grows and builds up reserves of nutrients in its first season then flowers, sheds seed and dies in its second season.

Biological control The use of a beneficial organism such as a parasitic insect to control another organism that is harmful to plants.

Boss A rounded protuberance; often refers to a crowded mass of stamens in the center of a flower.

Bottlebrush A flower head shaped like a bottlebrush, with a mass of slender flowers arranged tightly along a slender stem.

Bulb A storage organ made up of a number of tightly packed fleshy scales. Often used more generally for any underground storage organ.

Bract A small leaflike organ positioned alongside a flower.

Cluster A group of flowers held together.

Coarse Describes leaves which are especially broad, thick, or rough.

Coir A fine, peatlike material made from coconut fiber.

Cold frame A low structure consisting of a timber, brick, or concrete frame with the top and sometimes the sides glazed with glass or clear plastic. Used to protect plants from cold weather and to harden off developing plants.

Compost Rotted vegetable matter.

Cross 1 To raise a new plant through combining the characteristics of two different plants by fertilizing one with the pollen of the other. **2** The plant resulting from such an enterprise.

Crown The part of a plant at or immediately below the soil surface from which leaves and shoots develop.

Cultivar A named selection of a particular species. For example: *Phlox paniculata* 'Fujiyama', indicates that 'Fujiyama' is a cultivar of *P. p.*, of which there are many other cultivars.

Cutting A piece of stem detached from the parent plant that produces roots and develops into a new plant, usually identical to its parent.

Deadhead To remove flowers as they die and before they shed seed; this promotes continuous flowering and prevents the seed being shed.

Deciduous Losing leaves completely in the fall or early winter.

Division The splitting of a plant into a number of small plants.

Dormancy Two meanings. **1** A resting period in which a plant does not grow. **2** A period in which a seed does not germinate because the appropriate conditions are absent.

Drainage The percolation of water through the soil. Well-drained soils allow water to percolate through them quickly, poorly drained or water logged soils hold water and remain wet for longer.

Drill A long, narrow, shallow trench in the soil in which seeds are sown.

Evergreen A plant that retains leaves throughout the year.

F₁ Hybrid A strain of seed-raised plants created by crossing two parent plants that are also the result of repeated selection for special characteristics.

Family A collection of broadly similar genera. For example: *Iris* and *Crocosmia* are both genera in the Iridaceae family.

Frond The leaf of a fern.

Fungicide A natural or synthetic chemical that kills fungus infections.

Genus *plural: genera* A group of related species having certain characteristics in common. For example, *Iris sibirica* and *Iris pseudacorus* are two species which belong to the genus Iris.

Germination The development of a seed into a seedling.

Ground-cover plant A dense, usually low-growing plant with a tendency to cover the ground and also to smother weeds.

Half-hardy A plant that grows well out side in summer but requires protection from the weather in winter.

Hardening off The gradual acclimatization to the open garden of plants raised in the protected environment of a cold frame or greenhouse.

Hardy A plant that will survive outside year-round without special protection.

Heavy soil Soil with a high clay content. Heavy soil is usually sticky, holds a great deal of water and also dries out slowly.

Herbaceous plant A plant whose leaves and stems die away every year, usually in late fall or winter. But see page 10.

Humus Well-rotted vegetable matter.

Hybrid A plant resulting from the crossing of two other plants.

Interplant The method of planting a number of individuals of two different plants among each other.

Leaching The draining through the soil of a solution of nutrients in water.

Leaf cutting A leaf detached from the parent plant that produces roots and develops into a new plant, ie usually identical to its parent.

Leaf mould Humus derived exclusively from rotted leaves of deciduous trees and shrubs and used to improve soil.

Light soil Soil containing a high proportion of sand or gravel. Light soil is usually very crumbly, holds little water, and dries out quickly.

Lime Material containing mainly calcium and used to reduce the acidity of the soil.

Liquid feed Describes fertilizer applied in liquid form.

Marginal 1 Describing plants that grow in moist soil, such as along the edges of ponds. **2** Describing the edges of leaves, usually in relation to variegation. **3** Describing plants that may not survive the winter.

Mediterranean plants Plants that grow in the wild in the Mediterranean region and areas with similar climates. They enjoy mild winters, plenty of sunshine, and good drainage.

Mulch Layer of organic matter or gravel spread over the soil to suppress weeds, prevent evaporation of moisture and improve the soil.

Native plant A plant that naturally grows wild in a particular area.

Naturalize To allow plants to develop with the minimum of interference; for example, to permit their seedlings to mature where they spring up of their own accord, or to allow plants to spread into one another.

Neutral (of soil) Neither acid nor alkaline; with a pH of 7.

Offset A new plant that develops at the base of a larger, established plant.

Opposite leaves Leaves that are positioned in opposite pairs at single points up the stem.

Peat Humus comprising partially rotted moss or sedge.

Perennial Correctly, a plant that lives for more than two years. But see page 9.

Pesticide A natural or synthetic chemical that kills insects or other creatures harmful to plants.

pH A measure of alkalinity and acidity. A pH7 is neutral; above 7 is alkaline, below 7 is acid.

Pinching The action of removing the tip of a stem to encourage the development of side shoots.

Pricking out The removal of a seedling from the pot or flat in which it germinated to an individual pot or a large flat, where it will have more space to develop.

Propagation The production of one or more new plants from an existing one.

Raceme An unbranched flowering stalk on which the flowers are carried individually on short side shoots.

Rhizome A stem that creeps horizantally, or just below the surface.

Root cutting A piece of root detached from the parent plant which then produces roots and develops into a new plant which is usually identical to its parent.

Rosette A cluster of leaves radiating from the crown of a plant with the new, smallest leaves in the center.

Run To spread rapidly, especially through the growth of roots.

Runner Stem that creeps across the surface of the soil, often rooting into the soil below.

Seed head A flower that is developing or has developed seeds.

Seedling A young plant resulting from the germination of a seed.

Selection A plant that is chosen as being noticeably distinct from others of its type. For example, it might have larger flowers.

Self-sowing Term that describes the tendency of some plants to shed seed which then germinates and develops into new plants nearby.

Slow-release fertilizer A plant food specially formulated to be released into the soil over a long period.

Species A naturally occurring group of almost identical plants. A number of botanically related species, sharing generally similar features (although these may not always be immediately obvious), are grouped into a genus. For example, *Iris sibirica* and *Iris pseudacorus* are both species in the genus *Iris*.

Specimen A plant grown for its striking or distinctive growth habit or general appearance.

Spike An unbranched flowering stalk on which the flowers are carried without individual stems.

Stake To support tall or floppy plants with canes, brushwood or steel rods.

Stolon A shoot that grows across the soil or arches above the soil and produces a new plant with roots at its tip.

Succulent Swollen or fleshy leaves, providing a store of moisture.

Tender Susceptible to damage from frost.

Top-dress To apply fertilizer to the surface of the soil.

Tuber An underground storage organ that is developed by the swelling of a root or stem.

Umbel A domed or flat-topped flower head in which each flower is carried on a slim stem attached to the top of the main stem.

Underplant To plant short plants around or underneath taller ones.

Variegated (of leaves) With edging, streaks, spots, splashes, or stripes of another color, usually yellow, cream, or white.

Variety A naturally occurring wild variant of a species.

Waterlogged soil Soil that remains very wet and rarely dries out.

Weed Any plant that is a nuisance.

SUPPLIERS

At the time of writing, all the nurseries listed below operated a mail-order service. It may be useful to telephone to find out catalog prices and hours open before ordering and visiting.

Blue Dahlia Gardens
Box 316
San Jose, IL 62682
Tel: 309-247-3210
(Mainly dahlia tubers)

Bluestone Perennials
7211 Middle Ridge Road
Madison, OH 44057
Tel: 216-428-7535
(Large stock of perennials sold as "starter" plants in flats)

Borbelata Gardens
15974 Canby Avenue
Route 5
Faribault, MN 55021
Tel: 507-334-2807
(Lilies, bulbs, and other perennials sold in pots)

W. Atlee Burpee
300 Park Avenue
Warminster, PA 18974
Tel: 800-888-1447
(Mixture of flowers, vegetables, and herbs; mainly seeds and seedlings)

Busse Gardens
P.O. Box N
Cokato, MN 55321
Tel: 612-286-2654
(Cold-hardy perennials)

Cooley's Gardens Inc.
P.O. Box 126
Silverton, OR 97381
Tel: 503-873-5463
(Irises and other perennials)

The Crownsville Nursery
P.O. Box 797
Crownsville, MD 21032
Tel: 410-923-2212
(About 1,000 perennials, with many asters and wide selection of rare species)

Houston Daylily Gardens
P.O. Box 7008
The Woodlands, TX 77380
Tel: 713-350-5577
(Specialize in [daylilies] *Hemerocallis*)

Klehm Nursery
197 Penny Road
South Barrington, IL 60010
Tel: 312-437-2880
(Famous for peonies and daylilies)

Mellinger's
2310 W. South Range Road
North Lima, OH 44452-9731
Tel: 216-549-9861
(Nice selection of perennials sold in pots)

Milaeger's Gardens
4838 Douglas Avenue
Racine, WI 53402-2498
Tel: 800-924-0737
(Common and unusual flowering perennials sold in pots)

Niche Gardens
Route 1, Box 290
Chapel Hill, NC 27514
Tel: 919-967-0078
(Native perennials and herbs sold in a variety of pots)

Park Seed Co. Inc.
Cokesbury Road
Greenwood, SC 29647-0001
Tel: 803-223-7333
(Mainly seeds. Free catalog)

Schreiner's Iris Gardens
3643 Quinaby Road NE
Salem, OR 97303
Tel: 800-525-2367 Ext 43
(Mainly irises in all colors. Free catalog)

Shady Oaks Nursery
112 Tenth Avenue SE
Waseca, MN 56093
Tel: 507-835-5033
(Excellent hosta selection plus other shade-loving plants)

Sunshine Farms and Gardens
Route 5H
Renwick, WV 24966
Tel: 304-497-3163
(Primulas and other perennials)

Swan Island Dahlias
P.O. Box 700
Canby, OR 97013
Tel: 503-266-7711
(Mainly dahlias)

André Viette
Farm and Nursery
Route 1, Box 16
Fisherville, VA 22939
Tel: 703-943-2315
(Huge variety of perennials, including rare species, sold in pots)

Wayside Gardens
1 Garden Lane
Hodges, SC 29695
Tel: 800-845-1124
(Choice perennials; many new hybrids)

Well-Sweep Herb Farms
317 Mount Bethel Road
Port Murray, NJ 07865
Tel: 201-852-5390
(Herbs and other perennials that are useful for fragrance, cooking, and medicinal purposes)

White Flower Farm
Route 63
Litchfield, CT 06759
Tel: 203-496-9600
(Rare and unusual perennials)

CANADIAN MAIL-ORDER SOURCES

Brackenridge Nursery
R.R. 7
Duncan
British Columbia V9L 4W4
Tel: 604-748-3165
(Unusual hardy perennials)

Brickman's Botanical Gardens
R.R. 1
Sebringville
Ontario N0K 1X0
Tel: 519-393-6223
Fax: 393-5239
(General perennials)

Cruickshanks Inc.
1015 Mount Pleasant Road
Toronto
Ontario L4G 1R1
Tel: 800-665-6505/416-488-8292
Fax: 488-8802
(Irises, poppies, and a small range of unusual perennials)

Delair Garden
35120 Delair Road
R.R. 4
Abbotsford
British Columbia V2S 4N4
Tel: 604-859-7919
(General perennials)

Ferncliffe Gardens
8394 McTaggart Street
S.S. 1
Mission
British Columbia V2V 5V6
Tel: 604-826-2447
(Irises, peonies, gladiolis, dahlias)

Gardenimport Inc.
P.O. Box 760
Thornhill
Ontario, L3T 4A5
Tel: 800-565-0957/905-731-1950
Fax: 881-3499
(Unusual perennials in limited range)

Hortico Inc.
723 Robson Road
R.R. 1
Waterdown
Ontario L0R 2H0
Tel: 905-689-6984
Fax: 689-6566
(General perennials)

Iris and Plus Enr
1269 Route 139
C.P. 903
Sutton
Quebec J0E 2KO
Tel: 514-538-2048
Fax: 538-0448
(Bearded and Siberian irises, hostas, daylilies, astilbes)

Les Jardins Osiris
818 Route Monique
C.P. 489
St-Thomas
Quebec J0K 3L0
Tel: 514-759-8621
Fax: 759-6571
(Siberian iris, hostas, daylilies, peonies, astilbes)

Mason Hoag Gardens
3520 Durham Road
1 R.R. 4
Uxbridge
Ontario L9F 1R4
Tel: 905-649-3532
(General perennials and hardy geraniums)

McMillen Iris Gardens
R.R. 1
Norwich
Ontario
Tel: 519-468-6508
(Tall and miniature bearded and Siberian irises, daylilies)

Pepiniere Charlevoix
345 Fraser
La Malbaie
Quebec G5A 1A2
Tel: 418-665-6435
Fax: 665-3015
(General perennials)

Prism Perennials
C-45, S-25
R.R. 1
Castlegar
British Columbia V1N 3H7
Tel: 604-365-3753
(General perennials)

Rainforest Gardens
13139 224th Street
Maple Ridge
British Columbia V2X 7E7
Tel: 604-467-4218
(General perennials, especially for shade)

Sherry's Perennials
P.O. Box 39
Cedar Springs
Ontario N0P 1E0
Tel: 519-676-4541
(General perennials)

Stirling Perennials
R.R 1
Morpeth
Ontario N0P 1X0
Tel: 519-674-0571
(General perennials)

PHOTOGRAPHIC ACKNOWLEDGMENTS

A-Z Botanical Collection 177 center, /Lance Beacham 170 left, /Anthony Cooper 133, /Terence Exley 132
Eric Crichton 139, 148 top, 148 below, 149 right, 149 below, 150 right, 152 right, 153 left, 153 right, 155 right, 156 left, 156 right, 157 top, 158 top, 158 left, 159 left, 161 center, 162 right, 162 center, 163 center, 163 right, 166 left, 167 below, 169 center, 169 right, 171 center, 174 left, 175 center, 178 left, 179 center, 180 center, 181 center, 182 left, 186 right, 188 right, 188 center, 189 right, 190 center, 192 right, 193 center, 194 right, 196 center, 198 left, 198 right, 200 center, 202 left, 202 center, 204 right, 204 center, 207 center, 209 right, 210 right, 210 left, 211 right, 214 right, 214 center, 215 right, 217 left, 220 left, 222 left, 222 right, 224 center
Elizabeth Whiting Associates 76 top right, 122
John Fielding 3 right, 3 left, 97 top, 145 below, 146 below, 147 right, 158 below, 159 right, 162 left, 168 right, 168 center, 173 left, 197 left, 207 right, 208 left, 211 left, 212 center, 213 center, 217 center, 219 right, 223 left, 224 left, 226 right
Garden Picture Library /Brian Carter 19, /Erika Craddock 13 center, /Elizabeth Crowe 17, /Ron Evans 100, /John Glover 16, 89, /Neil Holmes 13 top, 127 top, /Michelle Lamontagne 47, /Jane Legate 97 below, /John Miller 96, /Clay Perry 81, /Gary Rodgers 52, /Brigitte Thomas 101, /Steven Wooster 128
Garden Matters /J. Feltwell 42
John Glover 43 bottom left, 91, 107, 120, 124, 130 top, 131, 134, 135, 147 left, 151 center, 155 left, 173 center, 177 left, 180 left, 182 center, 182 right, 184 right, 186 top, 193 left, 193 right, 194 center, 195

left, 200 left, 201 right, 201 left, 205 left, 213 right, 215 center, 215 left, 216 left
Jerry Harpur 2, 4, 8, 9 right, 15 right, 28, 41, 45, 46, 64, 76 left, 82, 83, 88, 92, 103, 105, 113, 117 below, 130 below
Marijke Heuff 115
Andrew Lawson 3 center, 18, 21 left, 38 top, 43 bottom right, 55, 57, 70, 86, 111 top, 112, 127 below, 129 left, 136, 144 left, 144 top, 144 right, 145 right, 146 right, 148 right, 149 left, 150 center, 150 top, 151 right, 151 left, 154 left, 154 right, 156 top, 157 left, 160 center, 160 right, 164 top, 165 left, 165 right, 168 left, 169 left, 172 right, 173 right, 174 right, 176 center, 176 left, 178 right, 179 left, 180 right, 181 left, 181 right, 183 right, 184 left, 185 center, 186 below, 187 right, 187 center, 189 center, 189 left, 190 left, 192 center, 194 left, 195 center, 199 right, 200 right, 207 left, 208 right, 211 center, 213 left, 217 right, 218 center, 220 center, 221 right, 221 left, 222 center, 224 right, 225 left, 226 left, 227 right, 227 left
Tony Lord 94, 99 right, 106, 110 below, 118 left, 119 top, 129 right, /Arley Hall 98 below, 104, /Broughton Castle 117 top, /Chatsworth 98 top, /Great Dixter 123, /Heslington Manor 75 center, /The Manor House, Heslington 119 below, /Kemerton Priory 121, /Aster Collection, Picton Memorial Garden 93
Clive Nichols 58, 227 center, /Designer: Sue Barker 142, /Brook Cottage, Oxfordshire 95 top, /Chenies Manor House Garden, Buckinghamshire 116, /Dartington Hall, Devon 90, /Eastgrove Cottage Garden and Nursery, Sankyns Green, Worcestershire 108, /Hadspen House Garden and Nursery, Somerset / Designers: Sandra and Nori Pope 125, /Longacre, Kent 95 below, /The Manor House, Upton Grey, Hampshire 30, /The Old Rectory, Burghfield. Berkshire 111 below, /The Picton Garden, Colwall,

Worcestershire 20, 65, /The Picton Garden, Carnwall 143 center, /The Priory, Kemerton, Worcestershire 74, /Red Gables, Worcestershire 0 back jacket, 14, /Sticky Wicket, Dorset / Designer Pam Lewis 102, /Turn End, Buckinghamshire 126, /Waterperry Gardens, Oxfordshire 6, /Designer, Anne Waring 109
Hugh Palmer 21 right
Jerry Pavia 13 bottom
Perdereau 1, 2, 12, 22, 50, 77 below, 85, 114
Photos Horticultural 31, 110 top, 137, 145 top, 145 left, 146 left, 147 center, 152 center, 153 center, 160 left, 161 left, 164 left, 164 right, 165 center, 166 below, 167 left, 167 right, 170 center, 171 right, 172 below, 172 left, 175 right, 176 right, 178 center, 179 right, 183 left, 183 center, 184 center, 185 right, 185 left, 187 left, 188 left, 190 right, 191 right, 191 center, 195 right, 196 right, 196 left, 199 center, 201 center, 203 right, 204 left, 205 center, 205 right, 206 left, 206 right, 209 left, 209 center, 212 left, 214 left, 216 center, 216 right, 218 right, 218 left, 219 center, 219 left, 220 right, 223 right, 225 center, 225 right, 226 center
Reed International Books Ltd. Picture Library /Jerry Harpur 154 center, 155 center, 166 right, 170 right, 174 center, /WF Davidson 161 right, /Jerry Harpur 177 right, 197 right, 198 center, 199 left, /Jerry Hapur 202 right, /Jerry Harpur 203 center, 212 right, /Mark Williams 26 bottom left, 26 top right, /George Wright 191 left, 192 left
Graham Rice 186 left
Harry Smith Collection 157 right, 175 left
Mark Williams 26 top left, 26 bottom right
Macmillan Publishers Ltd 229 supplying information for the European zone map
Reader's Digest Association 229 supplying information for the N American zone map